JEWELS AND JACKBOOTS

Hitler's British Channel Islands

JEWELS
AND
JACKBOOTS
Hitler's British Channel Islands

In the thrilling final days of the Western campaign, Luftwaffe pilots landed in these, the former British Channel Islands.

They immediately surrendered. And so it was that these jewels in the British Imperial Crown passed into German hands.

Erich Hohl, Deutsche Inselzeitung, 1st July 1943.

John Nettles

About the Author
John Nettles

Actor John Nettles, who became famous for his portrayal of Jersey's TV detective Jim Bergerac, then Tom Barnaby in *Midsomer Murders*, is the author of this fascinating addition to the history of the Second World War in the Channel Islands.

As well as being a much-loved actor around the globe, John is also a graduate of History at the University of Southampton, where he specialised in the Second World War.

He is the author of two previous books on Jersey, where he lived for twelve years during the filming of *Bergerac*. During this time he developed an abiding interest in the Channel Islands and their people, to whom this book is dedicated.

Published in 2013

by

SEEKER PUBLISHING
&
EWM DESIGN & ADVERTISING

Copyright © 2013

Cover design and production by EWM Design & Advertising
www.ewmdesign.co.uk

Printed & bound by CIP Group (UK) Ltd

ISBN 978-1-905095-42-1

www.jewelsandjackboots.com

Acknowledgements

This book could never have been compiled without the enormous help I received from a great number of people in the Channel Islands. The number is indeed so great that there is simply not enough space here to mention them all by name, but they all have my heartfelt thanks for sharing with me their knowledge and wisdom about the Occupation years.

Most thanks for his untiring research in my behalf must go to Howard Butlin Baker, who discovered so much about the Occupation that it would take a dozen volumes to tell it all.

Appreciation is due, too, to those three great survivors of those days: Bob Le Sueur and Michael Ginns in Jersey, and Henry Winterflood in Guernsey. Their conversations with me were among the most pleasurable experiences I had in the whole process of compiling this book; through them I was able to hear the true Island voice speak of those difficult times all of seventy years ago.

Paul Sanders and Hazel R. Knowles Smith, two of the foremost historians of the Occupation years also gave of their time to explain to me the complexities – and they are complexities – of the Islands' response to being invaded and occupied by the Germans. Not only that of the men in high places but also that of the ordinary Islanders who were kept largely in the dark about what was going on. They were difficult times and good historians are needed to make some kind of sense of them and explain them in all their many aspects. Paul and Hazel are very good historians indeed. They performed that task for me without thought of reciprocation, and I cannot thank them enough. The same goes for Freddie Cohen, whose work on uncovering the fate of the Islands' Jews is a model of fine historical research and a welcome counterbalance to some of the more hysterical approaches to this most difficult and contentious matter. He, very kindly, took time out from his States duties to talk me through what had happened to the Islands' Jews during the Occupation, and the story that emerged was quite an eye-opener.

Especial thanks must go to the Société Jersiaise library folk, and Anna Baghiani in particular, for finding and sending me all kinds of material on the Occupation. It was an invaluable help. As indeed was that given so freely to me by the staff of the Priaulx library in Guernsey and the staff of the Jersey

Archive in St Helier – a more helpful and friendly group the aspiring writer could not wish to meet.

The pictorial content of the book is most important in the telling of the Occupation story and I am more than grateful to those kindly Islanders who allowed me to use photos from their collections, the better to illustrate the tale. Chief among these is Mark Lamerton who has what must be the best Occupation photos in the Islands. Looking through them counts as one of the pleasantest experiences in the research process.

I spent many a happy hour too in Richard Heaume's wonderful Occupation Museum in Guernsey. Apart from documents, German notices and proclamations, he actually gave me an excellent photograph of Schmettow with which to adorn the chapter on the Occupiers. I thank him for that.

In Jersey, may I thank the staff who showed me around the War Tunnels – so expressive of Nazi energy and hellish ambition that they take the breath away. They opened up their extensive archives sparing no effort to find the very best material to use in this book. I am only sorry we could not include more.

Finally, my deepest appreciation for their help and understanding goes to Simon Watkins for publishing and Eddie McGrath for the design and artwork of this work on the Occupation.

Working on this book has been a richly rewarding experience for me, not least in meeting and talking to so many Islanders who have so generously given of their time to tell the story of the Occupation. I am deeply indebted to them all.

John Nettles
October 2012

John Nettles

Acknowledgements

The publishers would like to acknowledge with thanks, permission to reproduce photographs and material supplied by:

Jersey War Tunnels

German Occupation Museum

The Channel Islands Military Museum

La Vallette Military Museum

The Imperial War Museum

The Channel Islands Occupation Society (Guernsey)

The Channel Islands Occupation Society (Jersey)

Jersey Heritage

Jersey Archive

Société Jersiaise Photographic Archive

Guernsey Archive Services

Guernsey Museum

Priaulx Library (Guernsey)

Adler Archive

Bundesarchiv

Deane Photographic Archive

Damien Horn Collection

Festung Guernsey Collection

Carol Toms Collection

Mark Lamerton Collection

David Gainsborough Roberts Collection

Franz Zurhorst Collection

Alan Allix Collection

Channel Island Publishing

The Guernsey Press

The Jersey Evening Post

Gareth Hawker

Gerald Palmer

Simon Watkins

Alan Blampied and the Blampied Family

William Ozanne

Pug Films

Deutsche Inselzeitung, 1943

I n the thrilling final days of the Western campaign, Luftwaffe pilots landed in these, the former British Channel Islands. They immediately surrendered. And so it was that these jewels in the British Imperial Crown passed into German hands. Through the power of the German sword, the European continent has effected a correction in its strategic security cordon on the Western Front, and in so doing showed up the absurdity of the historical-political situation that existed in these waters around the Cherbourg peninsula. As shown by centuries of British hostility toward mainland Europe, the English entirely understood the economic and strategic value of holding on to these Norman Islands and of consolidating and constructing from this oddity a permanent condition of advantage. The French, in thrall to the English for a hundred years and more, would not take offence and had submissively just accepted this peculiar situation.

But the sharp German sword has removed this aberration in European politics, wiped it from the map! Since the 1st July, 1940, around the rocky coasts of the islands, German soldiers have kept watch, and from the towers, those same strong towers built along the beaches by the English against a feared Napoleonic attack, German soldiers gaze out over the Channel, always looking for the enemy.

The face of the Island has changed!

For three years the Islanders have watched in amazement this miracle of German organisation unfold right before their very eyes, the planned utilisation of each and every natural feature, brilliantly surmounting all the technical and geographical difficulties to bring about a structural and military transformation in the Islands.

Any Englishman wanting to impress his countrymen by mounting any sort of attack will quickly find out how effective that transformation can be. For then the camouflage netting would be cast aside, the fiery battery mouths would gape and thousands of ammunition rounds would be unleashed from bunkers and bases.

Against the enemy would be concentrated all the mighty fire-power of coastal defence of which he got merely the slightest foretaste in the Dieppe adventure!

From being a playground for pleasure-seeking Englishmen and an open-air retirement home for shrivelled-up sterling millionaires, these Norman Islands have now been incorporated as an integral part of the huge defensive system of the Atlantic Wall, protecting Europe against the British sea-pirates.

They are outposts of Fortress Europe, ready to attack when the time comes. That Germanic genius which has transformed the coast of France into a cordon of concrete and steel, an invisible network of bunkers, bases, machine-gun emplacements, artillery posts, transformed B-posts, has erected heavy tank walls at all likely landing places and strung the beaches with minefields and wire entanglements – that same genius has also been at work in these Norman Islands. Day and night, hammers pounded, construction machinery stamped, machines steamed and hissed. And in this way, these islands renowned for nothing so much as early potatoes and tomatoes, have been transformed into floating outposts of the European continent, and where in previous years the hedonistic culture of sun and sea clouded the mind, today there beats a powerful rhythm of determination, alertness to duty, and the exercise of the will.

Behind this great wall of iron and concrete, the German soldier stands in the calm certainty of his power. Discipline, countless hours of preparation for hardship, training in the ways of ruthlessness, has turned him into a true fighter, and a fighter who awaits his hour. And when it comes, then he will show that there is steel in the heart of the fighting man!

The German soldier in the Norman Channel Islands knows what he has to do. He is aware of his task. While his brothers-in-arms far away in the vastness of the Russian steppe are engaged in a life and death struggle with the Bolshevik, he, on this lonely outpost in the Channel, guards the coasts of Europe from enemy attack.

No matter how much the agitating Jews across the Channel may whip up clarion calls for invasion into a frenzy, no matter how great the attempt to sweep the shameful memory of Dieppe beneath the carpet, his power will bring their hopes crashing down.

Erich Hohl, 1st July.

Contents

Timeline

1940

14 June

The Lieutenant-Governor of Jersey, Major General J.M.R. Harrison, and the Bailiff, Alexander Moncrieff Coutanche, know the Home Office has a lot on its plate, what with Dunkirk and the massive military collapse. Nonetheless they make yet another enquiry to the rather vague Charles Markbreiter, who is in charge of Channel Islands affairs, as to whether any decisions have been reached about what the Islanders should do now that the Germans are on the doorstep. They are told that nobody has decided anything or, indeed, thought very much about the fate of the Channel Islands at all!

16/17 June

The Channel Islands' Dunkirk! British troops retreating before the overwhelming German forces are trapped around St Malo. They desperately need to be evacuated. An urgent request for help is sent to Coutanche who is immediately on the phone to the commodore of the Jersey Yacht Club asking him to organise a relief operation to shift the beleaguered elements of the British Expeditionary Force away from France.

On the night of 16–17 June, dozens of fishing boats, yachts and other vessels set out from St Helier and make toward St Malo. They arrive in the early afternoon of the 17th and set about ferrying the troops from the land to the big ships waiting offshore in the bay. All the troops are successfully evacuated. The operation is a success. But only just! As the last man is leaving the first German soldiers are entering the outskirts of St Malo.

19 June

At last a decision – of sorts! The Islands' governments are told that the Islands are to be demilitarised but that they should keep as quiet as possible about it for 'reasons of security'. This sotto voce dissemination of the news results in only a minority of the Islanders learning of the Islands' new military status and the Germans – who should have been the first to know – not knowing anything about it at all! The policy of the British during this whole affair was characterised by Charles Cruickshank, author of the magisterial official history of the Occupation, as bordering on the 'criminal'.

20 June

The Tommies say goodbye! The last British soldiers leave the Islands with some speed. The local militias are stood down. The Channel Islands are defenceless – but the Germans don't know.

21 June

Everybody knows the Hun is coming and they know he's coming fast. Everybody knows the Germans are rapacious, sadistic, bloodthirsty and murderous. Everybody is afraid. Fear and primal panic spread across the Islands. For many the urge to run is irresistible. 23,000 in Jersey register for evacuation and thousands crowd into St Peter Port with the same aim in mind.

In Jersey, Alexander Coutanche manages to steady the ship with a speech addressed to the frightened crowds in Royal Square. He says that he and his wife are going to stay and tough it out, as should every true Jerseyman. They are rooted to the soil and will never leave.

His words have great effect, for of the 23,000 registered for evacuation from Jersey, in the event only 6,600 actually go. There is no equivalent intervention by the Guernsey Bailiff, and when the ships leave for England they are carrying away the enormous number of 17,000 Guernsey folk from a population of 42,000. The majority of the Guernsey children are gone.

The Dame of Sark, Sibyl Hathaway, declares, in her endearingly patrician way, that all those with a home and a stake in the land should stay:

I am not promising you that it will be easy. We may be hungry but we will always have our cattle and crops, our gardens, a few pigs, our sheep and rabbits.

In Alderney almost the entire population leaves. By 24th June only 19 people remain in the Island.

26 June
The Islanders can see the Germans across the sea on the Cherbourg peninsula. See the fires. See the smoke. CIGS (Chief of the Imperial General Staff) are still dithering about whether or not to tell the Germans that the Islands are a demilitarised zone. They have a lot on their minds, what with Dunkirk and the threat of imminent invasion.

The Germans assume the Islands are still defended and ...

28 June
.... attack! The War comes to the Channel Islands. There are bombing raids on St Helier harbour in Jersey and on St Peter Port harbour in Guernsey. 44 people are killed: 11 in Jersey and 33 in Guernsey. Many more are injured.

This would not have happened if the German High Command had been properly informed that the Islands were a demilitarised zone. The sound of stable doors being bolted fills the air as ...

30 June
... Joseph Kennedy, the American ambassador in London, is requested to formally notify Berlin that the Channel Islands are a demilitarised zone.

1 July
No more bombs.

Major Albrecht Lanz lands in Guernsey. He is to be the first military commander in the Islands.

Captain Gussek arrives in Jersey. Coutanche is forced to give up his gardening to receive him, and the Attorney General helps himself to the Bailiff's excellent port to steady his nerves.

2 July
Alderney is occupied.

4 July
Sark is occupied. Major Lanz and Dr Maass pay Dame Sibyl a courtesy call. She is highly impressed by their good manners. They wipe their feet on the mat. Obviously gentlemen.

7 July
Second Lieutenant Hubert Nicolle, a Guernseyman and chosen for that reason, lands in the Island on a reconnaissance mission. He discovers much information

about the disposition of German troops and the activities of the Luftwaffe. It is a highly successful venture, in fact the only successful venture of its kind in the whole of the War. On his way back to England he meets, down on the beach ...

10 July

... Second Lieutenants Philip Martel and Desmond Mulholland, in plain clothes, who are the advance party for a much larger three-pronged attack by 140 men scheduled for ...

15 July

... The raid is a failure. Two of the attacking parties fail to land in Guernsey at all. The third party does manage to land but achieves precisely nothing. Their leader, a rueful Durnford Slater, admits as much, saying that the whole commando exercise has got to be sharpened up. Churchill, the instigator of this type of raid, is not pleased. And neither is Ambrose Sherwill. He very much fears German reprisals against the civilian population if such raids continue. Meanwhile Philip Martel and Desmond Mulholland are unable to escape from the Island. They are hidden by their families. Such concealment is a crime in German eyes and, indeed, just knowing of the presence of 'enemy' agents in the Island without informing the Germans is a punishable offence. The situation is dangerous in the extreme, but the brave and resourceful Ambrose Sherwill comes to the rescue! And on ...

28 July

... he finds British army uniforms for the two officers and sends them, thus attired, off to the German military to surrender themselves. The uniforms Sherwill acquired for them ensures that the two men are treated as POWs and not shot as saboteurs. Martel and Mulholland are sent to France and spend the rest of the War as guests of the Third Reich.

The Germans have been here a month now and, on the whole, they are behaving very well indeed. Nobody is getting hurt; the tone of the Occupation is polite and courteous. Things are not too bad at all and certainly not as bad as expected. Ambrose Sherwill is very pleased, to the point of ...

1 August

... responding to a request from his German masters to broadcast a speech to be transmitted by Radio Bremen and aimed at a British audience, in which he extols the virtues of the Germans:

I imagine that many of you must be greatly worried as to how we are getting on. Well let me tell you ... The Bailiff Mr Victor Carey, and every other Island official has been, and is being, treated with the greatest courtesy by the German Military Authorities. The conduct of the German troops is exemplary.

It is a propaganda coup by the Germans.

9 August

German bureaucracy arrives in the Islands in the shape of Civil Affairs Unit *Feldkommandantur* 515, commanded by Colonel Schumacher. He is responsible to the military government in Paris, but it is fairly clear from the outset that the Germans are going to treat the Channel Islands as a special case.

4 September

It's replay time! Despite Sherwill inveighing against incursions and commando raids by the British, Second Lieutenant Hubert Nicolle returns to the Islands with fellow-Guernseyman Second Lieutenant James Symes on an intelligence-gathering mission.

Most importantly they want to find out if the Germans are going to use the Islands as a launching pad for the invasion of Britain. They gather what information they can and after two days return to the coast to await the boat that will take them off the Island and back to England. But no boat appears. Exactly like Martel and Mulholland before them, the two men are stranded in enemy-occupied territory and dressed in civilian clothes. Capture in this state means death by firing squad. They go into hiding with family and friends for nearly eight weeks. More and more people know of their presence. More and more people are at risk. The situation is intolerable and on ...

18 September
... Sherwill is called into action again, and again he finds British army uniforms for the two soldiers. He brokers a deal with the compliant Germans whereby the two men, now dressed in army uniform, will be treated as prisoners of war and not shot as saboteurs. Most importantly, all their friends, loved-ones and family who knew of their whereabouts and gave them refuge and succour, will not be punished in any way. However, the German Military Command in Paris reneges on the deal. Nicolle and Symes are tried as spies and sentenced to death. Ambrose Sherwill himself is arrested, along with twelve family and friends of the two soldiers, and they are all sent to the Cherche-Midi prison in Paris. There is a suicide. Symes' father kills himself. Other people are about to suffer.

21 October
The First Order against the Jews is registered in the Royal Court in Jersey.

23 October
The First Order against the Jews is registered in the Royal Court of Guernsey.

This is the first step in the Nazi programme to identify the Jews – to find out who they are and where they live so they can easily be found when the Germans next come-a-calling. Worse is to come.

11 November
Wireless sets have to be handed over to the Germans. This is a straightforward reprisal measure for acts of resistance directed against the Occupiers.

30 December
Good news! The Nicolle – Symes affair has been referred to a German Court of Honour in Berlin. The Paris judgements are overthrown. Nicolle and Symes will not be shot but rather treated as POWs and imprisoned for the duration of the War in a German POW camp. The civilians are all released from Cherche-Midi prison and return as happy as may be, given the suicide, to Guernsey.

There is a downside to all of this. The Germans declare that they can no longer work with Ambrose Sherwill and he is stripped of the presidency of the Controlling Committee. The Island loses an invaluable servant but gains a new president in the shape of John Leale. Leale's thinking as to what the behaviour of the Islanders should be towards the Germans is exactly the same as Sherwill's.

1941
28 January
A Rosenberg hit squad sacks the Masonic Temple in Jersey and sends the loot back to Berlin to be put on show. The Masonic societies are regarded by the Nazis as Jewish front organisations, there to promote Jewish aims, and, as such are anathema to them. There are mighty protests against these sequestrations from both Jersey and Guernsey. These are quite successful and

the larger part of Masonic wealth is turned over to the States of Guernsey, re-branded as States assets and as such kept out of the reach of the Germans.

1 February
The Germans think the Salvation Army is a potential threat. They are a little misled by the use of the word 'army', and ban this amiable organisation along with the Boy Scouts and the Girl Guides, and indeed any uniformed association apart from the local police. Most remarkably they ban the St John Ambulance Brigade. Perhaps their uniforms were a little too similar to the Hugo Boss-designed outfits worn by the SS.

A man from St Ouen, a Mr H.P. Turpin, is discovered in a designated Military Zone by a German patrol. He fails to respond to a sentry's challenge. He is shot in the back and killed.

3 February
The trial begins in the Old Committee Room of the Royal Court in St Helier of François Scornet and his 15 fellow-Frenchmen who tried to escape to England but only managed to get as far as Guernsey where they were arrested by the Germans. Sentence of death is pronounced on Scornet, and long prison terms are handed down to the others.

12 March
Germans grow tired of the Islanders hooting, singing patriotic songs, booing, jeering and laughing at German newsreels and propaganda films. Such demonstrations and outbursts are now expressly forbidden; in fact any demonstration of any kind is *verboten* on pain of a less than condign punishment. However the Germans take less than two days to realise that they have gone a little too far and on ...

14 March
... Island cinemagoers are told that they are allowed to laugh at the comedians and cheer and clap the heroes. 'Hurrah!' they can shout as the blond Aryan hero leaps up the endless stairs to rescue the blond Aryan heroine from the clutches of the filthy Jew in *Jud Suss*. And they can loudly cheer and laugh along at the sight of the subhuman and very black Algerian soldiers taken prisoner by the Germans and forced to dance for their captors.

And there is a death in Jersey on ...

17 March
... François Scornet is taken to St Ouen's Manor, tied to an ash tree in the lower garden and shot. His last words are 'Vive Dieu!' and 'Vive la France!'

June
The nature of the War in the West has changed. Hitler is turning towards the East and Russia, He needs to secure his Western Front by the creation of defensive positions. A start is made on the fortification of the Islands. Of more immediate interest to the Islanders, on ...

25 June
... all drivers are ordered to drive on the right.

Following exhortations from the BBC, 'V' signs begin to appear all over the Islands.

The Germans are not pleased and threaten bloody reprisal. The Bailiff of Guernsey, Victor Carey, is not pleased either. He doesn't want his fellow-Islanders shot, nor does he want the delicate relationship with the Germans harmed in any way.
So on ...

8 July
... a notice appears, signed by Carey, offering

a £25 reward to anyone who will tell the authorities who is putting up the 'V' signs.

5 August
The Germans threaten to shoot anyone harbouring crews of British aircraft which have crashed in or near the Islands, but a reward is offered to all those who report these crashed aeroplanes.

3 September
Dr Wilhelm Casper, whose name appears on nearly every piece of anti-Jewish legislation enforced in the Channel Islands, takes up his post as chief administrator of the *Feldkommandantur*.

12 September
German agents, engineers and citizens working in Persia (Iran) have been interned by the British, acting in concert with the Russians. It is believed, on very good grounds, that the Germans want to secure the oilfields and warm water ports of that country the better to prosecute the War. An armed force actually enters neutral Persia to ensure that Allied war aims are not thus compromised. It is an undoubted breach of international law, much like the invasion of neutral Belgium in 1940.

Hitler is hugely annoyed by this attack on German nationals in a neutral country and casts around for ways of reprisal. His eyes light upon the only British people in his power, the Channel Islanders. He demands that for every German detained in Persia, ten Islanders should be shipped out to the dreaded Pripet Marshes in far-away Eastern Europe. His demand is lost in the bureaucracy between Berlin and Paris, and between Paris and the Islands. The Islanders have been reprieved but only for a short while!

20 October
Hitler issues his Fortification Directive. The Islands are to be turned into 'impregnable fortresses'. Paragraph 1 reads:

Operations on a large scale against the territories we occupy in the West are, as before, unlikely. However, under pressure of the situation in the East or for reasons of propaganda, small scale operations at any moment may be anticipated, particularly an attempt to regain possession of the Channel Islands which are important to us for the protection of sea communications.
To prevent this, a huge programme of fortification is envisaged in which:
The strength of these fortifications and the order in which they are erected will be based on the principles and the practical knowledge gained from building the Atlantic Wall.

And in the building of this fine wall, foreign labour, especially Russians and Spaniards but also Frenchmen, may be used. And of course the man to organise the mighty workforce to fulfil Hitler's wishes is none other than Dr Fritz Todt, father of the famous autobahns, creator of the Siegfried Line and altogether the master builder of the Third Reich. He comes to the Islands in ...

November
... to supervise the first arrivals of the Todt workers. There are 16,000 of them. The condition of these forced labourers and the way they are treated by the Germans causes considerable revulsion amongst the Islanders, who quickly revise their opinion as to the nature of the occupiers.

1942
January
The civilised and very sensual Baron Hans Max von Aufsess is appointed head of the Civil Affairs branch of the Military Administration. This is a 'good thing' from

the Islanders' point of view as he tries constantly to protect them from the harsher effects of the edicts that pour out of Berlin and Paris. He says this of the last ten months of the war:

It was probably without precedent in the annals of military history and international law. These small islands, so foolishly transformed by Hitler into 'Island Fortresses', planned to withstand the heaviest attack, and, similarly heavily garrisoned, were marooned in the backwaters of war: bypassed by the Allies' advance and left isolated from the continent and all sources of supply. On them, cut-off and cooped up together, lived 35,000 German soldiers and 60,000 Islanders.

Fortification work begins in earnest in Alderney. Work is commenced on building the first labour camp, Lager Norderney. There are three more to be established: Helgoland, Borkum and Sylt. This last, Lager Sylt, is to be the most notorious of the four, housing as it will, political opponents of the Nazis and, inevitably, Jews. It is to be run by the SS.

February
Below-belt needs of the German soldiers are addressed. Three brothels are to be opened. The female operatives in these establishments are classed as heavy manual labourers when it comes to food rations. There are a lot of soldiers and they are a long way from home.

21 April
'April is the cruellest month'. Implementation of the 'Final Solution' takes Therese Steiner, Auguste Spitz and Marianne Grünfeld from Guernsey shores. It is the beginning of their via dolorosa. Their final destination will be Auschwitz.

May
The Guernsey Underground News Service, pleasant acronym GUNS, begins publication of its news sheets. The men behind this endeavour are brave and honourable, which is more than can be said for 17 members of William Sculpher's Guernsey police force who in this same month are accused of stealing large quantities of foodstuffs, liquor and other items from German stores. But they have not confined themselves to purloining enemy provisions. Apparently they have been stealing food from the Islanders' own stores as well, in effect robbing their own kith and kin. Confessions are beaten out of the men. Teeth are lost. Bruising and bleeding occurs. Ambrose Sherwill does not mount any kind of defence for them in court. He believes they thoroughly deserve what they are going to get. Their plea in mitigation, that they were playing Robin Hood, stealing in order to redistribute the goods among the poor and needy, is not accepted. Heavy prison sentences are handed down.

3 May
A tragedy occurs just off Green Island on the east coast of Jersey. Dennis Audrain, one of three teenagers attempting to escape from the Island in heavy seas, is drowned when the engine of their little boat fails and the boat is dashed against the rocks and overturns. The other two boys, Peter Hassall and Maurice Gould, are arrested when they swim back to the beach. They are tried in accordance with the infamous *Nacht und Nebel* terror decree, by which those who carry out anti-Nazi activities are just 'disappeared'. No one – family, friends or their governments – are told of their whereabouts, or even if they are dead or alive. Peter Hassall cleverly manages to survive, to live with the memory that it was his own mother who

had betrayed the boys to the German harbour police. Maurice Gould, however, dies in the concentration camp.

26 June

All wireless sets belonging to the civilian population have to be handed in to the Germans in accordance with Article 53 of the Hague Convention. The Germans' right to do this is disputed in Bulletin No.1 of the British Patriots in which it is stated quite bluntly that Article 53 of the Hague Convention quite definitely does not give the German authorities the right to confiscate cycles, wireless sets or any other form of personal property. The German authorities have neither legal nor moral right to confiscate wireless sets.

The Germans are aware that any half-way competent radio engineer can convert a radio receiving set into a rudimentary transmitting set, and they do not want information about the fortification programme to reach Britain. A good reason for the confiscation.

All protests are ignored by the Germans and thousands of sets are surrendered.

July

In informal conversation, Hitler mentions his plans for the Islands once the War is over:

With the fortifications we have constructed and the permanent garrison of a whole division, we have made certain that never again will the Islands fall into British hands. When the War is over they can be handed over to Ley for, with their wonderful climate, they would make a wonderful health resort for the 'Strength through Joy' (Kraft durch Freude) organisation.

8 August

A daring commando raid on the Casquets

Lighthouse. The British mistake some of the German soldiers for women as they are wearing hair nets to keep their long locks tidy while they sleep. Seven Germans are taken prisoner.

September

Hitler discovers that his instruction to deport British-born Islanders in retaliation for the internment of German nationals in Persia has been forgotten or ignored. He re-issues his order and this time it will be carried out. On ...

15 September

... the instruction arrives in the Islands. The Island Authorities vigorously protest that such an order is in breach of international law. The Germans, Brosch in Guernsey and Knackfuss in Jersey, tell them that such protest is futile as the order comes direct from Hitler, who will countenance no opposition to his 'unalterable' will.
So between ...

16 and 29 September

... just over 2,000 British-born Islanders are deported to internment camps Biberach, Laufen, Dorsten and Wurzach. Their worst fears are not realised, for these are not concentration camps and the regime is relatively civilised. Leaders of the camp communities are appointed and community life organised. And, most importantly, they are in receipt of Red Cross food parcels.

The deportations mark a serious deterioration in the relationship between the Islanders and the Germans. The Occupation is not quite as 'model' as it was thought to be. And the atmosphere is about to get a whole lot worse for on ...

3 October

... there is a commando raid code-named

Basalt on Sark. It is not the finest hour for the British. The small force manages to take prisoner five Germans quartered at the Dixcart Hotel. Their hands are tied and the commandos then try and take them back down the Hog's Back to the waiting boat. But the Germans try to escape and the commandos shoot two of them dead. Hitler is outraged at this shooting in the back of bound prisoners and orders all Allied prisoners to be shackled as a retaliatory measure. And more than this, on ...

27 December

... Hitler orders more deportations of Channel Islanders. This time they will include Freemasons, Jews, army officers, churchmen, people with criminal convictions and any prominent and wealthy citizens who might be working against German interests. The families of all these categories are included in the lists.

Not a happy end to the year for the Islanders, but an even worse beginning to the new year for hundreds of Alderney slave workers who in ...

1943
January

... find themselves aboard the two German transport ships, the *Xaver Dorsch* and the *Franka*. They are being shipped out to Cherbourg, but a storm blows up and the two ships are thrown onto the rocks just outside Braye harbour. And here they will stay for 14 days in truly appalling conditions. Scores of the workers, already weakened by conditions in the Alderney work camps, die in the holds of the wrecked ships.

12 February

Following Hitler's order of December 1942 the second deportation takes place, although it is not as large as had been at

first feared. In the event 201 Islanders are deported. They include Ambrose Sherwill and Elisabet Duquemin, her husband and their baby daughter.

March

The SS arrive in Alderney. Maximilian List, who bears an uncanny resemblance to Himmler, and Kurt Klebeck, take over Sylt camp. This is to be the place where the particular enemies of Hitler – Jews, German communists etc, are to be corralled and, of course, treated abominably.

3 March

Germans begin arresting Jerseymen in connection with the illegal possession of wireless sets and the dissemination of news in the Island. These include Canon Clifford Cohu, acting Rector of St Saviour's and Hospital Chaplain, his churchwarden, the parish clerk and the gravedigger. They are tried on ...

9 April

... and all found guilty. Harsh sentences are handed out and on ...

13 April

... the Germans issue this notice explaining why the punishments are so harsh:

Although in June 1942, i.e. 10 months ago, the handing over of wireless sets was ordered, and furthermore, in December, 1942, another Order was published by which persons who were still in possession of apparatus were given the opportunity of delivering up the same without suffering punishment, wireless sets are still being found in possession of the local population.

Therefore at the sitting of the court martial last weekend, it was necessary to inflict heavier punishment than given last year on those persons retaining wireless sets.

Furthermore the news bulletins broadcast by the BBC have been spread both verbally and by leaflets, although the persons concerned were well aware of their criminal actions. The three persons chiefly concerned were, therefore, sentenced to punishments ranging from one year to three years imprisonment, while the rest received lighter sentences.

Clifford Cohu will end up in Zoschen camp.

May
There has been a good deal of Royal Navy and RAF activity in the Channel. Essential supplies to the Islands are being disrupted and reduced. The Germans propose to reduce the food rations saying that the Islanders will 'know who to blame' for their consequent distress. The Islands' authorities see the German action as a reprisal measure and complain bitterly. The Germans backtrack furiously, wishing above all to avoid the accusation that it was in fact a reprisal, and on ...

7 May
... the following notice appears in the Islands' press. It includes this disclaimer from the from the Field Commander:

The delegation received the assurance of the Feld Kommandant *that the 20% reduction of the present bread ration of the entire civil population over 21 years of age is dictated by the existing war situation and is in no sense a punishment against the civil population.*

September
Disastrous naval action in the Channel! A Royal Navy task force attempts to attack and destroy a German convoy. In the engagement the nimble and lethal German E-boats completely outmanoevre the British ships and two of them, HMS *Charybdis* and HMS *Limbourne* are sunk. 500 men are killed or drowned.

16 November
Wilhelm Casper, instrumental in the killing of Steiner, Spitz and Grunfeld, leaves the Islands to join forces with Werner Best, *un Nazi de l'ombre*, who is the big German controller in Denmark. The position of Chief Civil Administrator in the Channel Islands is taken over by the Baron von Aufsess.

17 November
41 of the naval personnel from HMS *Charybdis* and HMS *Limbourne* are buried with full military honours in Guernsey. Over 5,000 Islanders turn out for the ceremony, turning it into a massive demonstration of anti-German feeling. Some people expressed that feeling a little differently as on ...

20 December
... a Jersey woman is found guilty of anti-German activity. She had had the temerity to hurl horse manure at a passing troop of German soldiers. She is sentenced to three months' imprisonment, which is doubled on appeal.

Horse manure is not the only thing being thrown at the hated Hun. The Islanders look up and can see scores of bombers flying overhead heading for targets on the Continent. The Islanders are much cheered by the sight. The War will be over soon. As the *Evening Post* puts it, in careful language so as not to annoy the German guests:

Standing today on the threshold of a new year, we gaze with brightened vision upon the days of 1944 which stretch out before us, and hope again springs up in our hearts as we long for the peace which will banish war and bring us to normal living conditions.

1944

2 March

Field Commander Knackfuss is hauled back to France to be tried for what are deemed to be 'defeatist comments' on the outcome of the War. His replacement at FK515 is Heider. The Germans are getting very nervous and apprehensive as the War, on every front, turns more and more against them. Hitler persists with his disastrous 'stand fast' strategy, and on ...

3 March

The Islands are declared 'Fortresses', or *Festung*, to be defended to the last bullet and the last man. It is a recipe for suicide as will be demonstrated bloodily over and over again, from Breslau to Bayreuth, as the endgame is played out.

May

The tempo of operations against the Germans is hotting up. There are increased air attacks along the Cherbourg peninsula. 25 ships are sunk. It is becoming increasingly difficult to get supplies into the Islands. In fact little or no food is getting through at all. The situation is becoming desperate.

19 May

The Germans are gearing up for what looks likely to be the final struggle, or 'Final Victory' as Goebbels calls it.

The German civil administration body, *Feldkommandantur* 515 is re-titled *Platzkommandantur* and its numbers severely reduced Its more able-bodied members are absorbed into units of the army and guns thrust into their hands. The fight is imminent.

And in Jersey Louisa Gould and her brother Harold Le Druillenec are arrested.

June 6th D-DAY

The Allies land on the Normandy beaches. The fighting is hard. The casualties many. The Americans in particular suffer a 90% casualty rate on their initial landing. But a foothold is gained and the great offensive which will lead all the way to Berlin is about to begin. The Islanders expect that the Allies will soon, if not immediately, turn their attention to them, attack and deliver them from the Nazi yoke. Alas for these hopes!

The invasion of the Channel Islands figures not at all in the plans of the Allied High Command. Just as they are, the Islands are making a great contribution to the war on the continent. A whole division of 26,000 men is bottled up here, unable to help their hard-pressed comrades across the water in any way. They are virtually POWs. A very satisfactory state of affairs from the Allies' point of view. Nonetheless, Hitler, still clinging to his belief that the Islands will be attacked, declares on ...

17 June

... that the Islands are to be defended to the last man. There will be no surrender. And it looks like there will be no food either, for all the supply ports, Cherbourg, Granville and St Malo, are captured by the Allies. The lifelines to the Islands are cut off one by one. Soon there will be no food, no coal and no fuel. The outlook is bleak.

July

German casualties from the ferocious fighting in France around St Malo are being shipped across the dangerous water to be treated in hospitals in Guernsey and Jersey. There is a chronic shortage of medical supplies and many operations on badly-wounded soldiers are performed without the aid of drugs or anaesthetic.

Coutanche and Carey appeal to the Germans to urgently address the problem of food supply by going to the Protecting Power who can then ask the British or the Red Cross for aid. There is little in the way of a positive response until ...

19 September
The Swiss Red Cross are informed by the Germans that the civilian rations are exhausted and on ...

27 September
... The Swiss government tells the British of the parlous state of affairs in the Islands. They also tell them that the Germans will accept either Red Cross aid to alleviate distress or, more dramatically, the wholesale evacuation of the Islanders. There is a move to accept the first proposal. But then Churchill himself steps in. With total disregard to the welfare of the Islanders, and in the name of military necessity, he wants the Germans to surrender. The grounds, which they themselves must recognise, are that they cannot fulfil their obligations towards the civilian population under their jurisdiction. The Germans, predictably enough, refuse to surrender on these, or indeed any other grounds. The going gets tough and the Germans get going. During ...

October
... they ransack the Islands for food. John Leale in Guernsey and Alexander Coutanche in Jersey protest that this taking of food from a captive civilian population is a crime in international law. It is in direct and obvious breach of the Hague Convention. Schmettow, taking a leaf out of Churchill's book, cites 'military necessity' as the justifying factor. The British and the Germans are both obdurately entrenched in their own positions. The Islanders, meanwhile, find the situation getting worse by the hour as ...

November
.... gas and electricity supplies are cut off or rather just stop. There is no food worth the name. There is hardly a dog, a cat, or a horse left to eat. There are no medical supplies remotely sufficient to the need of the increasing number of patients in the hospitals. Doctors are forced to introduce a system of selection when treating the sick.

They prioritize certain patients such as the young and those with a better prospect of recovery. It is a hard time. People die because proper medical care cannot be provided.

The situation cannot be allowed to continue. There is a massive increase in the pressure on Churchill to alter his view. He had maintained that to send food to the Islands would be to provide sustenance to the enemy – which should always be denied.

This is the iron law of warfare according to the British war leader – but he does eventually hear the many voices speaking persuasively into his ear about the pitiable state of the Islanders. The Allies are now miles into France. The Germans in the Islands are no conceivable threat being so far behind the front. Churchill now sees that the Channel Islands are best viewed as a rather large POW camp. This is a good thing and yes, of course, permission will be given for the Red Cross to go in with food and medical supplies and on ...

7 November
... The War Cabinet formally agrees that the Red Cross may supply the Channel Islands, with the proviso that the Germans will continue to guarantee basic rations. A month almost to the day after this decision is made, on ...

8 December
... This notice appears in the Islands' newspapers

I am officially informed by the German Military Authorities that a Red Cross ship was, weather permitting, due to leave Lisbon on Thursday, December 7th, for the Channel Islands. The ship will call at Guernsey first, en route for Jersey.

The good ship *Vega* does not however leave on this day but on ...

21 December

... the BBC announce that she has left Lisbon and is heading up through the Bay of Biscay towards the Islands. She won't arrive in time for Christmas but whenever she does arrive, which she does on ...

27–30 December

... she will be very, very welcome!

1945

28 January

The year opens with a coup in the German ranks, and one that bodes no good for the Islanders. Von Schmettow, the military commander, is manoeuvred out of office by the hard-line Nazi, Vice-Admiral Hüffmeier. How 'hard-line' he is, the Islanders are yet to discover. But before they do, they can rejoice that on ...

7 and 11 February

... The Vega pays a second visit to Jersey and Guernsey with her very welcome cargo of 700 tons of food, and medical supplies. And on ...

6 and 9 March

she comes again.

7 March

The Islanders are happier now the relief has arrived. But many of the German soldiers are not happy at all.

They see the War as lost, and lost because of Hitler and his Nazi party. Their beloved Fatherland is in ruins.

Their brothers-in-arms have died, are dying, in their millions and all for nothing. Mutiny is in the air. Up the road from St Helier at Bagatele, there is an explosion in the Palace Hotel. One German officer and eight NCOs are killed in the blast. It is thought that the explosion was all the greater because much of the material, explosives, munitions etc, for the Granville raid was stored there. This Granville raid takes place on the night of ...

8–9 March

... and is a qualified success. A number of American prisoners are taken and a small quantity of coal obtained. The Germans can still bite. And on ...

25 March

... Ex-commander of the *Scharnhorst*, *Inselkommandant* the Vice-Admiral Hüffmeier delivers in Hitlerian style (he holds a minute long pause before he begins) a mighty speech to the troops in which he vows never to surrender, never to give in until the last breath has left his body. He expects his men to be with him in this Armageddon.

He repeats these sentiments in his speech on Hitler's birthday on ...

20 April

.... which is the last birthday the most evil man in the history of the world will spend on this earth, for despite the announcement that Hitler falls 'fighting to the last' against the forces of Bolshevik Jewry, in fact on ...

30 April

... Adolf Hitler commits suicide deep inside his Berlin bunker. Admiral Doenitz is appointed as his heir to govern what little is left of the Third Reich. A little of that little is the Channel Islands. What will Hüffmeier and his soldiers do? Will they fight on to the bitter end or will they surrender quietly and without a fight?

Hüffmeier finally obeys his new commander's order for the surrender of all German forces in all theatres of war and on ...

9 May

... the Germans surrender to the British. Brigadier Snow and his Force 135 land triumphantly on the Islands to start picking up the pieces.

The War is finished. The Occupation of the Channel Islands is over.

Prologue

The twentieth century was the bloodiest century in the history of the modern world. There were two World Wars and innumerable smaller conflicts in the course of which millions of people were captured, enslaved, tortured and killed. No place on earth escaped the fighting, no soul in the world was left untouched by the killing frenzy.

It was thought that the First World War of 1914–18 was the war to end all wars but it proved to be nothing of the kind.

The victorious Allies imposed a peace on Germany which was not a peace at all but a revenge, as Hitler himself bitterly pointed out, and it reduced the country to grinding poverty, economic ruin, starvation and great suffering. It was rumoured that mothers in Hamburg were killing their babies because they had no way of feeding them. These were the years of the Weimar Republic – years of great decline and massive inflation with all their attendant evils.

Of course in such circumstances, discontent and revolutionary thinking flourished, indeed every form of radical thought found expression – violent expression – most obviously on the streets of the great German cities like Munich and Berlin. Two political groupings came to dominate the struggle for power: the Nazis on the right and the Communists on the left. In the end it was Adolf Hitler's Nazi Party that came to power in 1933. The new Fuehrer joyfully joined the select club of dictators, Stalin, Mussolini and Franco, who bestrode the world in these turbulent times. His ambitions for himself and for Germany were expansionist and avowedly racist. He wanted Germany restored to her pre-War shape and eminence as a leading European nation, and more than that he wanted to expand the territory of the restored Germany far into the east to provide the superior Aryan race with the living space they so badly needed. As for the Poles and Russians who lived in this great space, Hitler was going to annexe all their lands so that they became part of the Third Reich. The superior Aryans would take, as a matter of right, everything from their unfortunate neighbours, who were racially inferior Untermenschen, and as such would be exterminated or enslaved, whichever Hitler thought best, along with the Jews, who were the most inferior beings of all.

They, of course, had, through an international conspiracy, brought about the disastrous war of 1914–18 that had created and perpetuated the hated Bolshevism threatening to engulf all

Europe. The Jews were the cancer in the Nazi World and they were to be cut out.

This is what Hitler said in his speech of January 30th, 1939:

'And one other thing I wish to say on this day, which perhaps is memorable not only for us Germans: In my life I have often been a prophet, and most of the time I have been laughed at. During the period of my struggle for power, it was, in the first instance, the Jewish people that received with laughter my prophecies that some day I would take over the leadership of the state and thereby of the whole people, and that I would, among other things, solve also the Jewish problem. I believe that in the meantime that hyenous laughter has been smothered in their throats. Today I want to be a prophet once more: If international-finance Jewry inside and outside of Europe should succeed once more in plunging nations into another World War, the consequence will not be the Bolshevisation of the earth and thereby the victory of Jewry, but the annihilation (Vernichtung) of the Jewish race in Europe.'

The Fuehrer was to achieve this Jew-free Aryan paradise by force of arms or through the threat of violence at home or abroad. There was little diplomatic subtlety about the conduct of Hitler's foreign or domestic policy in the years after his assumption of power in 1933. Every day it seemed there were headlines trumpeting some new violation of the Versailles Treaty: the reoccupation of the Rhineland, Sudetenland, rearmament on a massive scale. Every day saw some new attack on political opponents of the regime, some new outrage or some new killing. Concentration camps and institutionalised thuggery were the order of the day, to say nothing of the subversion of the entire judicial system to the point where it became an instrument of Nazi tyranny. The law became an expression of the Fuehrer's will.

So it went on and on, chapter after chapter in the Great Nazi History Book, recording dangerous times in a dangerous world – a world far-removed from the Cotentin Peninsula and the people living in those little islands just offshore.

During these years of the 1930s when Hitler was killing his political adversaries or corralling them in concentration camps, while he was indulging in state terrorism and spreading fear and alarm all about him, far away from all of this, in peaceful isolation, the Channel Islands of Jersey, Guernsey, Alderney and Sark went about their business in a gentle, quiet and insular fashion, as they had done from time immemorial. They were certainly a part of the British Isles, but they were an atypical part. To extrapolate from their wartime experience general conclusions about how the rest of British society would have behaved during a German occupation, as has been done many times in post-War histories of the time, is a flawed exercise. The Islands were very much peculiar and not to be used as an exemplary instance of British society.

Jersey, the largest of the Islands, but still only nine miles by five with a population of around 35,000 was, then as now, famous for its cows: saddle-backed, large-eyed and of a beautiful light brown colour. Famous too for the Jersey Royal potatoes grown in the rich soil of the cotils under great layers of vraic, or seaweed, dragged off the beaches around the coast. The great Jersey artist Edmund Blampied, who designed the Occupation stamps and banknotes, has, in one glorious painting or etching after another, recorded many a vraic-gathering scene, great horses against a roaring sea under a blazing sun.

It looks idyllic, which indeed it was, though it must be said there was not a little poverty in the Island, particularly among the tenant farmers who lived in tiny cottages with dirt floors, no gas or electricity and no inside toilet. This last lack was apparently of great importance in the German evaluation of racial status, at least as far as one German officer on the Eastern Front was concerned. He averred that what distinguished the racially superior from the subhuman man was the possession of an indoor lavatory. On this evaluation most of the Island population (to say nothing of the British mainland population) would have been of an inferior species and outside the pale.

There was a little banking in the Island, not as much as now but nonetheless a substantial part of the Island income came from this source. And then there were the holidaymakers, all anxious to get away, if only for a few days, from the disquiet and unease on mainland Britain, spend a little precious time lounging on the warm sands of St Brelade's Bay, swimming in the crystal-clear water and then perhaps enjoying a delicious Jersey cream tea in one of the rather splendid hotels. The Isle was full of delights, a world away from troubled Europe and mad dictators.

Jersey, like the other Channel Islands, was historically part of the Duchy of Normandy. When William the Conqueror became king of England after the Battle of Hastings in 1066 he continued to rule them as the Duke of Normandy. Although over the centuries England gradually lost all of her possessions on the French mainland, the Channel Islands remained steadfastly loyal to the English crown. They were, and are, a 'peculiar of the Crown' and are answerable to, and ruled ultimately, not by the British parliament but by the Queen in Privy Council or a committee thereof. The Islands enjoy an enviable degree of autonomy in most matters except defence. Domestic legislation is passed in the States, the Island's parliament, which is presided over by the Bailiff who is, in effect, the First Minister.

In 1940, when our story begins, the Bailiff of Jersey was the gloriously-named Alexander Moncrieff Coutanche, about whom we shall hear much more as the Occupation story unfolds.

The Bailiff of Guernsey was the elderly, somewhat portly but equally grandly-named Victor Gosselin Carey (he spent an unhappy 69th birthday greeting the first German occupiers of the Island). Each of the two Islands of Jersey and Guernsey had a Lieutenant Governor: Major General Richard Harrison in Jersey and Major General A. P. D. Telfer Smollet in Guernsey.

Guernsey, though not quite so fortunately formed for agriculture, nevertheless produced enormous amounts of tomatoes under glass for export. Jersey had her potatoes; Guernsey had her tomatoes. Very little of anything else apart from flowers was produced at this time, but this was to change radically during the years of the Occupation.

A little offshore from Guernsey lies the most unspoilt and beautiful of the Islands. It is Sark. Three-and-a-half miles long and one-and-a-half miles wide, the tiny island is guarded by soaring 300-foot-high cliffs which are extremely difficult to scale (as the men on the night-time commando raids were to find out to their cost). Easier access to the island is via a small harbour and up through a tunnel hewn through the rock. The chief occupations of the Sarkese were fishing, dairy farming and a little holiday trade. At the time of the outbreak of war the 600-strong population was looked after, in time-honoured fashion, by the formidable Dame of Sark, Sibyl Hathaway, née Collings. An Islander born and bred, her great-grandfather, John Allaire, had been a privateer, a species of licensed pirate, who made a great fortune from robbing merchant ships sailing up and down the Channel. As the Dame herself remarks, he was a man 'of unchristian temper, debauchery and iniquity,' but the money he made enabled his daughter, Mary, to become the Dame of Sark.

Mary married a Guernseyman, Thomas Collings, Sibyl's grandfather. And so the title of Seigneur was passed down through the family until by 1940 it was held by Sibyl Hathaway (as she had become after her marriage to the American, Bob Hathaway). The fact that he was a US citizen and had been an officer in the Royal Flying Corps during the First World War was to have serious consequences for the Dame come the deportations of 1943.

Sibyl's proper title was 'La Dame de Serq,' the female equivalent of the Seigneur. She presided over the governance of the Island through its own parliament called the Court of Chief Pleas, with its attendant Court of Justice. There was no income tax, no death duties and not a car in sight! It was a lovely little Island paradise caught in a feudal time warp: private, quiet and completely hidden away from that dangerous world across the sea on mainland Europe.

A short trip over the water from Sark will bring you to the last of the four main Islands, Alderney, which, it is generally admitted, appears less immediately pleasing to the eye than Sark. In fact in 1940 it was a rather bleak, inhospitable place and, it must be said, rather backward. There was farming it is true, but it was all rather primitive, subsistence farming. A few of the more enterprising bred pedigree calves for export to Guernsey and there was some granite quarrying, but that was all apart from the inevitable smuggling from time to time. The communication system within the Island was almost non-existent. There were no telephones and – very unfortunately for the Islanders in June 1940 – there was no underground cable linking the Island to Guernsey. It was the town crier, paid half-a-crown a time, who was used to convey news around the Island, and it was the wireless that was used to talk to the outside world. Alderney had no legislative chamber of its own and no courts of justice. Constitutionally it was part of the Bailiwick of Guernsey. The local man in charge of the Island was Judge French, an Englishman and an ex-soldier. It was he who led the Alderney folk away across the Channel leaving the Island for the Germans to take vacant possession.

In the summer of 1940 all the Islands, 'little pieces of France fallen into the sea and scooped up by Britain,' as Victor Hugo described them, lay in the hot sunshine, defenceless in the face of the advancing Germans. There was no help to hand. No British troops to defend them.

The bad news came on the back of an envelope.

Major General Harrison was the Lieutenant Governor of Jersey from 1939 to 1940. In June 1940 he received a phone call from Major General Percival, Assistant Chief of the Imperial Staff at the War Office. He wrote down the conversation quickly on the back of an envelope before going to deliver the news to the States of Jersey Assembly.

It reads:

War Cabinet decision is that the Island of Jersey is to be demilitarised. All troops to be withdrawn.

Further issues regarding Lieutenant General will be sent.

From Major General Percival

Chapter 1
Betrayal and Buffoonery

'We shall go on to the end. We shall fight in France, we shall fight on the seas and oceans, we shall fight with growing confidence and growing strength in the air, we shall defend our island whatever the cost may be. We shall fight on the beaches. We shall fight on the landing grounds, we shall fight in the streets, we shall fight in the hills ...'

Winston Churchill

'We shall fight everywhere but in the Channel Islands' he might have added...

Lord Portsea, otherwise known as Bertram Falle, a doughty 80-year-old Jerseyman, scathingly characterised the British government's handling of the Channel Islands in the weeks leading up to the disaster of June 28th as 'sheer stark buffoonery!' More than that, he declared the Islanders had been 'betrayed' by the British government, 'left in the lurch', utterly defenceless and so vulnerable to every kind of assault by the enemy. It is difficult to disagree with the noble Lord's assessment, for certainly it is true that when the Heinkels came out of the clear blue summer skies that awful Friday evening, the Islanders had not a weapon with which to defend themselves, no militia and not a single British soldier to offer any kind of protection.

Lord Portsea was right. The Islanders had been abandoned and he was angry:

'If the Islands could not have been held by the Islanders for more than a few weeks, those men at least could have died, and died decently, instead of being slaves. And how could they have died better? Fancy a British Government, an English Government, saying the odds were too great, a thousand to one, people would be killed! We have heard of Agincourt...'

The Islanders had indeed been abandoned and also 'betrayed', but in a more subtle way than Bertram Falle imagined at the time.

The story of this 'betrayal' is one of panic, naivety, political and military ignorance and, most significantly of all, a gross if unthinking failure to properly care for and protect the lives and welfare of the beleaguered Island folk.

This unfortunate and unpleasant turn of events was to have a profound effect on the relationship between the British Government and the Islanders, particularly in an immediate post-war period which was full of accusation and recrimination. This is how the action unfolded. This was the timetable of events leading up to that evening of Friday 28th June:

Wednesday 5th June

The Chief of the Imperial General Staff, General Sir John Dill, presented a paper to the Chief of Staff Committee of the War Cabinet in which he declared, after a long, detailed and totally unnecessary account of the military history of the Channel Islands since AD600, that there was no danger of a full scale invasion but:

'If the enemy effected a landing it would be necessary to eject him as a matter of prestige.'

In this last remark there is some recognition of the potential propaganda value of the Islands. If Sir John had developed this line of thinking a little further he might have concluded that if indeed it would be necessary to eject the enemy as a matter of prestige, the enemy might think it equally necessary to invade and occupy the Islands for precisely the same reason. What a propaganda coup it would be if German forces set foot on British soil! Of course such thinking would have seriously weakened the notion that in all probability the Germans would not bother to attack the Islands.

This judgement, that there was no immediate danger to the Islands, was based on the belief, held for many a long year, that the Channel Islands could have no strategic value for either side. In other words there was no military point in either attacking them or defending them. So in all probability the Germans would just ignore the Islands. They would simply leave them

be to advertise themselves as a holiday haven in the sunshine away from the horrors of war.

Wednesday 12th June

On this Wednesday morning, Sir John Dill read his paper for a second time but this time to the War Cabinet, saying again that the Channel Islands had no strategic value or importance. Nonetheless on the grounds of prestige alone some defence arrangements should be made. The Chiefs of Staff agreed with this and it was decided to despatch two battalions to the Islands.

Events, however, were moving extraordinarily swiftly. This was no re-run of the First World War, a war of attrition and stalemate. It was emphatically not a positional war. This was a war of rapid movement, improvisation, lightning manoeuvres and blitzkrieg.

At the very moment this meeting was taking place, news came in of the imminent and triumphant arrival of the enemy on the coast of France. A second urgent meeting of the War Cabinet was convened in the afternoon. It was decided, in the light of this latest information, to review their earlier decision to despatch the two battalions across the water to defend the Channel Islands.

Thursday13th June

Next morning General Sir John Dill, CIGS reappraised the situation of the Channel Islands.

With the enemy in Cherbourg and thrusting towards St Malo, it was absolutely clear that the Germans would soon have absolute control along the entire French coastline.

There was nothing to stop them.

This being so, the cable link from France to Jersey and to mainland Britain, the existence of which had provided a small reason to defend the Islands, would be rendered ineffective. There was now not even the smallest strategic reason to try and defend the Islands with the two battalions. Besides, these two battalions would be needed urgently to defend the mainland against imminent invasion by the enemy.

The decision was rescinded. No British troops would go to defend the Islands.

Friday 14th June

The Germans had crossed the Seine at Quillebeuf. The saturnine Bailiff of Jersey, Alexander Moncrieff Coutanche, clever, able, and with a razor-sharp brain said:

'I happen to know that part of the country very well. If the Germans have crossed the Seine at Quillebeuf there is nothing whatever to stop them coming here.'

He was right. There was not and he was fearful therefore.

Accompanied by the Attorney General, Charles Duret Aubin, the Bailiff hastened to meet with the Lieutenant Governor Major General James

Harrison. He asked him to ring up London as a matter of urgency, to find out what they thought of this dangerous situation and what the Islanders should do, as they had not had a peep out of the Home Office all this while.

Very concerned himself, Harrison put a trunk call through to Charles Markbreiter, the Assistant Secretary at the Home Office with special responsibility for the Channel Islands. Charles Markbreiter seemed remarkably unconcerned about Jersey's situation:

'I haven't thought about it very much, but it does not appear to me to have changed significantly.'

Coutanche expressed the entirely opposite view – that the situation had indeed changed, drastically and for the worse:

'When did you last get an appraisal from the War Office?'

asked the Bailiff. Markbreiter replied:

'Oh I don't really know, but there hasn't been anything to disturb us very much.'

Coutanche, in a remarkably restrained and polite manner, asked the vague Assistant Secretary if he would be kind enough to please get in touch with the War Office to find out exactly what they thought. Markbreiter did just that and discovered that the War Office, like Coutanche, were not at all happy with the situation and indeed they wanted the Bailiff to fly across to London that very afternoon for a conference with them as a matter of urgency.

Events, however, overtook the plan. Instead of flying to London, Coutanche was required to stay in the Island to organise and oversee the evacuation of British troops from St Malo, trapped there by the rapid German advance. Jurat Edgar Dorey was sent to London in his place.

It was decided on this Saturday that the Islands would be demilitarised but that both the Islands' airfields must be defended on bases from which the RAF could help British troops up in the north-west of France for as long as possible.

'Thereafter the policy of demilitarisation will rule.'

At this point no formal declaration of demilitarisation was made, but nonetheless the War Cabinet had definitely decided that the Channel Islands were to be demilitarised at an 'early date'.

Sunday 16th June
On this Sunday orders to immediately evacuate all troops from the Channel Islands were issued.

Tuesday 18th June
At last the Islanders were to be informed about what was planned for them. Jurat Dorey, who had flown to London in place of Bailiff Coutanche, was informed on this Tuesday of the decision taken by the War Cabinet three days before, on Saturday 15th June, to demilitarise the Island. Jurat Dorey was also told that 'in the interests of the inhabitants,' no attempt would be made to defend the Islands, which would be declared 'open towns'. All armed forces would be withdrawn and shipping would be provided for any civilians who decided to evacuate.

The Lieutenant Governors would be recalled and the Bailiffs would take over their titles and their duties.

What exactly those duties would be was set out in a letter from Sir Alexander Maxwell, the Permanent Undersecretary of State to the Lord Lieutenant which read:

Sir
I am directed by the Secretary of State to say that in the event of your recall it is desired by His Majesty's Government that the Bailiff should discharge the duties of Lieutenant Governor, which would be confined to civil duties and that he should stay at his post and administer the government of the island to the best of his abilities, in the interests of the inhabitants, whether or not he is in a position to receive instruction from His Majesty's Government. The Crown Officers also should remain at their posts.

I am sir, Your Obedient Servant
A. Maxwell.

It is important to note that the reason for the demilitarisation of the Islands was to serve the interests of the inhabitants, to save them from being bombed, assaulted and killed by a ruthless enemy; the laudable and proper intention of the British Government being to preserve the life and safety of the Islanders, even if they could no longer guarantee their liberty in the face of such overwhelming odds.

Unfortunately, and fatally for the Islanders, this intention was not carried through in the days leading up to Friday 28th June.

Wednesday 19th June

At a sitting of the Jersey States (the Island parliament) the lieutenant governor, General Harrison, was busy explaining to the assembled and very apprehensive Jurats and Deputies what the situation was, when a phone call came through from London. The formal decision had been taken to demilitarise the islands. Churchill himself disliked the decision with a passion, saying that:

'It would be repugnant now to abandon British territory which has been in possession of the Crown since the Norman Conquest!'

He was very much at one with Lord Portsea in believing that the Islands should be fought for and defended as a matter of national pride and honour. In the event, however, he bowed to the informed judgement of Vice Admiral Tom Phillips, that a military defence of the Islands was impossible given their proximity to the German front line and also given how stretched British military capabilities were in the region.

Fortunately for the Islanders, the British war leader, unlike his German counterpart, would take advice from his commanders in the field. Had there been a really concerted effort to defend the indefensible, it is true beyond peradventure that civilian casualties would have been enormous.

In Guernsey on this same day, 19th June, it was announced in the evening paper that the Islands were to be demilitarised.

There was, crucially, however, no formal declaration through the proper and accepted channels that demilitarisation had indeed taken place.

The Germans were not told and unless they had a spy in the Jersey States or had read the Guernsey evening paper they would not know of the new military status of the Islands.

They didn't have such a spy nor had they read the Guernsey newspaper. They did not know the Islands had been demilitarised. Consequently the Channel Islands remained for the Germans a legitimate military target.

The Islanders were now in grave danger. Green Arrow, the German operation to invade the Islands, was being planned for the end of the month. The Channel Islands were defenceless.

EVACUATION!
Thursday 20th June

On this Thursday all the remaining British troops were taken off the Islands aboard SS *Marlines* and SS *Biarritz*. The cable to France was cut. The two lieutenant governors packed their bags and left.

The Islanders were on their own: defenceless, vulnerable.

Panic set in. Stories of the inhuman savagery of the Germans, who were just a few short miles away, spread like wildfire. There were stories of rape, arbitrary killings, mass murder of civilians and the mutilation of children, to feed the terror. Given the terrible news from Poland these stories had a deal of foundation in fact. In Guernsey the Reverend Douglas Ord writes in his diary:

'It all looks like the end of the world – or of this little world at least.

June 20th. The margin of time for registration proved too narrow last night. Crowds besieged the Constables' offices and the suggested timetable was thrown out of gear. Under cover of darkness, children have been leaving. Now with coming of day all roads lead to St Peter Port. Thousands throng the street. Normal life is completely suspended. Everywhere the same questions are heard: "What shall we do?" and "Where shall we go?" Long queues formed as early as 6 a.m. in Lefebvre Street, which was so packed with humanity that movement was impossible. Those who came to register found that a queue four deep filled the length of the street. One might have walked on the heads of the crowd. Those who fainted could only with difficulty be attended. A fearful target for aircraft! But no orders for dispersal were issued. The Registration Order was so worded that many supposed it was obligatory. Hence great numbers registered as a precaution, myself included, though, as it proved, unnecessarily.

Mr Sherwill did his best and spoke of arrangements that were being made , adding that it was most unlikely that the mass of Guernsey folk could hope to evacuate. Men of military age, while not compelled, should go to England and do their duty there. To remain would court the possibility of slave labour' though in the speaker's opinion that would prove unlikely. He said he really did not know if the Germans would come to the Island. Perhaps we might escape the rigours of an occupation after all. The food problem would be the most serious thing they would have to face. Hence the evacuation of the young. And so with further cheering words he sent the people away.

(*Diary of Reverend Ord*)

It was an ambiguous and cloudy message from the Attorney General.

People were unsure what to do for the best.

Best to err on the side of caution. A mass evacuation took place: 17,000 out of 41,000 Guernsey folk left; 6,500 out of

50,000 in Jersey; all but 18 in Alderney, and 129 out of 600 in Sark. It was a fearful time for the Islanders, particularly in Guernsey where there was genuine panic and no clear direction from the Island leaders.

People did not know what to do for the best, but the general feeling was that to leave was the wisest course, children first. Crowds rushed down to the harbour of St Peter Port to get on whatever boat was going westward – if one could be found:

'I was just started school and I remember ever so well in that classroom, the hustle and bustle going on, being given a gas mask and labels to put on my coat and that, and the next thing was we were sent home because the boat hadn't arrived to take us.'

(Eileen du Mouilipied)

'We didn't know what was happening. We didn't know if a boat was coming to fetch us, and then the headmaster said, "I'm sorry, you must all go back home and come back again at 2 o'clock tomorrow morning." So we all went back and I, my mum and dad, brought us to the school, there was a lot of other people there and there were buses waiting for us and about dawn it was, it was daylight.'

(Stanley Martin)

Eileen and Stanley did eventually get away, but over in Jersey Marion Rossler recalls that:

'We stayed. I believe my brother wasn't

very well, but I don't know if that was a bit of an excuse for my father to stay because he was an out-and-out Jerseyman and he wouldn't have wanted to go. That I know, though we had the opportunity.'

But 6,500 other Jersey folk left as quickly as possible:

'We watched the cars drive down onto the pier and people tumbled out of them dragging suitcases, and the cars were left with the doors open and the ignition keys in them and they just went on board the boats and that was it.'

(Leo Harris)

Those who remained were now in a very dangerous situation, and more dangerous than they knew, for no one told either of the bailiffs that the Germans had not been informed of the demilitarisation. They were utterly and completely defenceless, yet still regarded by the enemy as a legitimate military target. Their only defence from attack was that they had no defence. But the Germans did not know that. They assumed, lacking any knowledge to the contrary, that in all probability the Islands were garrisoned and strongly defended. They would act accordingly.

Saturday 22nd June

The Chiefs of Staff requested that the Foreign Office formally declare to the enemy the demilitarisation of the Islands. A press notice was prepared declaring the Islands demilitarised, but this notice was withheld on the grounds that it would be read by the Germans who would regard it as an open invitation to just walk in. So there was at this point still no formal declaration. The Germans still regarded the Islands as legitimate military targets.

Monday 24th June

A message from the King arrived in the Islands.

'For Strategic Reasons it has been necessary to withdraw the armed forces from the Channel Islands. I deeply regret this necessity and I wish to assure my people in the Islands that in taking this decision My Government has not been unmindful of their position. It is in their interest that this step should be taken in present circumstance. The long association of the Islands with the Crown and the loyal service the people of the Islands have rendered to my ancestors and myself are guarantees that the link between us will remain unbroken and I know that my people in the Islands will look forward with the same confidence as I do to the day when the resolute fortitude with which we face our present difficulties will reap the reward of victory.'

It was accompanied by a gnomic instruction to communicate the message to the Islanders:

'In such a manner as may seem to you advisable having regard to the interests of national security.'

In other words let as few people as possible know of this message for fear the enemy find out about the demilitarisation. The upshot was that very few Islanders knew of the King's message and the small crumbs of comfort it contained. They knew nothing of the King's care and concern for them at this dreadful time. Their sense of abandonment was complete.

By this day, too, there was still no formal declaration of demilitarisation. The Chiefs of Staff did however repeat their suggestion that the Foreign Office should make such a declaration.

There was a meeting. The subject was discussed.

It was again suggested that such a declaration would amount to an open invitation to the enemy to walk in. The possibility that without such a declaration the Germans would march in anyway, but with all guns blazing, was not discussed.

It was also asserted at this meeting, in a somewhat paradoxical fashion, that they did not need to make a formal declaration of demilitarisation because the Germans probably knew about it anyway through their intelligence network. As a matter of fact the Germans did not know of the demilitarisation. Their intelligence was not that good.

They had not read the Island newspapers. They did not have spies in the Islands' parliaments and they had not heard the King's message.

The Germans, who should have been among the first to know, still did not. The Islands remained a military target and time was running out.

Friday 28th June

It was a beautiful sunny day. The Islands were bathed in summer heat. Children were playing on the beaches. Down on the docks in St Helier and St Peter Port there were long lines of lorries loading up the ships with potatoes and tomatoes.

In Guernsey too, cattle which had been abandoned in Alderney and rescued by a Guernsey task force were due to be landed. A large meeting was planned, at which Major Ambrose Sherwill, the Attorney General, was going to speak.

The bombers came in the early evening, first to Guernsey and then to Jersey. First the long lines of lorries were bombed and then the whole dockside area was machine-gunned. The Guernsey lifeboat was attacked as she was travelling between Guernsey and Jersey. Tragically, Harold Hobbs, the young son of the coxswain, was killed.

Altogether, 44 people were killed. It is more than probable that no one would have been killed had the enemy known of the demilitarisation, had there been a proper formal declaration of demilitarisation.

To make such a declaration was now, of course, an absolute necessity, lest more bombers came and more Islanders be slaughtered. Ambrose Sherwill, who was to figure so largely in the Occupation history, said as much and forcefully too. It so happened that he was on the phone to Markbrieter at the Home Office in London arguing this point when the bombs began to fall on St Peter Port. 'Here they come,' he said, and held the phone up for the Secretary to hear. It had the desired effect. That night on the 9 o'clock BBC news the Islands were declared a demilitarised zone.

As it happened, the much-vaunted German Intelligence failed to pick up the broadcast.

Sunday 30th June

At last, on this last Sunday of the month, the Foreign Office was stirred into action and did what it should have done two weeks before. Joseph P. Kennedy, United States (still neutral) ambassador in London was now asked to relay a note to the Germans via the United States embassy in Berlin which read:

'The Islands are demilitarised and cannot be considered in any way as a legitimate target for bombardment.'

If the declaration had been made sooner, then in all probability the tragedy of 28th June would have been avoided.

The policy of keeping the

demilitarisation secret from the Germans was mistaken and dangerous. Concealing demilitarisation from the enemy would, at the very best, have meant the Germans continued to believe the Islands were defended and caused them, perhaps, to pause for a few hours, before advancing if they so wished. For the sake of these few hours, no proper, unambiguous declaration was made to the Germans and as a consequence the Channel Islands were left open and vulnerable to the terrible assault of 28th June. The main concern of the British Government was plainly not, as it should have been, the safety and welfare of the Islanders, but in delaying a possible German invasion by a couple of days.

The Islanders paid a heavy price for this confusion of priorities, born of an understandable panic and confusion though it might have been. Lord Portsea's accusation that the Islanders were 'betrayed' had real force, and how keenly the British Government felt it to be true is a key to understanding their attitude towards the Islanders when the days of reckoning came at the War's end.

But that was five long years away.

Chapter 2

The Bombing

The Jersey Bailiff, Alexander Moncrieff Coutanche, was absolutely correct in his judgement of 14th June that the Germans' all-conquering advance across the Seine would not suddenly stop at the coast of France. Without doubt they would attempt to cross the few miles of water, invade and occupy the Islands. Indeed Hitler clearly announced his determination to take over these little parts of Britain in a directive unambiguously declaring that the Channel Islands were 'to be occupied as a matter of urgency.' He was aware, as London often seemed not to be, of the huge propaganda value in having German boots on British soil. It would be seen as a massive victory for Hitler and the Third Reich, a glorious opening scene in the final act of the War in the West which, it was confidently expected, would end in a matter of weeks rather than months.

Apart from the undoubted propaganda worth of such an occupation, it is also true that the German estimation of the strategic value of the Islands differed markedly from that of the British. We have already discovered that it was the deeply embedded belief of CIGS in London that the Channel Islands were of negligible strategic use to any side in the conflict and, more than that, because of their location and geography, they were indefensible. This belief was not new. It had been held from as early as 1932. Some thought had been given to providing the Islands with some military protection when the cable joining England to France via the Channel Islands had been a viable installation, but with the Germans on the coast of the Cherbourg Peninsula it ceased to have any use and was cut on 13th June. Some attempts were also made to protect the Islands' harbours and airports in order to safeguard the evacuation of defeated British and French troops from France, but they had all gone through by 20th June. At this time, to all intents and purposes, the Channel Islands ceased to be of any strategic importance whatsoever to the British. There were no troops there, no harbours or airports that were of any use, and no communications system to be defended. The Islands were completely demilitarised but, as we have seen, the Germans did not know of this (from their point of view happy) state of affairs.

In fact, the German High Command saw the Islands as a very real and very near threat to Germany's western flank, from which attacks on the French mainland could be launched. So allied to the propaganda value of occupying the Islands there was also a perceived military imperative to attack. This being so, the practical questions to be answered were, 'How well defended are the Islands?' and, 'What sort of force will be needed to take them?'

In order to answer the second question the Luftwaffe set about trying to answer the first, by launching reconnaissance flights to observe and photograph the Islands. Of course if the Germans had been informed of the British decision, taken on 15th June, to demilitarise the Islands they would have had the answers to both the questions: which is to say the Islands were not defended at all and therefore no great force would be needed to occupy them. Sadly the Germans were not so informed and continued with the reconnaissance flights as a preparation for activating Operation Green Arrow (*Grüne Pfeile*) to capture a little piece of Britain for Adolf Hitler.

The reconnaissance exercise produced varying and ambiguous results – yes there were many military-looking installations in Jersey, Guernsey and Alderney but (as Michael Ginns the great expert in Occupation matters has pointed out) many of the photographs were taken from such great heights that it was often impossible to determine their correct vintage or their capability. As many, if not the majority, of the military installations, forts and gun towers in the Islands had been built over a century before during the Napoleonic Wars, this difficulty with proper identification was a severe hindrance in the attempt to make a

proper assessment of the Islands' defensive capacity. Even the fact that not a single shot had been fired at the observer planes flying over the Islands was taken to mean not that the Islands were undefended, but that, in all probability, the Islands' garrisons were lying low, not giving their positions away and keeping their powder dry.

By 28th June there was still no certain knowledge about the military status of the Islands. The Germans had still not been correctly and formally told that the Islands were undefended and a demilitarised zone. They believed that more aggressive methods had to be employed to discover what was going on over in the Islands. So it was, on the afternoon of June 28th, that the Heinkels took off from Cherbourg to carry out an 'armed reconnaissance'.

The mission, to carry out bombing raids on St Helier and St Peter Port.

The aim, to provoke an armed response, the size of which would provide the invaders with a proper understanding of the Islands' defensive capability.

The chosen aeroplane used for this 'armed reconnaissance' was the Heinkel III which was the main type of bomber used by the Luftwaffe in the early days of the war. It was a twin-engined medium bomber, a bit slow it must be said, with a top speed of 200 mph when fully bomb-laden. But in addition to the bombs, it was armed with a murderously efficient 7.92 mm machine gun, the MG15, which could fire at the rate of a thousand rounds a minute, each round travelling at 1691 mph.

No doubt about it, the Heinkel III was a highly efficient killing machine.

And so it proved that summer's evening of 28th June when they swooped down on the Islands: bombing, strafing, killing.

The pilots probably did not see Mary, Bernard and Eva crouched, hiding under the bench by La Rocque harbour. But the children had seen them:

'We saw the planes, you could see the planes. Mary Roberts, Bernard and myself were standing there. We'd been down to the beach all day, swimming, and Uncle Frank, all the children called him Uncle Frank, Mr Gallichon, and there was a bench there, and he just put us under there to save us, because otherwise we would automatically just run across the road home. So we stayed there until it was clear, he let us go. Our mother put us under the bed before they came to machine-gun. They made a kind of circle, machine-gunning everything and then we went down to Mrs Mauger's to stay the night in case they came back and for a long time I was frightened of planes and I would dive under the table and even now, I don't like them it just turns me.'

And Yvonne Bouteloupe tells of a miraculous escape:

'I was waiting for my brother and mother to come home. They had gone for an interview with Mr Gallichon at the Bakery. Eddie was being accepted for an apprenticeship there. I was standing in the doorway of our cottage which is on the far side of La Rocque, when I saw three aeroplanes. I thought they were the aeroplanes I had seen earlier in the day flying towards France and thought it was them coming back. Then suddenly I heard this whistling sound and – crump! – crump! I knew we were being bombed. I ran back down the passage to my grandmother who was sitting in the kitchen. She was crippled and wouldn't have gone anywhere anyway, and I buried my face in her lap shouting "Grandma they're bombing us!" And then later they started machine-gunning and of course I didn't know where my brother and mother were, I was worried about them. Later they returned to the house and it transpired they had been for the interview with Mr Gallichon and on the way back they had stopped their bicycles to talk to the Major who was up here waiting for a bus. Then they had gone on because it was time to go home. So by the time they had gone right round the corner on their bicycles the bombing occurred and Mother said "Oh! Come on Eddie! We must hurry! We must hurry!" And then as the aeroplanes came back machine-gunning, they threw their bicycles down anyhow on the road and dived into the green bushes that were there.

When my mother got into the house she found out how near she had been to being killed because she had a double hole in the sleeve of her (new) coat where a bullet had passed through – "and this coat at that!" she said. But neither of them was hurt. We didn't come out of the house until the next morning when the leaflets were dropped. And then of course we heard about poor Mrs Kitchen, the bullet had come straight through the little scullery window and straight into her throat, and Mum found bullet holes in the walls and especially on the Monday, when we had to put out those big white sheets after they dropped the leaflets ordering us to. We helped Mum. Eddie went on the roof with her to tie the sheet to the chimney breast and I was leaning out of an attic window you know tying it so it would not blow away. That's when she saw the bullet holes. We were lucky!'

And on that evening of 28th June a certain W. Bertram Payne, all of 18 years old, was sitting with his mum on top of the granite sea wall opposite the family farm, exotically named Côte d'Or, in Grouville, a few yards from the northern side of La Rocque harbour. The time was 6.45 p.m.

'I was talking things over with my mother – farm business and the like and she said, "Look!" and at the same time I saw three dots in the sky behind Seymour Tower. They were coming straight towards us getting bigger and they were coming from the French coast direction. I thought maybe they were German so the two of us ran over the road (La Grande Route des Sablons) and we crouched down behind the hedge that separated our place from the coast road. No cover at all really when you think about it!

Then we could hear the planes and suddenly things happened in a rush. There were some really very loud bangs, bombs going off and then came the sound of tiles slithering off the roofs of houses round about. Next thing we went down to the slip down by the harbour and there were several people we knew there. A visitor waiting for a bus by the slip had been killed and across the road at a cottage called Harbour View. One of the local air raid men, Mr Thomas Pilkington, had been hit and was lying dead in his open doorway. There was also a Mrs Farrel lying at the same place and she had blood pouring from her neck … I got the farm lorry and we wrapped her in a tarpaulin and put her in the back but she bled to death before we could get her medical help.

…I think we were all very shaken of course – you can imagine it can't you – very shocked and it had been such a nice evening as well and then all that happened to us.'

After bombing and strafing La Rocque the Heinkels flew slowly down to St Helier harbour. It took them over a minute to make the journey. On the dockside they could see lines of lorries. They were loading their Jersey potatoes onto a transport ship.

But the German pilots did not know this. As they had done on the earlier reconnaissance sorties, they assumed that these were military vehicles and therefore legitimate targets. First they bombed and then they strafed.

Direct hits were recorded on the vehicles. A number of yachts and small boats in the harbour were destroyed. Eleven people were killed and nine injured either by shrapnel from exploding bombs or by rounds from the lethal MG15 machine guns. On the pier itself three people were killed, Mr L. Bryon, Mr W. Moodie and Mr R. Fallis.

A wretchedly sad and dispiriting story attaches to the last named, Robert Fallis.

He was the resident toll keeper responsible for the collection of mooring fees due from the vessels that docked in the harbour. A nice little perk came with the job – he was provided with a modest but comfortable apartment built into the structure of the Albert Pier's upper promenade. As Fallis lay dying on the harbour side a hit and run raid of a very different type was to take place on the Albert Pier and this time the target was very specific – it was the little home of the toll keeper. Taking advantage of the chaos caused by the German attack, someone slipped unnoticed into the toll keeper's apartment and made off with a gold watch, sundry valuables and the sum of eight pounds in cash. Now eight pounds was a hefty amount of money in those days. It was three times Mr Fallis' weekly wage. The *Evening Post* of 3rd July 1940 published an article with the headline 'Despicable Thief' alongside the details of the toll keeper's funeral.

In Guernsey the assault was more savage and the damage greater than in Jersey. The death toll was more than three times as high: 27 were killed and 36 injured.

At 6.45 p.m. across the water, Ambrose James Sherwill, the Attorney General of Guernsey, had just finished addressing a large crowd, answering their questions and trying to allay their fears.
He returned to his office:

'... soon after Markbreiter of the Home Office rang me on the telephone. Just as we were ringing off, I heard the sound of aeroplanes and the stuttering of machine guns from the direction of St Samsons. (They must have been machine-gunning the little steamship Courier bound from Alderney to Guernsey with a cargo of pigs rounded up in Alderney by our people after the total evacuation of that Island). I remember saying to Markbreiter, "Here they come", and held the receiver to the open window so that he, too, might hear.'

The first bombs fell on Guernsey at 6.54 p.m. on Friday 28th June 1940. We can be that precise about the timing because one of those bombs fell on the harbour weighbridge, stopping the clock at exactly that time.

The three German bombers saw the lines of lorries lined up in the harbour, much as they had seen them in Jersey. They assumed that these were carrying military equipment which made them a prime military target.

They attacked with incendiary bombs and machine gun fire. There was panic. People ran for cover beneath the pier. It was a mercy that the tide was out for otherwise there would have been no shelter there.

In a worse state were the drivers of the tomato lorries.

They flung themselves beneath their vehicles hoping to save themselves from the German terror. But of course there was no safety there at all beneath those flimsily constructed, mostly wooden lorries.

The bombs rained down. Murderous strafing followed. Fuel tanks exploded. Raging fires began to burn. Men died horribly, their blood mingling with the tomato juice that streamed and puddled along the pier road.

There were however, valiant attempts to defend the harbour and fight back against this outrageous airborne assault.

It so happened that the little mailboat the *Isle of Sark*, under the command of Captain Golding, was alongside at St Peter Port when the Luftwaffe came calling on this Friday 28th June. Painted grey in recognition of the state of war that existed, she was also armed with four Lewis automatic machine guns. The gunners reacted instantly to the attack and threw up a continuous barrage against the incoming bombers with such success that neither the *Isle of Sark* herself nor any other ship in the harbour was damaged in any serious way.

Nevertheless great damage was done at the weighbridge and all along the Esplanade during the hour-long raid. Not content with that, the Germans went on a shooting spree to other places about the Island. There was no concern and no attempt at all to identify legitimate military targets.

They did a sweep across the island, machine-gunning the haymakers in the fields, indeed anyone they saw moving, just as they were to do in Sark a little later on. They met with little success here but out to sea they managed to kill Harold Hobbs, the coxswain's son, when they machine-gunned the St Peter Port lifeboat on her way to Jersey.

Later, Ambrose Sherwill had a conversation with the newly-arrived German, Dr Maass, a graduate of Liverpool University and a fluent English speaker:

'I tackled Dr Maass about the raid. He said the German airmen had mistaken the tomato lorries for lorries carrying war munitions. I then asked him, even if such a mistake had been made, how he accounted for the machine-gunning of the plainly marked lifeboat. He replied, I remember, "There are lunatics in the armed forces of all nations."'

Chapter 3

Shaking Hands with the Germans

What do you do with the Germans when the more important question is what are they going to do with you? The arrival of the forces of the Third Reich in the little Islands was preceded by such tales of cruelty and outrage, murder and mayhem as to arouse more than a little apprehension in the native breast. Stories of rape, mutilation, the casual lopping off of infant arms, the massacre of entire villages, were the talk of the threatened community. In Alderney, the island closest to the French coast, Judge French assembled his little flock. He was not going to stay and shake hands with any Germans. 'We are in danger of our lives,' he declared, watching the great pyres of smoke from the burning oil installations on the Cherbourg peninsula as the Germans got closer and closer. 'What shall we do?' he asked them. 'Let's go!' they shouted in reply. And go they did, and as fast as was humanly possible. Almost the entire population left for mainland Britain, leaving behind half-eaten meals on the table, pet dogs and cats running in the roads, horses dying in the fields for lack of water, and cows unmilked, wild with pain.

In Alderney there was scarcely a person left to meet those most unwelcome of unwelcome German visitors.

Many people left Guernsey too, but not the entire population. By 23rd June, 17,000 out of a population of 42,000 had left Guernsey, including most of the school children. The leader of the community at this time was 69-year-old Bailiff Victor Gosselin Carey who, along with his opposite number Alexander Coutanche in Jersey, had been sworn in as acting Lieutenant-Governor. It must be said that Carey has not had a good press from anyone at all. His fitness for the post was questioned from the outset and his conduct during the Occupation has been heavily criticised as being collaborationist and cowardly.

His grandson says that at the end of the War the British did not know whether to hang him or knight him, so mired in controversy was his tenure of office. (In the event and in the spirit of reconciliation adopted by the returning British, Victor Carey was knighted.)

Ambrose James Sherwill gives us some flavour of the thinking about the Bailiff in his *A Fair and Honest Book*:

'Victor Carey, when he came to the office of Bailiff, was most slenderly equipped for the post. As Attorney General I have listened to many a summing-up of his in a criminal case. I do not know what effect it had on the prisoner in the dock but I do know it terrified me. His drafting abilities were very mediocre and his clerk,

Louis Guillemette, and I must have rescued him on scores of occasions from predicaments in his drafting of forewords in the Billets d'Etat issued by him when convoking meetings of the States.'

The general feeling was that Carey was too old and inept to be of any use during the Occupation, and indeed it is true that in two infamous instances he betrayed what has been termed an insensitivity towards the feelings of his fellow Islanders and an offensive degree of pusillanimity in the face of the occupying powers.

The first instance was the 'V' sign notice issued on 8th July 1941, which he composed himself. It was not a German creation. In this notice the Bailiff offered a £25 reward to anyone giving information about people putting up the 'V' signs around the Island. Offering rewards to people who informed on fellow-Islanders for acts of resistance against the hated Germans was certainly not the way to improve his reputation or increase respect for him. Of course, Carey's main desire was to save the Islanders from German reprisal punishments by stopping the 'V' campaign, which had reached epidemic proportion, dead in its tracks. As he saw it, he was acting 'to the best of his abilities, in the interests of the inhabitants,' as all the Bailiffs and Attorneys General had been told to do by the Secretary of State in the letters of 19th June 1940. Unfortunately, as Sherwill remarks, he carried out this duty in a most clumsy fashion. The

Guernsey folk did not see in the notice the hidden desire to keep them safe, they saw only the offensive invitation to betray for money those of their brave countrymen who were prepared to stand up against the invader. To them, this smacked very much of collaboration.

The Bailiff was not a popular man and he brought more obloquy about his ears when he issued another notice concerning those Islanders who concealed British agents.

Attention is called to the fact that, under the order relative to Protection Against Acts of Sabotage, dated October 10th 1940, any person who hides or shelters escaped prisoners of war shall be punished with death. The same applies for the hiding or sheltering of members of enemy forces (for instance, crews of landing aircraft, parachutists etc.). Anyone lending assistance to such persons in their escape is also liable to the death sentence.

Victor G. Carey
Royal Court House
August 9th 1941

Eagle-eyed seekers for evidence of collaborative tendencies spotted immediately the hapless bailiff's reference to the English commandos as 'enemy forces'. His authorship of this notice is not absolutely established but it was assumed by everyone in the Island. If he did compose it, it certainly bears out all Sherwill's strictures about his ineptitude and clumsiness when it came to drafting important and very sensitive documents.

Even more heinous than this notice, at least according to a report sent to the Home Office on 17th August 1945 by British Intelligence investigating charges of collaboration, is this letter, in his own handwriting, sent to the *Inselkommandant* on 23rd June 1941:

The Lieutenant-Governor and Bailiff requests the pleasure of the company of the Inselkommandant, his adjutant, Prince Oettingen and Dr Reffler with the Interpreter to take wine with him at Le Vallon on Sunday, July 6th at 5.30 (17.30).
Le Vallon
23rd June 1941
Guernsey

However, the adverse judgements hurled at Carey's head do seem a little facile, a little uninformed. There is no doubt that on occasion he expressed himself in a somewhat unfortunate manner but there is not a scintilla of doubt that Victor Gosselin Carey cared, and cared deeply, about his Guernsey people.

He worried himself sick about their welfare. In particular he fretted about the London government sending over young, raw, inexperienced and untrained young Guernseymen like Nicolle and Symes on ill-planned raids. Like Sherwill, he saw that these raids would place in mortal danger not only the young men, but also the wider civilian population. He inveighed against

the attacks in private and declared that he would go and see Churchill himself after the War to ask what right he had to send soldiers into a demilitarised zone endangering everyone in the Island.

Victor Carey did not, in the event, make that trip to London. Perhaps he should have done, for it would have been a very good question to put to the great war leader.

Not that any of this mattered as much as it might have done because, though Victor Gosselin Carey was the titular head of the Guernsey civil administration, as a matter of fact, the real leadership of the island was in the hands of the Controlling Committee which had been set up in the weeks immediately preceding the Occupation.

This committee, established on 21st June by a somewhat unconstitutional process on a proposition of Jurat John Leale, comprised eight members, all there to provide the Island with a fleet and flexible administrative body to deal with the difficulties, trials and tribulations that lay ahead. John Leale, in proposing Ambrose Sherwill as the president of this new body, laid out what was to be the official policy of Guernsey for the duration of the war:

'Should the Germans decide to occupy this Island, we must accept the position. There must be no thought of any kind of resistance, we can only expect that the more dire punishment will be meted.

51

I say this, the man who even contemplates resistance should the Germans come is the most dangerous man in the Island and its most bitter enemy. The military have gone. We are civilians.'

AMBROSE SHERWILL

Ambrose Sherwill was a remarkable man.

He was a hero of the First World War. While serving as a signalling officer he had, under heavy enemy bombardment, relieved a brigade signalling post, becoming quite severely wounded in the process. For this act of outstanding courage he was awarded the Military Cross.

In words which found their echo across the water in the sister Isle of Jersey, Ambrose Sherwill talks of his theory of the Occupation:

'As head of the local administration in Guernsey when the German Occupation started, I was determined to out-Job Job himself and that my administration should act as a buffer between the occupying forces and the civilian population. Now a buffer, to be effective, must above all else be resilient. It must give when pressure would otherwise be irresistible and it must always come back in readiness to resist other and lesser impacts.'

Bailiff Alexander Coutanche in Jersey could not have agreed more. On a more personal note he continues:

'It sounds terribly pretentious to say so

but I attempted initially, so far as I could, to run the German occupation for them, in so far as it touched the civilian population. I recognise now of course that this was a fatuous thing to do, but at the beginning the German occupying force was so small and I was in such close touch with the commander and his staff that it did not seem to me impossible.'

'To act as a buffer,' if it could be done, would truly be government 'in the interest of the inhabitants,' and truth to tell, in the opening months of the Occupation it all seemed wonderfully possible. The Germans who came to the Island were by no means the monsters, looters and rapists many Islanders had fearfully expected. On the contrary they were quietly spoken, well educated and altogether rather civilised, or so it appeared in these first months of Occupation. Along with everyone else, Sherwill was pleasantly surprised. As he says:

'It seemed to me to be the strangest and most peaceful invasion of all times.'

The Commandant, Major Doctor Albrecht Lanz (a doctor of Philosophy and Law) was:

'absolutely straight and kindly. I grew to like him very much and I believe he was adored by his men.'

And as for his Chief of Staff, Dr Maass, well he was altogether a 'very remarkable man.' He held a degree in tropical medicine from Liverpool University and spoke fluent English.

Sherwill rejoiced in him:

'He was an enemy but oh such a pleasant one.'

Over in Sark, the formidable Dame Sibyl Hathaway, while she shared Sherwill's opinion of Lanz, did not think so highly of Maass:

'There was something about Maass which made me distrust him. His face was too smooth for my liking and I could well imagine that while in England he had sent back a lot of valuable information to Germany that had nothing to do with tropical diseases.'

Sherwill did trust him however and considered that he could do business with both him and Lanz. He sat down with them to agree and accept the conditions of the German Occupation. It was, by Sherwill's own account, a reasonably affable affair, and he came away with what he saw as significant concessions by the Germans. Yes, wireless sets could be kept. Yes, prayers could be said for the British Royal Family and yes, divine worship in church and chapel would be allowed to continue. Lanz mentioned at this stage that he was obliged by international law to permit such congregations to continue so long as they were not made:

'the vehicle for any propaganda or utterances against the honour or interest of, or offensive to, the German government or forces.'

The mention of international law, and by implication the observance of the Hague Convention, must have further encouraged Sherwill in his belief that he could run that model occupation so dear to his heart. He laid out his vision of the future in this speech delivered to the States of Guernsey at their first meeting since the beginning of the Occupation. With Lanz and Maass by his side he said:

'May this occupation be a model to the world. On the one hand, tolerance on the part of the military authority, and courtesy and correctness on the part of the occupying forces, and on the other, dignity and courtesy and exemplary behaviour on the part of the civilian population. I do not know how long the Occupation will last ... when it is over, I hope that the occupying force and occupied population may each be able to say: of different nations, having different outlooks, we lived together with tolerance and mutual respect.'

Across the water in Jersey, the Bailiff and Lieutenant-Governor, Alexander Moncrieff Coutanche and his government officers were facing up to the imminent German occupation in much the same way as their Guernsey counterparts, though there were significant differences. In Jersey as in Guernsey, a commitee was formed as an emergency administrative body the more efficiently to handle the governance of the Island during the Occupation. Unlike Guernsey however, based on a judgement of competence, the Bailiff was not side-lined at all, far from it. Coutanche was in complete control of the grandly titled Superior Committee. Coutanche was the man who dictated the Island response to the Germans, and his idea of what that response should be, though less grandiloquently expressed, chimed very much in accord with that of Ambrose Sherwill. In accordance with the instruction received in the Island, 'to administer the government of the Island to the best of his abilities, in the interests of the inhabitants,' Coutanche, using the same language as Sherwill, saw a duty to provide:

... *'some kind of buffer between the Jersey people and the Germans.'*

ALEXANDER COUTANCHE

Alexander Coutanche was described by Baron von Aufsess as 'cunning and vulpine'. Alan and Mary Wood in their excellent book *Islands in Danger* describe him as:

'... dark and swarthy, something of a thruster and a showman, but with a saving sense of humour.'

A lawyer by profession, he spent much of his early career away from the island, first of all in Birmingham and then in Belgium. In 1935 he was created Bailiff of Jersey and was hugely successful in that office, directing the Island on a course that, by 1939, had made it the wealthiest of the Channel Islands. In that opening year of the War, Coutanche was 47 years old, over 20 years younger than Victor Carey and

at the top of his game. He needed to be as he undertook to shelter his countrymen from the rigours of the Occupation. However his first meeting with the German commander, Captain Gussek, was a bit of a comedy.

Coutanche had returned to his home after his initial meeting with a group of junior German officers up at the airport. He was, as might be expected, more than a little depressed at the catastrophic turn of events and sought to calm himself by doing a little gardening. He put on his old and torn grey flannels, donned an ancient sports jacket and began the therapeutic excercise. While he was thus engaged, the German invader in the shape of Captain Gussek, two soldiers and six officers, arrived in the drive. Coutanche hurriedly dropped his hoe and went into the house to meet them:

'(Gussek's) method of expressing some surprise at my appearance was to put a monocle in his right eye, the better to take me in. In those days I used on occasion to wear a monocle myself and it so happened that I had one in the pocket of my jacket now. I was, therefore, able to repay the compliment and I did so. We took good stock of each other.'

Through his monocle and over Gussek's shoulder, Coutanche could see his Attorney-General, Duret Aubin, who had come down from the airport with the Germans, helping himself to a glass of his finest port.

The two men, Gussek and Coutanche, the niceties of the first introduction having been completed, got down to the real business on the following day in St Helier town hall.

It was not a difficult meeting. The German view was that the War would almost certainly be over by Christmas and at this point the requirement was for an expedient and easy arrangement to be put in place for the short period to the end of hostilities when a more permanent settlement might be imposed on the Islands. In June 1940 military objectives were the priority, not civil administration.

The Jerseymen could go on governing themselves subject to certain restrictions and changes laid out in the proclamation of 8th July 1940. Coutanche points to three provisions which he had agreed to and which defined the legal relations between Jersey and the occupying power.

'The Civil Government and the Courts of the Island will continue to function as heretofore, save that all Laws, Ordinances, Regulations and Orders will be submitted to the German Commandant before being enacted.

Such legislation as in the past required the sanction of His Britannic Majesty-in-Council for its validity, shall henceforth be valid on being approved by the German Commandant and thereafter sanctioned by the Bailiff of Jersey.

The Orders of the German Commandant heretofore, now and hereafter issued shall, in due course, be registered in the records of the Island of Jersey, in order that no person may plead ignorance thereof. Offences against the same, saving those punishable under German Military Law, shall be punishable by the Civil Courts, who shall enact suitable penalties in respect of such offences, with the approval of the German Commandant.'

In short, the civil administration would stay in place and would be used as the most expedient way of imposing German rule in the Island. Jersey's government officers, Jersey's bureaucracy and Jersey's courts would become instruments of occupation as and when the Germans so required.

Coutanche accepted these provisions because he had to. It was an exercise in *force majeure*, but he saw that in this arrangement there were possible opportunities to moderate the terms of occupation in the best interests of the Islanders. That is, for him and for his Superior Council to indeed act as a buffer between the Germans and the civilian population, just as Sherwill and his Controlling Committee intended to do over in Guernsey.

They would try and make the best of a very bad job.

THE DAME OF SARK
On June 24th the Dame of Sark, the feisty and redoubtable Sibyl Hathaway,

heard the bombs exploding in St Peter Port, saw the smoke rise in the air and wondered if the enemy planes would pay Sark a visit. She did not have long to wait. Twenty minutes after the raid on Guernsey the Heinkels swooped down low over the little island. Mercifully they had no bombs left to drop and contented themselves with machine-gunning the fishermen and their boats along the shoreline. Luckily for the Islanders, the German gunners must have been a little tired by then, and contrived to miss all their targets. Not a boat was touched, not a fisherman hurt. But nonetheless it was a frightening experience for the Island folk who now waited with trepidation the arrival of the Hun. The telephone link with Guernsey and the outside world had been cut.

They had no idea what was happening and they were frightened, very frightened. News of the barbarities visited by the Germans upon defenceless Polish men, women and children chilled the blood, as did the stories told by the dozens of French refugees who had passed through the Island fleeing from further German outrage. With the awful enemy now at the door, many an Islander must have wished that they had not heeded the Dame's advice to stay put, but had got out while the going was good.

Dame Sibyl Hathaway was naturally apprehensive, very apprehensive, about the imminent arrival of the Germans. The protection of her people was her very first priority and:

'There were many things to be considered. First, the inherent character of the Sark people, who are a close-knit community, caring for nothing and nobody outside the island. To these self-reliant, self-confident people, many of whom are direct descendants of the first forty families brought over to protect the island during the reign of Elizabeth I, anyone visiting Sark, even an English tourist, is a foreigner and therefore should be treated as a guest who is entitled to courtesy no matter how tiresome he may be.'

In all of Europe there had not been a response to the German invaders like this one. The niceties of social etiquette would be observed in this part of the world. There would be proper, civilised and well-mannered behaviour between the occupier and the occupied. In this way, Sibyl believed, her island community could live protected and safe from the worst horrors of enemy occupation.

The Dame was encouraged in her belief that the Occupation could be carried on as a polite dialogue between herself and the Germans by the fact that she was an upper-class, nay aristocratic, lady and she expected to be talking to upper-class Germans. As she herself says:

'I had spent some time in Germany after the First World War and since then had met a sufficient number of Germans to know something of their national *characteristics. Moreover, my name and status were included in the* Almanac de Gotha, *which in those days could be guaranteed to make clear my rights and authority when dealing with upper-class Germans.'*

The *Almanac de Gotha* was a prestigious and authoritative who's who of European aristocracy.

Sibyl was banking on the German 'guests' recognising her great status as a European aristocrat and, for that reason, affording her, and by association her island people, preferential treatment for the duration of the Occupation.

And it worked!

Major Lanz and Doctor Maass duly arrived on 3rd July aboard the old Guernsey lifeboat. They were conducted by the Seneschal to the Seigneurie on foot, there being no cars on the island. It was a bit of a walk but at last, perspiring somewhat in the summer heat, they arrived at the Dame's abode. They wiped their feet carefully on the mat. This impressed the Dame very much. As she said to her husband Bob, 'That is most reassuring. It is a gesture of respect to the house.' Then they were ushered in to meet the Dame. She spoke to them in German. They were hugely impressed, particularly Major Doctor Lanz. He, of course, presented the orders of the Commandant of the German Forces in the Channel Islands to be obeyed by the Islanders, but then

he sweetened the pill by saying that:

'if ever I found difficulties I was to communicate directly with the Commandant of the Channel Islands in Guernsey.'

In other words there was to be something of a special relationship between the Germans and the lady from Sark, and one which she could exploit in the interests of her little flock.

'I was treated with great courtesy by the senior officers and I in turn extended to them the hospitality of the Seigneurie which is due to all visitors in this island who are made known to me.'

However, what the Dame regarded as a proper courtesy to be extended to her visitors, the British Intelligence in their post-war investigations regarded as collaboration with the enemy, as in this report from the Intelligence Officers of section 1(b) attached to Liberating Force 135:

The Dame of Sark, Mrs. R.W. HATHAWAY, has also been guilty of friendly and ingratiating behaviour towards the Germans. Major Albrecht Lanz, the first German Commandant of Guernsey, in his report on the Channel Islands, says that when he arrived for the first time on Sark, he was formally and politely received by the Dame, who explained that a large proportion of the Sark people were descendents of the Vikings who had come from the far north. After settling official business,

Major Lanz and his staff were invited to a good lunch. The Dame was a particular friend of Dr Mass (sic), Prince von OETTINGEN, AND General von Schmettow, who were frequent visitors at weekends. At Easter 1945 ZACHAU, Schneeberger and others were invited to a lobster lunch. The Dame of Sark has preserved her property and privileges intact throughout the Occupation; her gardens have not even been modified by wartime agriculture.

In The Channel Islands in wartime it was not judged to be patriotic or right to invite the enemy to eat and drink with you as if they were friends of some kind. The idea that by treating the German commanders in a civilised fashion they would be encouraged to respond in kind to the benefit of the well-being of the Islanders as a whole did not occur to the rather bleak-eyed officers from British Intelligence like Stopford, Dening and d'Egville, who busily conducted the post-war investigation into charges of collaboration and treason.

In something of a contrast, the behaviour of the Jersey Bailiff was adjudged to have been somewhat better than that of his counterpart across the water. There was to be no junketing with lobster and wine up at Alexander's house, indeed the astute Bailiff deliberately ruled out any such friendly occurrences:

'Schmettow and I reached an early agreement which actually worked during the whole of his time in the Island. We

agreed mutually that we were enemies and that there must be no sort of social intercourse between us of any kind whatsoever. Within those limits, however, we could still both behave like gentlemen.'

He was not going to behave in the same way as Victor and Sibyl towards the Germans. He would avoid the charge of over-familiarity but not by much, at least in the judgement of British Intelligence.

'In Jersey the attitude of the States and of the Bailiff, Alexander Moncreiff Coutanche, does not seem to have been so "gratuitously friendly" as it was in Guernsey, but it was still very far from being satisfactory. Over one question, that of the deportations, there is almost universal bitterness. The States provided the Germans with the names and addresses of all persons likely to be wanted by the Germans for this purpose. Their doing this is bitterly resented, the general comment being that the Germans should have been left to do their own dirty work.'

There might not have been any feasting and carousing up at Alexander's house but, it was alleged, there was an even worse form of collaboration in which his 'best abilities' were certainly not used in the 'interests of the inhabitants'.

Indeed the whole bureaucracy of the Island was deployed to facilitate a course of action which was wholly and clearly inimical to the best interests of a large number of the civilian population.

Where, in all of this vexed business of the deportations, it was asked, was the notion of the civil authority as a buffer, there to protect the otherwise defenceless islanders? What was going on in the deliberations of the Bailiff and his Superior Council?

It is very much worthwhile taking a closer look at the issue of deportations because it was, in many ways, a defining moment in the conduct of the Occupation. The principles informing the attitudes and behaviour of the Superior Council towards the German occupiers, left happily and a little vaguely implicit before, suddenly became unhappily and very clearly explicit.

On 12th September 1941 the British interned nearly 500 German nationals working in Iran (Persia), considering their activity to be inimical to the Allied cause. Hitler was angered by this, as he saw it, unethical action, and cast about for some way to respond. The chosen way of reprisal was to issue an order in October 1941 that ten British-born Channel Islanders for every German hostage be transported to the dreaded Pripet Marshes in Poland. This intractable, sodden, marshy and unfruitful area in the General Government was intended as a prime dumping ground for all enemies of the Third Reich, primarily of course, Jews, but also communists and anti-Nazis of whatever political persuasion. It was not a pleasant prospect.

But then for some reason which is not altogether clear, though it probably had a lot to do with Hitler's preoccupation with the Eastern Front and Moscow rather than the Western Front and the Channel Islands, the initial order for the deportation got lost somewhere in the system and was never carried out. Perhaps it was deliberately lost, because it is known that Colonel Knackfuss objected to such a deportation on the grounds that it would remove a strategically valuable hostage population from Festung Jersey. However this may be, in September 1942 following an enquiry by the Swiss to the German government about supposed Channel Island prisoners, Hitler discovered that his order of the previous year had not been carried out, and promptly issued a new order. This time he kept a very close eye on its implementation.

In the Island, lists of all British-born residents, of those who had served in the British armed forces, and those with criminal records were carefully drawn up by the Island authorities. In fact, in that year of 1942, every single Islander was compelled to carry an identity card containing the name, address, occupation and place of birth of the owner.

The Island government had always been willing to provide the Germans with whatever list they wanted, but it is true to say they were not always aware of the purpose to which these lists would be put. The Chief Aliens and Registration

Officer in Jersey, Clifford Orange, talking after the War about these lists said:

'Amongst such lists was one containing particulars of British subjects resident in the Channel Islands who did not belong to the local population, and another containing particulars of British Regular Officers (Retired) registered as residing in Jersey. Both of these were supplied in November 1941. As from September 1942, when it became obvious the purpose to which lists of persons supplied long before were being put, I refused to supply any further lists to the German authorities.'

But in September 1942 such a refusal meant little. The Germans had already got all they needed from Clifford Orange in the way of information about the British-born Islanders who were to be deported.

Bailiff Coutanche was taken entirely by surprise at the news of the intended deportation:

'At a few minutes before noon on Tuesday, September 15th 1942, I received a telephone message from the Feldkommandantur 515 (Sonder Fuehrer Hermnsen speaking as interpreter) to the effect that the Feldkommandant wished to see me, with the twelve Constables, at 2pm at his headquarters at College House, with regard to the evacuation from Jersey to Germany of the English-born members of the population.
I said I had no previous knowledge whatever of this matter, and that I would

naturally wish to discuss the matter with the Feldkommandant, in presence of the the Attorney General, before the meeting with the Constables.'

And later:

'We were told that twelve hundred people would be required to leave the Island on the next day, that the Constables would be consulted as to the persons to be evacuated, and that the Constables would be required to serve the evacuation notices.'

Coutanche faced a crisis. The words of that final letter from the Home Secretary that:

'he should stay at his post and administer the government of the Island to the best of his abilities in the interest of the inhabitants.'

must have been ringing in his ears as he struggled to find the best way forward. It was not easy. Here he was being asked to organise and preside over the forced deportation of hundreds of Islanders whose interests he had been commanded to protect. More than that, he was being asked to help the enemy carry out a reprisal measure in contravention of the Hague Convention, and which would condemn a sizeable number of his Island flock, men women and children, to God knows what horror on Mainland Europe.

When, after the War, Alexander

Coutanche was asked what he had done in the Occupation, he replied, 'I protested.' And it was on this occasion that he protested most strongly.

During an interview with Knackfuss:

'I said that I was shocked and protested against the proposed measure, and asked whether I could do nothing to stop it, or at least to delay it. Colonel Knackfuss replied that the order came from the Fuehrer himself, that no one had the power to vary it in the slightest degree, and that it would be carried out to the letter whatever I might say or do.
I said that in view of what was proposed, I and any other member of the Island government who wished to do so would be entitled to resign and that I must have time to consider whether that step were not the proper one to be adopted by me and the members of the government and to be urged upon the Constables.
Colonel Knackfuss replied, without conceding my right to withdraw from the government, that it was clearly in the interest of the people of Jersey that the government should continue in office.'

That last remark of Knackfuss was the sting in the tail of the conversation, for he was reminding Coutanche, with just a hint of menace, what the alternative to a civil government through the Superior Council would be, though, naturally, he did not say what that something was in so many words. Lots of velvet round that iron fist! The alternative was of course to impose unmediated, direct German rule in the

Island, most probably by the SS and their constant friends from the Gestapo. The 'buffer' between the occupied and the occupier would be removed. That relationship with the Germans, which had worked quite effectively up to that point, would be destroyed; that little but precious bit of sovereignty still exercised by the Jerseymen would be gone and, as Coutanche knew only too well, an occupation run entirely by the invaders might be a very brutal affair.

Coutanche admitted defeat and decided to stay in office.

He had lost this battle but there would be others to fight and he, as leader, needed to be in the strongest possible position to fight them, in the interests of his fellow Islanders:

'For the moment, at any rate, we were serving the best interests of the population by remaining in office and doing whatever we could to alleviate this hardship.'

Coutanche stood by the decision for him and his Superior Council plus the Constables to stay in office. Long years after the War, in his autobiography he states:

'We finally decided, and in this I am sure that we were right, that we could do far better by continuing to act as some kind of buffer between the Jersey people and the Germans.'

Coutanche then went on to do what he

could for the deportees, in actions which perfectly described the limits of the civil government's power. They could provide the bandage but they could not prevent the wound. They could stand up and be a buffer but there would surely be an impact. They could soften but not prevent the blow. And in the case of the deportations this is precisely what they did:

'The Government, by remaining in office, was enabled to supply the evacuees with emergency rations and clothing for their journey, and with transport for themselves and their baggage to the ships.'

Through the Occupation years, then, this was the role of Coutanche's government: to stand and protect, as far as they were able, the Jersey folk from the excesses of German Occupation rule. The alternative to active cooperation was always the imposition of direct German control in the shape of the SS – which would undoubtedly be inimical to the interests of the Islanders. It was this threat of direct German rule that informed all the activities of the Superior Council in their attempts to act as the buffer between the Germans and the Islanders.

And were they praised for their efforts? No they were not!

They received very little by way of praise. In many quarters, particularly among the young, the reverse was the case. Indeed the government 'gang', the

'self-interested oligarchy' were noisily reviled. Coutanche and his government were accused of grovelling acquiescence to every German demand, of outright collaboration, pusillanimous at best and traitorous at worst. And it is true that the behaviour of the Superior Council would, to the uninformed observer, appear to be that of a quisling administration. There seemed to be only a very small number of cases in which the Jersey Council did not do the German bidding. The overwhelming majority of German orders were registered in the Jersey courts without demur and with no objection raised. Lists of people, lists of animals, lists of food and fuel stocks, lists of everything the Germans asked for were supplied with due expedition, no questions asked, no time wasted. In this way the Jews could be registered, persecuted, imprisoned, excommunicated and robbed. In this way the British-born Islanders, men women and children, could be forced from their homes, crowded onto stinking boats and exiled to camps across the water. The cynical and casual observer might be forgiven for thinking that the Germans were using Coutanche, the Council and the Constables as convenient instruments of occupation. If the Jerseymen chose to believe that staying in office and complying with German orders and requests and, more than that, actually enforcing German occupation ordinances in the civil courts, was the best way to care for their community, then all well and good. If they chose to dress up their near-absolute cooperation with the enemy as being an exercise in ensuring the greatest good for the greatest number, well that too was a good thing, for it would provide an exculpatory philosophic justification and explanation for a course of action that might otherwise be described as morally reprehensible.

And if they were under the impression that there was some sort of implicit contract between the Jersey government and the occupiers – a contract based on the observance of the Hague Convention by which the life, liberty and well-being of the population would be preserved and protected in return for properly quiescent civilian behaviour in accordance with internationally-agreed principles – then the Germans were only too willing to promote this fiction because again it provided the Jerseymen with a principled course of action which side-stepped the issue of untoward collaboration but still gave the Germans everything they needed in terms of Island cooperation. Everyone could be happy.

There were, however, occasions and events which prompted a more robust and confrontational stance from the Island authorities, but these were few and far between. In general, in both the Islands, the attitude was 'don't rock the boat' or worse will befall!

Nonetheless there were exceptions to this, and in a handful of cases when the Island authorities decided to do battle

with the Germans they achieved a measure of success to such a degree that some commentators with easy hindsight have declared that the Island governments should have fought many more battles with the Germans than they did. The Island governments, living in the presence of the enemy, were more uncertain of their powers and chose which battles to fight with a circumspection born of a well-founded fear of terrible consequences. This, predictably, was not enough for some people. In particular it was not enough for the MI5 officers Major J.R. Stopford and Captain Dening, investigating the issue of collaboration with the enemy after the war, as they said in this report to the Home Office:

'Many of them are people of no particular loyalty and on the whole concerned with their own welfare more than anything else. All the reports which have become available tend to show that a perfectly correct attitude could have been adopted by the States officials without incurring any more special hardships than were incurred through entire friendliness and cooperation, and the Germans themselves regarded the people as subservient to a remarkable extent.'

One battle neither Guernsey or Jersey chose to fight was that on behalf of the Jews, the people who needed help more than any others. There was, it is true, one solitary objection raised, at the time of the registration of an Anti-Jewish Order, by Abraham Lainé in Guernsey, against the wearing of the yellow Star of David by all the Jews. Ambrose Sherwill recalls the events of that time:

'The honour of refusing to concur in its registration fell to Sir Abraham Lainé, KCIE, who, when called on as a jurat to vote upon the matter, openly and categorically refused his assent and stated his grave objections to such a measure. He has now gone to his rest, but this courageous act of his should never be forgotten. As I sat listening to him, I realised how right he was.'

He may have been right and Sherwill may have been ashamed, but the objection had no effect whatever on the registration of the Order. At the time Sherwill considered that:

'No purpose would be served in advising the Royal Court to refuse to register it. If I had, presumably the Germans would have threatened the Royal Court by marching in armed soldiers.'

It is also true that, in contrast to the general attitude in Guernsey, Alexander Coutanche in Jersey, along with his Attorney General Duret Aubin, chose to ignore the very real danger in crossing the Germans when they strenuously objected to the imposition of the Eighth Order which would have forced all Jews to wear the yellow star.

Their objection was successful and the Eighth Order was never registered in Jersey. But all the others were without any protest whatsoever. This absolute compliance with German wishes in Jewish matters, critics point out, contrasts sharply and unfavourably with the Island governments' attitude when it came to the Freemasons. As in this report sent by Intelligence Officers to the Home Office:

'When the Germans proposed to put their anti-Jewish measures into force, no protest whatever was raised by any of the Guernsey States Officials, and they hastened to give the Germans every assistance. By contrast when it was proposed to take steps against the Freemasons, of which there are many in Guernsey, the Bailiff made considerable protests and did everything possible to protect the Masons, of whom he himself is the senior representative.'

Despite these protests the Masonic Lodges in the Islands were stripped of their regalia, furnishings of all kinds, and their libraries, which were then transported to Berlin to be put on show. By this time, however, the Island authorities, acting in concert, had contrived to transfer most of the Masonic assets into the care of the States where they stayed, safe from grasping German hands, for the rest of the War. More importantly, not a single Freemason suffered in the way the Island Jews had. As a direct result of opposition mounted against proposed German legislation by the governments of the Channel Islands, the anti-Masonic measures were never registered in the Islands' courts. It was a battle won.

The question that critics raise over and over again is whether a similar degree of success could be achieved in the matter of the Jews. It is one of the great 'What ifs' of the history of the Occupation, and though we may guess at the answer we can never know for certain because, as we have seen, that particular battle was never fought. There was certainly a 'buffer' for the Freemasons but not for the Jews.

Of the three Island leaders, Alexander Coutanche, Ambrose Sherwill and Sibyl Hathaway, who faced the invading Germans in that hot and terrifying summer of 1940 , two were still in office at the end of the Occupation. Admittedly Coutanche and Hathaway were much thinner in 1945 than in 1940 but they were still in office while Ambrose Sherwill was not. As noted elsewhere, he had been deprived of office after his involvement in the Nicolle–Symes affair had put him on the wrong side of the Germans. The presidency of the Controlling Committee passed to a Methodist minister, 'Bible' John Leale, an intelligent, articulate exponent and practitioner of the quietist approach to the German occupiers. Unlike Coutanche across the water, Leale provided posterity with an extremely full and very detailed account of the workings of the Controlling Committee during the Occupation. More importantly than that, he also gives us a comprehensive insight into the philosophy and the thinking that informed the attitudes and actions of the Guernsey leaders.

THE REVEREND JOHN LEALE

John Leale was a Methodist minister who in a previous incarnation had been a Cambridge don. Tall, grey-haired and on his own admission, 'the wrong side of 50,' he was a man of considerable intellectual acumen, having a special expertise in economics and finance, which was to serve him and Guernsey well during the Occupation. He was also, and unusually for a man of the cloth, a very wealthy man, for he was the owner of a successful property firm in the Island.

When Ambrose Sherwill was removed from his office of President of the Controlling Committee of the States of Guernsey in the wake of the Nicolle–Symes affair, John Leale it was who stepped up to the plate to take over his responsibilities. There was a degree of continuity here because Leale and Sherwill were absolutely as one in their thinking about the Occupation.

Both men believed with a passion that the Islanders should strive with the Germans to conduct a 'model occupation' in the spirit and the letter of the Hague Convention. There should be no resistance, 'for we can only expect that the more dire punishment will be meted out,' declared the reverend gentleman, and anyone who even thought about such actions would be considered as a criminal and as an enemy of the state.

The boat must not be rocked. Civilian lives must not be put at risk by reckless acts of sabotage and violence. A principled accommodation with the enemy in their midst was the best hope of the Islanders and, at the War's end in his speech to the States (the longest speech ever delivered in that august place), Leale claimed a large measure of success for this approach.

The worst excesses of enemy occupation had by and large been avoided:

'The behaviour of the people has, except for a few isolated instances, been seemly, sensible, realistic and in harmony with the rules of international law. Ours has indeed been an occupation in which neither side went to spectacular extremes. When one hears in other places of war criminals and quislings and the Gestapo as being its chief actors one rather heaves a sigh of relief that ours was not that sort of occupation.'

It might not have been 'that sort of occupation' but still it had not been easy. Leale bemoaned the fact that the man in the Guernsey street was not aware of all the fighting and the struggles between the Committee and the Germans that had gone on behind closed doors to run this 'model occupation' as much as possible in the interests of the Islanders. Many times the Committee had confronted the Germans and many times they had to back down:

'Disquieting things kept happening, and it was perhaps not unnatural that a

public, tired, fearful and irritated, should at times take a somewhat jaundiced view of some of our activities. They saw taking place what appeared to be unnecessary injustices and, knowing nothing of our interviews, protests and letters, they took our failures as meaning that we were just letting things take their course. They did not see the picture as a whole. They saw only a part and that part hurt a great deal.'

Which was precisely the same as what happened in Jersey.

And, as in Jersey, the most troublesome issue Leale and his Committee had to deal with was the deportation orders of 1942. Like Coutanche, Leale considered resigning:

'We had to decide whether we should cut ourselves completely adrift on the grounds that the thing was unclean, or take the point of view that if the deportations were due to take place there was nothing that we could do to prevent them. If we accepted the latter as our standpoint, we could work to ensure that everything was conducted in an orderly fashion; we could try and get the maximum number of exemptions; we could organise so that everything that was humanly possible was done to lighten the burden of those who had to go. We chose the latter alternative.'

John Leale, just like Coutanche, decided that it was much better to stay in office than to resign and have the Germans, and quite possibly the SS, take over entirely the civil administration of the Island. Admit defeat in this instance but live on as a government prepared to fight other battles, perhaps more successfully, in the future.

The Director of Public Prosecutions, Theobold Mathew, pronounced himself a little disappointed at the response of the Islands' authorities to the deportation orders and thought that a more robust opposition to them would have produced a better result for the Islanders. This was a general criticism of the civil administrations in both Islands during the Occupation. 'If only they had been more courageous,' so the argument goes,' and had the guts to stand up to the German bully boys, what wonderful successes might have been achieved!'

'There seems to be an idea prevalent, that if only one were firm enough the Germans would give way. I don't know on what basis this theory is founded. I know of no kind of proof that can be brought forward to substantiate it. It assumes at heart that they were a pack of cowards, but even if they were, which isn't proved, it doesn't become any clearer why they should be frightened of anything we could do to them. They were always at the right end of the gun and up to the last few months they were confident beyond a shadow of a doubt that they would win the war.
Underestimating one's opponents is a very common form of human error. With individuals it brings its own punishment and is therefore just foolish. With

governments the punishment is passed on to the community and it is therefore unpardonable. To have underestimated the Germans, either in intelligence or courage, would merely have brought more suffering on the public.'

In other words, it would have been irresponsible of the Island authorities to be aggressively confrontational in their dealings with the Germans when the consequences for the civilian population could have been so dire. As John Leale said, the Island government had other things to do besides adopting histrionic attitudes. They were facing real life, not acting in a melodrama:

'It is easy to talk big when you have no responsibilities on your shoulders. We all met the type whose fierce hostility to the Germans varied in inverse ratio to their proximity to Grange Lodge.'

Captain J. R. Dening, who had been a very long way from Grange Lodge for the whole of the Occupation, might characterise the administration of the Islands during the Occupation as 'pusillanimous', but to John Leale and his small band of helpers it was a largely successful exercise in war diplomacy, necessarily reticent and circumspect given their extremely dangerous enemy, conducted in the best interests of the Islanders. They had stroked the savage dog and come away largely unscathed.

The achievements of the Islands' leaders during the Occupation was recognised by a grateful government so happy that, despite a few allegations to the contrary, the honour of Britain had not been compromised or besmirched by the Islands' leadership.

Victor Carey did not feel the rope about his neck, but the touch of the royal sword on his shoulder. He was knighted in December 1945, as was John Leale and of course Alexander Coutanche. Ambrose Sherwill had to wait a bit for his elevation until 1949 but he did receive a CBE for his outstanding service to his country at the War's end – and, many would say, his was the most deserved honour of them all.

Chapter 4
Those Who Were left

They began clearing up the mess from the bombings, dressed the wounds of the injured, prepared the dead for burial and awaited fearfully the arrival of Hitler's all-conquering army. German boots on British soil, Island folk as *Wehrmacht* prisoners. What would become of them? What was their future? Would they have any future?

Many thousands of the Islanders had decided not to stay and find out the answer to these life-and-death questions but had packed their bags and shipped out for the comparative safety of mainland Britain. Almost half of the Guernsey population, and one fifth of the Jersey folk had fled. In Sibyl Hathaway's fiefdom of Sark, by way of contrast, only a few, a very few English-born chose to do so. In Alderney everyone upped sticks and ran. The place was left deserted.

There was hardly a soul left to observe the Germans as they turned it into a massive fortress and committed the grossest crimes against humanity in the history of the Channel Islands.

But in the beginning of July 1940 those that were left got the first view of their German visitors. And weren't they magnificent? Or so thought many who squinted nervously through the sunlight at these young *Wehrmacht* warriors parading, victorious, through the Island streets.

'And everyone said they don't look like Germans and no, they were more like us and many of them were blond and blue-eyed and so, so smart. Their uniforms were absolutely terrific!'

Not only were they good to look at but, unexpectedly, they all behaved very well, as Ambrose Sherwill remarked in his infamous radio broadcast. Sibyl Hathaway was very impressed over in Sark:

'We found out later that the first troops sent to occupy the Island were specially picked to impress on the British people that the Germans were well-behaved, well-disciplined and withal kind-hearted. The behaviour and discipline of these troops was excellent and it was rare to see a drunken German soldier in those early days.'

As a matter of fact, according to Jersey historian Michael Ginns, all the German soldiers at this time were young, fit and impressive, the troops were not specially chosen at all but they might just as well have been, so handsome were they and so exemplary their conduct. Initial fears allayed, everything settled down. Violet Carey records in her diary for 3rd July 1940:

'Mr Gorrel told James he was working in his field and a young German officer came up to him and patted him on the shoulders and said, "Don't be frightened old man, we don't fight civilians." People are much less frightened now and the German soldiers are still polite and do not molest anybody. Some of them say the War will be over in three weeks time and they will be back in their own country.'

In the meantime the Islanders got their first taste of Occupation rule in the shape of German orders published in the *Star* in Guernsey and the *Evening Post* in Jersey.

Orders of the Commandant of the German Forces in Occupation of the Island of Jersey.

1. All inhabitants must be indoors by 11 p.m. and not leave their homes before 5 a.m.

2. We will respect the population of Jersey, but, should anyone attempt to cause the least trouble, serious measures will be taken.

3. All orders given by the Military Authority are to be strictly obeyed.

4. All spirits must be locked up immediately and no spirits may be supplied, obtained or consumed henceforth. This prohibition does not apply to stocks in private houses.

5. No person shall enter the airport at St Peter/La Villaize.

6. All rifles, airguns, revolvers, daggers, sporting guns and all other weapons, whatsoever, except souvenirs, must, together with all ammunition, be delivered at the Town Arsenal by 12 noon tomorrow July 3.

7. All British Sailors, Airmen and Soldiers on leave, including Officers in this Island, must report at the Commandant's Office at 10 a.m. tomorrow July 3.

8. No boat or vessel of any description, including any fishing boat shall leave the harbour or any other place where the same is moored without an Order from the Military Authority to be obtained at the Commandant's office. All boats arriving in the Island must remain in Harbour until permitted by the military to leave. The crews will remain on board. The Master will report to the Harbourmaster and will obey his instructions.

9. The sale of motor spirit is prohibited except for use on Essential Services, such as Doctors' Vehicles, the delivery of foodstuffs and Sanitary Services where such vehicles are in possession of a permit from the Military Authority to obtain supplies. The use of cars for private purposes is forbidden.

10. The Blackout Regulations already in

force must be obeyed as before.

11. Banks and shops will be open as before.

12. In order to conform with Central European Time, all watches and clocks must be advanced an hour at 11 p.m. tonight.

13. It is forbidden to listen to any Wireless Transmitting stations, except German and German-controlled Stations.

14. The raising of prices of Commodities is forbidden.

Given that there was a war on, these orders did not appear too harsh at all. A return to something like normal life could be expected. True, the Germans had an irritating if not to say downright dangerous practice of driving their vehicles much too fast on the wrong side of the narrow Island roads. Joyce Le Gallais was killed in Jersey. But on the other hand the Germans seemed anxious to encourage the social life of the Island and to join in with it themselves.

Special dispensations were granted to people working in the entertainment field, theatres, cinemas and dance halls. There were a few unpleasant incidents; an Islander was knifed by a German soldier in a drunken brawl at the Alexandra Hotel. A few 'hotheads' vociferously proclaimed their disapproval of a German propaganda film being shown at the Forum Cinema in Jersey, but as Leslie Sinel reports in his diary entry for 31st July:

'After a month of German Occupation the life of the Island is more or less normal but stocks of certain commodities are diminishing and purchases of some goods are restricted. The tugs and barges used by the Germans have taken away potatoes, spirituous liquors, motor cars and other goods on a small scale, while the troops have made substantial purchases, mostly of clothing, jewellery and tobacco, especially cigars; new arrivals are to be seen standing in front of shop windows with their mouths open! Rabbit keeping is now an Island-wide proposition.'

On Monday 23rd September between 2.30 and 5.30 the RAF paid a visit to the Islands to drop cheery news on small quarto sheets from the skies.

TO CHANNEL ISLANDERS.
All you, His Majesty's loyal subjects on the Channel Islands must keep asking yourselves two great questions: "How long must we put up with the German occupation," and "How are our friends on the mainland?"

This news sheet brings you the heartening answer. We on the mainland are in good heart. By subjecting our women and children to the wickedest form of warfare known to history, Hitler has only stiffened our backs. And the events of the last three weeks have only served to confirm Mr Churchill's words of

August 21st that 'the victory may not be as long as we expect. Nor may the day be so distant when we shall come to your relief.

The boys from the RAF returned on 30th September in more reflective mood. The news sheet was headed 'Leaves and News':

Autumn leaves are falling as well as your copies of News from England. They may seem a gloomy enough reminder that the summer is over and a second war winter is setting in, this one under the heel of Germans bent on war domination. But remember that the leaves must seem far more ominous to the Germans; they remind them of the Kaiser's promise in 1914 "You will be back before the leaves fall," and of Hitler's proposed victory parade which was to celebrate the occupation of London in August. As the inhabitants of their great industrial towns huddle in their air raid shelters through the coming winter nights, the suspicion will gradually spread among them that the war cannot be won, that their dream of world conquest and plunder was only a dream and that dawn will break not so very far ahead on a Europe free from gangsters and ruled by its own peoples.

On 5th October the RAF returned yet again, but this time to drop bombs and not bits of paper.

The Islanders were rather pleased that the planes had come:

Saturday 5th October

'More gunfire at 5.15 p.m. at British planes – shrapnel fell all over the Island, most of it in the Braye Road district. The tale of the day is that a German Officer stopped a Guernseyman in the Grange last evening and in broken English said "Heil Hitler! Which is the way to the Regal?" The Guernseyman replied "God save the King! First on the left!"

Another heard in Westminster Bank earlier in the week was that an English resident considered the Guernseyman to be the most patriotic of the King's subjects – McDude asked him why – he said whenever he took shelter the invariable remark when the all-clear sounded was "Bugger!"'

(Diary of Violet Carey of Guernsey)

But the war was not, despite British and German predictions, going to be over any time soon. The Germans settled in. There were great changes in Island life. The Occupation Reichsmark was introduced, valued at roughly seven to the pound sterling.

There was an instant fuel shortage. All private cars were taken off the road. Yachts and high-powered boats were commandeered.

Horse-drawn vehicles appeared once more on the street. Busy barges came from France to fetch tons of potatoes for German troops on the mainland of Europe, aeroplanes performed the same service for tomatoes. Income tax was raised from 9d in the pound to 4/- in the pound, and most ominously of all, six days after they arrived, the Germans introduced food rationing.

On 6th July an order was published limiting the provision of meat to ¾lb per person per week, and the allowance of butter, cooking fats and sugar to 4oz per person per week. This order presaged five years of shortages and privations in the supply of food and nourishment. Food, and the supply of food, was the major preoccupation of the Occupation for occupiers and occupied alike. The years passed, the supplies dwindled until finally starvation came in the cold winter of 1944 – the Islands' very own 'hunger-winter'.

FOOD

We're all quite well but getting thinner
Not much for tea, still less for dinner
Though not exactly on our uppers
We've said adieu to cold ham suppers

Indeed it's getting quite the fashion
To queue up for our weekly ration
Butter, sugar, tea and flour
Salt we wait for by the hour

Men miss their beer, we can't get hops
Children have no lollipops
What put most people in a hole
Was when they had to ration coal

In peace time those who wished to slim
Tried diet, massage, baths and gym
We'll tell the stout of every nation
The secret's solved by OCCUPATION

The anonymous Jersey poet who wrote this ended by saying:

Little Jersey bombed and mined
To us war fates have proved unkind
But after all the stress and strain
To greater height we'll rise again

Yes, but in the meantime the order of the day was to keep the wolf from the door, food in your mouth (and the Germans off your back). And what a lot of mouths there were to cater for. Despite the June evacuations, 41,101 men, women and children remained in the Island. In Guernsey, where 17,000 had left, the figure was just under 23,000; in Sark, 470.

One thing was for certain. They could not feed themselves. They were Islanders living on islands which depended on supplies from overseas. Prior to the arrival of the Germans, these had come from France and in large measure from England. Now England was cut off, and France alone would have to victual the beleaguered Islands. It was a matter of urgency, and from the very start the Island authorities acted with commendable alacrity to address the problem. A Purchasing Commission was hastily set up to cross the sea to Granville on the Normandy coast and see what could be done to buy the much-needed supplies of all kinds from the French. The Commission was headed up by a Guernseyman of outstanding ability and his name was Raymond Falla, the Chief Agriculture Officer. He spoke fluent French, (which is somewhat different from the native

Guernsey patois) and had a terrific talent for wheeling and dealing in the French and very dodgy black market.

Money for the enterprise was provided by the Germans themselves who paid for all the cars they had requisitioned, not in sterling of course, but in Reichsmarks. The Guernsey authorities also provided money to fund the Purchasing Commission by auctioning off the antiquities, carpets and paintings belonging to the former Lieutenant-Governor of Guernsey, Major General J. R. Marshall-Ford. Taking the money across the Channel in battered suitcases and old sugar boxes Falla pitched camp in Granville Hotel and worked from there to buy all the necessaries he could for the Islands.

But despite his best endeavours the supply of essential commodities diminished significantly as year followed weary year of Occupation.

It has been remarked forcefully by no less a person than Joe Mière, historian, self-confessed hooligan, patriot and thorn in the German side, that the greatest heroes of the Occupation years were the women of the Islands: the housewives, the mothers, not of course those involved in 'collaboration horizontale' but those, the majority, engaged more in 'resistance culinaire.' He has a strong case.

For five long years these women worked hard and long to put food on the table. They would stand for hours in long queues to buy foul tasting 'bread', whatever vegetables were available, sometimes no more than a carrot or two and small and diminishing amounts of meat.

April 10th 1944

'In town this morning the grocer told me that he could supply this week four things only: butter, sugar, and two other commodities. Of course in the usual exiguous amounts. Every month the screw is tightened a little. Had they put us on this fare right off we should have died before the first Christmas. Only a tiny meat ration too this week. The demands of empty bellies begin to override conscience. I recall what a German woman said of the blockade in 1918: "The time my conscience died." So it begins here.'

(Diary of Reverend Ord)

There were scores of instances in which mothers went without themselves in order that the children could eat. Where to get food was the overwhelming concern of the Islanders and became even more so as months passed by and the hopes of an early end to the War faded utterly. There were shortages of everything, even, towards the end of 1944, a shortage of pet cats and dogs to kill for food.

WHAT CAN WE EAT?

John Lewis, the wise and kindly doctor in Jersey at the time of the Occupation writes this of those times:

'Let me make it plain before I go any

further that the Germans' broad policy was to preserve, as far as their own interests allowed, the basic individual liberty and welfare of the Island community. Shortage of supplies and the consequent deprivation we suffered were by no means entirely their fault, but rather that of the strip of sea which separated us from the French mainland. The considerable harassment (especially towards the end) by our own RAF naturally increased their difficulties and hence ours.'

Whatever the causes of the great dearth, shortages to the point of extinction there were. The Islanders, with a few exceptions, lost weight. Even the mighty suffered diminution. Alexander Coutanche ended the Occupation looking not so much vulpine, as von Aufsess described him, but more like an anorexic bloodhound. Over in Guernsey Victor Carey lost much of the opulent rotundity he had possessed in 1940 and appeared drawn and haggard by the time of Liberation. His weight had dropped from nearly fourteen stone to eight stone. In Sark, Sibyl Hathaway, thirteen stone and smiling when she was photographed with husband Bob greeting Albrecht Lanz and Dr Maass in July 1940, lost over six stone and weighed just seven stone by 1945, and this despite the lobster dinner she was condemned for having with Zachow and Schneeburgur in the Easter of that year. The Dame looks positively skeletal in the pictures of her at the time. (She managed however to put it all back on in time

for her appearance with Bob Hope and Bing Crosby in Hollywood in 1946.)

But almost everyone was affected. Here is Ruth Ozanne, a 56-year-old Guernsey spinster, living with her aged mother in St Peter Port, writing as early as 1941:

'I am now almost elegantly slim and weigh nine stone twelve pounds. I wish I knew what I weighed before but have certainly lost three stone and probably more. My friends frequently 'cut' me now and all say how much I have changed. I went to a funeral in Mother's dress and coat so that shows how much flesh I have lost. I feel all the better for it but my poor face does look lined and old. Everybody has lost weight and all look old and haggard. A lot are suffering from mild dysentery due to all the vegetables they have to eat.'

Often vegetables, mostly root vegetables, were all that was on offer – weeks could go by without any meat at all. Scarcity was everywhere and the Islanders began to suffer the effects of malnutrition as evidenced by this diary entry for Sunday 19th April 1942 (just after the wireless had been returned by the Germans), written by Violet Carey:

'In the news they told us there was an appeal by the food ministry not to waste bread, that [in England] too much bread was found in 'dustbins'. Words fail me! Don't the authorities know that a huge majority of the proletariat will not eat anything but fresh bread, will not eat the

heels of loaves! The poorer they are, the more snobbish they are on the subject. It makes us nearly burst with impotence and rage, when we think of our poor people here literally starving, our poor men weak from want of bread and meat. I think that what they miss more than anything, when they had two large slices of meat cut right across the sirloin and unlimited bread at every meal. Now they have two mouthfuls of meat and carefully-cut slices of bread, and when there are children both parents are giving up their bread.'

There are now eighty cases in the emergency hospital of 'Occupational malnutrition'. The Germans object to that name, but the *doctors formally use it*.

Things were bad and getting worse. Lord Portsea angrily demanded of an uncomprehending Parliament why food couldn't be sent to the Islands. He received the dusty answer that 'it was impossible to send food to the few remaining people there,' the 'few' numbering 60,000!

Given the lack of almost everything, invention and improvisation became the order of the day. Watermills were reinstated in Jersey, old millers dragged from peaceful retirement to do the work. Seawater was scooped up and used for cooking and for its salt, as featured in M Le Huguet's Occupation Alphabet:

A
Stands for the mighty Atlantic

By the pint for salt we bought it

Which indeed was the case, at 6d a pint from the water-carts the parish thoughtfully sent about the Islands. And M Le Huguet says:

B
Is for Bramble with lime tree
Gave leaves which made a substitute tea

Not that it tasted all that good but the real stuff was impossible to come by legitimately. On the black market it could however be bought for a hefty price of £16 a pound!

M Le Huguet might also have included under the letter 'B' a reference to beet, as in sugar beet, which was used to make a rather tasty sweet syrup which could be spread on otherwise unpalatable lumps of hard baked bread. It was quite difficult to make, difficult to get the boiling and reducing process exactly right, and you had to have a lot of sugar beet. The usual amount was 1cwt. These then had to be washed and cleaned using ordinary household scrubbing brushes. After this they were boiled in a washing tub, a copper or any large metal drum until they were soft and malleable. Then they were pressed and pressed until all the juice was expelled. This juice was then boiled and constantly stirred to make it into a syrup. It was hard work and the process took up to three days to complete, by which time the original one hundred weight of sugar beet would have yielded only around half a dozen standard size jam jars of tasty treacle.

M Le Huguet did include under the letter 'M' a mention of the ubiquitous use of Irish or carrageen moss.

M

For the slimy carrageen moss. Which made milk blancmange when at a loss.

Carrageen moss is a rather pretty form of seaweed, red to purplish in colour and found all around the Islands' coasts. During these Occupation years it was harvested, bleached on trays in the sun and sold in packets. It was then boiled and made into a kind of gelatine which in turn could, by additions sweet or savoury (sometimes even alcoholic) be transformed into blancmange or a soup. The Islanders, particularly children, were very grateful.

The great lack though, was meat. Weeks could go by and no meat at all could be obtained except on the black market and then at exorbitant prices. At many points in the Occupation Alexander Coutanche had more chance of getting meat for his dog than legitimately for himself. Some enterprising folk living near the slaughterhouse would beg blood and offal of slaughtered animals. The intestines were boiled to make a yellowish fat which was then used to fry black pudding made from the blood. Nothing was wasted, everything exploited to feed the hungry people but still there was not enough.

January 1942

'Some 30 RAF machines were visible and shrapnel was falling all over the town. To civilians death does not come so quickly as to those on active service. Old Colonel Rundle of Ivy Gates died this week from sheer starvation and over-exertion says the doctor. All he did was to go to town to draw his pitiable rations. At Les Banques a man pushing a small handcart just dropped down suddenly and was found dead. The papers contain long lists of obituaries and the hospital is full of starvation cases. Nor is it just humans who are affected. I saw with deep pity, a man trying to persuade his two horses (no whip of course being used) to drag a van load of furniture up Smith Street, but to no avail. The animals just could not move.

It is said that as many as fifteen typhoid cases have been notified, two being civilians.'

(Diary of Reverend Ord)

THE BLACK MARKET AND BARTER

Money talks and money gets. Those without it went without, those with it bypassed the rationing system paying way over the odds for whatever they wanted, and for whatever was available and on the black market. For most of the Occupation, most things were available at a price – even meat.

It is a commonplace of Occupation history that the experience of the townies differed markedly from that of the farmers and the country dwellers. Put simply, the farmers had the food in abundance, townies had none at all. The traffic was all one way. Much of the food, meat and vegetables went into the rationing system but there was a lot that didn't and was 'available' unofficially from some farms on the local black market. If you had enough money you could get what you wanted. How well you ate had a lot to do with the size of your purse.

Almost everyone in the Islands was involved perforce with the black market in foodstuffs: over 90% is a figure often quoted. If you weren't involved you suffered. Bob Le Sueur tells of the very high-minded and Very Reverend Matthew Le Marinel, the rector of St Helier, who refused to use the black market on principle. As a consequence the saintly gentleman lost 58% of his body weight, his dog collar hanging loose about his scrawny neck like a ring on a skeleton's finger, virtue intact, still very reverend, but now very thin.

Then there was barter. You could try and get what you wanted by a system of exchange of goods. This could be done by placing an advert in the local press or by going down to one of the exchange shops. These had previously been ordinary retail outlets conducting business for cash. Now however they were places to which Islanders brought goods of all kinds to be exchanged for other goods they might need more. The shopkeeper himself took a percentage of the notional value in money of the objects exchanged.

There was some bizarre trading too – wellington boots were exchanged for eggs, shoes for a tree, sawdust for flour and almost anything for tobacco.

Sonia Hillsden records in her book *Occupation Remembered* that there were even adverts in the *Evening Post* which offered food as the reward for finding lost property. For example the following advertisement appeared in the *Evening Post* on 26th April 1941:

'Lost: Red Horse Rug. Reward: 12 eggs. Apply Evening Post.'

The barter shops were kept extremely busy and among their chief patrons were the German soldiers. Having bought up all the luxury goods at the very beginning of the Occupation with his Reichsmarks they now returned with another form of currency – their cigarettes. Those of us who are, or have ever been, slaves to nicotine will understand all too readily the lengths the addict will go to satisfy his desire for a lungful of smoke. The German soldiers knew this very well, and took a proportion of their rather generous tobacco ration along to the barter shops and could obtain in exchange anything they wanted that was available.

Those Islanders who could not obtain tobacco or cigarettes in this way resorted to rather inventive ways to satisfy their craving. The leaf of any bush or plant that could be dried was used to make cigarettes: dock leaves, rose leaf or coltsfoot, it didn't matter – if it could be dehydrated and shredded it was pressed into service. The next job was to find suitable paper in which to wrap the ersatz tobacco. Toilet paper (of a rather harder kind than the softer tissue we caress ourselves with nowadays) was the obvious choice in the early days of the Occupation, but this ran out rather quickly. The good Islanders turned to the Good Book not for enlightenment but so that they could light up. The thin tissue on which the word of God was inscribed was ideal for rolling up a cigarette, but here again, despite the religiosity of the natives, there was still not enough paper to answer the need.

A solution to the problem came from Guernsey. It came in great quantities and in the form of wrapping paper used to pack the famous Island tomato. What a godsend it was! Even the Jersey folk had to admit that this precious paper served many purposes apart from providing a smoker with the means to make fags. It was also used as substitute toilet paper and it could be used as writing or typing paper. There were even drawings and paintings created on these sheets of humble wrapping paper, the gift from Guernsey.

But still it was food, or rather the lack of it, which concerned the Islanders most of all. You don't die if you don't smoke. You do die if you don't eat – and the Islanders did not eat or at any rate not enough.

From the end of 1943 onwards things got steadily worse for the civil population and it was only the arrival of SS *Vega* in December 1944 that prevented mass starvation such as was seen in Holland during their *Hongerwinter*.

But it was not just food that was lacking, important though that was; the Islanders also lacked news of what was going on in the War all around them. Rumours they had a-plenty – many wild and fantastical, many terrifying, the stuff of nightmares and very few to bring peace of mind and tranquillity. There was another lack which the Islanders felt most keenly, and that was the lack of any contact between the British Government and themselves. It was bad enough to have been 'left in the lurch', even 'betrayed' by the mother country, but it was rubbing salt in a very deep wound to have no direct messages of comfort and hope from across the water. Lots of commando raids putting the lives of the Islanders in mortal danger came from that direction but not a word was addressed directly to them for the entire duration of the Occupation. They felt abandoned and alone.

Friday December 6th 1940

'The rumour had gone around that Churchill was making a speech on the wireless and had good news to give to the country. We were all keyed up knowing that somebody would be sure to hear the speech, but it was a false report as he has not spoken.'

(Diary of Ruth Ozanne)

Nor did the great war leader ever speak to the Islanders during the War, and he did not visit the Islands after the War either. 'Our dear Channel Islands,' they might have been, but from 1940 to 1945 Churchill and the War Cabinet saw them as purely military factors in a hard war. The Germans were there to be attacked and defeated. That was the overriding concern. The welfare of the civilian population in this harsh scenario was, to put it mildly, very much a secondary issue.

The Islanders felt their isolation very keenly and there was widespread incomprehension at the treatment meted out to them by the British. Nonetheless, in diary after diary there can be found expressions of great loyalty to King and Country remarkable in their intensity. Even more remarkably, these multiplied as the Occupation ground on and on and as the true nature of the German Occupiers became more and more apparent. It became clear that this was going to be no gentle exercise. People were going to get hurt, many Islanders were going to suffer and a few were to die.

THE IRON FIST AND THE VELVET GLOVE

As has been remarked, the first Germans to arrive, the polished and burnished soldiers of the *Wehrmacht*, were instructed to treat the Islanders in a polite and courteous fashion and so they did, up to a point. There was nonetheless a sense of entitlement, however restrained, about the behaviour of these first German invaders which expressed itself in admittedly small but irritating ways.

They always jumped the queue in the shops demanding to be served first. They assumed the right of way over the native Islanders as they walked, noisy and laughing, along the pavements of St Helier and St Peter Port. The local policemen on the beat were obliged to salute the German officers, though some went to great lengths in order to avoid humbling themselves: doubling back when they saw a German officer approach or suddenly finding something extraordinarily interesting in a shop window which meant actually turning their back on the officer until he had passed. The farmers and, particularly of course in Guernsey, the glass-house cultivators were annoyed to take instruction from imported German farming 'experts' with no idea at all about Island agriculture. The German lorry drivers had no idea either about the peculiarities and difficulties of driving on the Islands. Some drove on the right after the continental fashion and they drove too fast; the need to get Hitler's work done far outweighed regard for public safety.

Driving on the right was introduced officially on 3rd June 1941. A man was killed, several severely injured and many frightened.

The ladies in the Islands decided to treat the invaders with coolness, at best an icy civility, thinking in a very English fashion that by over emphatic exercise of good manners they could best express their disdain for their unwelcome German visitors. There were of course other women in the Islands who were not considered ladies, and who behaved in quite a different fashion towards the handsome young invaders. These were infamous 'Jerry bags,' the horizontal collaborators who indulged in every kind of relationship with the German soldiery, *Wehrmacht* privates, *Wehrmacht* officers, it made no difference. The men could get sexual satisfaction and the girls (and they were mostly very young girls) would get food and presents, cigarettes, drink and car rides by way of return. But it would be a mistake to be cynical or judgemental about all these liaisons with the occupiers. Many a truly loving relationship was created in those days and, indeed, there were a number of marriages.

There were, of course, many children born to German fathers. The numbers are disputed. The British press, with its characteristic disregard for accuracy when reporting Channel Island affairs, put the number as between 2,000 and 3,000. This number is about 1,000 more than the number of all infants born in the Occupation.

The Germans themselves believed that only 80 children had been born to German fathers in all the Islands. The German records also contain the following:

All mothers with children already born, *insofar as they comply with our racial specifications, will be transferred to Germany, and that pregnant women will be taken to* Lebensborn *homes in France.*

Lebensborn means 'spring of life' and was the name given by Heinrich Himmler to a programme that provided medical and financial help to 'racially pure' and biologically fit Aryans. More particularly, in the occupied countries of Western Europe it provided care for unmarried mothers who had been in relationships with German soldiers.

Many of these women were ostracised by their own community and the *Lebensborn* homes were the first port of call for aid and succour.

Here the women would be cared for, the offspring relocated. Of course in such a thoroughly SS organisation with its thinking about eugenics and social engineering the women considered for *Lebensborn* help had to satisfy certain racial criteria – they had to be Aryan or at least have a fixed number of Aryan characteristics. It was here that the Island women fell down. According to German records most of them failed the tests, they were 'not up to standard'. They would have to stay in the Islands and risk obloquy and opprobrium from the community.

Only there was no vilification or maltreatment of the women or their children from within the Island society.

The British press did not report, perhaps

because it did not fit in with their agenda of attacking the reputation of the Islands, the story of how these children born of German soldiers were treated after the War ended.

In many countries women who had consorted with German soldiers and had their children were treated abominably. Their hair was cut off, they were verbally and physically attacked and sometimes even killed. Very often the child was separated from the mother. This was particularly so in Norway. Anni-Frid Lyngstad, the beautiful singer with Abba, suffered a great deal because of the treatment meted out to children born of German fathers. Her mother was forced to flee from the dangers in Norway across the border into Sweden, so great was the hatred directed towards her and her child. And so it was in most of Western Europe – but it was not so in the Channel Islands. Here the women and their children were quietly absorbed back into society. There were very few, if any, instances of mother or child being abused or ostracized in any way in the post-war years. The Islanders could be proud of themselves for such restraint in an intolerant and rather inhuman post-war world.

The thought expressed by Leslie Sinel that things would get back almost to normal and that the Islanders would get on in quite a reasonable fashion with the courteous invaders was gradually, bit by bit, destroyed as the Occupation went on. Things happened which

demonstrated all too graphically the true nature of the Nazi regime in the Islands. The German high command might send a lot of doctors and members of the near and actual aristocracy, to say nothing of a couple of princes, along to impress the Islanders with their culture and breeding, and it is true to say that many were initially seduced by the civilised appearance they presented.

But as Donald Rumsfeld famously remarked, in war, 'stuff happens', despite the best intention and endeavours of the belligerents – and 'stuff' began to happen in the Islands. Violent incidents occurred and not a few threats against the civil population were posted in the Islands. News that a Frenchman had been shot for keeping pigeons which the Germans thought were being used to send messages to the enemy was disseminated throughout the Islands, with the obvious implications that the same fate would befall any Islander who kept pigeons for the same purpose. In the event the Germans considered the entire pigeon population in the Islands as a threat to their security. Also at very great risk of being shot were those who gave any sort of help or refuge to agents of the enemy, such as Second Lieutenants Hubert Nicolle and James Symes, Guernseymen of the Hampshires, who came to Guernsey on that commando reconnaissance mission on 4th September 1940.

These two officers gave themselves up, were tried and sentenced to death.

Not only were they arrested but with them all their family and friends, along with Ambrose Sherwill, were taken into German Custody and sent to the Cherche-Midi prison in Paris.

As has been noted elsewhere, conditions both psychological and physical were extremely bad and James Symes' father, Louis, committed suicide by slashing his wrists. It was a terrible experience though still not as awful as it might have been, for the family and friends of the two men were released just after Christmas 1940 and Nicolle and Symes had their death sentences commuted to imprisonment in a POW camp for the duration. This had all been achieved through the intercession of von Schmettow appealing their case in a Court of Honour, but it was a near death experience for all concerned and a salutary reminder of the realities of war.

More were to follow.

THE DEPORTATIONS

September 15th 1942

NOTICE

By order of higher authorities the following British subjects will be evacuated and transferred to Germany:

a) Persons who have their permanent residence not on the Channel Islands, for instance those who have been caught here by the outbreak of war,

b) All those men not born on the Channel Islands and 16 to 70 years of age

who belong to the English people, together with their families.

Detailed instructions will be given by the Feldkommandantur 515

Der Feldkommandant
Knackfuss
Oberst.

Despite the evacuations of June 1940 there remained a sizeable minority of English folk still in the Islands. These people found themselves at risk through no fault of their own.

Winston Churchill, holding his nose and acting in concert with the Russians, decided to take action in Persia in order to secure oil supplies and warm water supply routes to the Red Army. There were around 4,000 German engineers, technicians and advisers in that country all very anxious to tap into her resources and use them to supply the German war machine on the Eastern Front.

'Taking a leaf out of Hitler's book,'

as Churchill put it, privately, but not of course, publicly. Not a good idea to acknowledge Adolf as a role model. Forces were sent into Persia in August 1941 to achieve the Allied goals. The Shah was forced to abdicate and his son Mohammed Reza Pahlavi placed on the Peacock Throne on the understanding that he would carry out the wishes of the Allies to the letter, particularly with regard to all the German nationals in his country.

On 12th September 1941 the British War Cabinet announced that it would intern all German citizens in Persia whom they considered to be actively engaged in activities directed against the Allied cause. That meant all of them.

The whole affair was in direct breach of international law which expressly forbade regime-change and forceful incursions into neutral states. Churchill confessed as much when he said:

'We had been doing something for which we had justification but no right.'

Hitler did not like this one little bit, in fact he disliked it so much that he ordered reprisal measures to be taken against the 'hostage' British population in the Channel Islands. Ten Islanders were to be taken for every German arrested in Persia and shipped forthwith to the dreaded Pripet Marshes, the dumping ground for all the 'undesirables' in the new German Empire. In other words the Islanders were to be used as pawns in the great war game. No notion here of a 'special relationship' based on respect for life and liberty between the occupier and the occupied. Not even lip service to the international conventions forbidding reprisals against innocent civilian populations. Quite simply the Islanders had no rights at all in this matter. Their lives counted for nothing so much as to serve German war aims.

However, despite the fact that Hitler certainly issued the instruction for all the British-born Island residents to be deported, something happened in its transmission from Berlin to Paris and then to the Islands, for it was not carried out for over a year. The reasons for this failure are largely unknown, many of the relevant documents having been burned.

In August 1941 the Island census was carried out recording the place of birth of all the residents. Towards the latter end of 1941, at the request of the Germans, certain names taken from this census were made up into another list by the Island authorities. The Island authorities did not know that the order for these lists to be made up had come direct from Hitler himself. He was looking in particular for British-born Islanders to figure in a 'reprisal action'; the kind of action that was, as the British Foreign Office pointed out, expressly forbidden by the Hague Convention.

The lists were drawn up by the ever compliant Island governments and deportations should have commenced almost immediately but they did not. It seems there was some obscurity in the wording of the deportation order. It was not clear if the deportations should indeed go ahead immediately or whether they should wait upon a more 'favourable political opportunity'. General Warlimont, who conducted the enquiry into what had happened to the Fuehrer's instruction (as recounted by Cruikshank in *German Occupation of the Channel Islands* p228) concluded that:

'The Foreign Ministry had believed that the military authorities were carrying out the deportation according to plan, whereas the military authorities were under the impression that the Foreign Ministry wanted it to be postponed on political grounds.'

Whatever the truth of that, the fact remained that a direct order from Hitler had got lost in a fog of inter-departmental misunderstanding and the Fuehrer was not a happy man when he discovered that his will had been so obstructed. He discovered this heinous non-compliance only twelve months later and almost by accident.

The Swiss, as a neutral mediating power, initiated discussions with the Germans in August 1942 about the possible exchange of badly-injured POWs. It was proposed by the Swiss that British-born Channel Islanders wanting to return to the mainland should be included in the number of British POWs to be exchanged. As there were thousands of prisoners both British and German involved in the Swiss plan, and because it was therefore of great significance, it was put before Hitler himself. Hitler immediately and testily demanded to know why any British people at all remained in the Channel Islands. Had they not all been deported according to his order of a year ago?

No, they had not.

Hitler issued the order again with a degree of vehemence and a certainty that this time it would be carried out with expedition and thoroughness. The British-born Islanders had unknowingly enjoyed a twelve month period of grace from deportation but now the time had come. All protest was in vain. And great protest there was. Coutanche berated Knackfuss and threatened resignation. Knackfuss commiserated with the Bailiff but said that the order had come direct from Hitler and there could be no gainsaying.

The deportation notices were issued in all the Islands.

By order of higher authorities the following British subjects will be evacuated and transferred to Germany:

a) Persons who have their permanent residence not on the Channel Islands, for instance those who have been caught here by the outbreak of war,
b) All those men not born on the Channel Islands and 16 to 70 years of age who belong to the English people, together with their families.

Detailed instructions will be given by the Feldkommandantur 515

Der Feldkommandant
Knackfuss
Oberst.

Leslie Sinel describes the impact of this in his diary entry of 15th September:

'The effect of such an order cannot be described, the evacuation of 1940 paling into insignificance in comparison. It is learned that it is a direct order from Hitler and that speed must be applied in carrying it out. The Bailiff, Attorney General and the Constables were summoned and the Germans gave their orders. The Bailiff and Attorney General made vigorous protests and the Constables refused to be the ones who would tell people they must be sent away to Germany. No logical reason can be given for this distressing order except that it is out of pure spite for the bombing of Germany by the RAF. Early in the evening and continuing throughout the night cars were rushing around the Island with German and local officials armed with lists of the first people to be sent away.'

It was bad news for Marie Françoise Augustine Richards, her two sisters and her mother and father. This is her story of the day of the deportation:

Friday 18th September

'Received our notice at 12 noon to be at the Parish Hall for 2.45pm or St Nicholas Church at 3.15. Went to the latter. Rushed up to Oakhurst to say goodbye to Mother and Dad. Both Bricks. Not a sign of their heartbreak. Rushed home. Bert taking our things down on his trailer. Sudden heatwave and dresses in several layers of warm winter underwear! Waiting for two hours in the sun. Buses arrive – inadequate room – another wait and at last we are on ... Weighbridge Hall – Huge crowd singing through town. Meetings and joyous reunion of friends.

All in good spirits. Much repartee – German officials courtesy itself. Particulars taken and numbers given out. Dick's 399 and mine 400. Gong! And numbers called, and people queue up for buses and taken to pier. Refreshments. Jam sandwiches and cups of milk. About 9pm last three buses returned and people back.

Then notice read out that no one else is going tonight – must all return home (cheers) but return in a week's time. Buses and cars requisitioned to take people home. German soldiers helping to carry children and luggage – seem as pleased as we do. Phoned up Augie and Bert to say we're on our way to spend the night with them. Joyous reunion and phone going frantically to inform Maman and friends.'

Monday

'Busy sorting out stuff and repacking – Tea at Tony and Mavis'. Week of mending and sorting. House and affairs to put in order. Evacuation order postponed until Tuesday 29th September. All up at Maman's for tea. Farewell party. Week of terrific rainstorms. "Desinent" on rocks. Weather improving. Monday – glass falling! Returning from Maman's Sunday night with foreign workers outside Pavilion. My knuckles very sore!'

Tuesday 29th September

'All in high spirits and Bert seeing us off with trailer for luggage. Rosie turned up in dreadful rain to give a hand and thorough brick. Rain clearing. Have had lovely dinner- stuffed marrows – refused to leave until eaten all we could! – Late arriving at Weighbridge. Missing lots of faces – informed they've gone on to boat – some bus loads going straight down to pier. Sorting ourselves out and finding friends. Watson's there. Parked with them and Dodsley's – Mallet going with Frankier family. A JERSEYMAN! Doesn't know why he's being sent!'

"They" are calling for families! Women and children to line up with Daddies to have best place on the boat. We're still waiting – We've no kiddies so can park anywhere. Beside we shall be able to help some harassed mother ... No refreshments this time. They are on the pier, handing parcels to people as they go on board ... Waiting is terrific, so tiring.

However...
There goes the gong! All crane to listen."There will be a little interlude"...
What does it mean? They said that last time before we were sent back. – Does it mean no more being taken? Impossible, such luck does not happen twice! – Spirits rising very high. Lunch baskets opened – almost too excited to eat! German officials all conferring together. Seem excited. What's happening? Another long wait.

Gong ! Everyone stands to listen. "There will be no further evacuation ..." FRANTIC CHEERS! "... for the time being!" More cheers. "You may all go back to your jobs! HEAVENS! It can't be true! It can't be! We stare incredulously. Then everyone goes mad! Where is our traditional sang froid gone? Everyone is hugging everyone else

– Some are weeping with blessed relief – Mrs Dodsley throws her arms around Dr Gow and kisses him, then grabs hold of another man and dances a mad polka! Germans are looking on and laughing. Arthur Chillingworth has gone to phone Augie and Maman – JOY! JOY! JOY!!! I pick up my rucksack and the strap breaks! Is that another omen? Last time the handle of my suitcase came away when I picked it up to go back home. Perhaps we shall remain. Conveyances for all, buses and cars. Back to First Tower. Augie mad with delight.

Neighbours coming in to find out why and wherefore. " Has so-and-so come back? Did so-and-so go with all her children?" etc. etc. etc.

Our thoughts are with those poor devils on board. What are they going to face? What of all those little ones? Surely all that is most unnecessary. What possible harm can we British do cut off in this little island?

Augie and Bert want us to remain with them for the time being until we know for certain which way the wind blows. Rumours already starting that it will only be until Christmas. Then we shall have to face all this all over again!

Well it's fate I suppose and we should be thankful that we've another three months of comfort left, before we attend the "luxury" attendant behind barbed wire fences. What a life! Many of the people gone today will never see their homes again – some are ill, some are old

– and there are little babies in arms, while some women are pregnant – oh my heart bleeds for them. Why hasn't there been an outcry to stop this awful thing? Someone will surely have to answer for this crime.'

And Marie spoke for many when she wrote:

'I can restrain myself no longer. The rotten curs! Soon, very soon, I hope and pray that our men will come and put an end to this filthy regime that hits back at babies and nursing mothers, I want to see them crushed and broken – It's all very well for these smiling beasts to help us with our luggage – I wouldn't let one of them help me this afternoon to carry mine – even though my arms felt they were coming out of their sockets – the sight of those mothers and babes this afternoon and last week especially – makes me feel that the very nearness of that hated uniform is pollution.

There is iron eating into my soul – I feel bitterness and hatred that I never thought I could ever feel so deeply – and its depth seems bottomless, for I am sure that I shall never forgive this. If such a thing can happen to people who have never crossed them in any way – what devilry do they perform on those who do?'

The answer to that last question was more terrible than anyone in the Islands could know.

The deportation orders were disastrous for the Islanders. Yes, the Occupation up to then had been uncomfortable and decidedly unpleasant but not unbearably so – food might be in short supply, shoes worn and clothing shoddy. The curfew was irksome and there were petty acts of violence and thievery but nothing like this – the wholesale uprooting and transportation of a large chunk of the population to some hellish place across the sea in Germany. And it wasn't just the menfolk. Women, wives, mothers and children were all included and told to get themselves down to the harbour by 9 o'clock on the 16th to embark for the Fatherland. Nor were the deportees permitted to take much luggage with them – 'no heavier than you can carry' was the rule. Your house had to be locked up and the keys handed over to the Constables.

Any jewellery and valuables had to be left behind, deposited in a bank.

'Should you fail to obey the order sentence a court martial shall be effected,'

declared Knackfuss.

This was only the first deportation.

There were more. They carried on until the January of 1943. No one knew where they were going, though urgent enquiries as to the destination of the deportees were made by Coutanche in Jersey and John Leale in Guernsey. There was no response from the Germans, which merely added to the fear and distress felt by everyone in the Islands.

Rumour was rife that they were going to be used as human shields in those great German cities that were being blown to pieces by the RAF or perhaps they were to be kept as hostages, bargaining chips in some desperate Nazi strategy. It was the not knowing that was terrifying and too much to bear for some. Mr John Sibley the Guernsey butcher ended the uncertainty by gassing himself, as did a British-born man and wife living in Beaumont, Jersey.

Over in Sark another married couple, Major Skelton, the Island's agricultural officer, and his wife Madge, were on the list of eleven people ordered to present themselves at the tiny Creux harbour prepared for deportation.

They failed to appear at the appointed time and the boat left without them. The Germans began a hunt for them and put up a notice demanding information about the Skeltons' whereabouts. In fact they were lying in a little field next to their house. Major Skelton was dead. He had slashed his wrists. By his side lay his wife Madge. She had taken poison and also been stabbed by her husband in this suicide pact. But she was still alive, half drowned and bleeding in the continuous rainfall but still alive. Madge was rushed to the Guernsey hospital where she was successfully treated for her physical injuries. Her mental injuries can only be guessed at. She came back to Sark in the July of 1946.

As far as the Germans were concerned, Major John Skelton was a prime candidate for deportation because he was an ex-British army officer who had served in the Royal Engineers and spoke fluent German. He fitted the profile of a British agent perfectly. He was also a Jew and it is thought that it was this, above all else, that caused him to take his own life.

He knew what kind of fate awaited him once he set foot on the *White Heather* waiting in the rain in Creux harbour.

'The scene could not have been more dismal when we gathered at the harbour. A bitter wind was blowing in from the sea, which was looking particularly sinister, and rain pelted down viciously from a leaden sky. By far the most pathetic figure on the Quayside was Mrs Pittard, who had not yet recovered from the shock of her imprisonment in Guernsey and was now about to face an unknown fate in Germany. Miss Duckett and Miss Page were also there. Although we were all cold and wet and miserable, those who were about to leave and those who remained tried to reassure one another.'

(Sibyl Hathaway, Dame of Sark p151)

In the larger Islands there were more heart-rending scenes as the Islanders bade farewell to those countrymen, women and children so cruelly taken from them. The Island authorities had done all they could for them.

They could not, despite their best

efforts, stop the deportations but they could provide the deportees with food and clothing.

Summerland, the marvellous little factory for producing woollies and boots, coats and jumpers from any material left to hand, went into overtime to produce stuff for the deportees.

The States of Jersey further provided a 1lb loaf of bread, a tin or jar of paste, a slab of chocolate, a tin of milk and a packet of cigarettes. (Sinel diary).

In Guernsey the deportees first went to the Royal Cinema:

After waiting some time in their seats the people had to file up to a table where two German clerks copied particulars from their identity cards, entering them on a register and giving out a ticket. Then they waited again and were sent on in batches by the Truchot exit to Murdochs Store to collect their luggage, then through another store where each received a chip basket containing 2lb bread, ½lb butter, ½lb biscuits, ½lb chocolate, a tin of liver paté and a tin of sardines, soap if they wanted it and razor blades for the men. The men also had tobacco and cigarettes.'

(Diary of Ruth Ozanne)

All this courtesy of the States of Guernsey fund specially set up by the Bailiff, Victor Carey.

Everything that could be done for the

deportees was done but still:

'Words fail to describe the wretched state of the Island at the moment, for those not affected have scores of friends who are; everyone is distressed and there is scarcely a dry eye tonight.'

(Diary of Leslie Sinel)

And all this despite the German assurance given to the Islanders back in July 1940 that:

'In the case of peaceful surrender, the lives, property and liberty of peaceful inhabitants are solemnly guaranteed.'

They got a musical send-off in Jersey:

'Suddenly a very clear voice began to sing "There'll always be an England" and we all joined in, we all knew the words, and then we sang "Red white and blue, what does it mean to you?" And they sang "God save the King" and all of a sudden the people of all the boats, by the time they were moving down the harbour, started to respond to us and singing back and joining in.'

(Theo Russell)

The Guernsey folk were a little more muted but calling out:

'"Au Revoir, Cheerio" and so on which made one feel rather lumpy in the throat, for all those going were laughing and waving to their friends. It made one very proud of them all for they were truly magnificent. All of them had had to give up their homes at two days' notice and

*were leaving behind their belongings and
in many cases their nearest and dearest.
I literally did not see one tear shed and
one dear old lady insisted on kissing us
all with hearty smacking kisses as we
stood in the entrance together.'*

(Diary of Ruth Ozanne)

A small measure of revenge for the
distress of the deportees was exacted by
a young Jerseyman:

*'One German officer already unpopular
in the Island was taking photographs of
these horrible, grotesque and
heartrending scenes when suddenly a
young chap jumped out and while the
German was bending over taking a
particularly good shot, he gave him a kick
up the backside as hard as he could kick
and the German practically ploughed a
furrow in the tarmac with his face.'*

(Lewis)

A little joy for the deportees but they
still did not know where they were
going – perhaps to Germany.

*'We were thinking that probably they'd
be going to be forced labourers
somewhere, possibly in factories on the
Ruhr where the RAF are bombing nightly.
They're going to be in trains across
Europe where the RAF is bombing the
railway lines. This is what people thought.
Here were these people with their
children, and nobody, absolutely nobody
was in tears. It was incredible.'*

(Bob Le Sueur)

There were exemptions granted for the
very old and the sick, and certain
essential administrators like Victor
Carey, John Leale and Dr Symons the
excellent Officer of Health, and
Raymond Falla so important in
providing the Islanders with food. It is
believed that Baron von Aufsess
exercised some influence in saving these
men. Ambrose Sherwill, William
Sculpher, the Guernsey police chief, and
Bob Hathaway, the Dame of Sark's
American husband were not so lucky
and must have cursed the Germans as
they clambered aboard the filthy
transports in rain and heavy seas to be
taken away for the rest of a very long
war, away from their Islands, away from
their loved ones.

FRANÇOIS MARIE SCORNET

In the western parish of St Ouens in
Jersey there is a great manor house with
sweeping lawns, a wide lake and
magnificent old trees. It was, and still is,
the ancestral home of the powerful de
Carteret family whose name appears on
almost every page of the Island's history.
It is a beautiful and tranquil place but it
was here on the 17th March 1941 that
a young Frenchman was shot by
German firing squad for the crime of
wilfully supporting Great Britain in the
war against the German Empire. His
killing angered and shocked the kindly
Island folk. Certainly they had been
victims of the bombing raid of 28th
June 1940. People had died, collateral
damage, but that had seemed to be an
unfortunate incident in no way
indicative of how the Germans would
behave once they left their planes

behind and were personally present in the Island and, moreover, acting in a quite civilised and gentle manner.

This shooting of François cut right across many of the assumptions the Islanders had made about the nature of the Germans and the murderous lengths to which they would go in the prosecution of the war – they would certainly not baulk at contravening the Hague Convention as and when it suited them, and it certainly suited them in the case of François Scornet.

François Marie Scornet was just 20 years old when he set sail with 15 companions in an open boat headed towards the southern coast of England. Once there, the plan was to join the Free French Forces under de Gaulle and fight on against the Germans in a war the Vichy Government had so shamefully abandoned. The 16 young men were in high spirits as they pulled away from the north Brittany coast – they were on their way to help salvage the honour of France and strike a blow against the hated enemy. But the night was dark and the seas were heavy and, alas, their patriotic fervour was much greater than their navigational skills.

After six hours tossing about on the rough waters off the Cotentin they spied land. England they thought.

They thought wrongly.

It was not the south coast of England but Vazon bay in Guernsey in which they found themselves. They saw German soldiers waiting for them on the beach, guns at the ready. There was no turning back for the young Frenchmen. They flung their weapons, such as they were, as quickly as possible into the sea and surrendered to the Germans.

At the beginning of the Occupation, the German military headquarters were in Jersey, so it was to St Helier that the 16 were sent to be examined by the High Command. They were interrogated and then tried by the German war court in the States of Jersey offices in Royal Square. Under the terms of the Franco-German Armistice signed in the June of 1940, any released French prisoner of war who carried out acts inimical to the German Forces would face the death penalty. François was one such as this and he took on the absolute responsibility for the entire episode.

He and two others in the group were sentenced to death. On appeal, the sentence on his two comrades was commuted to life imprisonment. They were sent to concentration camps. But François' conviction was upheld.

So it was on a dull March morning that a strange convoy set off from St Helier and made its way towards St Ouen's Manor. In the centre was a truck with a coffin in the back. On this coffin sat François Scornet. Either side of him, cradling their rifles, sat the German firing squad. Behind the lorry came a couple of local taxis containing assorted German officers and, more importantly, the Reverend Père Marie, the Catholic priest from St Thomas' Catholic church in St Helier.

On that miserable morning, they drove west along the Esplanade and then turned north up the long, steep Beaumont Hill, passed St Peter's village and finally drove through the stone archway into the grounds of St Ouen's Manor.

Here the gallant young Frenchman was taken from the lorry and marched the last few yards to an ash tree in the hollow before the eastern walls. He was tied to this tree. He refused the blindfold. Père Marie embraced François and then held out the crucifix for him to kiss.

The firing squad raised their rifles. Scornet cried out, 'Vive Dieu! Vive la France!' The Germans then shot him.

In François Scornet's last letter to his mother and father he wrote:

'I believe the end of my existence has come. I will die for France, bravely facing the enemy. In an hour it will be finished … Be assured that I will die a good Christian … For the last time I embrace you.'

The ash tree is long gone but if you go there now you will find a little memorial plaque put there in honour and remembrance of this gallant man.

The effect of this execution on the Islanders cannot be overestimated. It was seen as an unforgiveable, disgraceful and repulsive act of savagery which added much to the loathing and contempt directed towards the invader as the War turned from a brief encounter to a long-drawn-out struggle.

The Islanders might have considered themselves in a terrible situation, frightened and isolated, deprived and threatened by their German masters, which indeed they were. But to their dismay and disgust they were soon to meet people many times worse off than themselves – the slave workers of the Organisation Todt (OT).

UNTERMENSCHEN

On 13th June Hitler issued an instruction for the fortification of the Islands. He thought them to have enormous strategic and propaganda significance, and this belief gained in intensity as the war in the East began to unfold. He was convinced that an Allied attack on Western Europe would begin with an attempt to take the Channel Islands, which must be prevented whatever the cost. The little Islands must be turned into mightily defended fortresses with great gun-emplacements, huge minefields, miles of underground tunnels to house stores and hospitals, and massive sea walls constructed against the invader.

This for Hitler was a serious ambition and on 20th October 1941 he issued the personal order for the intensive fortification and embattlement of the Islands of Guernsey, Jersey and Alderney.

Dr Fritz Todt was despatched to the Islands. As head of the OT it was his task to estimate what had to be done to fulfil Hitler's wishes and then find the human and material resources to complete the job. He might have thought the War unwinnable but this did not stop him working flat out to satisfy the labour needs of Hitler's Third Reich. The human resources of labour he used came in the main from Russia. It was a late realisation on the part of the Germans that it was a much better idea to use captured Russians to work for them rather than letting them starve by the million in barbed wire compounds or in open railway carriages.

Germany suffered increasingly throughout the war years from a chronic shortage of labour, and turned more and more to forced labour imported from all over their new empire. And so it was that many Russians came to the Islands to pour the concrete, dig the ditches and build the walls needed to turn them into the strongest section of the great Atlantic Wall that stretched all along the Western European seaboard from Norway to the northern edge of Spain.

Their appearance in the Islands shocked all who saw them. Their treatment by the German guards appalled them even more.

THE OT SLAVES

The Islanders might have very little food

but compared to the Russian slave workers they were living high on the hog, for these men had hardly any at all. Though the work of these OT men was heavy, the calorific value of their diet was extremely low, less than half that of the Islanders. There was little or no meat but lots of thin, very thin, vegetable, usually cabbage, soup; small pieces of coarse bread and quantities of ersatz coffee. They were dressed in rags, mostly old sacking and they were often without any footwear beyond bits of cloth wrapped around their feet.

Unwashed and verminous, gaunt and hollow-eyed, the appearance of these prisoners from the East and their brutal treatment by their captors provoked feelings of disgust amongst the Islanders. Alexander Coutanche himself was moved to protest to von Schmettow after seeing them:

'... prisoners being driven to work by their guards when their feet were so sore that they were wrapped up in sacks.'

He had seen them:

'... take the weight off their feet by walking on their elbows on the walls which abounded the roads.'

Many Islanders witnessed gross acts of violence against these Russian *Untermenschen*, including this little boy who saw a gang of Russians building a military road in Jersey:

'They were working hard. They had no

clothes and there was one guy who had no shoes and he'd dipped his feet in tar and stuck gravel on the soles of his feet and that's how he had to work.'

(Messervy Norman)

Dr John Lewis recalls his first encounter with Russian slave workers:

'Very early one morning, on an urgent visit to a patient in St Lawrence, I had just passed Meadow Bank, when I became aware of an extremely unpleasant smell – a compound of urine and faeces, but above all of mice. Rounding the bend I saw a column of men being herded (and "herded" is the word) by Nazi soldiers. They were of all ages, bearded, some with shoes in various stages of decrepitude, but many with just rags wrapped around their feet. They all looked worn and emaciated, and one old man, propped against the hedge would probably never reach the top of the hill alive ... I learned that this particular batch were inhabitants of a village in German-occupied Russia, where some sort of sabotage had been committed. In retaliation the Germans had rounded up every male between 16 and 60, locked them all in unfurnished, unheated, covered trucks and sent them across Europe as forced labour. Having never set foot outside the trucks, which were not opened until they were transhipped into France, and being devoid of any sanitary facilities whatsoever, it was small wonder they stank the way they did.

I did not see them again except working at a distance, but I gathered they were put in a camp somewhere round Ville du

Bas, St Lawrence. Subsequently I got to know a Russian from the same camp ... He told me that a number of the original group had died within days of their arrival.'

Their condition was pitiable and the Islanders would sometimes try to help these transplanted Russians by secretly passing food to them, but it was a risky business. A few Russians managed to escape, men like 'Bill' Polykapovitch, and were given refuge by the Islanders, but most of them stayed where they were. Wretched and starving, they did their work as best they could, often in full view of the local people. And it was this experience which changed many an Islander's view of the Germans and their occupation.

'The Germans have a large camp here of Russian prisoners, who are working for them, and are in the most dreadful state of starvation and dirt. These poor wretches are dying off like flies, and there is a large "Strangers Cemetery" opened in the field near here, where the poor things are buried.

They dig a large grave and put the first one in, and then leave the grave open till enough coffins arrive to fill it, and then shovel it in. They are just buried like dogs, and no prayer said over them, or any decency of any sort observed. I believe they just die of starvation and overwork; no one has heard of any particular disease among them. The people out in the country are very afraid of them, as they come and steal any food they can lay their hands on, and in one case the householder came down and discovered the thief, and they came to blows and the householder was killed and the Russian got away. The Germans could not identify which of the men who had broken camp was the one who had killed the Jerseyman, so they shot all the suspects to make sure! Poor things – it is awful for them, and nobody can talk their language – it is awful to think what misery is going on in this little Island.'

(Diary of Alice Mainland, Jersey)

'Great changes have taken place in both ourselves and in the Germans. Gone is the initial "courtesy," gone also is their boisterousness. Our people become progressively more determined.'

(Diary of Reverend Ord 1941)

And, he might have added, more deprived.

NO WIRELESS

Many things were taken away from the Islanders in the course of the long Occupation: food, liberty, their prosperity and even sometimes their lives. One of the losses they felt most keenly was that of the wireless, and it is not at all difficult to understand why. The normal emotional state of the imprisoned Island folk during the Occupation was one of high anxiety – as they would say, 'we were living on our nerves':

'We feel from time to time our hearts beat slower and slower, not because we doubt the ultimate outcome, but because

we can only stand and wait without chance of serving. And all the time a dog that may turn savage at any moment is roaming loose amongst us.'

(Diary of Reverend Ord 1941)

The Reverend Ord was absolutely right about the danger of the German Occupation. People knew that when push came to shove it was highly unlikely that their German visitors would shrink from savage reprisals. But not many of the Islanders could have shared the Reverend's optimism as to the outcome of the conflict, at least during the first two years. They just did not know what was going to happen. If they listened to, or read, Goebbels' propaganda they might believe the War would end with the defeat of Russia and a glorious and comprehensive German victory. The Islanders would be occupied forever!

It was an uncertain world for the Islanders, a world of rumour, half truth and downright lie, but their lives, their futures were at stake. Consequently there was an overwhelming desire to know what was really happening. They turned, of course, to the BBC to find out how the War was really progressing, and also they longed to hear some words of comfort and support from Churchill or the King addressed directly to them. They got the information they wanted but no words of comfort and encouragement which mentioned the Channel Islands by name. They were mightily disappointed by this, and felt their isolation even more keenly

Hitler triumphant! Hess to his right and Göring first left.

Hitler, Franco and Mussolini appear in the Battle of Flowers float 1939 one month before the outbreak of war. It is depicting the famous Peace in our time speech. Neville Chamberlain to the left.

An island prepares!

Jersey little ones await the Germans.

The bombing of St Helier Harbour, June 28th, 1940.

Potato lorries wait on the dockside in St Helier.

The bombing of St Peter Port harbour, June 28th 1940.

Burnt out lorries at White Rock, Guernsey harbour.

Bombed out clock tower.

The Germans on their way to the French coast.

Bailiff Coutanche urges his people to stay put and tough it out

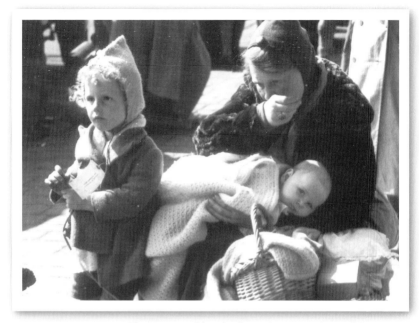

The youngest of the Islanders to leave.

Evacuees waiting for the boat to take them away

A nervous Duret Aubin and Alexander Coutanche greet the very first Germans to arrive in Jersey.

Jersey's Attorney General, Duret Aubin, says hello to the invaders

The Swastika on British soil.

The British Guernsey flag and some German officers in a propaganda photo.

Alexander Coutanche, Bailiff of Jersey.

Victor Gosselin Carey, Bailiff of Guernsey.

Ambrose James Sherwill,
Attorney General of Guernsey.

The luftwaffe enjoy some Guernsey tomatoes.

Major Albrecht Lanz sits next to Bailiff Victor Carey in the Guernsey States.

Triumphalism in St Peter Port

Major Lanz and the conquering heroes.

The Germans took many photos like this to send back home.

Detente! Making friends with the Islanders.

because of it, but still they could keep themselves up to date with a relatively truthful account of the conflict via the wireless. It was their lifeline to the world beyond the Islands, the one certain centre in an increasingly disordered world.

The first time the wireless sets were confiscated was in the autumn of 1940. This was quite simply a reprisal action taken by the Germans as a punishment for the aid given to Nicolle and Symes, the British Commandos, when they came to Guernsey. They were however given back after a few weeks. But then, in June 1942, the Germans took the radios for a second time and this time they held on to them until the end of the War and of the Occupation. The penalties for possessing a wireless set were harsh: imprisonment and possibly transportation. The order for the confiscation came direct from Berlin and could not be changed, or so Coutanche was told when he protested about it to Schmettow and his second in command, von Helldorf, in 1944.

The Germans thought they had good reason to take the Islanders' radios away from them. It was thought that the Second Front would soon be established in the West, and that the BBC in London was broadcasting appeals to the peoples of occupied countries to rise up behind the German lines and help the Allies when they crossed the Channel. It was assumed that the Allies would invade the Channel Islands and further assumed that the Islanders would obey the calls from London and attack the occupying German forces with every means at their disposal. From the German point of view it therefore made absolute sense to interrupt their enemy's communications by confiscating their radios.

'It is awful – there is such a feeling of fear everywhere, and a "What will happen next?" feeling. Can you imagine life without letters, newspapers or wireless? Talking of wireless we had them taken away six months ago. A good many people who had more than one set sent in one and hid the other for use after the War – as of course the one sent in will never be seen again. My second one is carefully hidden away – and I don't think it could be found if they searched the house. We get the news in driblets from people who still dare to listen in. My vicar tells me all he hears and one Sunday (November 15th) I was very early at church and he was doing something in the chancel and saw me come in. Presently he came to my seat and passed me a note. When I opened it I read "Sing Te Deum lustily today – Good news – the American troops are in Tunisia!"'

(Alice Mainland)

It must also be added that by June 1942 the Germans were discovering that the War was going to be a little more difficult, a little more drawn-out, than they had first imagined. It was not going to be a case of one glorious victory after another. There had been, and there were to be, setbacks and defeats, vacillation and retreats, all of which had to be handled very carefully by Goebbels and his Propaganda Ministry. The news from the front particularly, as it was broadcast over German radio, had to be dressed up in a language that could change defeat into victory, pointless death into heroic sacrifice and a major disaster into a little hiccough on the way to the inevitable triumph. On no account was the morale of the German people or the will of the German armies to be undermined by bad news, and the best way to ensure this did not happen was to exercise absolute control of the radio broadcasts – in Germany certainly, but also in all the occupied territories. There should be no broadcasting which would give hope and encouragement to enemies of the Third Reich: the BBC must not be heard! The safest way of preventing this was to confiscate all the radios in the Islands.

Many wireless sets were handed in to the Germans, but many more retained by the Islanders and concealed in a variety of hideaways. As we saw, Louisa Gould in Jersey hid her set under the steps in her garden leading down to the chicken coop. Many were concealed in out-houses or in barns, others under window seats or up chimneys. At the Regal cinema in Guernsey, the organist Kennedy Bott actually hid his radio set in the console of the cinema organ, stops and knobs looking much the same from a distance.

There it stayed, in plain view for the whole of the occupation. Things were not so good across the water at the other Island cinema.

The manager there failed to hide his wireless set from the *geheimepolizei* and was whisked off to a German internment camp. He left behind one of the chief sources of entertainment for the Island's population, both military and civilian.

THE SILVER SCREEN

The Nazi hierarchy, almost to a man, loved films. All Germany did. Hollywood of course was the biggest producer of films, but Germany during the thirties and forties ran it a close second. Adolf Hitler himself spent an inordinate amount of time watching the silver screen – time, some critics said, which would be better spent thinking of a way out of the terrible military mess into which he had led his country. The same was true of Goering. Up there in Karinhall when he wasn't hunting or caressing diamonds by way of therapy, the fat *Reichsmarschall* liked nothing so much as sitting in his sixty-seat private cinema and watching movies. Goebbels too had more than a passing interest in films and in fact, by direct and indirect means, he controlled most of the German movie output. He knew better than anyone the power of the moving image and how that power could be used for propaganda purposes in pursuit of German interests. Goebbels was not immune either to the charms of the beautiful actresses who graced many of the more romantic films of the time. But it was the ability of film to speak so eloquently to the servants of the Third Reich that impressed Goebbels the most. A film like *Der Ewig Jude* or *Jud Suss* could so dramatically reinforce Nazi racist ideology as to be indispensable in the struggle for hearts and minds. Both these films were sent to the Island cinemas during the Occupation. They are both very powerful films notable for their vilification of Jews and all things Jewish. According to these films Jews were money-grabbing, bestial, filthy criminals, racially inferior to the Aryan Germans. In *Jud Suss* they are portrayed as robbers, and in the case of the protagonist, as a rapist. This latter film, *Jud Suss*, is a technically wonderfully-shot film. The shooting is fluent and involving, the framing of individual shots brilliant but the message is as ignorant as it is hideous – that the Jews as a race are so far removed from decent society that they deserve extermination.

People were almost persuaded. People like Jersey boy Peter Hassall who said this after viewing the movie:

'The final scene depicted the German damsel struggling to protect her virtue from (Jud Suss) the Jewish baddie, while the Aryan prototype ran up the dozens of castle steps. The film ended in thunderous applause. [There would be a mixed audience of Germans and Islanders in the cinema. Peter doesn't say who contributed most to the applause.] *When the Jew met his end [he was hanged, a kinder death in fiction than that dealt out in reality to many a million Jews in the Holocaust] I hate to admit that I came away ... somewhat influenced by it. However, the Germans' conduct against the handful of Jews remaining on the Island quickly washed away any anti-Jewish sentiments I may have unconsciously harboured'.*

Coutanche may not have heard of any Jews who suffered. Peter Hassall obviously had. Peter Hassall was later on to learn all about the kind of ill-treatment you could get from the Germans for he was sentenced to eight years hard labour under the *Nacht und Nebel* (Night and Fog) laws for attempting to escape from Jersey, as we shall see.

There were, of course, the more straightforward propaganda films to be seen in the Islands' cinemas.

Every account of the Occupation will have a picture of either the Forum cinema in Jersey or the Regal cinema in Guernsey proudly proclaiming that the great German movie *Sieg im Westen* was being shown there. This film, thoughtfully provided with subtitles for the locals, showed how Hitler had achieved the subjugation of nearly all of Western Europe in such a remarkably short time. Happy times for the Germans. Some of the Islanders watching German propaganda movies like this vented their dislike and disapproval by booing and catcalling, even on one occasion singing the famous Flanagan and Allen hit version of 'Run Rabbit, Run Rabbit, Run, Run,

Run,' which they changed to 'Run Adolf, Run Adolf, Run, Run, Run', as did the impertinent Island folk when Hitler appeared on the screen. The Germans did not see any humour in this vociferous display of anti-Nazi sentiment and promptly issued an order which read:

'Instructions should be given to picturehouse proprietors to notify the public by means of notices posted in the halls, that no demonstration of public approval or the reverse will be tolerated. Contraventions will result in eight days' closure and the instigators will be severely punished.'

This order was later amended so that the cinema-goers could cheer the heroes of the films and of course applaud the appearance of the Fuehrer on the screen. In fact it was made obligatory to clap him – a directive more honoured in the breach than the observance – at least by the Islanders sitting in the stalls on the left side of the cinema. The Germans sat on the right.

'The Island police shall see to the compliance with this regulation.'

All this Teutonic toughness did not stop the wags and the 'rowdies' having their say. This from the diary of the Reverend Douglas Ord over in Guernsey:

'At least one joke at the expense of the Germans comes to hand each week. Here is one: A German propaganda film was being shown in Jersey featuring British

and American soldiers dying by the hundred in battle. Not so much as a single casualty was sustained by the Germans! ... It was finally rounded off by a special 'shot' of a German funeral ... A hero's honours were accorded. The coffin was borne slowly past amid the respectful silence of the audience, when a sepulchral voice from the pit broke the spell of amazement, 'That man died of indigestion!' Immediately the house rocked with great gusts of laughter. Swiftly the Germans reacted. They stopped the performance, locked the doors and made valiant efforts to identify the culprit, but in vain.'

(*Diary of Reverend Ord, 1942*)

When the Occupation began there were a few, mostly American, films left in the two Islands of Guernsey and Jersey – musicals and feature films. Very much enjoyed they were too, but there were not enough to last five years. It is true that the 'donkeys' and the 'crapauds' exchanged their meagre stocks of movies but still there were not sufficient to satisfy demand. The great gap in supply was unsatisfactorily filled by German, mostly propaganda, films with English subtitles. The Islanders, who did not see the Germans in quite the same light as the Germans saw themselves, did not like, and did not want to see such movies. There had to be better ways of passing the time than watching films lauding the achievement of the increasingly hated Germans.

The people turned their back on the cinema and returned, in their droves, to the theatre and home-grown entertainment.

NO BUSINESS LIKE SHOW BUSINESS
Guernseyman Basil C. de Guerin wrote this in *Theatre World* in October 1945:

'The German Occupation of the Channel Islands had the effect of stimulating that life of the theatre which was always an outstanding feature of the social life of the Islands.
After the initial period of adjustment of existence to the rule of the Nazi, the public began to tire of the cinema with its compulsory injections of German propaganda and, as no alternative was possible to procure from an outside source, sought the remedy in its own ranks.
The search was definitely successful both as to quantity and quality.
On Guernsey alone no less than five distinct companies of players; two casts for musical comedies; a stock variety company, and numerous concert parties were all well patronised on each of the frequent appearances on which they appeared.'

The Royal Players alone put on 16 plays in those war years including *The Wind and the Rain, Night must Fall, A Murder Has Been Arranged* and of course that wonderful dramatic piece by Arnold Ridley, *The Ghost Train*.

Across the water in Jersey the Island Players were even more ambitious in their choice of play, putting on a Shakespeare work, no less – The

Merchant of Venice.

Given the extreme sensitivity, or rather insensitivity, of the Germans to all things Semitic they might have foreseen the trouble that came their way.

First of all it was objected by the German censor that Mr Whinnerer's characterisation of Shylock was not nearly nasty enough. He did not portray the man in accordance with the irredeemably bestial Nazi-created stereotype of the Jew as it appeared over and over again in films like *Der Ewig Jude* and *Jud Suss*. Why, the Jersey thespian had made Shakespeare's character almost human! This would never do, for it was clearly contrary to right-thinking Nazi wisdom according to which the Jew was a bacillus causing disease and not, certainly not, a human being demanding sympathy. The Island thespian would have to change his performance.

A review of the play was published in the *Evening Post* which picked up on this sympathetic portrayal of the Jew and hinted that maybe, just maybe, certain people such as, for example, the Germans, were wrong in their judgement of the Semitic diaspora.

The rabidly Nazi censor was more than a little annoyed at such a subversive thought being published and went gunning for the writer of the article.

Now the reviewer always had a pseudonym, so aptly-named censor

Hohl commanded the *Evening Post* editor M. A. Harrison to give him the name of the heretical journalist. But Harrison knew, better than most, what such a disclosure might mean. After all, his paper had published, pre-Occupation, a score of articles and reports on the Jews and the attitude the Germans took to them. He knew full well what might become of a 'Jew lover' at the hands of the Nazis. He said he would not reveal the name of the reviewer. Hohl insisted.

Again Harrison refused to obey. Hohl left muttering dark threats, and it must be said that in those days he had the means in overplus to carry them out, no matter how dark they were. However, for reasons which are anything but clear, nothing was done. The reviewer remained undiscovered and Harrison unmolested. It was a happy and rare victory for press freedom. And, most importantly, the characterisation of Shylock remained as human and sympathetic as before. An unlikely triumph in the Occupation world.

Outside the opera house, in that other theatre, things were not so rosy. The War seemed never-ending. The isolation of the Islanders more intense than ever. The food and fuel shortages were worse and the presence of the Germans became more and more oppressive and resented.

Resistance was impossible and there was seemingly no way to express their loyalty to King and Country – though one congregation in a Guernsey church was invited to:

'Think silently through the national anthem at the end of the service.'

Otherwise the beleaguered Islanders felt sat-on very heavily by the invaders, imprisoned and rendered dumb. But then an occasion arose in which a very full expression of where the Island loyalty lay was possible, and it was brought about by the unhappy sinking of HMS *Charybdis*.

'In the death which follows and results from duty done, the heart knows no frontier lines, and mourning becomes international.'
(Graf von Schmettow's funeral oration at Foulon cemetery)

HMS *Charybdis*, a Dido class cruiser, was sunk on 23rd October 1943 at 2.30 a.m. off the coast of Normandy by no less than six enemy torpedoes. She had been engaged in 'Operation Tunnel', along with five other Royal Navy ships. Their mission was to attack a large German convoy sailing down the French coast. In the short battle the British force was totally outmanoeuvred by the German escort ships. Not only was HMS *Charybdis* hit and sunk, but her sister vessel, HMS *Limbourne*, was also torpedoed. *Limbourne* did not sink immediately despite her forward section having been blown away. But she was mortally wounded and shortly after the initial engagement the *Limbourne* was scuttled 'to keep her out of enemy hands'.

It was a massive victory for the Germans. Two Royal Navy warships had been destroyed and 464 British sailors had died. It was a heavy defeat in the Channel War.

A few days after that black Saturday of October 1943 the sea gave up her dead. The bodies of 19 Royal Navy and Royal Marine crew were washed ashore in Guernsey. The Germans, which means von Schmettow, gave orders that the men should be buried with full military honours at the Foulon Cemetery on Wednesday November 17th. A notice to this effect was published about the Island.

So it was that on a cold but sunlit autumn afternoon the 19 coffins, each draped with a Union Jack and carried by German sailors, slow-marched into the Foulon Cemetery. But the Germans weren't the only ones there.

The Bailiff, Victor Carey, was there, along with 5,000 of his Guernsey people bringing with them 900 wreaths to honour the fallen sailors. These formed a great carpet of flowers by the side of the burial ground as the Dean of Guernsey passed from grave to grave softly speaking the words of the Final Benediction. The biggest of the wreaths carried the bold message:

FROM THE RAF – WE WILL CARRY ON.

It was an intensely moving experience to be in Foulon cemetery on that day along with 5,000 of your fellow Islanders to pay heartfelt tribute to the men of the British Royal Navy. It was also, as the Germans immediately recognised, a massive demonstration of anti-German sentiment. The Germans ensured that no similar ceremonies ever took place again.

VICTOR CAREY IS ASHAMED

Not all the Islanders behaved in such an upright and honourable fashion as the 5,000 in Foulon Cemetery. Far from it. The wrongdoers were addressed thus at the end of the civil trial by Bailiff Victor Carey:

'As police officers you must realise and understand that you have brought shame and humiliation on every single soul in the Island from the Royal Court downwards.

Clothed in the uniform of the police you were given certain privileges by the German Army of Occupation in being allowed out after curfew. No one else was allowed out after curfew, you alone, and what have you done, clothed in the uniform? You have broken into your own property, you have stolen and carried on in the most terrible way and you deserve everything that you can possibly get and you will be looked upon with contempt by the whole of your fellow Islanders.

I can assure you that I am filled with shame and I only regret that we have not been able to inflict greater punishment on you than we have done today.'

Sixteen Guernsey police officers were

then taken down to White Rock and pushed onto a filthy coal ship that had just been emptied. They were thrust into the hold and taken across the Channel to the prison in Caen. It was an ignominious end to a criminal venture that disgraced the name of the Guernsey police force.

The convicted Guernsey police officers had been breaking into stores, mainly foodstores belonging not only to the German military and the OT but also to the Island civilians. The States dairy was also systematically raided. The amounts of foodstuffs that were stolen were not small; sackfuls of stuff were taken and scores of tins of assorted food removed. But the most heinous aspect of all this thieving was that many of the accused, acting in concert, had stolen from the Essential Commodities store in Trinity Square, St Peter Port, which housed all the provisions for the civilian population. They were stealing from their fellow countrymen, their own kith and kin. It was the kind of robbery that the Bailiff was referring to when he accused the officers of 'breaking into your own property,' with the implication that they were taking food out of the mouths of starving people.

The defence advanced for such grand larceny was succinctly expressed by PC Bill Burton:

'I, in common with other police officers, entered German stores in order to take foodstuffs and to distribute it among people in need. About 75% or 80% of the *stuff we took from German stores. The remainder was taken from people who were dealing directly with the Germans and distributing it on their behalf.'*

So they were playing a Robin Hood game of taking from the rich and giving to the poor. Very laudable. But the courts, both military and civilian, before whom the accused appeared, refused to view it as a mitigating circumstance. No doubt they were swayed in their judgement by the sheer quantity of stolen goods found in the accuseds' homes.

The accused men were treated abominably by their German interrogators, headed up by the notorious Wolffe of the *Geheimepolizei*. The assault on Constable Fred Short in the course of his interrogation was typical.

'They didn't take me to Grange Lodge for interrogation, they took me to Ash House, the house next door. I was taken up to a room at the top of the house and they battered hell out of me. They ripped my uniform and kicked me in the face, splitting my lip and smashing my false teeth.

The first thing Major Oeser did was to take his revolver out of his holster and place it on the table in front of him and say pointedly, in broken English, 'Now, these have been known to go off accidentally.'

And so it continued. PC Short was beaten unconscious, again threatened with a gun, had his head smashed against the wall. Finally he signed a 'confession' written in German, a language he did not understand.

It was the same for most of the accused Guernseymen. Their confessions were beaten out of them. As Ambrose Sherwill, who represented the officers at the military trial, noted:

'I received a message through the German Feldgendarmerie that the accused wished me to represent them at their trial. I then obtained permission to visit them and saw them all in the absence of any Germans. A number of them had been beaten up to secure admission of guilt but it was clear that, however much I deplored the method of obtaining such admissions, these admissions were in accordance with the truth.'

So obvious was the men's guilt to Sherwill that he felt unable to mount a proper defence but merely to plead extenuating circumstances. The accused could not have been too pleased when they heard the ex-Attorney General tell the court by way of prologue to his somewhat half-hearted attempt at a defence of the men:

'Had I been the prosecutor in this case, I might have asked for sentences perhaps not differing from those suggested by the German prosecutor.'

Sherwill shared Carey's outrage at what the men had done:

'The trial has brought a sense of shame and disgrace to the Island and which has profoundly disturbed and shocked the people.'

The German prosecutor got his way. All the 16 defendants bar one, Sergeant E. Pill, were found guilty and sentenced to terms of imprisonment ranging from four years six months with hard labour for Sergeant J. Harper, to just four weeks imprisonment without hard labour for PC P. Bretel.

The big question throughout all of this affair was 'how far in the know' was the Chief Inspector of Police, William Sculpher? Even if he were not aware of what was happening on his watch, didn't at least a formal responsibility for his men's actions exist, which meant that he should resign his office forthwith?

There is no evidence to suggest that Sculpher did know what his men were up to. Prince von Oettingen (yet another aristocrat shipped across to impress the Brits), who conducted much of the prosecution, believed that Sculpher was innocent of complicity in the robberies and that he did not know what his men were doing. The Prince opined that the reason Sculphur was not aware of the criminal activities of his force was because this ex-Brixton sergeant was a lazy, inefficient policemen, carelessly indifferent to what was going on around him. That was enough. The man had to go. And go he did, to be replaced by a Mr Langmead

– but not quite with Sculpher's old powers.

The Prince von Oettingen issued instructions:

'In future, the whole of the island police will be placed under the direct supervision of the Feldkommandantur. The Chief of Police will be directly responsible to me for the proper functioning of the police duties.'

This action signified a tightening of German control, the very thing Sherwill, Leale and every member of the Controlling Committee had fought so long and so hard against. And the excuse for carrying this through had been wilfully supplied by the local and largely criminal police force. In its new form the Guernsey Police force became a helpful subsidiary arm of the German Feldpolizei. It was the heavy price to be paid for such gross and unthinking dereliction of duty.

Meanwhile the food situation continued to be desperate. There was simply not enough to go round. There were too many troops. There were too many Islanders. The Islands were too small. The supply lines too vulnerable.

'In the afternoon I visited a house where the shortage was obviously being felt and where the parents were beginning to fear they would never more see their two children, now in England. The telephone rang while I was there. A relative was thought to be dying on her feet – and not always on her feet for she had been found lying in a faint a number of times. The doctors say that drugs are useless could they be got: food alone is needed and the food she needs also cannot be got. Only German officers of high rank can get that.

People who ought to undergo operations prefer to run the risk of delay rather than go through with them now that there is nothing to build them up afterwards. Swollen feet and legs are a common sight and again the doctors are helpless. The effect of the vicious cutting of the bread ration, the stopping of the meat ration and the cut in the sugar together with the general shortage of everything, becomes more and more evident. With a shock one sees people worn to skeletons, the skin drawn tightly over the facial bones. It is quite possible to pass a person in the street without recognition – so great a change may have taken place in a few weeks. Shops are all but empty. All that a greengrocer could offer this week was a quantity of lettuce, radishes and a few leeks that had gone to seed. Whatever else there may be is necessarily limited in amount, and Germans often stalk in behind the counter and requisition what they mind. Add to this the strain everyone feels and the continued deferring of hope and there is no wonder that there is depression. In their despair some doubt now they will live to see their release.'

(Diary of Reverend Ord)

Britain's great leader was not about to help.

'LET THEM STARVE.'

(Churchill)

In an insightful interview Count Graf von Schmettow gave in Jersey to *Topic* Magazine in 1967, he remarks on the special treatment that was afforded the Islanders throughout his kindly intercession with the German High Command:

'My pleas for favoured attention for the Channel Islands became something of a joke. I remember when I was visited by General Obert, head of the 16th army and he opened his talks with me by saying, "Don't tell me – we're going to hear more about your special circumstances," I was able to reply that conditions certainly were special in comparison with all the sabotage, resistance and trouble that he was having in France.' I was, soon after my arrival, able to get permission to modify or rectify, on my own responsibility, the regulations which were supposed to govern the Channel Islands.'

But however kindly-disposed towards the Channel Islanders he might have been, he was powerless to prevent the gradual deterioration in the state of their well-being during the last two years of the Occupation, a deterioration which became increasingly rapid after the D-Day landings. And it was not just the civil population that suffered.

Schmettow's own troops were suffering too from a shortage of all the necessities of life. Perhaps they were suffering more because they were forced to stand idly and helplessly by as Germany was bombed, battered, blasted and pulverised on its way to a terrible defeat.

'On their way to the islands, one German soldier obtained ten days leave to visit his home in Mannheim. He left the troop train at a junction where he expected to get another to be home within a couple of hours. No trains were running. Apart from an occasional lift in a farm wagon he had to walk, and it took him two days to reach Mannheim. A cycle could not be obtained for love or money. Nearing his home he saw roofs and windows damaged in many of the villages but when he reached Mannheim he had the shock of his life. The town is a heap of ruins and where his house once stood was one huge hole. He spent the remainder of his leave trying to trace the whereabouts of his wife and children but without success. These two men were so down and out that they blamed Hitler for all the world's troubles – they would both give themselves up at the first opportunity to the British as prisoners of war.'

(Diary of Reverend Ord).

There was hardly a man in their number without a friend, lover, mother, father, sister, brother, son or daughter maimed or killed as all of Germany's great cities were reduced to rubble, dust and ashes in the massive Allied bombing raids.

Easter Monday 1945

'A strange rumour is going round that the bombing of German towns is affecting the spines and nervous systems of the *people. Another story is that of a German soldier who shows a matchbox full of white hair –"the hair of my small child". This it is alleged turned white through terror.'*

'On Good Friday during the singing of Stainer's "Crucifixion" the lights went out as they were singing "There was darkness over the land!"'

(Diary of Reverend Ord)

The future looked bleak for Germany and for her soldiers. There was some comfort and consolation for the Island's German garrison in that they were not fighting the savage and relentless Bolshevik hordes edging ever closer to Germany's eastern frontier. Even so, the Channel Islands, which they had seen when they first arrived as a land flowing with milk and honey, had turned into some sort of prison camp in which, it seemed, they would either starve to death or be annihilated.

'We heard this morning that at one house in St Martin, when the lady of the house answered the door, a German soldier stood outside and feebly asked for a glass of water. The lady who had some coffee hot, asked him to come into the hall while she got him a cup of coffee. When she returned, the soldier's head was bending forward on his chest and he was taking his last breath. By the time she had called her husband, the poor fellow was dead. A fortnight ago, Mr Brouard the florist had 60 wreaths to make for the Germans.'

(Unnamed diarist)

They were not a happy band of soldiers and as their situation became worse, so dissatisfaction grew.

There was disaffection and mutinous mutterings and not just among the men. The officers commanding the garrison became increasingly restive as more and more of them saw where Hitler was leading them. To hell in a handcart. And it looked as if the Islanders would accompany them.

A disaster was in the offing.

'The Bailiff of Jersey has written a statement to the occupying forces informing them of the state of things in Jersey – they are rather worse off than we are here. They have had no gas since September 2nd, no medical supplies after the middle of October, hardly any fuel for heating hospitals or for cooking in the communal kitchens, no paraffin or petrol, clothing and footwear absolutely inadequate, no fuel for civilian heating and so on.'

(Diary of Ruth Ozanne, 16th October 1944)

This entry was written around the time that the Germans tried to impose food cuts as a direct reprisal for the RAF bombing the ships carrying supplies of food 'kindly guaranteed by the German Army'. The Reverend Ord tells what happened:

'On Friday afternoon, April 30th, the German military authorities thrust the Bekanntmachung *peremptorily before*

the Controlling Committee together with the ultimatum that the rations were to be cut 'at once'. Bread would be reduced from 4½lbs a week to 2lb 5oz; meat from 4oz to 2oz and all cooking fats to 1¾oz. As this meant sentence of death to a high proportion of the civil population and grave physical injury to all, the Committee made the most energetic protests and sought to play for time.'

There was a hurried phonecall to the Bailiff of Jersey, Alexander Coutanche. The Jerseyman was once asked at the end of the hostilities what he had done during the Occupation. He replied that he had 'protested' and never was this more true than on this occasion. Victor Carey too, joined in protesting to the German command that such action, taken as a reprisal, constituted a war crime.

Coutanche sent a now-famous memorandum to the beleaguered von Schmettow on 31st August 1944. He himself calls it 'perhaps rather rhetorical'. It certainly made good reading for the British Intelligence men who conducted the investigation into allegations of overweening collusion and collaboration levelled at the Islands' leaders at the War's end.

'Sooner or later the clash of arms will cease, and the powers will meet, not only to consider the means to an enduring peace, but also to pass judgement on the authorities, be they civil or military, upon whose conceptions of the principles of honour, justice and humanity the fate of peoples and places, and not least of occupied peoples and places, has temporarily been determined.

The Insular Government believes that, at that day, it, or such of its numbers as survive, will stand with a clear conscience born of the conviction that it has failed neither in its duty to the people of Jersey nor in its interpretation and observance of the rules of international law.

May the Insular Government be spared the duty of adding to the problems which will face the powers on allegations that, by an unjustified prolongation of the siege of Jersey, the military representatives endangered the health, and indeed the lives of the people of Jersey.'

And the lives of the Islanders were indeed in jeopardy. The Germans wanted to opt out altogether from their responsibility to care for the civilian populations. The desire was to abandon them to starvation and death.

In October 1944 in the Guernsey States, Abraham Lainé painted a grim picture of the state of the Island's supply of essential commodities. There was not enough flour to last beyond Christmas. There was no meat. There were no stacks of coal or coke. There was no petrol for civilian use. Electricity supplies would cease by 1st January and the same was true for gas supplies. Medical supplies were practically non-existent. There were no drugs to treat a civilian population now so vulnerable because of malnutrition to all kinds of disease. In September 1944 the Channel Islands were facing a winter of hunger which threatened to rival that which the Dutch people had to endure in their *Hongerwinter*.

The German troops too were in desperate straits and for much the same reasons:

'The perils and uncertainties of the situation are increased by the growing hunger of the troops. They are 'kidnapping' and slaughtering cats and dogs everywhere. They made an application for permission to shoot seabirds, chiefly, of course, gulls, with carbines. Fortunately Heine turned this down on the grounds of endangering public safety. Up to January the soldiers had stolen 900cwt of potatoes. House breaking, robbery and the procurement of goods under a false assumption of authority are the order of the day. Furniture is smashed and floorboards wrenched up for use as firewood.
The first cases of soldiers dying of malnutrition have been reported from Guernsey.'

(*Diary of von Aufsess*)

Von Aufsess further remarked:

'My impression of Guernsey is that it is even more like a sanatorium for the weak and the ailing than Jersey. The soldiers look pale and undernourished, the civilians even more so.'

The Germans were facing a huge problem of supply. There was simply

not enough food to meet the military and civilian demand. Serious consideration was given to diverting all food supply to the German troops and just letting the Islanders die, but even then there would not be enough of anything to last more than a few months into the New Year.

'So the question we are again facing is whether the doubtful gain of holding out in the Island fortresses for a few more useless months would be worth achieving at such a frightful cost in human life. Never must the German soldier be made the instrument of such a hideous crime, totally irreconcilable with his military honour or the duty of his country, as the wiping out of the Island population.'

An appeal was sent to the War Cabinet to send supplies to the civilian population. Churchill refused point blank to countenance the request on the grounds, it is assumed, of military good sense. Any food sent from Great Britain he thought would end up in German hands. He would be victualling the enemy which is not a good way to go about defeating him. 'Let them starve', said the British War Leader by way of a decision in the matter. It is charitably suggested that of course Churchill wasn't referring to the native population in 'our dear Channel Islands' but just to the Germans.

But starve the Islanders would, unless a new source of food could be found.

In November 1944 a crisis point had

been reached. Thousands of lives were at risk. Something had to be done. Alexander Coutanche, keenly conscious of the doomsday scenario beginning to unfold, decided to make a direct appeal to the Protecting Power, through the Swiss Ambassador in Berlin. He pointed out the dire straits they were in and appealed for help as a matter of great urgency. Coutanche says there was no conversation with Guernsey to coordinate appeals, but almost simultaneously Victor Carey sent an appeal directly to the Red Cross.

There was nothing more that could be done. All the Islanders could do was wait and pray that life-saving help would soon be on its way.

In the event, the actions of the Island leaders brought quite a swift response – and a good one at that. On 8th December von Schmettow himself delivered the news that a Red Cross ship would leave Lisbon, Portugal, laden with foodstuffs and bound for the Channel Islands.

On 13th December Coutanche published the following notice:

The Befehlsfaber *has informed me that the Home Secretary has made the following statement in the House of Commons:*

'Supplies of food, medicines and soap are to be shipped to the Channel Islands. The German Government had approached the British Government with a view to sending supplies to the Channel Islands. In view of reports received, the British Government had decided that it was right to send additional supplies of medicines, soap and food parcels. The food parcels would take the shape of those sent to prisoners of war. Final arrangements had not been completed but it was believed the ship would be ready to sail next week. She was a Swedish vessel sailing from Lisbon. It was hoped a representative of the International Red Cross would be able to sail and carry out further investigations into the actual situation of the population of the Islands and arrange for further supplies.'

A similar notice was published in the Guernsey press. Joy in the Islands was unbounded. The SS *Vega* would soon be on her way and even, with a bit of luck, deliver her cargo of goodies in time for Christmas day. Alas that 'bit of luck' proved elusive.

The departure of the *Vega* from Lisbon was delayed by storms in the Bay of Biscay and she did not reach the Channel Islands until 27th December. She docked first at White Rock in St Peter Port, Guernsey at 6 p.m. in the moonlit winter night.

'It was one of those moments in our lives that we will never forget - not even the slightest detail!'

While the Vega *was being unloaded, virtually every Islander went down to the Esplanade to stand and admire and,* indeed, pay homage to the ship that had brought us our next meal and our next and our next – the ship that brought us life. I stood on the Esplanade and admired the ship with its Swedish Flag proudly flying from its stern and proposed a silent toast. The *Vega*, *God Bless her.*'

(Bill Green, Guernseyman)

Leslie Sinel over in Jersey was equally delighted with the arrival of the *Vega* though he expressed himself in a more restrained manner:

'*After weeks of anxious waiting our hopes were realised at 5.45 this evening (December 30th) when the International Red Cross ship* Vega *entered St Helier's harbour and took up her berth at the end of Albert Pier.*'

The Jersey *Evening Post* in its New Year message to its readers stated with some truth that:

'Only those who have knowledge of how so many of the poorer inhabitants have lived during the last months can imagine what this will mean. Medical supplies, foodstuffs, soap, all urgently needed are being provided, and a commission will decide what other supplies are required. So the year ends on a brighter note and we enter the New Year with the knowledge that, though hard and difficult times still have to be faced, our position is less serious than it might have been.'

THE FINAL YEAR

The situation in the Channel Islands was

indeed less serious now that the good ship *Vega* had discharged her cargo, but it was still very serious for everyone in the Islands, particularly the poor German troops. They could see the Red Cross parcels, indeed they oversaw their unloading and storage, but they were not allowed to touch. Neither, incidentally, were the Irish contingent left in the Islands.

These numbered about 500 but as they were nationals of a neutral country they had no right or entitlement to the Red Cross parcels. For the ragged German army it was back to a diet of ersatz coffee and cabbage soup while the Islanders could enjoy their tins of ham, salmon, sardines, prunes, cheese and marmalade to say nothing of the tea and chocolate in each oh-so-welcome parcel packed courtesy of Canada or New Zealand. It must have been agonising for the German soldier to see so much largesse so near and yet so far.

He was reduced to killing cats and dogs, shooting seagulls out of the sky, scraping at walls with his bare hands to find snails, digging in the winter-cold earth for worms and acorns, taking anything and everything for food.

And of course there was widespread recourse to common thievery. Desperate men do desperate things, and the German troops were increasingly desperate in those last months of the War. The number of robberies rose and many of them turned violent. Islanders were often fired upon or knifed when they tried to prevent attacks on their food and property. Nothing was safe, it seemed: seed potatoes, carrots, cabbages, cauliflower, wood, even handcarts and tools were all taken in raids by the German soldiers, acting usually in ones or twos. Still it was not enough, nowhere near enough to satisfy their need. They were in dire straits. And yet hardly a Red Cross parcel was touched by the German soldiers. It is said that an empty stomach has no morals, well here was the exception to that rule and a remarkable exercise in restraint by men in extremes of suffering. So extreme was their suffering that all forms of physical exertion were banned and the soldiers were ordered to sleep in the afternoon to preserve their woefully depleted resources of energy. As Sinel records in his diary entry for 30th January:

'There has been a meeting of German doctors and it is understood that they are greatly concerned with the health of the troops and the lack of medical supplies. Many soldiers are looking extremely ill and some have collapsed in the street; they now have reveille an hour later and must rest in the afternoon, while all sport is stopped.'

This ban on sporting activities applied, albeit to a lesser extent, to the locals as well, for in February of this year all football matches were cancelled because the medical authorities considered that the shortage of food, particularly bread, would endanger the players' lives.

The German commanders were deeply concerned by their troops stealing from the civilian population, particularly from farmers. In Guernsey, where thieving had, as in Jersey, reached epidemic proportions, the following notice was issued to their men. It was also published in the *Star*.

In order to prevent thefts from fields more effectively than heretofore, guards and patrols, beginning April 5th 1945, 8.00 p.m. have the following orders:

DURING THE DAY, to prevent every theft from fields and glasshouses by arresting such thieves and to make immediate use of their firearms, if they should try to escape.

DURING THE NIGHT, on principle NOT TO CALL but to shoot sharp, aiming at every person committing larceny (i.e. stooping and taking vegetables or potatoes, or breaking into a glasshouse).

In other words the situation had become so desperate that a shoot-to-kill policy had to be introduced.

Times were tough for the German garrison but despite the physical weakness in their ranks, and despite the increasing hopelessness of their position from a military point of view, the German commanders planned to carry out a risky and daring raid on Granville on the Normandy coast.

A LAST HURRAH!

There were two attempts at 'Operation

Port Granville', the purpose of which, besides the destruction of Allied materials, was most importantly 'to obtain supply goods necessary for the Islands by capturing loaded steamers'. It was an extraordinary venture, born of desperation, to be carried out by a force of 200 men. The first attempt on Granville took place on the night of February 7th 1945 but the storms blew up, the seas rose and to cap it all there was widespread mechanical failure in the attack boats.

The Germans wisely aborted the mission and limped back to the Channel Islands.

But, nothing daunted, a month later on March 8th they tried again, and this time the gods of wave and wind were with them – conditions were perfect. The 200 men, strengthened by feeding on reserved rations, landed in the French port.

Von Schmettow gave this account of the adventure:

'At 0200 hours the force broke into the port of Granville and landed in the northern part of the town.

The Commander's boat, a minesweeper, had touched the ground when landing in the port and had to be blown up. As provided by the plan, the combat patrols entered the port area and the northern part of the town. In the ensuing fighting the enemy, who was completely surprised, suffered heavy losses of killed and wounded.'

The group of artillery carriers encountered one American vessel, guard boat PC 564, south-west of the Chausey Islands, put it out of action and captured prisoners.

'The combat patrols made 30 prisoners, among them a Lieutenant Colonel. Five ships were effectively blown up. Tonnage about 4.800 tons. Fourteen cranes, locomotives, railroad freight cars, fuel depot, were blown up or destroyed. The sluice was destroyed once again. The port set on fire. 55 German parachute troops were freed and taken along. The steamship Eskwood *was captured and brought back along with its own power to the Islands. Unfortunately the steamers lying in port had unloaded their cargoes.'*

So the main purpose of the daring raid was not fulfilled. No supplies so desperately needed by the Channel Islands garrison were obtained. What they did capture instead were 30 American prisoners, some taken from the American patrol vessel taken by artillery carriers just south-west of the Chausey Islands. The raiding party also freed 55 German paratroopers from Allied captivity, not altogether a good result for it meant that, back in the Islands, there were 85 more mouths to feed from small and ever-dwindling stocks of food.

The American prisoners, needless to say, were mightily unimpressed with the amount of food on offer, to say nothing of its quality, and they did not receive Red Cross parcels.

THE YANKS COME ... AND GO

The Americans taken prisoner in Granville and brought back to the Islands were by no means the first of their kind. Captain Edward Clark had arrived in Jersey months before in August 1944. He had been searching for his unit just outside Dinan and drove slap bang into a troop of Germans occupying the little village of Lanna Valle. He and his driver, Sidney, were surrounded and, an obvious discretion overcoming a mortal valour, promptly surrendered. Their German captors seemed more interested in taking the cigarettes they were carrying than in extracting information about the enemy.

The two men were offered some cognac, which Sidney, the jeep driver, gratefully accepted but Edward refused, and then marched into Dinan.

'We walked into the city of Dinan with French people on every side of the street watching us. None of them smiled, and none of them said "hello". However, every now and then when we would look at them closely we would see them with their hands down along the side of their trousers or along the side of their dress with their fingers in a "V".'

The interrogation by the Germans was, to say the least, perfunctory – there was no intimidation, no shouting or violence of any kind. In fact, the senior interrogating officer, who spoke English quite well, far from pressing Clark to reveal sensitive military information, entered into a somewhat rueful conversation with him and he told Clark that:

'... he was married and had two children and that he was getting mighty sick of war. He said that I didn't have to worry for he figured that within the very near future that rather than I being his prisoner, he would be my prisoner and at that point he offered me a cigarette and by that time I had got to the point that I accepted any cigarette that was offered.'

Edward Clark liked his nicotine fix very much. He remembers with gratitude a Jewish hotelier running out to the truck in which he was being taken to St Malo, and offering him cigarettes, and how grateful he was for that act of kindness.

Clark and a small group of fellow American prisoners, together with about ten wounded (some very seriously indeed), were shipped out of St Malo during a bombing raid. It was a clear moonlit night – very good for bombers, who could see their little ship quite clearly. But somehow they all reached St Helier safely.

'The people in the streets would only stare at us. No one waved at us. They just stared. Finally we arrived at what turned out later to be an old English prison camp for delinquent English soldiers.'

And they were very well treated, these big and brash men from the New World. Compared with the Russian slave workers, they were treated like royalty. Clark even had 'an excellent bed with springs, good mattress and sheets.'

The food, however plentiful by 1944 Occupation standards, did not begin to approach those levels of gastronomic excellence the hearty eaters from the US expected as a matter of course:

'Our food was practically always the same, although it got a little less all the time. For breakfast we had two slices of black bread and a cup of substitute coffee which we always swore was made out of stable sweepings. For dinner we had another cup of substitute coffee plus either a plateful of potatoes with gravy that was practically water, or we would have soup that consisted of different types of vegetables or cabbage that had bugs floating around on the top of it. For supper our ration, anywhere from one to three times a week, would consist of one meat ball – darned small – and two slices of bread which was usually black. Actually we weren't starving to death, but we were always hungry.'

The American prisoners were helped, however, by the Islanders through the good offices of Jerseyman Dr Shore. The kindly Jersey folk sent in apples, grapes and peaches in season, vegetables, and every once in a while, luxury of luxuries, rolls and cake!

All in all, life in the prison camp was not too bad for Edward Clark. He even made a halfway friendship with the ardent Nazi corporal in the camp, Corporal Kammon. They would give each other cigarettes when either was short and he:

'... would tell me about his wife in Germany. He would tell me about the last time he received a letter from her. He would tell me about his beliefs. He thoroughly believed in Hitler. He thoroughly hated the Jews. He said that he knew the Americans were going to win the War. However, although he seemed to me a very nice fellow, he said that when he got back to Germany if the Jews started coming into Germany again he would kill them, and every other German would act the same way. He was about 38 years old.'

Well, the life in the camp might have been bearable enough, what with a soft bed, nearly enough food and reflective conversation, to say nothing of running water and proper sanitation, but Edward Clark was not a happy man.

His thoughts ever turned to ways of escape from the camp and from the Island, a difficult enterprise not helped by the fact that it was by now January in one of the coldest winters ever. Nonetheless Clark kept thinking and planning how to get out and here he got lucky. It was a fortune born of misfortune.

Lieutenant Haas was a field artillery observer for Company Contingent B of the Sixth Armoured Division who had been shot down over France. The pilot managed to crash-land the plane in an orchard. He died on impact. Haas' leg was broken in the crash and then broken again by a bullet from a soldier of the German reception committee that was waiting on the ground.

But Lieutenant Haas recovered sufficiently from his injuries to take part in an attempt to escape from the camp by tunnelling under the perimeter fence from the latrine which provided perfect cover for the digging.Unfortunately for the would-be escapees the Germans were more vigilant than their fictional counterparts in *The Great Escape*, and poor Lieutenant Haas was caught in the act of digging and put into St Helier's Gloucester Street Prison. His fellow inmates thoughtfully cheered him on his way by singing 'If I had the Wings of an Angel' and 'Should Auld Acquaintance be Forgot'. Lieutenant Haas smiled, although the expectation was that he would be very badly treated in his new confinement. Amazingly things turned out quite differently, and much to the advantage of Edward Clark's escape plans.

Lieutenant Haas was indeed put into solitary confinement. But in the cells next to him were all those Jersey folk who had been arrested for offences against the German rules of Occupation such as reading pamphlets dropped by the Americans and the RAF, listening to or concealing a wireless, attempting to lower the morale of the German troops, and so on. Hass, by talking along the pipes that ran by the prison wall, and through a small hole in the ceiling of his cell, was able to make contact with the civilian prisoners. From them he found out the names and addresses of the people who could, and would, help the Americans in their escape.

It was not just the other prisoners who helped Haas gather that information – the German sergeant in charge of Haas' block was an anti-Nazi. He allowed Haas into his room to check out the addresses he had been given on a large-scale map of Jersey hanging on the wall. He'd also been allowed to listen to the BBC and to share in the Christmas food that had been sent in by the Jersey folk to their imprisoned countrymen.

Moreover the 'good German' had provided Haas with no less than nine blankets to keep him warm on those bitterly cold December nights. Haas was still smiling when he was returned to his friends in the prison camp.

Haas imparted his news to a delighted Clark. Now he had the information he needed to make an escape. He and Haas would go over the fence, make contact with those who would help them to a boat and thence to France and freedom. It was a heady prospect.

Clark and Haas went over the wall on the night of 7th January using Haas' crutches, that he had wisely kept, joined together as a scaling ladder. A stove poker bent into an inverted 'J' shape was attached to the end of the 'ladder' to serve as a hook to gain purchase on the top of the fence. They hit the ground outside the camp, ran across a field and climbed over a second smaller barbed wire fence.

No guards!

And down onto the road towards their first destination, Oscar Laurens' house, some three miles away.

Their reception was not quite what they were expecting. Mr Laurens was not willing to take them into his house at all. He was nervous – as well he might have been. As the notice posted about the Islands on 8th January unequivocally stated:

'Anyone who takes in or extends help in any way to Captain Clark or Lieutenant Haas will be punished by death according to paragraph nine of the Order for the Protection of the Occupying forces.'

But Laurens did his best. He directed the two men to a place behind a row of small trees and bushes that acted as a windbreak. Here they hid in the snow and hail for two days and nights. Mrs Laurens supplied them with tea and some bread. They also enjoyed some tinned sardines from Laurens' Red Cross Parcels. Predictably though, Clark's greatest comfort came from the two packets of Jersey cigarettes he had with him.

After three days it was time to move on, this time to Bertram's farm on the way to Gorey harbour where a boat might be found in which to escape. The Laurens family had provided the men

with some equipment for the sea-trip: a compass and a large knife. There was also tea and food stuffed into their pockets, enough to last them the voyage, though quite how they would be able to make tea on the open sea was never made clear. What did become very clear however, was that the man at Bertram's farm would not help the two American officers in any way. No, he wouldn't let them into the house to hide until the wind died down, no he would not give them food. No, he had no boat he could let them have. In fact he could not, would not, do anything for them at all apart from telling them that 'his cousin down the road might help them as he had been the one that had helped launch the Jersey civilians during the summer of their escapes.'

This was good news. The man's cousin was no less a person that that distinguished Jerseyman, Deputy of the States William J. Bertram who lived at the farm called East Lynne at Fauvic.

The man was a godsend. Yes, they could come in. Yes, he knew who they were. Yes, they would get food in his house. In fact nothing seemed too much to ask. The two freezing soldiers were ushered into Mr Bertram's house and sat in front of a fire 'burning with the roots of trees they had dug out of the ground', and given cheering hot milk and then fried eggs and potatoes. William then dug out his illegal radio, literally dug it out for he kept it buried in the garden during the daylight hours, and turned on the BBC news. It was the first proper news Clark had heard for nigh on six months and it was not altogether good. The Battle of the Bulge had begun and Guderian's German troops were pushing the surprised American forces back in their drive for Antwerp. More than that, though this was not on the news, the men under the command of crack Nazi commander Joachim Pipon were taking no prisoners and killing unarmed US soldiers in cold blood. That was in the Ardennes. The two American officers in Jersey were safe for a short while at least.

William Bertram was looking after a nearby house for an English couple who had been forced to leave Jersey in the 1942 deportations, and it was in this house that he told the two escapees to hide. But though he really wanted to help the men he advised against trying to leave from Gorey harbour. It was heavily guarded he said, and there were always at least three guards on duty, each one with a perfect view of the whole harbour.

Despite this warning Clark and Haas talked each other into making the attempt to escape. The plan was deceptively simple. Wade, up to the waist, to the pier's end and then a further five hundred yards out, in the falling tide, to where three fishing boats lay at anchor. Clamber aboard, slip the anchor and let her drift out with the tide towards France

Under cover of darkness the two men had just begun their cold wade out to sea through the harbour full of German boats, in fact they could hear the German sailors chatting and laughing on the decks above them, when disaster struck in the shape of a strong wind which sprang up quite suddenly. That would not have mattered but it was blowing in the wrong direction. It was a powerful and rising wind blowing from the east to the west, away from France and towards Jersey. It was, quite literally, a dreadful blow. Their boat could not possibly drift gently off on the tide towards France. Instead they would be blown, and blown forcibly, back on to Jersey. There could be no escape that night.

They spent the rest of that stormy night in the cabin of a half-wrecked boat they found lying in the harbour. All through the next day they waited in their cold, damp refuge. Through the portholes they could watch the Germans working in the harbour along with a couple of locals. Most importantly they saw that quite near to them were moored twelve small rowing boats. There was an answer to their prayers. One of those little boats could take them across the narrow sea to Normandy, and the boat they picked to carry them thither was a twelve foot fishing boat.

Back to William Bertram's house they went at nightfall. They explained to him the new plan, which was to get fresh supplies together, and, most importantly, dry socks, and wait for the wind and sea conditions to be favourable for a trip to France.

The great day arrived. The weather forecast was not all that good but not all that bad either. They had to go. And go they did after an emotional goodbye to William and his family, their mentors and saviours, who had risked their own lives in helping these two American soldiers.

Clark and Haas hid once again in their half-wrecked boat in the harbour and waited for nightfall. The wind was blowing strongly during the morning, and the waves were banging against the sides of their hideaway. But then at around midday the wind dipped away to nothing and the seas slackened. Things were looking good, and even better when at nightfall a gentle breeze began blowing, and this time away from Jersey and eastward toward France.

They climbed from their little home in the cabin-boat and crept towards the little rowing boat. George Haas got in at the stern, Edward Clark got in amidships carrying the oars. He settled himself, pushed out the oars and began to row. George was on the tiller:

'I was more scared than I would ever be again. Any second I was expecting that 38mm to boom out. An unhappy thought kept entering my head – maybe the Germans have just been playing cat and mouse with us. If so, killing us would be perfectly legal. I could hear them explaining – "Haas and Clark were escaping in a row-boat – we hollered 'halt.' The only thing left to us was to use the 38mm."

As I kept rowing Haas crouched down in the stern splashing the tiller back and forth with no success whatever in guiding us. Just when I was wondering and splashing the oars because the boat didn't move, the half moon came out in all its glory. We were sunk!! Not only could we not buck the tide but we couldn't get back to our cabin boat and now we were in plain view of the Germans, enabling them to have some sport at our expense. By the time we got out to the end of the pier I was worn out. I couldn't lift one of those oars to save our lives. "George," I said, "take over these oars, I can't go any further."

"God Clark, get us out round this pier, out of sight of the German security."

I replied "I can't do it." So after practically capsizing the little boat, George took the oars and I took the tiller.

As our little boat was rounding the pier we really realised what fools we were. The groundswells were at least 15 feet high and every one seemed greedy to capsize us. "Ed, we can never make it and we can't get back to Jersey alive. Anyway we've beaten those Germans." This was little comfort to me. I didn't care much about beating the Germans if they found me later floating face down. "George, as long as it doesn't get any worse than this we've got a chance."

At this time the wind was blowing and the now friendly moon had hidden itself again. The wind was blowing directly at our stern and the direction we wanted to go. George saw it was useless to row so he busied himself by checking the course with our little compass (which meant not a damn thing because we had to go with the wind and keep our boat perpendicular to the trough of the sea) and watching the waves loom up behind us swaying a little right or left to keep me from capsizing us. After what seemed hours to us we had come to believe our chances were pretty good, I looked back to see the island still in plain view. Were we going to get out of the range of the German guns before daylight? If we weren't, they could really have some long range target practise on us.

I was beginning to become cramped and very cold, fighting that tiller, trying to keep us afloat. Later, the wind died down and George began to row again, but the sea became choppy. Shortly thereafter George excitedly exclaimed to look to our stern. As I looked I could see a ball of black steadily growing larger and as I looked I realised there was not a breath of air stirring. Then it was upon us with all its fury – a snow storm! The snow was stinging our bare skins and was travelling at breakneck speed, parallel to the whipped up sea. It immediately became so dark that George sitting four feet away from me appeared to be nothing but a dark blot. I couldn't see the tips of our oars. The sea immediately became rolling ground swells but George couldn't see them coming behind us and I could not see the trough before us. Then it was I found a use for these ears of mine that stick out so from my head. If the snow was hitting both my ears I knew that the

wind and the sea were directly at our stern. If the snow was hitting the side of my face and only one ear, I knew that the tiller had to be used accordingly. This went on for what seemed to both of us an eternity.

I became so cramped and cold finally that I had to have a cigarette or die. All I had was some home-grown Jersey "roll-your-own" that John had bought to me. George couldn't roll one and wouldn't try, so in spite of it all, holding the tiller with my knees which had taken all I could muster before with both hands, I rolled a cigarette and managed to find a dry match to light it with. That, undoubtedly, was the best cigarette I ever smoked, although it must have been made out of one of the world's worst tobaccos.

The smoke bucked me up for a while but my condition then became worse. I wanted to stretch my aching muscles, exercise, in order to keep my blood circulating. I just couldn't stand this any longer.

"George, you've got to take this tiller for a while."

"God, no Ed, I'll capsize us."

"I don't give a damn if you do! Are you coming back here?"

"No."

"Well I'm coming back up there then."

George scrambled back to the tiller as I moved to the bow in time to keep us from shipping but little water. God, I was tired. I crawled underneath the seats in the slopping water – too tired to live and not giving a damn if I did or did not. Just as I was becoming comfortable in my dazed condition stretched out in the bottom of the boat, George cried out "Ships, Ed, ships! You can see their lights." I scrambled up and started screaming as I saw the lights also. Then, nutty as I was, I started striking matches and throwing them into the air hoping to attract attention as the lights faded out, and in spite of George I slumped back into my comfortable coma. Shortly thereafter, we shipped at least half full of water – did I come out of it. It will always amaze me how a person will fight for a spark of life. Here we were, our little boat half full of water, not a ghost of a chance now to stay afloat, and the tiller wouldn't answer at all in the trough, huge monsters crashing down on us from all sides. I picked up the oars and frantically straightened up as best I could. George and I both felt that this was the end. He talked calmly about it then. We felt sure we would drown in two minutes in that sea – that wouldn't be bad. At least the Germans wouldn't find us floating face down. We were too far away from Jersey for that.

We both talked about our families – wondering if they would ever know what happened to us. I thought about my wife – patriotism or not she was one of the big reasons I had taken these chances and now I would not see her again. I told George if there was a second world I hoped that the first person I would meet there would be my brother Jack. It wouldn't be bad if he were there.

For some reason, God only knows the reason, we stayed afloat during our conversation. Then I began to worry as land began to get closer – what about rocks. I had heard the beaches of France had many. Suppose we got near shore and capsized? In this rough sea we would both drown.

About this time another snow squall hit us and my hands were plenty full. Now I could really see what mountains these groundswells could become and how choppy they were. This seemed, or every squall seemed, to be the worst of all. It was all I could do to hold the tiller. Then WHOOP, we shipped water and the tiller was knocked out of its slots. Between the two of us we got the tiller back in place and George started pumping again.

Then I began to worry about whether I could take this little boat through the heavy breakers that were beating against the shore. The coast guardsmen do it on the Gulf of Mexico with their whaleboats, but I was not a coast guardsman. George said if I could get him within 200 yards of the beach he would swim the rest of the way. I still doubt that he could have but I know he would have given a good exhibition.

When we got within about 500 yards of the beach, George started taking off his overcoat and loosening his shoes. As for me I didn't take off a thing because I knew I couldn't swim a stroke – I was too badly whipped.

As we raced into shore, George could see there were no rocks and he got ready with the oars, in case of necessity. There was no need. With the waves cracking down on us we slid right onto the beach. When, to our dazed amazement, a shot was fired and some soldiers came running down towards us. For one horrible moment I thought we had landed on another of the Channel Islands, Guernsey, and that those were Germans coming towards us. But then an American Lieutenant and an American soldier came up to us.'

Captain Edward Clark and Lieutenant George Haas had done it! They had beaten the Germans and beaten the roaring seas to make it into the embrace of their comrades in arms.

Their voyage, which to them had seemed to last an eternity, had in fact lasted for 15 hours. It had been a hellish time but it didn't' matter any more to Edward and George as they gratefully sipped their hot coffee in the Command Post in Coutances. They were happy men. There was however an unhappy man they had left behind in Jersey, and that man was the owner of the little rowing boat they had taken, Mr L. Godfray the Gorey harbourmaster. The angry Germans suspected that Mr Godfray had knowingly provided the Americans with the escape boat, and the punishment for doing that was to be shot. However the harbourmaster was able, after a lengthy interrogation, to persuade them that he knew nothing of the daring escape from the South Hill

POW camp in St Helier and that, moreover, he had certainly not given any kind of permission for his precious boat to be taken across to France. The loss of the boat was quite a blow to Mr Godfray and immediately after the War he hurried to claim compensation.

Haas and Clark returned to the Island on 7th January 1995, the 50th anniversary of their escape. They unveiled a plaque at Gorey Pier commemorating their escape. A large crowd had gathered and at their head was another notable escapee, Sir Peter Crill, Bailiff of Jersey. Clark delivered a speech in which he said:

'I'll never know how we made that trip to France that night – someone was sure watching over us. And I'll tell you this right now – if you offered me a million dollars to do it again, I'd turn down the offer on the spot.'

NACHT UND NEBEL: NIGHT AND FOG

Edward Clark and George Haas were among the last to attempt escape from Jersey. There had been many before. Many had succeeded, like Dennis Vibert in his tiny boat *Ragamuffin* in September 1941 who, despite engine failure and unfavourable winds, made it all the 150 miles to mainland Britain. Or like Roy Mourant, John Floyd and the future Bailiff of Jersey Peter Crill. These three boys, as they were, set sail in the *Alouette* from Fauvic – always a favourite place from which to start, and managed to make triumphant landfall near Coutances on the French coast.

And there were others, many other successful escapees, particularly during the latter period of the Occupation in 1944. There were however some terrible failures.

It has been noted before that the seas around the Islands can be very dangerous. The seas can be rough, very rough, as Clark and Haas found out, and the tides are among the highest in the world. Set out from the Islands during the winter months of the year and you must expect mist, fog and storms as a matter of course.

Many of the would-be escapees were drowned, tumbled out of their little boats into an unforgiving sea. But a worse death awaited Maurice Gould when he set sail with his two teenage friends, Peter Hassall and Dennis Audrain on 2nd May 1942.

Leslie Sinel's diary entry for 3rd May 1942 reads:

'An attempt to leave the Islands ends in tragedy when the boat containing three youths overturns off the south-east coast, and one of them (Audrain) is drowned; the other two named Hassall and Gould were taken prisoner by the Germans. It was subsequently learned that the attempt was made from Green Island and that when the boat was taken there a party of Germans helped the boys to launch it!'

It was a dangerous enterprise the young lads had embarked upon but, despite warnings from Captain Sowden and a friendly Jersey policeman Albert Le Cheminant (who interestingly did not see it as part of his duty to report their intended offence), the boys loaded a little dinghy on to a horse and cart that carried it through the St Helier streets under the very noses of the Germans, out along Havre des Pas and the eastern coast road to the launch site at Green Island. On arriving there a small group of young German soldiers, scarcely older than Maurice, gave them a hand to get the dinghy off the cart. That was the last fortunate thing that happened to them that day.

The boys had planned to push off from Green Island at 10.00 p.m. in the dark on an ebb-tide that would carry them quietly and gently out to sea and towards the Normandy coast. But the turning sea blew up quite rough, choppy with a heavy swell. They waited in the rather forlorn hope that the wind would drop and the sea conditions improve. It didn't, and after 45 minutes, impelled by a youthful bravado, they threw necessary caution to the winds, launched their dinghy and headed for the open seas. When they were about a quarter of a mile out, and clear of German coastal guards they thought it time to start the little engine. But as they were attempting to do this, the boat lost way in a deep trough, turned half sideways against a huge oncoming wave and was lifted up and hurled against the emerging rocks. The dinghy turned over and the three Jersey boys found themselves plunged into the frothing sea and one of them could not swim. Dennis Audrain was drowned. Peter Hassall, who was nearest him, did his best to save him but could not hold him up in the heavy seas. Dennis was swept away and under the water. It all happened in a minute. Meanwhile, Maurice Gould was at first carried away from the shore but eventually succeeded in turning around and swimming back to safety. Peter Hassall had also made it back to shore and it was here that another terrifying ordeal began, as they fell victim to Hitler's *Nacht und Nebel* decree.

The 'Night and Fog' decree was a draconian measure directed particularly against civilians who sought to resist or fight in any way the rule of the Germans. *Die deutsche Sicherheit gefährden.*

Heinrich Himmler informed the Gestapo all about it on 7th December 1941:

'It is the Fuehrer's will that the measures taken against those who are guilty of offences against the Reich or against the occupation forces in occupied areas should be altered. The Fuehrer believes that in such cases penal servitude or even a hard labour sentence for life will be regarded as a sign of weakness. An effective and lasting deterrent can be achieved only by the death penalty or by taking measures which will leave the family and the population uncertain as

to the fate of the offender. Deportation to Germany serves this purpose.'

As Wilhelm Keitel (who was hanged for his *Nacht und Nebel* offence among others) expounded:

'Efficient and enduring intimidation can only be achieved either by capital punishment or by measures by which the relatives of the criminals do not know the fate of the criminal.
Any prisoners not executed within eight days are to be transported to Germany secretly, and further treatment of offenders will take place here; these measures will have a deterrent effect because: A. The prisoners will vanish without a trace. B. No information may be given as to their whereabouts or their fate.'

They would just disappear into the Night and the Fog. No one, not their friends or their families, would know what had happened to them.

And this is what happened to Maurice and Peter. As soon as they stumbled and crawled from the sea they were arrested by the German police. The photographs and maps of the German military installations in Jersey that the boys were carrying with them meant that they fell into the category of enemy agents as defined by the *Nacht und Nebel* directive. They could be treated as terrorists and they were. For ten days they were imprisoned in the Gloucester Street prison and underwent continuous and 'rigorous' interrogation.

They were not allowed any form of communication with the outside world. They could not talk to their parents. They had no legal representation. After ten days the two teenagers were transported to Fresnes Prison in Paris and further interrogation ensued. Only this time it was truly rigorous. In fact the boys were subjected to torture. They were immersed in baths of cold water and their heads forced under the surface and held there for an injurious length of time. What the torturers wanted was a confession, naming and placing the British agents they assumed must have assisted the two in their bid to escape. Peter and Maurice did not give the Germans any such information because they couldn't. There were no British agents who had organised their venture. The German assumption was mistaken.

The two Jersey boys were then sent to an SS camp called Hinzert and it was here that things became really bad, particularly for Maurice. He was always picked to do the hardest and most soul-destroying work. Moreover, he was beaten repeatedly and savagely by the camp guards. So savagely in fact that, as Peter said after the war, Maurice lost the will to fight on through his adversity, lost the will to live. Starving, beaten, weak and ill, Maurice, along with Peter, was transferred to another prison camp at Wittlich in July 1942 where conditions were a good deal better than at Hinzert, but it was too late to help him. Maurice was mortally ill with the great killer disease of the camp, TB. Peter recalls the sad time:

'By the end of September 1943 Maurice had almost stopped eating – symptomatic of the final stages of TB. I often went over to him and sponged his face and hands to make him as comfortable as possible. He had been bed-ridden so long that his back was covered with large sores. During his final days as I attended him, he again said to me, "When the war is over, Peter, please come and get me! Don't leave me here!" I did my best to comfort him, and told him that I would see that he got back to the Islands after the war. I disliked having that nature of conversation with Maurice, as it brought home my own vulnerability, however, I would have done anything, or said anything, to give him just one second of comfort and happiness. I did not want to see my tall gentle friend die, as we had been through so much together, and I knew that when he was gone, a large piece of me would go with him. It was a sad time and there were moments when I was not certain that I really wanted to live, despite my promise to Maurice. At nights, as I lay in my bed, I often thought how brave Maurice had been. I had never heard him complain about his lot, and at times when I expressed my trepidation about returning alone, he comforted me by saying that I was a hero, and the Bailiff of Jersey and the Attorney General would see that I was honoured – that always raised a little chuckle between us.
On the morning of 1st October 1943 while I was changing a patient's dressing, I heard choking sounds coming from Maurice's bed. When I got to his bed, he sat upright and reached out for me. I held

his hands, then pulled him to my chest, where I hugged and cradled his head on my shoulder. I begged him not to leave me alone, but he looked at me and weakly whispered, "Remember, Peter, tell my Grandfather what happened, and please don't leave me here!" and with those words Maurice Gould died in my arms, and as he died, the prison clock clanged twice. It was 10.30 a.m., 1st October 1943, and my dear friend and companion was gone. I was now alone but able to console myself that Dennis and Maurice were now together. I sponged the blood from the corner of his lips, washed his face, then straightened out his body, and finally I gently closed his eyes, after which I pulled his blanket over his face.'

Peter carried on in the camp for two more years and was then taken to Breslau (the Festung that suffered such a hideous fate at the hands of the Red Army) and actually given a trial. At this trial Peter conducted his own defence and did it very well and very cleverly and, perhaps most importantly of all, he spoke in very fluent German. The court was impressed and he was not sentenced to death but to four years in prison. Here again Peter was fortunate.

Nacht und Nebel prisoners were generally sent to one of three camps: Natzweiler, Gross-Rosen, or a place like Schweidnitz. The first two were notorious for their appalling conditions and high mortality rate, the third less so. Natzweiler was the only concentration camp on French soil, created as it was up in the north-east corner of France by the Vosges mountains. And it wasn't just a concentration camp. It had its very own gas chamber on site for it was an extermination camp.

Gross-Rosen in Lower Silesia, where Peter Hassall should have ended up, was not an extermination camp, but prisoners died there nonetheless, and in their thousands, for this was the camp whose inmates worked in the great granite quarry. Many of them worked to death but fortunately not one of its most famous prisoners, Simon Wiesenthal, who survived to become the great Nazi hunter in the post-war years. Peter Hassall was sent, not to either of these two death-dealing *Arbeit macht Frei* horror camps, but to Schweidnitz, and in this he was fortunate.

Schweidnitz was one of about fifty sub- or satellite camps of Gross-Rosen. Conditions in these *arbeitslager* were hard, bordering on the inhuman. There was little food and what there was, was of a poor quality. They were filthy, dirty, verminous and disease-ridden, but, and it is an important 'but', a man could survive incarceration there, particularly a man like Peter Hassall, who had the strength of will to endure all the suffering and the hardships of his captivity, never losing hope he would, one day, be released.

In the bitter cold of January 1945, thousands upon thousands of refugees, fleeing the horrors of the Red Army advance, poured through the town of Schweidnitz.The Russians would soon be there to liberate the camp. But for many an inmate it was too late for that.

The winter of that year, 1945, was apocalyptically terrible; temperatures way below freezing, snow, ice and cruel wind everywhere along the Eastern Front, and in the Schweidnitz camp, famine, disease and death. Many of the young *Nacht und Nebel* prisoners died in that winter of 1945. But liberation was indeed at hand for those who managed to survive. On a morning in early February Peter Hassall woke up to hear the thunder of the Russian artillery fire not more than ten miles away.

Deliverance was near! But the Germans dashed the expectations of relief by moving Peter Hassall and all the other prisoners who could walk. They were marched to Hirschberg prison, 30 miles to the west of Schweidnitz and here they stayed for another three months. That was the time if took for Russian armies to advance their line up to and beyond Hirschberg. Peter's German captors didn't bother to try and move their prisoners further west for a second time. Hitler's empire was dust and ashes, the Red Armies were in the streets of Berlin, the Fuehrer defended only by old men and children. There was no point in going on. The cells of the Hirschberg prison were thrown open and all the *Nacht und Nebel* prisoners simply ordered to leave. Peter Hassall joyfully obeyed. He was free to make his way back to Jersey. His war was over.

An unpleasant footnote:

'In captivity, Maurice and I often went over the events leading up to our captivity, and given the curfew, the timings of the escape, the arrival of the Water Police and the Feldgendarms, there was no doubt that we were denounced by my mother. However when I returned to Jersey, and based on information 50 years later, I was assured by our lone confidant that someone other than he had learned of our escape plans, including location and timing, and informed my mother.'

And Peter's mother went straight round to her friend from the Harbour Police, *Oberwachmeister* Linde, at the Pomme d'Or Hotel and told him of the planned escape. Peter's own mother had informed on him. She had betrayed him and his two companions to the Germans.

Why had she done this?

'Over the long years I had reconciled her betrayal as an act of motherly love – an act of a terrified mother desperate to get her son back safely, and during all the years I had forgiven her, as I think I understood her dilemma on the night of 3rd May 1942.'

Peter Hassall believed that his mother had told the Germans of his planned escape because she was frightened that her son would surely die in his little boat if he succeeded in getting offshore and into the dangerous Channel waters. She was mightily concerned with his well-being. Telling the Germans was not so much a betrayal as an act of motherly love.

But yet doubts lingered in Peter's mind for years after the War. There were blank spots, pieces missing from the story of that dreadful night when Dennis was drowned and Maurice and Peter were arrested by the Germans.

In the summer of 1991 Peter, by this time living in Canada, wrote to his brother to ask for an answer to the question that had haunted him for so long, 'What happened at Winchester House on the night of Sunday 3rd May 1942?'

His brother took his time in replying but at last, just after Christmas 1991, the letter arrived. It did not make pleasant reading.

'She (my mother) knew you had this boat quite some time before the ill-fated trip. That's why on the night of May 3rd 1942 she asked why you were not at home and the curfew gone by. I said I did not know anything. She then twigged, put two and two together and in her usual lady-like way screamed at Dad and I and said off the top of her head, "The little wretch, I bet it's that boat, he's leaving the island." She then shouted, "We will all be arrested for his stupidity." Then Dad and I tried to calm her down, and Dad said, "If he's gone, good luck to the boy and God speed him. Please do not go to the Wasserschutzpolizei (German Harbour

Police)." "No! No!" she screamed. "We must inform them, then they will look at us more kindly. Then they won't arrest us all." There was nothing that Dad or I could do. She stalked off down Winchester Street, towards the Pomme d 'Or. It was no use pleading with the b***h.'

Peter was shocked as he had forgiven his mother in the belief that she had tried to act in his best interests. But now:

As I re-read my brother's letter, I asked myself, "Was she afraid of punishment, or was she frightened of losing her lucrative black market operation?" Reading my brother's letter almost 50 years after the event was painful enough, but the fact that she might have been responsible for Maurice's death made matters worse – had she not denounced us, and even if the tragedy had taken place, we had a contingency plan to go into hiding, and we might have succeeded in hiding out until the end of the war – others did.'

Then in the summer of 1992 another letter, bearing three French stamps, arrived for Peter. It was from his mother, who was still alive and living in Paris.

This was amazing news, for Peter had believed that Elma was dead and yet here she was after decades of silence, writing to the son she had so selfishly betrayed.

There was a little note inside. Elma had written:

'Is it so hard to forgive? x'

Peter found it very hard:

'Now that she was alive, would Maurice want me to forgive her? I thought deeply and tried to connect with Maurice, and when I did, or believed that I had, I experienced a chilling reply.

I thought over my mother's plea for forgiveness. I then went over to my desk, where I typed a short reply. Forgiveness was not mine alone to give. I had to include Maurice's option in my letter, and I felt no joy nor vindication when I mailed my reply the following day – but then I am not a very forgiving person. I still carry an enormous amount of guilt and my nights are always long. However, from my mother's short plea for forgiveness came one consolation: she seems to acknowledge her guilt and needs forgiveness – perhaps that will help ease things a little.'

Chapter 5

Who Are These People and Why Are They Here?

'When I see your wonderful men march up the street, then my heart is bleeding about this war between brothers.'

(an Island journalist as reported by Pfeffer in 1941)

Everybody knew that Hitler's great obsession was with Russia and the Jewish Bolsheviks away to the east of the burgeoning Third Reich. Anyone who had read Hitler's lengthy and hate-filled book on his political philosophy that he had penned in his rather comfortable cell in the Bavarian state prison would know that the great struggle of the twentieth century would be against the *Untermenschen*, the Jewish Bolsheviks, the near-animals living their disgusting lives in the vast territories beyond East Prussia, territories in which the German leader wanted to settle his own people. Such a war would be waged ruthlessly and ferociously without regard to any rules of combat or international law in the name of Aryan supremacy, and it would result in the triumph of the racially superior over the racially inferior. The victory cried out for in the Nazi shout 'Sieg Heil' was a victory in the East, not in the West.

The mighty Fuehrer did not want a war with any of the Western powers, nor during the years leading up to 1939 did it seem likely that there would be such a conflict. A policy of 'appeasement' was pursued by the two powers of France and Britain, informed and underpinned by a feeling that Germany had been hard done by in the Versailles Treaty, that too much punishment had been meted out to the stricken foe, and that Hitler did have legitimate territorial claims and was justified in pursuing them. This being so, there was but little appetite for opposing Hitler when his army reoccupied the German industrial heartland of the Ruhr, few voices raised when Czechoslovakia was dismembered. Hitler became convinced that he could act with impunity, for neither the French, with their endlessly-changing governments, nor the British under Prime Minister Neville Chamberlain, it appeared, had the courage or the will to stand up to him. He was wrong in his belief, for Chamberlain, the man from Birmingham, finally did abandon his policy of appeasement – and he abandoned it because of the invasion of Poland. The British prime minister saw this for what it was: an act of naked aggression with no possible justification.

He had bent over backwards, terminally ill as he was, to empathise with and find some justification for Hitler's armies marching hither and yon all over Europe, but this Polish action was a step too far and he said so in no uncertain terms in Parliament. To see the film of Neville Chamberlain's speech to the House on that September day in 1939 is to watch a man in agony, appalled by the actions of the German dictator, weary to the soul of fighting for peaceful answers and peaceful solutions, and fearful of the horrors that were about to be unleashed. He spoke plainly, without adornment, and bitterly to the point:

'Everything that I have worked for, everything that I have believed in during my public life has crashed into ruins. There is only one thing left for me to do: that is devote what strength and power I have to forwarding the victory of the cause for which we have sacrificed so much.'

And then he said:

'We have a clear conscience we have done all that any country could do to establish peace. The situation in which no word given by Germany's ruler could be trusted, and no people or country could feel itself safe, had become intolerable.

Now may God bless you all. May He defend the right. It is the evil things we shall be fighting against – brute force, bad faith, injustice, oppression and persecution – and against them I am certain that the right will prevail.'

Hitler was stunned by Chamberlain's declaration of war. On hearing the news he turned, bewildered, to Ribbentrop and the assembled generals and asked

'What now?' for there had been no real belief that Britain and France would go to war for Poland, an action which, militarily, made no sense. Why had the miserable, appeasing 'worms' he had encountered in Munich suddenly turned so absolutely against him and his aggressive expansionism? But turn they had, and thus there was a war to be fought in Western Europe. The Eastern Front was secured by the extraordinary Ribbentrop–Molotov Pact: an unprincipled and very expedient accord struck with the sub-human Russians, and leaving the Germans free to organise and prosecute the Western conflict.

But Hitler was reluctant to open hostilities. There was a lengthy pause in proceedings known as the 'Bore' war or the 'Phoney' war. But then in May 1940 the guns opened up, the Luftwaffe hurtled about the sky and the panzer divisions scythed with incredible speed around the Maginot line. The British and the French were driven towards the Channel, towards Dunkirk and, most importantly and dangerously for the Channel Islands, towards the Cherbourg Peninsula and St Malo. General Rundstedt might very kindly, if mysteriously, have stopped the advance of his rampant panzer divisions allowing an entire army of 320,000 British and French soldiers to be ferried across the Channel to the safety of mainland UK, but there was no stopping the Germans eventually gaining control of the entire French coast facing across the water towards England. And as the victorious Germans looked out from along the

Cotentin Peninsula, from Granville and St Malo they could see before them the Channel Islands: Jersey, Guernsey, Alderney and Sark. British territory at last, ripe for the taking. What a triumph it would be for the Third Reich and for the Fuehrer to have German boots on British soil, the Luftwaffe in English skies and the *Kriegsmarine* in the Island harbours. Whatever legitimate doubts the all-conquering Germans might have entertained as to the strategic military value of the little Islands, there was absolutely no doubt that the great propaganda value alone of invasion and occupation would justify a military operation. And so the Germans came to the Channel Islands and, in the event, not a shot was fired against them, not an arm raised in protest.

The bombing raids of 28th June 1940 demanded absolute submission to the will of the enemy, and they got it in very short order. The Luftwaffe took control of the airports in Jersey, Guernsey and Alderney. German soldiers marched smartly along the streets of St Peter Port and St Helier, turning the head of more than one fair Island girl. Every member of the occupying force was in high spirits – they were on British soil and they were everywhere victorious. The opposition had disappeared like a morning mist before a stiff breeze. It was such a happy time for the Germans and in particular for Major Doctor Albrecht Lanz who was to be the very first Island Commandant. In his diary he wrote of the experience of flying out of

Cherbourg to take the Islands into German possession:

'With many good wishes from all those left behind who envied us our glorious task, we rolled to the top of the runway. With a drone of engines one Ju followed the other across the field. Soon the ground vanished beneath our feet. A few seconds later, the machines turned out to sea in a great loop and arranged themselves in ordered formation. We had scarcely left the mainland when there was a slight jolt to the stomach, and the Jus dived down towards the foaming waves, for we could only fly between 25 and 50 yards above the wave crests in order to keep out of sight of British fighters and remain hidden.

Evenly the engines droned their former song, already in the distance the first contours of the longed-for Island began to show themselves. Then someone began to sing and in a moment everyone in the aircraft joined in. With steady voice and shining eyes the song resounded through the aircraft. "Wir denn fahren gegen England." ("We are marching against England.") Now at last we really were. An unforgettable moment.'

Major Lanz was a personable *Wehrmacht* Officer and held a doctorate in Law and Philosophy from Heidelberg University. He was a very able soldier who had distinguished himself in action and was very popular with his men. He also impressed the Dame of Sark, Sibyl Hathaway, when he came calling along with Dr Maass on 1st July 1940:

'Instinctively I judged Lanz to be a fair-minded man, who would never trick anyone by low cunning.'

For his part Lanz recognised Sibyl as:

'La Dame who very energetically wears the breeches.'

Lanz, in a spirit of great cordiality:

'... went so far as to say that if ever I found any difficulties I was to communicate directly with the Commandant of the Channel Islands in Guernsey. I took advantage of this throughout the war, and it paid big dividends.'

Major Albrecht Lanz also endeared himself to the President of the Controlling Committee and leader of the Guernsey people, Ambrose Sherwill:

'Dr Lanz was every inch a soldier, not very easy to get to know but absolutely straight and kindly. I grew to like him very much and I believe he was adored by his men.'

Lanz tells us in his diary:

'The Attorney General of Guernsey, Mr Sherwill, is a responsible leader, a man with grown-up children who has himself often been to Gemany. He told us that even he had fallen for the British propaganda that if we came, "the islands would be overrun by a horde of wild cannibals."

It was thought that we would cut off children's hands and violate women and girls. Therefore in the first days we were here, scarcely a single person was to be seen in the streets. The feminine sex very timidly held themselves back.

Before our arrival they had shot their dogs by the hundred so that the barbarian could not torture them to death and eat them! Mr Sherwill's wife told us that her eleven-year-old son was very eager to see a German soldier. When they met one, and the mother pointed out the German soldier to her son, he was hugely disappointed and said "Why mummy, they're only men, exactly like us!"'

The Guernsey President of the Controlling Committee was also favourably taken with Lanz's helpmeet, Dr Maass. This was in contrast to Dame Sibyl, who found him a little shifty. Sherwill, however, thought Maass:

'... a very remarkable man. He had been a prisoner of the English in the 1914–18 war, held a degree in tropical medicine from Liverpool University and spoke English remarkably well. His cheery face was a tonic in those depressing days and there can be no question but that his presence and friendly activities helped the situation enormously. When he left to take up another job, we really missed him. He was an enemy but oh such a pleasant one.'

Over in Jersey Bailiff Alexander Coutanche, peering through his monocle, was less impressed by his visiting German come to present the terms of Occupation. This was a Captain Gussek, appointed by Lanz to be *Inselkommandant* in the Islands:

'There was nothing very remarkable about this Captain Gussek. He was a fighting soldier, short, neat and polite who went briskly about the business in hand.'

Captain Gussek made it clear that the Channel Islands were to be just a very small part of the north-west German command in France for the duration of the War, which he firmly believed would be over by Christmas at the latest.

This idea that the War would be over in a matter of weeks was one shared by almost all the Germans, officers and men who came to the Channel Islands in that blisteringly hot summer of 1940. Some thought they were already in Britain and asked where the red double-decker buses were, others bought up stocks of cloth to be made up into suits when they got to London's Savile Row in a few weeks' time. Every one of them was pleasant and polite, indeed they were commanded to be so.

Sweets for the kiddies, a 'Good day Madame,' here, an 'Excuse me Sir,' there, sugared the pill of Occupation. This was not to be the roughhouse of Poland or the killing fields of Ukraine. Children were not to be killed or mutilated, or villagers burnt in barns, and nor were women to be raped – although there was one poor soul who suffered such a gross sexual assault in the first few days of the Occupation.

The person in question was a maiden lady over 70 years old living in the Vale in Guernsey. Two inebriated German soldiers had entered her little house and one of them raped her at gun-point. The other soldier, who took no part in the attack, was, on the contrary, very solicitous towards her and 'afterwards patted her hand in sympathy'. Ambrose Sherwill was informed of what had happened and he in turn informed Dr Maass, who immediately went to the house with Adjutant *Oberleutnant* Mittlemüeller. The good doctor was at first not inclined to believe the offence had taken place because of the great age of the woman, but then he listened to her doctor's report and instantly changed his mind. He set about finding the culprit with commendable expedition. Every single soldier in the still-small German force was called to answer for his whereabouts at the time of the rape.

Inside three hours the guilty man was found, and the very next day a military court of enquiry was convened up by the airport at 9 o'clock a.m. The soldier, identified as the suspect rapist, was then immediately shipped over to Cherbourg for a full military trial, in fact a court martial. The soldier was found guilty and shot. Ten days was all it took to deliver justice for an offence which would have been winked at on the Eastern Front.

The correct and kindly Germans were not so bad as they had been painted, not by a long chalk. Or so thought Ambrose Sherwill, along with many others in these early days. He said as much in his broadcast, transmitted on German Radio Bremen in August 1940, addressing the rest of unoccupied Great Britain:

'I imagine that many of you must be greatly worried as to how we are getting on. Well, let me tell you. Some will fear, I imagine, that I am making this record with a revolver pointed at my head and speaking from a transcript thrust into my hand by a German Officer.

The actual case is very different. The Lieutenant Governor and Bailiff, Mr Victor Carey, and every other Island official has been and is being treated with every consideration and with greatest courtesy by the German Military Authorities.

The Island Government is functioning. Churches and chapels are open for public worship. Banks, shops and places of entertainment are open as usual.'

And later:

'The conduct of the German troops is exemplary. We have been in German occupation for four and a half weeks and I am proud of the way my fellow Islanders have behaved and grateful for the correct and kindly attitude towards them of the German soldiers.

We have always been, and we remain, intensely loyal subjects of His Majesty, and this has been made clear to, and is respected by, the German Commandant and his staff.

On that staff is an officer speaking perfect English – a man of wide experience, with whom I am in daily contact. To him I express my grateful thanks for his courtesy and patience.'

Everything Sherwill says in his broadcast was true. Contrary to expectations this was no savage invasion.

There are, however, reasons why the German invaders behaved so differently in the Islands, and the first and major reason has to be the positioning of the Islanders in that racial index which put the Jews at the bottom and the Aryans at the top. The Reverend John Leale pointed to this in his great speech to the States of Guernsey at the close of the War:

'The Germans believe in treating people according to this estimate of their culture. We received favoured treatment because we were regarded as belonging to a different order of civilisation, from, say, the Poles.'

It is also true to say, and this is another compelling reason, that the Germans who took control of the Islands both from a military and a civil point of view were of a very different mentality from that of their SS and Nazi bosses. Some of the Germans in the officer class were highly educated, many held doctorates – not this is in and of itself a guarantee of proper behaviour; eight of the infamous 15 at Wannsee were doctors – and, perhaps more importantly, a number of them were members of the German aristocracy from whom might be expected nobility in action as well as nobility of title. None of the Germans who came to the Islands of Jersey, Guernsey and Sark was an SS man. There were no hard-line Nazis here before the autumn of 1945 and, though many an Islander thought otherwise, there was no Gestapo. But there was the *Geheimefeldpolizei* – the army secret police.

THE MODEL OCCUPATION

The Islands were to become part of the North West, Zone A, French Department of La Manche, with its headquarters in Paris. Civil affairs in the Islands were dealt with by *Feldkommandantur* 515. This administrative unit had its headquarters in Jersey at Victoria College House overlooking St Helier, with a Guernsey branch or *Nebenstelle* located up the hill going out of St Peter Port at the Grange Lodge Hotel (still there, as is Victoria College House). The First Commander, or *Feldkommandant*, was Colonel Schumacher; an army man through and through, and certainly no Nazi. He was short and spherical, thick-lipped and flat-nosed. He was also a sick man enfeebled by illness, and it is probably for this reason that he kept himself in the

background for quite a lot of the time. But when he did come forward to do business with the Superior Council, they found him a very courteous, gentlemanly and amenable administrator who would act, when he could, to serve the Islanders' interests, sometimes as if they were his own.

This passage from the diary of Edward Le Quesne is eloquent on the point:

'For once the news to be recorded today is good news. We are to be permitted to retain our wireless sets. This is due to the influence of Colonel Schumacher, the German Island Commandant to whom the Islanders owe a debt of gratitude, for at great danger and inconvenience to himself he went to Paris and interceded on our behalf with the high German authorities who had issued an order for the confiscation of our sets.'

In that instance the *Feldkommandantur* was as much a buffer between the civil population and a potentially oppressive Occupation rule run from Paris as were Coutanche and the Superior Council, or Sherwill with his Controlling Committee. The Islanders were, as they themselves acknowledged, extremely fortunate to have him in place during the opening months of the Occupation, and equally fortunate in the Germans who came after to the Islands in that they conducted the Occupation, within the constraints of the perceived 'military necessity', in a relatively benign and moderate way.

The *Feldkommandantur* in particular seemed on many occasions to try and soften the effects of harsh edicts coming from Paris and Berlin. Louis Guillemette, the tireless and hugely effective secretary to the Guernsey Controlling Committee, (they had stolen him from the Bailiff, Victor Carey), says this in his dairy of a meeting with the *Feldkommandantur* at the time it was planned to deport a large number of the Islanders:

'It may sound strange to say that the conversation was friendly when it must affect adversely so many of our people, but we know what the public don't know, and that is the Feldkommandantur are the only friends we possess and the talk was mainly an assurance that he would do his utmost on our behalf.'

Louis Guillemette, Ambrose Sherwill, John Leale and Dr Symons went to Grange Lodge to talk over the projected deportations with Baron von Aufsess, Chief Civil Administrator for the Islands.

And Von Aufsess did do his utmost to at least moderate the order in favour of the Islanders. Together with his fellow officer, Colonel Knackfuss, they had spent hours with the military commander, General Graf von Schmettow, trying to get exemptions to the deportation order. In the event they were only partially successful.

Schmettow's hands were firmly tied, for the order came from the very top of the command chain – from Hitler himself, in fact – and was not to be disobeyed.

But the *Feldkommandantur* had tried to intervene and that fact marked them down as friends.

Feldkommandant Schumacher let go his benign grip on the Islands' civil affairs in the August of 1941. Ageing, tired and mortally sick, he resigned. He was much too ill to carry on and he shuffled off this mortal coil a few months later. On 8th September 1941, the post of *Feldkommandant* was taken over by Oberst Friedrich Knackfuss. He was small and rotund like Schumacher. Unlike Schumacher he was bumptious and bursting with good health. Like Coutanche and Gussek he was fashionably be-monocled. Edward Le Quesne didn't take to him. This is his diary entry for Saturday 10th January 1942:

'Spent part of the day attempting to modify an order issued by the German Command preventing us cutting down trees without their permission. The reception I had up to now was unsatisfactory. Unfortunately, in dealing with Colonel Knackfuss, the Island Commander, we are not dealing with a gentleman of the Colonel Helldorf type; Colonel Knackfuss is a true overbearing kind of Nazi who seems to consider it his especial duty to be as nasty as possible to those he has, at present, at his mercy.

He is rude to the Bailiff and considers the members of the Council as beneath his contempt. I have to meet this 'gentleman' again on Monday and must make sure that my temper is under full control. We have been lucky up to now with Captain Gusseck, Colonel Schumacher and von Schmettow, and I suppose the law of averages compels us to have a rotter now and again.'

Le Quesne was a little hasty in this judgement of the busy, bustling German officer. We have already noted one instance in which Knackfuss acted totally in the interests of the Islanders – there were to be others – and he was certainly not a 'rotter', in fact he was almost aristocracy. Friedrich Knackfuss was the son of a famous court painter of Kaiser Wilhelm II, though he inherited none of his father's talent.

His administrative skills too were called in question. As the German war effort began to stall and essential food supplies to the Islands were destroyed by RAF planes off the Cherbourg Peninsula. Knackfuss came close to committing a war crime.

On 27th April 1943, Leslie Sinel has this entry in his diary:

'Great excitement in the early evening when a convoy from France en route for Guernsey was attacked by British planes in the vicinity of Noirmont. A supply ship named the Helder and a patrol boat which was towed into harbour eventually sank; a fourth ship – the Maas – was laden with coal and though badly damaged in the stern was towed to the new North Quay for discharge. Residents assert that about 20 planes were seen. Among the vessels machine-gunned was

an oil barge on which were three Guernsey buyers returning from France. The number of casualties cannot be correctly ascertained, but it is understood to be in the region of 30.'

On 30th April Knackfuss published the following notice in the *Evening Post*:

'Wherever German forces have occupied territory they have safeguarded the supplies of foodstuffs and essential commodities for the civilian population. To this the British Channel Islands have been no exception.

The British Command, on the other hand, does its worst to hamper and interrupt the steady flow of supplies to the Islands, regardless of the fact that the population of the Islands are their own fellow countrymen. Since as a result of these nuisance raids the rations of the civil population have to be reduced, they may thank their countrymen across the Channel for such measures.

Mr Churchill and the men behind him will not achieve any military results with their nuisance raids. But it is typical of their well-known ruthlessness and lack of consideration that they do not refrain from exposing their own countrymen to hardship and sufferings which might well be avoided.

At least however, the Island's population ought to know the guilty party.'

It was immediately seen that this reduction of already very small rations was nothing more or less than a reprisal, a vengeful act against a defenceless civilian population, and as such was a contravention of the Hague Convention. Coutanche, in consultation with Victor Carey, the Guernsey Bailiff, decided to protest not only to Knackfuss at the *Feldkommandantur* but also to Switzerland, the neutral protecting power, that such a reprisal measure constituted a war crime.

At this point Schmettow and the second in command, Helldorf, intervened. They were not going to allow any letter of protest to go to Switzerland or anywhere else. In stark and brutal contrast to the war in the Eastern theatre, in the West the niceties of the Hague Convention were definitely to be observed – even though Germany itself had not been a signatory to that agreement.

Knackfuss was hauled over the coals for precipitating this crisis in the relationship between the Germans and the Islanders and told in no uncertain terms to back down from any such reprisal action. He did so.

On 7th May this notice appeared in the *Evening Post*:

During the past few days the Feldkommandant and a delegation of the Council have held conferences with reference to the sinking of ships by Allied forces in the waters adjacent to the Channel Islands and to the possible

effects of such sinkings on supplies.
The delegation received the assurance of the Feldkommandant that the 20% reduction of the present bread rations of the entire civil population over 21 years of age is dictated by the existing war situation and is in no sense a punishment against the civil population.

Future events will show the time during which it may be necessary to continue this reduction.

On behalf of the Council
A.M Coutanche. Bailiff

THE BARON VON AUFSESS

If Friedrich Knackfuss didn't quite make the cut as a true aristocrat, Hans Max von Aufsess certainly did. Tall, handsome and very certain of himself, Von Aufsess was a member of the old Bavarian aristocracy. His family had lived in their splendid castle in Franconia for near on 1,000 years (it is now an excellent hotel). He brought a certain aristocratic detachment to his work as the head of the civil affairs branch of the Military Administration, and towards the islanders he behaved very much like the patrician conservative he was. He was, most certainly, no Nazi. He characterised the Nazis variously as 'dangerous animals, beyond reason,' and 'utterly ruthless in furthering the 'cause'.' There were, it is true, a small number of the 'better sort of Nazi', driven by an outdated belief that a better Germany could be created by following the great Fuehrer to leaven the brutal mix.

Aufsess himself, in common with all the officer class of the German army, became increasingly alienated from the Party and the Fuehrer as Germany's fortunes declined more and more from 1941 onwards. His own wife was arrested and imprisoned in the massive round-up of those thought to be opposed to Hitler in the days of the July assassination attempt by Stauffenburg.

The Baron ended the War inveighing against Hitler as an upstart 'lunatic', the man responsible for all the nation's woes. It was a realisation that came a little late, for by this time Hüffmeier had arrived in the Islands and the Islands had been declared fortresses to be held to the last man. Annihilation was staring them in the face.

It was all so different from how it had begun back in the summer of 1940 when it seemed the conflict would be brief, and to be in the beautiful Channel Islands more of a holiday than an act of war.

Von Aufsess fell in love with the Islands, especially Jersey. It was a pretty, gentle place with wide sandy beaches where he could gallop his horse Satan, and warm seas where he could take his long swims. It was all a long way from the Eastern Front. No millions of fanatical, death-dealing Soviet troops here. No flesh-destroying frostbite either, only the occasional cold. Most importantly for the Baron, there was more than the occasional woman. He was a serious and serial womaniser, a

delighted sensualist, given to comparing the lovemaking of the French and the English women he had experienced:

'The Englishwoman is astoundingly simple, effortless and swift in her lovemaking. While the Frenchwoman involves herself totally in the game, which she likes to be conducted along intellectual lines, for the Englishwoman it is a surprisingly straightforward physical matter. The direct and uncomplicated fashion of making love is not to be underrated; in its openness and honesty it precludes all that is wanton or furtive. If the Frenchwoman, after prolonged kissing, would murmur some word of love or quote a romantic couplet, the Englishwoman would surely only laugh at such tactics'.

The Baron had such a good time. Satan, sex and social intercourse of every kind filled his days and nights in a very pleasant manner.

While he was in Jersey in the autumn of 1944 he made the acquaintance of Ethel Mae Fielding and her daughter, Elaine Fielding, who resided at 5 Wellington Road, St Saviour.

They were a highly cultured twosome and it had not escaped the Baron's notice that Elaine was very pretty indeed – a 'budding beauty' as Aufsess called her. Elaine's father was a university professor working in Mexico and the mother and daughter had been unable to get a passage to join him because of the outbreak of war. They were marooned in Jersey.

And the German aristocrat was on the prowl, but initially:

'The mother must have noticed my interest in the growing daughter and had possibly warned her to take no notice, as the girl looked rather embarrassed and averted her gaze, even when I encountered her alone.'

Elaine Fielding's reserve was not to last long.

Out on one of his walks in the woods above St Helier one evening, Aufsess came across the two women indulging in the very illegal activity of gathering wood. At first he did not recognise them in the gathering gloom but:

'Drawing abreast I was genuinely surprised to recognise the Fielding ladies, generally so soignée, but now dishevelled, flushed and disconcerted. I simply had to laugh. I relieved them of their burden right away, with mock threats, and hoisted the spindly branch of oak on my shoulder, and with much exchange of banter on the way, in which they participated with great good will, I deposited the corpus delicti at their door ... And having arrived at the door, I could not resist the heartfelt invitation of mother and daughter to come in for a cup of tea.'

The relationship with the Fieldings blossomed from then on. The Baron became a regular visitor to their house

and was, as he says:

'Deeply moved by my rich reward in having gained the confidence and affectionate regard of these two Englishwomen.'

They had many cultural evenings *a trois*. Mrs Fielding played the piano 'beautifully' for him, and every evening they spent together, the two women would think up some new cultural delight with which to entertain him. The two women certainly took Von Aufsess' mind off the parlous state of Germany in general and the fate of his wife in particular, if only for a few precious hours.

And, of course, Elaine Fielding fell in love with the German. 'A happy gift of fate,' as he put it:

'Yesterday evening Mrs Fielding was invited out and left me alone with Elaine, with an observation I felt worthy of the Marschallin in Die Rosenkavalier, *that she was leaving behind "a lucky girl and a well-balanced man."'*

More importantly this 'well-balanced man' moderated, or attempted to moderate, the effects of many of the orders and directives coming from Paris, and the harsher and more oppressive ones that came direct from the Nazi headquarters in Berlin. He represented and pursued a policy of moderation in the interests of the Islanders and many times interceded on their behalf.

Towards the end of the War, in the springtime of 1945, he opposed Admiral Hüffmeier's 'get tough' policy towards the civil populations and, if his diary is to be believed, actually contemplated killing the Admiral who had declared his intention of holding out to the last:

'We are close to the time when the Admiral will have to be put out of action and that one of us will have to do it.'

That would have been the most extreme expression of Aufsess' philosophy during the Occupation years, which was to try as far as he was able to prevent the worst excesses of Nazi policy. In this endeavour he received considerable support from his superior, the Military Commander of the Channel Islands, Graf von Schmettow: tall, hawk-faced, tubercular and something of a friend to the Islanders.

INSELKOMMANDANT GRAF VON SCHMETTOW

The General had impeccable military credentials. Born into a Silesian military family, von Schmettow had fought in the First World War as a cavalryman on the Eastern Front where he was quite seriously wounded. On his recovery he was sent to serve on the Western Front in command of an infantry division but his luck ran out again for, like Hitler, he was gassed in the course of the vicious trench warfare. The inhalation of the poison was so injurious that he had to have his right lung removed. Immediately prior to his arrival in the Channel Islands he had seen victorious

action in Poland commanding his Hamburg Infantry Division. A recurrence of trouble from his old war wounds meant that he was invalided back from the East to a sanatorium in France, and it was while he was lying there in bed that he heard the good news of his new posting. In the September of 1940 he was appointed Commander of the British Channel Islands (*Belfshaber der Britische Kanalinsel*). He set up his command centre in St Helier, Jersey.

He was a pleasant, able, and above all, just man. According to all accounts including his own, he was well disposed towards the Islanders. He was well liked by his subordinates. Von Aufsess in particular speaks of him with great affection, calling him the 'little Saxon,' and found him a man who could be amusing and formidable by turns. Even in the dark days of autumn 1944 the General could make von Aufsess smile:

'This evening invited to the General's. We pulled the little Saxon's leg about his practical ways of dealing with small problems of life with astonishing results. He promptly emptied out the contents of his trouser pockets: knife, keys, cigarette lighter etc and happily demonstrated how he suspended these objects in his pockets so they could not get lost or damage the lining. Then having really got into his stride, he went on to expound the method he had devised to drain manure off his garden! In his enthusiasm he started to stutter, and we were hard put to it to restrain our laughter.'

But Schmettow was far from being a soldier-buffo when it came to the business of running the Occupation. As one Jerseyman remarked, echoing the sentiments of many, 'We were lucky to have him.' Nicolle and Symes would have endorsed that sentiment. As we have seen, these two British soldiers would have been shot as saboteurs had it not been for the intervention of Schmettow.

Some years after the War he was asked about his treatment of the Islanders during the Occupation and in particular about the accusations of 'softness' that, at the end of the war, were levelled at his head by his Nazi masters in Berlin. He replied:

'It was never a matter of being soft but of being sensible. I felt that when I was given the command that if the people acted correctly and I could instil into my troops strict and correct behaviour also, then the Occupation could go on without human unpleasantness leading to reprisals and, perhaps, death. I am sure that had we not started off on this correct footing then the people of the Islands would have retaliated and most of our time would have been taken up with dealing with the population instead of letting us get on with our job of having a strategic base. It was for this reason that I asked for the Channel Islands to come under its own administration unit and not to be grouped under the administration for France. I protested to my superiors that to carry out the repressive measures of France in the *Channel Islands, where conditions were so different, was illogical.'*

It can be said that he behaved almost to the very end of his tenure with an admirable even-handedness and humanity towards the Islanders. Towards the end, however, he did have an angry exchange of views with an unusually exercised Victor Carey.

The occasion which prompted this outburst was, almost inevitably, the supply, or rather the lack of supply, of food for the native Islanders. Von Schmettow said:

'In the Island one did not know war; one did not know what war means. They are unable to realise the effect as felt by German towns, the whole of France, London and south England, nor the sacrifices and sufferings which the affected countries have to live through. Compared with this the Islanders have not even felt a breath of it. They only had to feel the burden of occupation – occupation however, the command of which, conscious of its responsibility, has made every effort to prevent every hardship that could be avoided.'

Von Schmettow spoke a good deal of truth. He and the *Feldkommandantur* had indeed on many occasions stood between much Nazi heat and the Islanders – a necessary and welcome shield.

However, thoughts of protecting the civil population were not uppermost in his mind in the September of 1944. It was rather the terrible defeats east, west and south that were being inflicted on the Germans that haunted his every waking and sleeping hour. In these desperate days the exercise of his military duty overrode any other consideration, including the welfare of the Islanders. He was not by any stretch of the imagination a Nazi, or even a Hitlerite, but he was a loyal army officer who would fight to the death, not for the NSDP or the broken Fuehrer, but certainly to defend the Fatherland. He said as much in a missive to Joseph Goebbels dated September 1944:

'The Island fortress will faithfully hold out to the last.'

If there had been a battle to take the Islands then, almost certainly very few Islanders would have been left to tell the tale, for the Islands were mightily fortified and there would be an almighty battle to take them. The carnage that would have necessarily have ensued can only be imagined.

What was von Schmettow's greatest memory of the Occupation?

'More than anything I think of the outstanding leadership in both Islands by the officials who found themselves in almost impossible positions. Their handling of the situation was quite exemplary. I remember too the intense loyalty of the people of the Channel Islands to the country and their king. I am firm in my belief that the Occupation will go down in military history as unique, in which mutual respect of the population and the occupying forces for each other was the ruling factor. It is my sincere hope that one of the pleasant memories of the population of the Islands, in what was an unpleasant five years for them, was the high standard of behaviour by troops who were, in effect, the conquerors for that long period of five years.'

THE ATLANTIC WALL

If you go to the Channel Islands today you will see the German legacy: huge, lumpen and intrusive. Great fortifications, gun emplacements and underground tunnels still disfigure the land and seaboard of what had become the Fortress Islands, to be defended to the death.

The Germans were in the Channel Islands to wage war. At first, in June 1940, they thought that the War would be short, over by Christmas even, and in this short conflict the Channel Islands might usefully serve as a platform for chiefly air attacks by the Luftwaffe on the English mainland. It had not escaped their notice either that they were the British Channel Islands, and to occupy British territory was a fantastic propaganda coup.

However, the nature of the war changed as the weeks went by. There was no quick victory. There was the Battle of Britain; Hitler's thoughts turned towards the east and the pressing need to fulfil his historic role of defeating the Jewish Bolshevik power of Russia. The plan was to defend the Western Front and attack on the Eastern Front.While he was thus engaged, marching into Stalin's state, his already-conquered Western territories would be defended and secured by the building of a mighty Atlantic Wall stretching from the Norwegian fjords all the way along the coastlines of Denmark, Holland, Belgium and France, right up to the northern Spanish frontier. It was a mighty feat of military engineering involving thousands of workers, millions of tons of concrete and thousands of tons of iron and steel. The Channel Islands became part of that Atlantic Wall. Along its whole length nowhere was more heavily fortified against attack than were the Channel Islands of Jersey, Guernsey and Alderney. One twelfth of all the material used to construct the wall came to the Islands. Forts built during the Napoleonic wars and castles built even further back were recommissioned and used to position anti-aircraft and machine guns. Over 650 new concrete fortifications, gun emplacements and observation towers were built in the Islands. The clifftops were mined and the beaches strewn with anti-tank devices.

Altogether it was a huge operation in the course of which many hundreds suffered and died – all for very little military advantage, or so it would seem. Some of the locals benefitted from this great German fortification programme as the Reverend Ord says:

'There is misappropriation of cement, and this is how it is made possible. The Germans force our men to drive for them. Presently the Guernsey drivers will find that friends would be glad of "a bag of cement" from time to time. This is easy enough to arrange. But in time hearts grow bolder. Time and rendezvous are fixed, and willing hands are inspanned for the occasion. The driver with whom the agreement is made possible goes rapidly to the ship for his first load of the morning. Once he has his three tons off he drives at top speed to the place where the Nazi OT boss is ready to receive it. It is unloaded and the boss signs for it, leaving the carbon copy in the driver's book. Immediately the driver flashes back to the harbour and reloads. This time he drives not to the fortification site but to the yard of the "friend" who is standing by to unload. Willing hands make light work, and never was the adage truer! Once the three tons are off, the driver returns for a third load to ship. He has in the meantime carefully traced the Nazi "boss's" signature into his book. After lunch he makes top speed to the site where an irate "boss" demands to know where he has been all this time. To this he replies, "If you would give us some oil to lubricate our vehicles they wouldn't drop to bits as they are doing! I've spent I don't know how long trying to patch up my lorry and I've nearly bust myself to get a second load to you and this is what I get for it!!" How much cement has been diverted from its destined place in the "Atlantic Wall" who can say? But it cheers us up to think of so much undetected sabotage. It makes up for the handful of rotten quislings with their anonymous letters about wireless sets'.

The British had decided as early as 1926 that the Channel Islands had very little if any strategic value, and it was on the basis of this judgement that the decision not to defend the Islands had been taken. The Germans shared this view that the Islands were of little military significance. Of course there was terrific propaganda capital to be made from occupying these tiny bits of British soil, but hardly anyone believed that there was any kind of significant military advantage to be taken from such a manoeuvre. Hardly anyone, that is, apart from Hitler himself who, in the teeth of military opinion to the contrary, came to believe that the Channel Islands had enormous strategic importance and should be fortified to the maximum degree possible, garrisoned with thousands of troops and turned into impregnable fortresses. This obsession the Fuehrer had with the Islands and their fortification was lunacy, and indeed it was known as Hitler's *Inselwahn* or 'Island madness.'

And so it proved, for when the great invasions of D-day came in June 1944 the Islands, with all their guns and a small army of 30,000 soldiers, were simply bypassed, confined to firing off a few hopeless shots at Allied aircraft flying overhead toward France. Men who, as Rommel commented, could have been usefully employed in the vital defence of the West European seaboard were cut off, locked away in what was virtually a POW camp. It was a desperate situation for the Germans, but a very pleasing one for the Allies –

another of those gifts that Hitler insisted on giving his enemies at crucial times during the War.

How did Hitler come to this view of the Islands and their strategic importance in the great German war plan?

The answer seems to be this. As we have seen, the nature of the War in the Western theatre changed absolutely from being a short offensive war to being a defensive war that might go on for a year or even more while the conflict in the East against Russia was being decided. To defend the Western European territories from invasion the Atlantic Wall had to be built. But where was the enemy likely to strike first?

It has been remarked many times and by many authorities that the commando raids on the Channel Islands were, to put it mildly, not very successful. Little or no useful information was gathered, many of the British soldiers were blown up or captured, and the civilian population was put at considerable risk. As military operations these pin-prick raids, these capture and butcher attacks must be seen as failures but, as declarations of intent, Hitler saw them as very potent signs that the Channel Islands would be the first places the British would attack. If this were so, and there were very few 'ifs' in Hitler's vocabulary, then they would be the very last places the British would take, and every effort would be made to prevent that happening. They would be fortified to an extreme degree.

The Islands were in German hands and they would remain so even after the Final Victory. France, Britain, Holland and Belgium might be given back some degree of autonomy, not so the Channel Islands. They would remain resolutely German and become a holiday retreat for the good Nazi *Volk* under the auspices of Robert Ley and his 'Strength through Joy' movement.

Hitler spoke of the Islands thus:

'The inhabitants of the Channel Islands, which we occupy, consider themselves as members of the British Empire rather than as subjects of the King, whom they still regard, not as King, but as the Duke of Normandy. If our occupation troops play their cards properly, we shall have no difficulties there.

I do not approve of the suggestion made to me that these Islands should be colonised by people from Friesland and Ems regions; for whereas these latter are primarily marsh dwellers and cattle drovers, the inhabitants of these Islands are first and foremost small farmers.

If the British had continued to hold these Islands, fortifying them and constructing aerodomes on them, they could have been a veritable thorn in our flesh. As it is, we have now firmly established ourselves there, and with the fortifications we have constructed and the permanent garrison of a whole division, we have ensured against the possibility of the Islands ever again falling into the hands of the British.

After the War they can be handed over to Ley, for, with their wonderful climate, they constitute a marvellous health resort for the 'Strength through Joy' organisation. The Islands are full of hotels as it is, so very little construction will be needed to turn them into ideal rest centres.'

On 15th June 1941 Hitler had issued the directive to fortify the Islands. In November of that year Dr Fritz Todt, who had created the Organisation Todt (OT), to supply labour to the German war machine, came to the Islands preparatory to providing a workforce to build the required and massive fortifications. He did not waste any time. The first OT workers arrived in the Islands a week later, and with them came a change in the nature of the Occupation and the Islanders' perception of it.

Sinel records that towards the end of the year:

'Thousands of foreign workers are being poured into the Island [Jersey]: these are of all nationalities and include Spaniards who, during the Civil War, were interned in France; the majority of these workers are very poor specimens – badly clad and shod and all of them terribly hungry; some were seen on Christmas Day eating raw limpets and acorns, while if they get a chance they are always ready to beg for a bit of bread.'

They were an unsettling sight but worse was to come, from the direction of Russia.

The spectacular success of German armies in the early stages of 'Barbarossa' had meant that thousands upon thousands of Russian soldiers were held in captivity in huge camps without food, shelter or any form of sanitation. The wretched men were simply left to die; what else did *Untermenschen* deserve?

However, as the war proceeded and the demands on the German workforce grew, it dawned on the Germans that here in these trapped vast armies was a potent source of labour. Much better to have the subhumans work for the Third Reich than to have them die pointlessly and profitlessly in some foreign field. The Organisation Todt pulled them out of the camps and transported them like animals in cattle trucks to all the places in the new German empire where their labour was needed. Many arrived in the Channel Islands. Battered, beaten and starved, the sight of them and how they were treated had a profound effect on the Islanders and on their opinions of the invaders. The Island folk had not seen such brutality and viciousness ever before within their shores; Coutanche was appalled by what he saw. He went directly to von Schmettow:

'I told him how I had seen these wretched prisoners being driven to work by their guards when their feet were so sore that they were wrapped up in sacks. I had seen them take the weight off their feet by walking on their elbows on the walls which abounded the road. He was sympathetic and promised to do what he could.'

Schmettow professed himself shocked by the relation of horrors such as these, but despite promising to investigate the circumstances of Russian enslavement there was, as so many regular army officers on all fronts had discovered, little he could do to ameliorate the conditions of those caught up in the workings of the Nazi war machine.

THE OTHER RANKS

'I must say it was almost like being at home. The Jersey people were so normal, they were relaxed and they were not afraid. They were in a relatively good situation, they were well dressed, they had beautiful houses, they had roads, in fact they had everything they needed, there were water-mains, and waste disposal was freely available. There were many, many things that we had at home too. We had this image of perfection. It was as if the War did not exist. It was as if we were on holiday.'

(Hans Kegelmann)

Certainly compared with Russia and the Eastern Front the Channel Islands were wonderful places to be for the ordinary German soldier. As many of them remarked, particularly in the early days of the Occupation, the Islands were a land flowing with milk and honey, and more especially a land in which they felt safe. They did not walk about the streets of St Peter Port or St Helier in fear of being knifed or shot. Everywhere else in occupied Western Europe – France, Holland, Belgium – German soldiers would go about armed with a knife and a sidearm, but not in the Channel

Islands for there was no need. There was no resistance to the German Occupation which expressed itself in assassination attempts on the servants of the Third Reich, in fact for the most part the ordinary soldier could say truthfully that:

'It was, yes, certainly a peaceful time. You see there was no fighting whatsoever. I can only say that it was a very peaceful and friendly atmosphere.'

(Karl Orban)

Though this atmosphere changed somewhat with the arrival of hundreds of Todt workers and Russian slaves to build the fortifications that would transform the Islands into fortresses:

'Jersey, Guernsey, Little Sark, Sark, Alderney were all covered in cement and it was horrible to see how many people from the Nazi Organisation Todt were shipped over to build these bunkers. It was disturbing too to see the resentment all this caused, particularly in the farmers for, you see, we had taken some of their best land on which to build.

The appearance of the foreign workers caused me great distress, to see them living in rough barracks dressed in rags and getting such small rations, working round the clock to build our German bunkers.

It often happened that when one bunker was finished, about three weeks later the pioneers would come along and blow it up because it was in the wrong place.

That was very bad and I was always saying to my comrades there are too many cooks preparing this pie here.'

(Werner Grosskopf)

But, by and large, and for almost the whole of the Occupation period, the ordinary German soldiers had a relatively good time in the Islands.

The natives were peaceful and often pleasant to the German soldiers. Apart from on a very few occasions they were not at all threatening. And there was, for most of the time before the final few months of the War, just about enough food to go round. The contrast with the Russian Front was very stark:

'I came from the Russian Front, from Army Group Centre where we had terrible battering ram battles. By good luck I was chosen as a soldier with experience at the Eastern Front, to be posted to where it was thought the western invasion would be launched. To begin with, I was not happy about leaving my comrades, but when I heard that I was to go to the Channel Islands, I was so happy about it, because for us soldiers the Russian front was so cruel, so terrible, that one could only be glad to get out of that chaos. I was glad to come to Jersey, especially as I had some knowledge of English from school and we had an instructor who had studied at Oxford. I knew, therefore, that I was coming to a people, and would have to fight a people, who are somehow related to us north Germans. For it is well known that the Angles and the Saxons went

over to England in 450. And so we could assume that the way of the English is somehow related, and similar, to ours. This is why one could not help but be pleased at coming to these Islands. We knew that we would be treated correctly and humanly on this English front, even as prisoners, which was not the case at all on many of the other fronts.'

(Private Killmann)

Killmann was right to be so delighted at the posting to the Islands, for all was relatively quiet on the Western Front, the British were not about to carpet-bomb their own people in St Peter Port or St Helier. Nor was it likely, despite Hitler's belief to the contrary, that the Allies would attempt a full-scale invasion of the Channel Islands, again for fear of hurting their own people. The German soldiers were as safe as they could hope to be in a conflict of such magnitude as World War II.

It was all quite peaceful. The only big fear that the German soldier had at this time was that an order might come from the German Supreme Command for him to go to the killing fields of the Eastern Front. Otherwise his days were spent in endless exercises and manoeuvres, inspection parades and guard duties. In his free time he could take himself off to the cinema, though as time went on the never-ending stream of German propaganda films began to lose its appeal. There was also the beach where he could go and exercise, take part in organised

sports days or just swim and laze about on the sand.

He might also try his luck with the local girls. Baron von Aufsess was not the only one on the prowl.

Or, if he were in Jersey and if he liked, he could take himself off to one of the soldiers' recreation centres in St Brelade or St Helier or:

'We could visit the Forum cinema. The front-line theatre came too sometimes. Also there were a few cafes, Maxim and Fortes, we visited them too. So out of working hours we had the opportunity to while away the time somehow. There was a front-line bookshop too, we could buy books; I did. There was no boredom there, at all events not for me.'

(Corporal Meissen)

There might not have been much boredom in the beautiful Islands, but there was the hunger and the starvation that came after the Allied invasion of Normandy in June 1944 which resulted in the Channel Islands being cut off from all their sources of supply in France.

'Then we started to save at every turn. Everything became scarce and it became particularly scarce in the winter of '44-45. I must say we had to go hungry then for all the soldiers' horses had been eaten up. There were no stocks left. Rabbits and breeding fowl were shot, and when they were eaten up, we went on to the cats and dogs. They were shot offhand and

openly and ended up in the soup pot. I can remember that once, after a big flood on the west coast – what do you call those creatures with a lot of arms – the cuttlefish were washed up and all units received orders to send troops to the beaches with buckets and to collect these cuttlefish and prepare them for eating. I must say, however, that they were so disgusting that we couldn't eat any of them at all!'

(Private Killmann)

'That was very bad. That was very very bad. There was nothing left, and at the end when the English finally landed here, they said we had to clear out our quarters. And that same night, a lot more came out, out came the tins, out came the beer, out came the cognac, out came everything, there was still plenty there! But it had all been kept in reserve. We could have held out much longer.

And then we had a right good booze up and a right good feast, and most of us got diarrhoea and shit our trousers, you see it was all too much, all at once.
And we lived another two or three days on the reserve and too much was eaten and too much was drunk, it was too rich and all that. But everything good!'

(Corporal Meissen)

THE ARYAN WAY

The Germans brought into all the occupied countries their ambitions to impose not only political control but also a thoroughgoing system of racial selection and exclusion as well as a policy of weeding out all those who fell short of the Aryan ideal because of their mental or physical incapacity.

They brought too the bureaucracy, the administrative apparatus needed to fulfil their ambitions. It was called the *Feldkommandantur* and was comprised of twelve officers who were not really proper soldiers but rather civil servants in uniform and as such were rather despised by the real military. But they wielded real power when it came to the running of civil affairs in the Islands.

The *Feldkommandantur* was a small outfit but it did not need to be all that big because the majority of the work that had to be done in order to run the civil side of the Occupation was done by the Island authorities themselves. The Island Royal Courts would register the German orders and so turn them into the law of the land which would be administered in large measure by the Islands' civil governments and their attendant bureaucracy.

If the Germans asked for anything they almost always got it without demur, without protest. And what the officers of the *Feldkommandantur* wanted most of all were lists: lists for this, lists for that, lists of foreigners, lists of natives, lists of the British-born, lists of shorthand typists, lists of farmers, lists of their produce, lists of everything it seemed – but, most ominously of all, they wanted lists of Jews, Freemasons and those hospitalised because of mental or physical incapacity, all of whom they wanted either to kill or incarcerate.

The driving force behind the rabid anti-Semitism of the Nazi party was of course provided by Hitler himself. A believer in the authenticity of the protocols of the 'Wise Men of Zion,' he had an extraordinary unblinking and a visceral hatred of the Jews. They were to blame for the corruption of German society. They were to blame for the humiliation of 1918. They were the cancer at the heart of the body politic.

'If ever I am ever really in power, the destruction of the Jews will be my first and most important job. As I have power I shall have gallows after gallows erected, for example, in Munich on the Marienplatz – as many of them as the traffic will allow. Then the Jews will be hanged, one after another, and they will stay hanging until they stink. They will stay hanging as long as hygienically possible. As soon as they are removed then the next group will follow and that will continue until the last Jew in Munich is exterminated. Exactly the same procedure will be followed in other cities until Germany is cleansed of the last Jew.'
(Hitler in conversation with Josef Hell 1922)

And later:

'I suddenly perceived the moral mildew of the chosen race. Was there any shady undertaking, any form of foulness, especially in cultural life, in which at least one Jew did not participate? On putting the probing knife carefully to that kind of abscess one immediately discovered, like a maggot in a putrescent body, a little *Jew who was often blinded by the sudden light.'*
(*Adolf Hitler,* Mein Kampf)

So Hitler wrote in 1924 whilst in prison in the fortress of Landsberg on the River Leck for his leading role in the Bürgerbräu Keller Putsch on 8th November 1923. His release and subsequent rise to absolute power saw no change to his anti-Semitic stance, indeed it got more and more rabid as the years went by.

The Nuremberg Laws were passed, effectively disenfranchising the Jews from all political and cultural life; they were excommunicated from all of German society. They were to become non-persons, beaten, robbed, incarcerated, deported, transported and eventually annihilated.

This thoroughgoing anti-Semitism came to the Channel Islands in the baggage of the officers of the *Feldkommandantur.*

As in Holland, Belgium and France it did not take long for the first *Feldkommandantur,* Colonel Schumacher, to present anti-Jewish orders for registration in the Island Courts. Schumacher arrived on 9th August 1940 – the first order was passed into law on 21st October in Jersey and on 23rd October in Guernsey. There were to be nine in all.

Clifford Orange, Chief Registration Officer in Jersey, and Inspector Sculpher, head of the Guernsey police force, got busy compiling lists for their German master entrusted with the implementation of these measures. In the first instance this was Dr Gottfried von Stein, but he was succeeded by OKVR Dr Wilhelm Casper who in civilian life before the war had been a lawyer. After the war he became, if not a liar, at least somewhat economical with the truth concerning the German treatment of the Jews found in the Islands, as Madeleine Bunting discovered in correspondence with him in 1995. In this exchange Casper says that the two Viennese Jews, presumably Therese Steiner and Auguste Spitz, had simply returned to Vienna. No mention here of Auschwitz, or of Marianne Grünfeld for that matter. He goes on to say:

'I had not permitted Hitler's persecution of the Jews in the Islands. It contradicted the German constitution and was not democratically legitimated.'

But, despite the Doctor's protestations to the contrary, the few Jews in the Islands were persecuted, as we have seen. Therese Steiner and Auguste Spitz did not just return to Vienna, they were, along with Marianne Grünfeld, and with the active connivance of the Guernsey authorities, carted off to a death camp where they perished. Dr Casper, by way of exonerating explanation, remembered many years after the war:

'Nobody at that time on the Channel Islands – neither the Bailiff nor I – knew what would happen with the evacuated Jewish people … we thought they would

be interned like the other people evacuated from the Islands.'

But this is not true. He knew full well that the Jews would not end up interned in the relatively comfortable camps of Biberach and Laufen along with the rest of the Islands' deportees.

They would end up in concentration camps like Ravensbruck, Auschwitz and Belsen, or, as he says in his communications with Paris headquarters, in Dachau, where he wished they could have been.

Casper, according to his own account, continued to shield the Jews from death and destruction when he was transferred from the Islands to Denmark to serve under Werner Best. He claims that he was a friend and ally of Georg Duckwitz, who was opposed to the Nazi actions against the Jews and who contributed materially to the escape of almost the entire Jewish population of Denmark at considerable risk to his own life. Casper writes this:

'After leaving the Channel Islands I was the negotiator of the German forces in Denmark with the Danish government in the headquarters at Silkeborg in Jutland, the continental part of Denmark. One day my friend Duckwitz, the German navigation officer for Denmark in Copenhagen, told me the day when the Jews in Denmark should be transported to the East. He instructed the chief of the underground organisation at Silkeborg, a high forest official with whom I had

connection. You can read in the history books that almost the whole population of Denmark escaped to Sweden. Duckwitz was the first German ambassador in Denmark after the war. We ventured our lives in wartime.'

There was another and, in the Islands, much larger group of people who were at risk from the Germans. These were the Freemasons – almost as much hated by the Nazis as the Jews. But in contrast, and, some have said, shameful contrast, to the Jews, voices were raised in high places to plead their cause. No protest was made against the registration of the first anti-Jewish orders in either Island by the Superior Council or the Controlling Committee. Ambrose Sherwill, it is true, says in his account of the time that Abraham Lainé did object to the very first order of October 1940, but there is some confusion here. According to Sherwill, Lainé was revolted at the idea of the Islands' Jews being forced to wear the yellow Star of David, but there was no such proposal in the first order. The instruction that all Jews over the age of six should be forced to wear the six pointed yellow star with the name 'Jew' at its centre was contained in the eighth order, published two years later in the June of 1942. This was registered without any recorded protest in the Royal Court of Guernsey. There was, however, a successful intervention in the introduction of the order made by Bailiff Coutanche in Jersey. He 'advised' Wilhelm Casper that:

'this order should not be registered or put into execution.'

(Bailiff of Jersey files)

Casper took the advice; the eighth order was not registered in Jersey, but yellow stars were ordered anyway. They never arrived.

Coutanche's protest is the only one for which there is documentation. Before this time of June 1942 there had been no protest on behalf of the Jews. It cannot be said that the best interests of the Jewish Islanders were well protected. On the contrary, they were sacrificed on the altar of good relations with the Germans. As has been said many times, the battle to protect the Jewish population was one neither the Jersey nor the Guernsey government was prepared to fight. Had they chosen to fight they would almost certainly have lost the battle but gained a great moral victory of inestimable value for the reputation of the Islands in the post-War years.

THE FREEMASONS
They were prepared to fight, however, when the Germans, in accordance with Nazi theology, went gunning for the Freemasons. Again the impetus for this action came from the very top, from Hitler himself, who saw Freemasonry as a vehicle for Jewish ambitions to dominate the world. Here is Hitler in *Mein Kampf* talking of how the Jew went about his task:

'In order to strengthen his political position, he directed his efforts towards

removing the barrier of racial and civic discrimination which had hitherto hindered his advance at every turn. With characteristic tenacity he championed the cause of religious tolerance for this purpose and in the Freemason organisation, which had fallen completely into his hands, he found a magnificent weapon which helped him achieve his ends. Government circles as well as the higher sections of the political and commercial bourgeoisie fell prey to his plans through his manipulation of the Masonic net.'

Hitler was quite clear. Freemasonry was an international political network of Jewish and Jewish-inspired men whose aims and philosophy were wholly inimical to the survival of the Third Reich, and as such all Freemasons should be rounded up and imprisoned and their property looted.

As with the Jews, it did not take long for the Germans to begin their destructive work in the Islands. In January 1941 the *Einsatzstab Reichsleiter Rosenberg,* a species of hit-squad under the direction of the head Nazi philosopher Alfred Rosenberg, came to the Islands with the express purpose of dismantling the Masonic temples. Rosenberg's men took all the ornate Masonic regalia, entire libraries, rooms full of furniture, even the carpets, from the Temples in Jersey and Guernsey and transported it all back to Germany, to Berlin where it was put on show for the Berliners to gawp at and learn what a threat Freemasonry was to the Fatherland.

These Masonic riches were never returned to their rightful owners. They couldn't be because they were destroyed in one of the hundreds of terrible bombing raids on the German capital which began in such deadly earnest in 1942.

But the Germans were not content with just this bit of pillaging. They wanted more – a lot more. In the November of 1941 an order was issued to sequester all the assets of the Freemasons. This was a step too far. Victor Carey was roused to action to forestall this act of grand larceny. Colonel Knackfuss had informed Coutanche and Carey that:

'According to a decree of the Military Commander in France, the property of the Freemasons' Lodges is to be liquidated.'

Guernsey's Lieutenant-Governor, Chief Mason and Provincial Grand Master, Bailiff Victor Carey, consulted Alexander Coutanche over in Jersey. He suggested rather cleverly that the best way to protect the threatened assets would be for the Masons to transfer them voluntarily to the States, that is to say to the treasuries of Jersey and Guernsey where, re-titled as government assets, they would be safe from thieving German hands. There was a distinct air of positive resistance about the whole Masonic issue.

Eschewing the avowed policy of complete cooperation with the occupying power, Victor Carey refused to countenance the Island government implementing the anti-Masonic Order:

'If nevertheless the exigencies of war require the dissolution of the Guernsey Lodges and the disposal of their property I suggest that this should be effected by German order rather than by local legislation.'

Victor Carey protested. He was not 'begging to report' the existence of half a dozen Jews in the Island this time, he was saying, 'Leave me, my Freemasons and our property alone!'

He was only partially successful in his protest. Much Masonic property was taken by the Germans, but in February 1942 the agreement with the Germans for the transfer of assets to the States was entered into, and approved by the Royal Court. This was a victory and most importantly it flagged up the willingness of the local authorities to fight for the interests of at least one group of Islanders. From that time forward the Freemasons were afforded a good deal of protection. For example, when, in the February of 1943, the German High Command in Berlin issued an order for the deportation of, among others, 'Jews and high ranking Freemasons.' No Freemasons were in fact deported. Indeed no Freemasons in the Islands suffered any inconvenience for being a Freemason for the rest of the War. Elsewhere they were pursued to the point of death but not in the Channel Islands. There were nine orders

against the Jews registered in the Royal Courts. There were no anti-Masonic orders registered at all. And yet the Masons were almost as much hated by the Nazis as were the Jews. Why was this? Why were the Island Masons granted an immunity denied their brothers on the continent?

The answer is possibly that the German officers running the Occupation in the islands were not SS officers, nor were they out-and-out Nazis. In fact they were rather frightened of being replaced by the SS if they failed in any way to keep the local governments acquiescent. The Islanders themselves were fearful of the same thing. With hindsight it is easy to say that there was therefore room for discussion, room for compromise and a space for protest, more perhaps than the Islanders were aware of. But they chose to err on the side of caution, as they were bound to do given that so many lives were at stake.

It seemed, too, that von Schmettow, von Aufsess, Prince von Oettingen, Bandelow and even Knackfuss sought, on various occasions, to moderate the orders from Paris in the Islanders' favour, to soften the blows from a rampant and triumphant Nazism. One thinks immediately of the 'lost' or 'forgotten' first deportation order or Schmettow's intervention in the Nicolle and Symes affair. Of course when the order came direct from the Fuehrer there was no room at all for local manoeuvre or resistance, but otherwise Schmettow's velvet glove was always more in evidence than his iron fist, and for that the Islanders were very grateful.

At the very last, when the circumstances of the Occupation became quite desperate, the luck of the Islanders ran out. A new man arrived on the scene – a navy man who was a dyed-in-the-wool Nazi, *Vizeadmiral* Friedrich Hüffmeier, whose presence meant danger for the starved and beleaguered Islanders.

ENDGAME

The appointment of a navy man was not too surprising after the July assassination plot of 1944 which had been devised and executed by army officers. But Hitler had never trusted his generals either from a tactical or, latterly, a political point of view. This dislike and distrust drove the ex-corporal to promote himself to Commander-in-Chief of the Army in 1941 – just as German military strategy in the East was beginning to fall apart: a move that was the greatest godsend to Stalin and the Allies in the whole of the War.

If Hitler could not place any faith in his army generals, nor in the obese and drug-addicted Goering in charge of the increasingly malfunctioning and under-performing Luftwaffe, who could he turn to for unconditional loyalty, unwavering and effective support? The answer came in the shape of the navy, and in particular Karl Doenitz, Grand Admiral of the Third Reich's navy, an absolute supporter of the Fuehrer and

one of the first to rush down to Rastenburg and the Wolf's Lair to wish the shaken leader well and to swear undying loyalty to the man after the July bomb plot.

Hitler must have been impressed, for when Goering and Himmler fell out of favour for reaching too far and too soon for supreme power in the fast-disintegrating state, Hitler excommunicated them from the Fuehrer temple and declared in his last will and testament that the great admiral should be his successor.

And while Karl Doenitz was up in Felspern by the Danish border running what was left of the Third Reich, another faithful navy man, *Reich Vizeadmiral* Friedrich Hüffmeier was down in the Channel Islands, far behind the Allied lines, cut off, beleaguered, but still determined to defend the Fortress Islands, and defend them to the point of annihilation of both civilians and soldiers.

Hüffmeier was a very good Nazi. But he was not such a good sailor. When he was commanding the *Scharnhorst* his ineptitude and his bad seamanship, so obvious to his ship's company, meant that he was not the most popular or highly regarded officer in the German Navy. The author John Winton describes the *Scharnhorst* crew's reaction to Hüffmeier:

'But it took only a short time for Scharnhorst's ship's company to decide *to a man that 'Poldi' Hüffmeier was a walking disaster area. They believed he owed his appointment more to social influence than to ability, and he quickly showed himself a poor seaman with almost no talent for ship handling.'*

Winton goes on to itemise mistakes and accidents that happened to the *Scharnhorst* while *Vizeadmiral* Friedrich Hüffmeier was in command. He ran the state-of-the-art battle cruiser aground off Hela while speeding at 26 knots. This was bad seamanship but more was to follow. Leaving Gdynia harbour, he drove his vessel across a buoy wire which consequently wrapped itself around the right-hand screw causing enough damage to require a stay in the dockyard when the cruiser was desperately needed to fight the war on the high seas. And then, before he was mercifully replaced by *Kapitan Zur See* Julius Hintze, Hüffmeier contrived to collide with a submarine, U523, on a training exercise in the Baltic.

In the summer of 1944 Hüffmeier was appointed Navy Commander of the Channel Islands alongside but subordinate to the Chief of Staff of Armed Forces, General Graf von Schmettow.

The admiral set about a process of undermining von Schmettow, who he characterised as being 'soft' in his attitude to the prosecution of the War; 'too lenient' in his attitude towards the Islanders; and an 'exponent of compromise'. He succeeded brilliantly. What Hüffmeier lacked in navigational

expertise, he more than made up for in skills in political in-fighting. Baron von Aufsess has this entry in his diary for 1st March 1945:

'Yesterday brought shattering news. At lunchtime, Heider informed me that the General (Schmettow) and Helldorf have been dismissed from office. From 12 hours midday, today, Hüffmeier takes over as Commander-in-Chief of the Channel Islands. Other far-reaching changes in Command have also been ordered. The whole business smacks of a putsch or coup d'état'.

The Baron was right in describing Hüffmeier's seizure of power as a putsch or *coup d'état*. It was exactly that. A successful attempt to take power away from the *Wehrmacht* officers who were more and more disinclined to cling to the *Fuehrerprinzip* and give it to *Kriegsmarine* admirals who were very much inclined to follow the Fuehrer into the very last twilight of the gods.

No reason was ever given for Schmettow's removal, beyond the bald statement that he had retired back to the fatherland for health reasons, though, as he himself remarked bitterly, he had not seen a doctor in years.

'Now he is returning to a Germany where he will not have a roof over his head, where his homeland has been overrun by the enemy and where his family must be on the road somewhere as refugees'.
(von Aufsess)

He would leave behind the Islands in the control of a second-rate sailor and a devoted Nazi, a man prepared, as he himself put it, 'to eat grass' rather than surrender.

Every one of the beleaguered and starving German soldiers in the Islands might die, but so be it. In the rhetoric of collapsing Nazism, better Wagnerian Armageddon than shameful 1918-style laying down of arms. Never must that happen again!

This order was published on March 3rd 1945:

Hail our beloved Fuehrer!
At noon on the 28th February 1945, I have taken over the command of the Channel Islands and of the Fortress of Guernsey from General von Schmettow, who has been called home for reasons of health. I have only one aim: to hold out until final victory, I believe in the mission of our Fuehrer and of our people. I shall serve them with inimitable loyalty.

> *Hüffmeier. Vice-admiral and Commander of the Channel Islands.*

And all of this meant one thing and one thing only for the Islanders. The great hunger might have been averted but now there was a huge danger of violent and comprehensive annihilation of the civilian population in a fight between the invading Allies and the defending Germans. Constellation attacks on the Islands had been abandoned for the reason that civilian deaths would inevitably be huge in the ensuing conflict. There could be no doubt about it, the Islands and the Islanders would be reduced to rubble and ashes just like all the other places declared to be 'fortresses' in those final desperate weeks of the War.

The admiral was undeterred by such a prospect. Von Aufsess records him giving a defiant speech on the occasion of Hitler's birthday:

'Hitler's birthday was celebrated by a rousing speech given by the admiral. He is certainly a worthy pupil of Goebbels. The cinema where the big gathering of troops was held was decked out in the best Nazi tradition, huge flags, floodlights attendant orchestra etc. The admiral and his adjutant (Reich), so sadly lacking in inches, appeared on the platform as 'the long and short of it'. Hüffmeier snapped smartly to attention and greeted the assembly with a loud 'Heil Hitler', which was vociferously returned.

Taking his stand on the rostrum, he allowed half a minute to elapse in solemn silence. Then this scion of a family of Protestant pastors began his Nazi sermon, with evangelical fervour, but on behalf of Adolf instead of God.'

And the burden of his speech was resistance to the bitter end, no matter how many German soldiers died, no matter how many civilians died.

In the end the looked-for Armageddon did not happen, but it took Hitler's

German soldiers pose with some rather apprehensive Islanders for propaganda photos.

The Guernsey housewives queue for food in St Peter Port.

And some of the Island girls have a good time.

The good ship 'Vega' in sight of Jersey.

Island policeman posing for yet another propaganda photo.

Major Albrecht Lanz.

Feldkommandant Colonel Knackfuss.

On the lookout in Guernsey.

Von Schmettow, the Islanders friend.

Observation towers which remain around the Islands today.

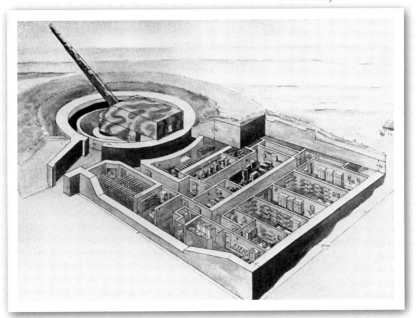

The great Mirus battery in Guernsey with its huge Russian naval gun – the biggest in the Islands.

Zimmerman's unwise salute.

Generalmajor Heine presents his I.D. to Captain Herzmark of the Intelligence Corps.

Taking orders before the surrender.

Generalmajor Heine signs the surrender document aboard HMS Bulldog.

HMS Bulldog

suicide to prevent it, for with the Fuehrer's death came the appointment of Hüffmeier's boss, Grand Admiral Karl Doenitz, one man who Hüffmeier would not, could not disobey. So when the order was passed to the admiral to lay down his arms and surrender peacefully, the *Kriegsmarine* man obeyed.

HMS *Bulldog* (the same ship that had captured the enigma machine) and HMS *Beagle* signalled instruction that the surrender to Brigadier Snow of all German forces in the Channel Islands should take place at sea, four miles south of Guernsey.

In the end, Hüffmeier sent the young, febrile and very Nazi junior officer *Kapitanleutenant* Armin Zimmerman as his representative to discuss not unconditional surrender as expected but the terms of an armistice.

Clutching his leather document case, young, pale and thin, he cut a somewhat forlorn figure on the deck of HMS *Bulldog*. He did not advance his cause very much by shooting out a straight-armed 'Heil Hitler' salute, not once but twice, before explaining his mission. He was told in fairly forceful terms that the British were not at all interested in discussing an armistice, what they needed was an unconditional surrender by someone with a few more pips on his shoulder than Armin. He remained belligerent, saying that the two warships should withdraw out of range of the Island guns because the general ceasefire signed in Rheims on 7th May did not come into force until 9th May and consequently they might well be fired upon. The young *Kapitanleutnant* must have enjoyed his little demonstration of power, much as the sailors aboard the British warships enjoyed seeing him getting a very wet bottom riding in the back of a little dinghy taking him back on a choppy sea to Guernsey and the admiral.

Zimmerman returned to the *Bulldog* a few hours later, but this time accompanied by a glum General Major Siegfried Heine, Admiral Hüffmeier's deputy and Commandant of Jersey. The articles of surrender were signed at 07.15.

It was the end of the war in the Channel Islands.

TERMS OF UNCONDITIONAL SURRENDER FOR CHANNEL ISLANDS

The Commander, GERMAN Forces, CHANNEL ISLANDS, hereby announces unconditional surrender of the Forces under his command to the Supreme Commander, Allied Expeditionary Force. The Supreme Commander, Allied Expeditionary Force, accordingly announces the following Terms of Surrender with which the Commander, GERMAN Forces, CHANNEL ISLANDS, undertakes to comply.

1. GERMAN Forces have ceased hostilities on land, sea and air; the GERMAN Commander has issued instructions to all forces under his command to cease hostilities at 0001 hours DBST on 9th May, 1945.

2.   a. All GERMAN armed forces and organisations equipped with weapons shall completely disarm themselves at once.

   b. GERMAN forces and all civilians accompanying the GERMAN forces will remain in their present position pending further instructions.

   c. All GERMAN forces shall be declared prisoners of war.

3. All aircraft shall remain grounded.

4. All GERMAN shipping and all shipping of the United Nations at the disposal of the GERMANS will remain in port. Crews to remain on board pending further instructions.

5.   a. The GERMAN Commander will hold intact and maintain in good condition and will hand over to the Allied representative at such time and places as may be prescribed:-

   (1) All arms, ammunition, military equipment, stores and supplies, aircraft, naval vessels and merchant shipping and all other war material, together with records pertaining thereto.

   (2) All military installations and establishments and all factories, plants and other civil institutions, together with plans and records thereof, as required.

   (3) All transportation and communications facilities and equipment, by land, water or air, and records thereof.

   (4) All livestock, crops, food, wines, spirits, fuel and water supplies under his control.

   (5) All submarine cables, telephones and telegraph installations. to be handed over in full working order.

   b. The GERMAN Commander shall provide all facilities for movement and land communications of Allied troops and agencies; he will maintain all transportation in good order and repair and will furnish the labour services and plant necessary therefor.

/6...........

Chapter 6
The Empire Strikes Back

The thought of British territory under the heel of the Hun was anathema to Winston Churchill. It was an unendurable state of affairs for the old Victorian cavalryman. Something had to be done. Plans should be studied to land British troops secretly by night on the Islands to kill or capture the invaders. Commandos should be sent in to carry out the task. But first, some kind of reconnaissance trip should be made to ascertain the disposition and strength of the German forces in the Islands, starting with Guernsey. Only six days after the Germans had occupied the Islands a man was on his way, his mission, to gather as much information as possible on the military status of the Island. How many enemy troops were there and was Guernsey going to be used as a springboard for the invasion of the British mainland? That man was Hubert Nicolle, himself a Guernseyman, but he was not the first choice; the first suggestion had been that a Captain Cantan should go because he had Sark connections. Very close connections actually, for he was the son-in-law of the Dame of Sark, Sibyl Hathaway, but he was passed over for the mission for the very good reason that if he were captured then that could be the cause of great embarrassment to his mother-in-law. So it was to be the 20-year-old Lieutenant Hubert Nicolle, late of the Guernsey Militia (which had been withdrawn from the Island as part of the demilitarisation process), who was to cross the dangerous seas to Guernsey. He was informed of the risks involved. He would not be in uniform and could therefore be shot if captured. He acknowledged the risk and bravely accepted the mission. Nicolle was to travel post-haste to Plymouth and board a Royal Navy submarine which would take him across the water to his native island. He was told to concentrate his investigative efforts on the St Peter Port harbour area and on the airport.

It was discovered a little late in the day that there was no boat provided that could take him on the last leg of his journey from the submarine to the shore. A canoe was hastily purchased from the toy department of Gamages stores in London and Nicolle, clutching the canoe in a brown parcel, rushed down to Plymouth to join the H43 which was to ferry him across the Channel. There was a small hitch when it was discovered that the canoe was too large to pass through the submarine's hatch. Crew member Lieutenant McGeoch turned ship's carpenter and cleverly remedied the situation by fixing hinges to the wooden framing so as to make it a collapsible canoe which could then very easily be pushed up through the submarine hatch and assembled on deck.

At 9.18 p.m. on Saturday 6th July the submarine crept slowly down the Plymouth Sound, out beyond Drake's Island and the as-yet-unbombed Plymouth, and set her course for Guernsey, 90 miles away.

This operation was named Operation Anger, and it was indeed anger that had created it: anger at the thought of Germans stepping on to British soil. Anger at the thought of British Citizens being enslaved by a foreign power,under the heel of the Hun.

On Monday 8th July Hubert Nicolle, the very first British commando, successfully landed in Guernsey at Le Jaonnet Bay, climbed up the cliff and commenced his work. He spent three days on the Island and did an excellent job in finding out how many troops were there, where they were concentrated and what the activity at the harbour and the airport was. He discovered that there were exactly 469 German soldiers in the Island and he could be absolutely sure of this because he knew the managing director of Guernsey's big grocery stores, Le Riches Ltd, Mr H. H. Collins. Le Riches supplied all the German troops with their food and consequently knew precisely how many there were in the Island. Nicolle was further helped in his mission by the fact that his father, Emile Nicolle, was a very senior civil servant, and as such had direct access to much of the information that his son was looking for.

After three days, his work done and as pre-arranged, Nicolle headed for the costal rendezvous where he boarded the submarine that was to take him home.

On the darkened beach, as he was leaving, he met two of his colleagues from the Guernsey Militia, Desmond Mulholland and Phillip Martel, who were coming into the Island to carry out phase two of Operation Anger.

On his return to London he was told that Prime Minister Winston Churchill wished to see him, as the operation in Guernsey was very near to his heart. Nicolle felt honoured by the great man's interest and looked forward very much to meeting him.

Unfortunately at the last moment the war leader was called away on urgent business. Hubert Nicolle was more than disappointed.

Desmond Mulholland and Phillip Martel had come as a forward party to facilitate the landing of the 140-strong No. 3 Commando Unit planned for the night of 12th July. This part of the strategy was called Operation Ambassador. Three raiding parties were to be landed under cover of darkness. One party was to attack the airport and destroy all the enemy planes they could, the other two to find and kill as many Germans as could be found at the old British barracks. It was an ambitious plan.

And it all had to be achieved within a

two hour period under cover of night. On the night of 12th July, Martel and Mulholland went down to La Jaonnet beach as arranged to guide the landing of one of the three raiding parties from No.3 Commando Unit. They waited all that night and for three long nights after that, but no one came. They did not come because it had been decided to postpone the landing for 48 hours because of unfavourable weather conditions in the Channel. There was no way of communicating this information to the two men.

When the raiding parties did eventually arrive in Guernsey waters, two of the three got lost, including the party due to land, at Martel and Mulholland's signal, on La Jaonnet beach.

HMS *Saladin* and HMS *Scimitar* successfully dispatched the three groups towards Guernsey but the party intended for La Jaonnet managed to miss Guernsey altogether, and ended up off Sark before giving up and returning to the mother ships. Another likewise returned because they did not receive the signal to land which they were mistakenly expecting. However the third raiding party, commanded by Lieutenant Colonel J. F. Durnford Slater, did manage to land at Petit Port – but that was only the beginning of their troubles.

The failures in navigation have been plausibly explained, not by incompetence or lack of preparation, but by the use of an anti-mine device known as the degaussing system. Major John Smale, who was part of Durnford Slater's group, explained:

'The degaussing system was a wire or a cable around the ship with an electric current so mines would not be attracted. It was not realised that it was upsetting the compass. We nearly missed Guernsey. It was only by Durnford Slater saying to the Captain "There is an Island over there, it is not ours by any chance?" So we did a left turn and got to Guernsey.'

Because of the 48 hour postponement of Operation Ambassador the tide was high when they finally came to the shore. The launches grounded on rocks and not on the expected smooth sand, and when the men jumped in, the water came up to their necks, their battle dress and boots filled up and their weapons got wet. Nonetheless they struggled ashore and started up the 300-foot cliffs. It was a long haul but a few minutes after reaching the top and starting on their mission a piece of good fortune came their way in the shape of an RAF Anson aeroplane circling just above their heads.

This manoeuvre had been preplanned in London where it was rightly thought that the noise from the aircraft would cover any commotion the raiders might make. Since Durnford Slater's men had seemingly woken the entire dog population of the Island and set them a-barking this contribution from the RAF was more than welcome.

But then things began to go wrong. Part of their mission was to attack a machine gun post on the Jerbourg Peninsula. One of their number, de Crespigny, broke into a little wooden bungalow to try and get information as to the whereabouts of German troops who might be in the vicinity. It was a forlorn enterprise, for the owner, Bill Crocker, had a stammer and when de Crespigny tried to question him he was so frightened he stuttered even more and in a very loud voice indeed. So loud was his voice in fact that the soldier, afraid that Bill's shrieking would alert the Germans to their presence, smacked him round the head with the butt of his rifle so hard as to render him unconscious.

When they did finally creep up on the machine gun nest, they found it unmanned, not a German in sight. No one to take prisoner or to kill. The same was true of the old British barracks which they entered next. No Germans! It was all going a bit pear-shaped. They had cut a few cables, it was true. They had built a barricade made of granite stones taken from Fred Veale's house to protect their escape route. But Durnford Slater's little group were very aware that their raid had not been anything like a success. They were also aware, because of the lack of any noise from that direction, that the projected attack on the airport, which had been the major objective of Operation Ambassador, could not have taken place.

And their time was up! In fact it was very nearly 3 a.m., by which time they should have been well clear of the Island. Durnford Slater's men ran back down the 300-foot cliff to the beach. Durnford Slater himself had almost made it to the bottom of the steep steps when he suddenly lost his footing and fell, his cocked pistol going off very loudly. The Germans manning the machine gun positioned on the other side of La Jaonnet Bay opened fire, but for some reason the fire was directed out to sea and not down onto the little beach. Durnford Slater could see the dim outlines of the launches waiting to take them off. They were a hundred yards out but they could not come any closer because the sea was too rough and the rocks too near. Instead a little dinghy was sent in several times to pick the men up in groups of two or three.

On the fifth run, however, disaster struck, for a great wave tossed the dinghy against the rocks. One soldier was thought to have drowned and the dinghy was a complete write-off.

A desperate Durnford Slater then ordered his men to swim out to the launches. At this point three of the men confessed that they could not swim. Durnford Slater was very far from pleased as he had, very wisely, specifically requested only men who could swim to form his troop for Operation Ambassador. Nobody had bothered to check whether that was actually the case.

He had no choice but to leave them behind. And so it was they became the first British commandos to fall into enemy hands. They remained prisoners until the end of the War.

Durnford Slater summed up the entire experience thus:

'The raid was of course a ridiculous, almost a comic failure. We had captured no prisoners. We had done no serious damage. We had caused no casualties to the enemy. Even the roll of wire for Lieutenant Smale's roadblock had proved too heavy to lift up the steep steps. There had been no machine gun nest, and to all practical purposes no barracks. We had cut through three telegraph cables. A youth in his teens could have done the same.'

Churchill was even less pleased, if that were possible, than Durnford Slater. He fired off an irate note to Combined Operations command:

'Let there be no more silly fiascos like those perpetrated in Guernsey. The idea of working all those coasts up against us by pinprick raids is one to be strictly avoided.'

The great war leader also inveighed against what he called 'fulsome communiqués' delivered after these raids which gave an unreal victorious gloss to what had been abject military failures. Another person who was not impressed by the commando raid was Ambrose Sherwill, President of the Controlling Committee of the States of Guernsey.

He was an angry man. He wanted to send a strong letter to Charles Markbreiter at the Home Office trenchantly making the case against any kind of military intervention in the Island. The message read:

'On the night of the 14–15 July an armed British force landed in Guernsey. They assaulted an old man living in the vicinity of the landing place, cut some private telephone wires, erected a barricade across the road and left behind a quantity of arms, ammunition, clothing and accoutrements. Certain of their number became detached from the force and have been taken prisoner. There were no casualties.

I do not know what the object of the landing was but to us it seems senseless. Until it was definitely established that an armed force landed, the German military authorities quite naturally suspected a locally-staged incident and although the truth soon became apparent, certain restrictions have been imposed as a result of the landing.

The object of this letter is to ask that you will make the strongest representations in the proper quarter to the effect that, it having been decided by the British Government, in the interests of the people of the Channel Islands, to demilitarise them, military activities of the kind referred to above are unwelcome to us and are likely to result in loss of life among the civilian population and generally to make our position much more unpleasant than it is. Please urge this very forcibly. The Bailiff was amazed when he heard of the landing and in writing to you thus I know I am expressing his views and that of many prominent people here.'

Sherwill's point is illustrated perfectly by the experience of the two officers, Mulholland and Martel, who were left stranded in Guernsey because their rescue vessel had not turned up. They were forced to shift for themselves in order to escape. They went to Perelle Bay, stole a little boat and set sail for England, as they thought. But the two knew little of navigation and even less of sailing. They almost grounded the little boat on the rocks and almost capsized before they gave up the idea of such an escape entirely and returned, with great difficulty, to shore.

Thereafter Martel and Mulholland managed to cross over to Sark in the hope of finding another boat in which to make good their escape.

Unfortunately for them the Germans had confined all the fishing boats to Creux harbour Those of you who have been to the Island of Sark will know that there is only one way to get to and from the harbour – through a narrow tunnel cut through the rock of the 200-foot-high cliffs. Of course, at the time of Martel and Mulholland's visit, this tunnel was very carefully guarded indeed. There was just no way that a boat could be taken from there without

the Germans seeing.

The two men gave up the attempt and returned, crestfallen, to Guernsey. Now Guernsey is a very small island and it was, and is, very difficult to pass unnoticed. They were seen and recognised by quite a number of people, and the longer they stayed the more they would be spotted. This meant that more and more lives were put in danger, for under Occupation law it was a capital offence to know of the presence of enemy agents and not to inform the German authorities of the *Feldkommandantur*.

Martel and Mulholland had had enough.

They knew that they would have to surrender to the enemy, but what was the best way of doing this? They went to Ambrose Sherwill, President of the Controlling Committee, for help in giving themselves up. Ambrose Sherwill gave them that help willingly but at enormous risk not only to his own life but that of his family.

The two officers were in civilian clothes. This being so, if they went ahead with their avowed intention to give themselves up, there was no question but that they would be shot as spies.

On the other hand, if they could appear in uniform they could, and would, then be treated as prisoners of war.

Uniforms had to be found, and quickly

too. It was quite literally a matter of life and death. There was a number of uniforms at the Town arsenal. Sherwill knew of this and organised a break-in. Two army uniforms were found. So far so good. But then Sherwill, as an ex-army man himself, saw with dismay that there were Royal Guernsey Militia buttons on the tunics instead of British army ones.

Something of a giveaway, it was thought. Fortunately for all concerned the wife of the Arsenal's caretaker proved a speedy and nimble seamstress and cut off the offending buttons and replaced them with those of the British army.

There was a further little hitch (literally), when it was discovered that one of the uniforms lacked braces. Ambrose Sherwill volunteered a pair of his own.

Thus attired in the uniform of the British army, Martel and Mulholland were taken by Sherwill to German headquarters in the Channel Islands Hotel and there they surrendered to Dr Maass. Curiously, and some might say with a Nelson's eye, Maass did not notice that the two men were dressed not in battle dress or fatigues, as would have been expected on such an expedition as theirs, but in ordinary service dress, that is to say in a 'walking-out' dress worn for semi-formal occasions. However that may be, the two men were not shot out of hand as spies but treated, as Sherwill planned they should be, as prisoners of war. They remained as such until the end of hostilities in 1945. Ambrose Sherwill was a much relieved man.

Three days after Martel and Mulholland had been taken off the Island by the Germans, another Guernseyman, Stanley Ferbrache of the Hampshires, not knowing what had happened, landed in the Island to rescue them and take them back to mainland UK on an MTB. He was too late. A last failure in a doomed operation.

Sherwill's letter begging that no more commando raids on the Island be carried out had not reached Charles Markbreiter. Sherwill had certainly presented his letter to the *Kommandant* to be forwarded to the Home Office. But it was never sent, and certainly never received or acted upon by Combined Operations, for towards the end of August, Lieutenant Hubert Nicolle was recalled to Combined Operations and given a task very similar to that of July.

He had to return to Guernsey to gather as much information as possible about the whereabouts of German troops, the defensive arrangements they had made and, most importantly, what sort of activity was going on at the airport and the harbour. Two men would be required for the job and Hubert chose a fellow-Guernseyman, Lieutenant James Symes, to accompany him on this dangerous excursion back to their home Island. The two were ideally suited for such an exercise, both being

Guernseymen born and bred and therefore possessing an intimate knowledge of the life and geography of the Island. Furthermore, and most importantly, Hubert's father, Emile Nicolle, was secretary of the Controlling Committee and therefore had access to every kind of information about the Occupation that would be of great value to British Intelligence.

Hubert Nicolle and James Symes landed at 3.00 a.m. on 3rd September. First port of call was to Hubert's uncle, Frank Nicolle, the deputy harbour master who could, of course, tell them of the shipping in and out of the Island, vital intelligence for the British.

Hubert Nicolle had been instructed to contact Ambrose Sherwill, which he did through his father, Emile. But Ambrose was very unhappy, to put it mildly, at the thought of yet more British agents in Guernsey. Here was more trouble for the Islanders. Emile got a message from Ambrose and it was:

'Don't send these people here because they only cause inconvenience and upset for the administration and are upsetting the local population.'

The same message that he had tried to send to Charles Markbreiter a couple of months before. The delicate and carefully-wrought accommodation that had been achieved between the occupier and the occupied was put in mortal danger by military operations of any kind aimed at the Island.

As the Nicolle and Symes venture unfolded, Sherwill's worst fears of a serious deterioration in the Islanders' relationship with the Germans were realised. The German dog, at first so well-behaved, was about turn savage.

But, to begin with, all went well with the Nicolle–Symes operation. They actually completed their three-day reconnaissance mission successfully and on the night of 17th September, carrying lots of valuable information about the enemy, Nicolle and Symes made their way to Petit Port from where they had arranged to be picked up by the Royal Navy. And it was then that the whole operation began to falter.

They signalled out to sea with their torch at regular intervals, flashing the letter R (for rescue) into the dark night. But answer came there none. No rescue boat appeared. They returned to Petit Port a second night and repeated the exercise again.When, once more, no rescue boat came in, Nicolle and Symes knew that they were stranded in exactly the same way as Martel and Mulholland had been two months before. They were trapped in enemy territory and they were in civilian clothes. If they were captured dressed like that, then they would be shot, no question. They had to escape somehow and so, just as Martel and Mulholland had done before, they tried to steal a boat. In a great spirit of daring-do they even hatched a plan to pinch the launch that belonged to the Guernsey German *Kommandant*, Major Bandelow (what a coup that would have been!). But this came to nothing because an intermediary they were going to use on the promise of a great deal of money, £1,000, was in the event most unwilling to risk his life by helping a couple of British 'spies'.

Hubert Nicolle and James Symes remained stranded in the Island.

Again it must be said that Guernsey is a very small island. It was virtually impossible for the presence of the two officers to go unnoticed:

'Many people got to know of their presence and there was much idle, but not, I think, treacherous talk concerning them. Whereas in the early part of their stay there was little difficulty in sheltering them, rationing and other difficulties increased until the situation became impossible'

So said Ambrose Sherwill, but it was he who played a pivotal role in rescuing the two men from the firing squad.Initially, however, when he was approached for help by Hubert Nicolle's father, Emile, he believed he could play no useful part in the affair:

'I told him that aiding espionage in wartime was a highly dangerous affair. I had got away with it in the case of Mulholland and Martel but that I had to remember, as head of the Controlling Committee, my first duty lay to that Committee and to the people of Guernsey. The possible discovery by the Germans that, whilst appearing to be co-operating with them I was aiding espionage, was likely to be followed by the Committee and me being swept away and by the full rigour of direct military government being imposed. In the circumstance, whilst I fully understood that he felt compelled to shelter his son, I must refrain from any part of it.'

Nicolle and Symes were now in a truly terrible position. If they gave themselves up to the Germans there was every possibility that they would be shot and, not only that, all those people who had helped them, including their families and girlfriends, would be subject to severe punishment. If they delayed surrendering to the Germans in the unlikely expectation of escaping undetected from the Island then it was inevitable that even more of their fellow countrymen would come to know of their presence in the Island and thereby also render themselves liable to punishment by the Germans. It was a very serious offence under military law for someone even to know of the presence of an enemy agent and not inform the Germans. Many people were already at great risk and the number would inevitably grow if they did not surrender. People would suffer if they surrendered. More people would suffer if Nicolle and Symes did not surrender and were later captured, as seemed inevitable. Nicolle and Symes did not want anyone to be hurt on their account but there was no course of action they could take to avoid at least a few of their nearest and dearest being hauled up before an unforgiving German tribunal.

The two men were in a jam. They could not go back, they should not go forward. Where to turn? What to do for the best when there was no best, just a choice of the bad?

At the moment of their greatest despair a way out of the impasse suddenly appeared and it came from, of all people, the Germans in the shape of General Graf von Schmettow and Major Bandelow. Von Schmettow was at this particular time in the process of taking over command from Bandelow, and together they decided the best way to flush out the British agents they knew were in the Island was to offer a sort of amnesty to the fugitives, and they would do this through the good offices of Ambrose Sherwill.

Bandelow told Sherwill that he knew there were British troops in the Island but, he said:

'If members of the British Armed Forces gave themselves up by the day to be appointed they would be treated as prisoners of war and nobody who had harboured them would be punished. He went on to say that if, however, members of the Armed Forces were discovered later, the Germans would select 20 prominent civilians and shoot them.'
(Sherwill)

Ambrose Sherwill had had a very good relationship with Major Bandelow. From their first meeting he described him as a man of geniality and integrity. He believed him to be a man of his word and that if Nicolle and Symes surrendered they would indeed be treated as prisoners of war, not shot as spies and that no one who had given them refuge would be punished in any way. That was the promise.

Sherwill also believed that the threat to shoot a score of Guernseymen if Nicolle and Symes did not give themselves up was a real threat.

Sherwill spent no time at all gazing into the mouth of this German gift horse. Quick activity followed close on opportunity. Emile Nicolle, fearful for his son's life, very much doubted that the Germans would keep their promise to all those involved in the affair, but Sherwill nevertheless persuaded him to go along with the planned surrender. The two boys would live. The 20 prominent civilians would not be shot. Bandelow would keep his word. Nobody would be arrested.

As in the Martel and Mulholland affair, Nicolle and Symes were provided with British military uniform to replace the civilian clothes in which they had landed.

The uniforms this time came not from the arsenal but from a German store of captured military uniforms down by the harbour. Now properly attired, Lieutenant Hubert Nicolle and

Lieutenant James Symes surrendered to the Germans at 6 p.m. on 21st October. They had been in the Island for 48 days.

But then the storm burst!

They were not treated as prisoners of war as Bandelow had promised. Instead they were summarily court-martialled by a German tribunal on the charge of spying and espionage, a sentence subject to confirmation by Berlin. They were found guilty and sentenced to be shot.

Had Bandelow, the instigator of the amnesty proposal, reneged on his promise too?

The truth was that the matter had been taken out of their hands by their superiors in Paris to whom they reported all the events in the Nicolle–Symes affair as a matter of course. The Paris men disliked intensely the idea of any kind of deal being struck with spies in general and with Nicolle and Symes in particular.

The prosecution of the case was effectively taken away from Schmettow and Bandelow. A special unit was despatched to Guernsey to conduct a more rigorous investigation into the affair, and this resulted in the arrests of all those Islanders who had helped the two British officers in any way, including their family members. Sherwill was now a very frightened man.

On the Saturday of 26th October he took his fears to the *Feldkommandantur*. The atmosphere was very cold and forbidding, the staff distant and withdrawn. Major Bandelow was apparently on leave, so Sherwill spoke, after some delay, to his deputy Dr Brosch:

'I got the impression of a deeply troubled man. I said, "Dr Brosch – before he went on leave, the Commandant gave me his word of honour that any member of the armed forces who surrendered by a given date would be treated as prisoners of war and that no one who had helped them would be harmed. They surrendered by the due date and since then you have been making a whole series of arrests. Are you going to keep your word?" Dr Brosch, not looking at me, replied, "We must keep our word, but it is going to be very difficult and only the Fuehrer can decide."

The answer chilled me to the marrow; if indeed that was true that the Fuehrer was being consulted, then I had no expectation of a favourable outcome.'

(Sherwill)

At this point none seemed likely. No mercy could be expected from the Fuehrer and none came.

Nicolle and Symes and all their immediate family, together with all those who had been found to have helped them, were rounded up, shipped out of the Island and thrown into the Cherche-Midi prison in Paris, an awful place notorious for its freezing temperatures and its lack of food.

Ambrose Sherwill himself was taken to

PROCLAMATION

Certain incidents have occurred in which, on the part of the inhabitants of the Island, acts have been committed which were against the safety of the Army of Occupation. Those who were guilty have been, or will be, punished according to the decree of Martial Law by Sentence of Death.

In their own interest I warn the Public most solemnly against perpetrating any further acts of this kind. Any person involved in such an act, either as Perpetrator, Participant or Instigator will, upon conviction by Court Martial, without power of Appeal be condemned to suffer the Death Penalty.

In view of the present economic situation the recent Prohibition in regard to Fishing has been modified. If, however, this act of leniency is misunderstood, and certain individual and irresponsible elements of the population perpetrate further acts which are detrimental to the safety of the Army of Occupation, the entire population will have to suffer the consequences of the reprisals which will follow.

People of the Island!   Your destiny and your welfare is in your own hands. Your Home Interests demand that you should refrain from and to the best of your power prevent, all such actions which must inevitably be followed by such disastrous consequences.

The Military Commander in France,

(Signed) v. STÜLPNAGEL,

General of Infantry.

the Paris prison having been found guilty of aiding and abetting the enemy agents Nicolle and Symes.

It was a far from pleasant experience for the First World War hero. Even less so for James Symes' father, Louis. He had been placed in a punishment cell, the only one available, while his own was being de-loused. The punishment cell, as might be expected, was a dreadful place.. There was little light and no bed or mattress, just a concrete block and the thinnest of thin blankets and a bucket.

Louis Symes was found dead with his wrists slashed on Monday 3rd December 1940.

Some said that it was not suicide at all but that the Germans had murdered him and dressed it up to look like suicide, but Ambrose Sherwill thinks otherwise:

'Louis Symes was suffering grave hardship. Presumably at the end of his tether through anxiety as to the fate of his officer son, who would quite likely be shot as a spy, worry about his prisoner wife and worry about himself, this final indignity caused his nerve to snap.'

Whatever the truth of that, Louis Symes was only six days away from release when he took his own life for, suddenly, on 29th December all the Guernsey prisoners were released and the command given, 'Anglais partir tout de suite.' The French was bad but the news delightful. Even more pleasing was the news that Lieutenants Hubert Nicolle and Jimmy Symes were to be treated as prisoners of war. They were not to face the firing squad after all but:

'Poor Mrs Symes; in what a turmoil of mixed emotions she must have been. Widowed, released from prison, her son saved from probable death. She was wonderfully brave and even joked with us as we drove through the countryside. We were in a jocular mood and yet conscious of what she was feeling beneath the brave face she was showing the world, again and again a ribald joke would be cut off half way as the joker caught sight of her tense face.'

They were going home, the sight of Guernsey never so lovely, but no such luck for the newly-alive Nicolle and Symes. They had to spend the next five years incarcerated as prisoners of war and when you are only 20, five years is a very long time.

But why had there been a change of heart towards the Guernsey people? Why had Nicolle and Symes been spared the execution squad?

Ambrose Sherwill provides us with the answer:

'On my return to Guernsey, I gathered that Major Bandelow had moved heaven and earth in his endeavour to keep his word. I obtained an appointment with him and asked him if this was so and he replied very modestly that he had done his utmost in the matter.'

Major Bandelow had indeed lived up to Sherwill's assessment of him as being a man of honour and integrity. He had returned from a period of leave and discovered the charges preferred against Nicolle and Symes and the way in which their helpers had been arrested. In other words everything that he had promised would not happen to these people, had happed to them. He had given his word of honour that Nicolle and Symes would be treated as prisoners of war, not as spies, and that their helpers would not be harmed in any way. He was outraged at this turn of events and considered that his honour had been impugned in a very nasty fashion. Major Bandelow hastened to rectify the situation as quickly as he possibly could. He demanded the convening of a Court of Honour, and in so doing threw his career on the line. For if that court found against him he would be required to resign his commission. On the other hand, if the court found in his favour then the obligation he had entered into as expressed in the notice of Monday 21st October 1940, namely:

'... Members of the British Armed Forces obeying this order will be treated as prisoners of war and no measures will be taken against persons who have assisted them,'

would have to be accepted by his military superiors. This matter of honour was referred all the way up to Berlin. The opinion of no less a military personage than General Field Marshall von Reichenau was canvassed and he produced the definitive response:

'When one gives ones word, one gives ones word'.

This was the result Major Bandelow had prayed for. And thus it was that Nicolle and Symes were saved from the firing squad and the Guernsey prisoners in the noisome Cherche- Midi prison were released to return home. Major Bandelow had kept his word. Ambrose Sherwill records that:

'I told Major Bandelow at the time that I regarded his action towards a number of British subjects in time of war, in the circumstances in question, as in the very highest traditions of chivalry and I still so regard it.'

It had been a narrow escape for all involved, but there were consequences of the kind Sherwill had written about in his letter to Charles Markbreiter at the Home Office:

'Military activities ... are likely to result in loss of life among the civilian population and generally to make our position more unpleasant than it is.'

and indeed this was true; the rather benign, not to say pleasant, relationship that had existed between the Controlling Committee and the Germans was severely damaged.

Ambrose Sherwill, who up to this point had been playing a pivotal role in running a 'model occupation' very much in the interests of the Islanders, was summarily dismissed from his office of President of the Controlling Committee:

'as further cooperation with the authorities is no longer possible.'

This was the worst of the fall-out from the Nicolle—Symes affair. At a stroke the best, the most able, the most intelligent and the bravest of the Islanders' leaders was thrown out of office. No one had done more to 'administer the government of the Island to the best of his abilities in the interest of the inhabitants,' as he had been exhorted to do by the British Government. It was the great fault of that same British Government to deprive the Islanders of their best servant by encouraging pointless, ill-planned military adventures.

By the end of December 1940 the Islands had been occupied for five months and Guernsey, in particular, had been at the receiving end of four commando operations. The biggest of them, 'Ambassador', had been, in the words of Durnford Slater, 'a comic failure'. Churchill himself called it 'a silly fiasco' for it achieved nothing of any use to the war effort. An old man had been assaulted in his home at two o'clock in the morning and clubbed to the ground with a rifle butt, four or five telephone wires had been cut and boulders had been removed from Mr Vedale's garden to create a barricade across the road by the Doyle Monument. No information was gathered, no enemy or enemy equipment destroyed, but three of the raiding party, who did not know how to swim, were captured.

In the course of the other three operations Martel and Mulholland were forced to surrender to the Germans. So were Nicolle and Symes, and as a result 20 Islanders were threatened with death, 13 Islanders were taken into France and imprisoned in Paris. One Islander took his own life there. Hubert Nicolle's father, the secretary to the Controlling Committee, and his uncle Frank Nicolle, Assistant Harbour Master, lost their jobs. More importantly, Ambrose Sherwill lost his and there was a damaging glitch in relations with the Germans. It is, by any standard, a somewhat sorry record and, as has been pointed out many times, the result of operations being mounted too quickly because of hurt pride rather than good military thinking. They were a knee-jerk reaction to the German Occupation of British territory and, most telling of all, the operations were, in this first phase of the Occupation, carried out by troops of the newly created commando force.

They were extremely brave men but at this time they were ill-trained and ill-equipped to do the job required of them.

The biggest single result of these military endeavours was to put the

Islanders' lives and liberty at risk.

Things had to get better. There had to be better training and planning, better equipment and an improved awareness of the situation in the Islands. As Brigadier John Durnford Slater himself records:

'We should go about this commando business properly or not at all and [Churchill] told Lord Keyes who was now Chief of Combined Operations to plan some really worthwhile raids.

As for me I was more than ever determined to mould a unit that would take any raid in its stride, and to bring back results. Only results matter. I knew now that I had a long way to go to achieve them.'

The British High Command had learned its lesson for it was two years before another raid was launched in the Channel Islands, and by this time things had definitely improved, at least from the military point of view. Combined Operations had got their act together.

The soldiers used in these later attacks were of a different calibre to those that went before – better trained, better prepared and altogether more deadly, but their success was still far from guaranteed.

There was one such raid that was, however, a complete success, and this was the attack on the Casquets lighthouse led by Major Gus March-

Phillips and his second in command, that remarkable officer Captain Geoffrey Appleyard.

The lighthouse was built in 1742 atop a bare rock standing six miles to the west of Alderney. When the Germans arrived in the Channel Islands they had quickly set up a radio station in the lighthouse and it presented an almost irresistible target for No. 2 Commando Small Raiding Force.

The twelve men of the SSRF duly arrived at the rock just after midnight on the night of 2nd September. There were no guards, no look-outs to raise the alarm. Most of the little German garrison of seven men were asleep. They were roughly awakened. Appleyard said:

'I have never seen men so amazed and terrified at the same time!'

The operation was a complete success. This is an account of the raid from an HMSO publication of 1943 entitled dramatically enough:

THE STEEL HAND FROM THE SEA
Shortly before midnight on the 2nd September 1942, Ober Maat (Chief Mate) Munte who had been a stoker in the German Navy, was seated in his office in the Casquets Lighthouse seized by his master when the Channel Islands were occupied in June 1940.
He was busy making up returns – an occupation well fitted to his rank and experience. A slight noise – it may have been the click of a door as it closed softly

– caused him to turn in his chair. Leaning against the door were two men with black faces, wearing crumpled khaki uniforms, somewhat damp around the ankles. Two Colt automatics, negligently poised, were in their hands. Chief Mate Munte got slowly to his feet, passed a hand over his eye, but when he dropped it, the figures were still there. He began to sway, and fell to the floor, fainting through terror. To bring him round the two black-faced men had to slap his face, and a short time afterwards he was in a small boat bobbing uneasily on the treacherous waters that surge about the lighthouse he had failed to guard. By then he was in the company of the six men who formed his command. They were the wireless operators and the guard of the lighthouse. Those who were not on guard duty were still in pyjamas and some were even wearing hair nets, which at first caused the commander to mistake one of them as a woman. By four o'clock in the morning, after a stormy passage, the Germans found themselves POWs in England.

The commando raid on the Casquets Lighthouse was an undoubted success.

The next venture into the enemy stronghold was anything but.

BUTCHER AND BOLT

Churchill had commanded shortly after Dunkirk that small-scale hit-and-run attacks should be made upon the enemy. Small groups of well trained soldiers, 'Leopards,' as he liked to call them, should launch lightning attacks

on German-held territory, cause as much damage as possible and then beat a swift retreat. They should 'butcher and bolt'. Operation Basalt was intended, in part, to be this kind of operation . It was to be a small-scale raid on Sark. Its purpose was pretty much the same as that of Operation Ambassador: to create as much mayhem as possible and also to find out what defence the Germans had established on the Island, how many troops were there, where they were, and what the conditions of the Islanders were after two years of enemy occupation.

The assault force was also to try and make contact with and take off an embedded, rather mysterious, Special Operations Executive (SOE) agent working on the island, and to take German prisoners for interrogation.

On the night of 3rd October, ten soldiers from the SOE's Small Scale Raiding Force, No.12 Commando, landed on the rocks below the Hog's Back, a large promontory with 300-foot cliffs which were extremely difficult to scale.

There were some very interesting characters in the commando party, not least their leader, Major John Geoffrey Appleyard DSO, MC and Bar. He had seriously injured his leg on the previous small scale (and very successful) raid on the Casquets lighthouse when all the Germans there had been taken prisoner and invaluable code books discovered. The limb was still not properly healed but Appleyard, or simply 'Apple' as he was affectionately known, was not going to miss out on this opportunity to assault the enemy. This ex-Cambridge Blue, international skier, athlete and scholar was described by Colonel Vladimir Peniakoff, the renowned Russian espionage ace, as:

'one of the few officers who had developed the technique of the small scale raid: the care he took of his men made him stand out among brother officers who were too excited by the prospect of adventure to think of anybody but their own selves.'

Alongside 'Apple' was 22-year-old Anders Lassen VC, MC and Two Bars. He was the cousin of Axel von den Bussche who was, as a member of Claus Stauffenberg's group, to try and kill Hitler in a suicide bomb attack. Anders himself was a dedicated anti-Nazi soldier and lethal in the field. His last act on earth, as he fell to the ground mortally wounded, was to fling a grenade at the enemy. The raiding party climbed up and over the Hog's Back. Appleyard knew the area reasonably well, having spent a holiday in the Island, but not well enough for his present purpose. They needed help and direction.

Mrs Francoise Pittard, living on her own in La Jaspallerie, was rudely awakened by the raiders breaking in. It must have been a frightening sight, unknown soldiers, their faces blackened, armed to the teeth, bearing down upon her.

Fortunately for the commandos she was made of much sterner stuff than poor Bill Crocker over in Guernsey who had so stammered and shrieked during Operation Ambassador. At first Mrs Pittard thought that Appleyard's party were members of the fire brigade. On being told who they actually were, the lady calmly got dressed and talked to them in the kitchen. Yes, she knew where some of the German guns were placed, yes she had a map of Sark and yes she knew where some Germans were stationed. They were in the annexe to the Dixcart Hotel just across the valley.

The commandos left La Jaspallerie and advanced towards the hotel. It was guarded, after a fashion, by one solitary soldier. Easy meat for Anders Lassen. He killed him quickly, efficiently, silently, with his knife.

Inside the annexe they found five Germans-one NCO and four engineers (who were doing some work on the harbour). They were roughly and immediately taken prisoner. From this point on the story is more than a little confused, for varying accounts have appeared of what happened next. It does appear, however, that the German prisoners were bound in some way – later official British reports described the prisoners as each being bound with a toggle to their captors. Other accounts say that the Germans had their belts removed and their flies opened to prevent escape. There are even stories of their mouths being filled with grass to stop them shouting for help. However this may be, it is certainly true that as soon as they were clear of the hotel one of the prisoners made a break for it and ran, shouting, back to the hotel. He was recaptured alive. Then some sort of struggle took place between the Germans and the commandos.

Appleyard threatened to shoot them if the noise and the fighting went on and when it did go on that is exactly what happened. Two Germans from the original group of six were shot and, moreover, shot in the back the Germans were later to claim. By this time German soldiers roused by the noise and the gunfire came running towards the Hog's Back in hot pursuit of Appleyard's commandos and their one remaining prisoner. They finally made it and escaped with their prisoner as they ran for dear life towards the waiting motor torpedo boat (MTB) and safety.

At some time during the escape there was a necessarily brief chat between Anders Lassen and Appleyard. Lassen was very much aware that to shoot bound prisoners constituted a war crime. British troops could not be seen to commit war crimes. Should he not go back up the Hog's Back and remove the restraints from the wrists of the shot Germans?

Permission to do so was declined. They had to make good their escape immediately. There was no time to re-arrange the dead bodies in accordance with the rules of international warfare. Alongside the Appleyard party on board the escape vessel was the SOE agent who had been successfully picked up by a separate group at a prearranged meeting place further round the coast. This SOE operative was quite an extraordinary character. Leslie Wright, a member of Appleyard's group, describes him thus:

'The SOE agent was a colonel in the free Polish Army which had reformed in England. He had fallen into the hands of the Gestapo for only a few days but that was sufficient to practically cripple him. His testicles had been crushed, his ankle broken and two of his toes had been cut off. His Christian name was Roman and his surname was Zatwadzki. We stayed friends but lost contact in 1947. During 1943 he had departed for another mission on the continent. He was a remarkable man.'

Their very frightened German prisoner eventually, it is reported, 'sang like a canary' about the military capabilities of the Island and about who, what and where the German soldiers were. A result to be applauded surely from a military viewpoint, but again one must refer to Ambrose Sherwill's points concerning such raids on the Islands, namely that such raids were 'unwelcome in a demilitarized zone' and that they would only serve to destroy any good relationship between the Islanders and the Germans. More than that, the civilian population would be put in considerable danger of loss of life and liberty because of reprisals which might be carried out. The question had to be asked: was the achievement of the raid – the obtaining of information and the killing of a few enemy soldiers, worth the suffering that was inflicted upon the Islanders and many others, because of it? The raid certainly had unfortunate consequences and, unlike any previous raid on the Islands, it had consequences in the larger theatre of war, far beyond little Sark.

On 7th October Berlin Radio repeatedly broadcast the following bulletin:

'16 British fell upon a German working party consisting of an NCO and four men, who they tied up in their shirts with thin but strong cord. The men were not allowed to put on more clothes, but were led off to the beach, and when they resisted this improper treatment, the NCO and one man were killed by bullets and bayonets and another soldier was wounded.'

The Fuehrer was enraged. As an immediate retaliation ordered that:

'From noon on October 8th all British officers and men taken prisoner at Dieppe will be bound.'

The troops captured and held in Dieppe were Canadian troops, and the Canadian military command, in its turn, ordered that all of the many German prisoners held in Canada should be chained. Hitler further ordered:

'In future, British and their accomplices, who do not act like soldiers but rather as bandits, will be treated as such by the German troops and will be ruthlessly eliminated in battle, wherever they appear.'

The gloves were off on both sides. Things were getting tougher everywhere. Here is an extract from the *British Handbook of Irregular Warfare* handed round at that time:

'Never give the enemy a chance; the days when we could practice the rules of sportsmanship are over. For the time being every soldier must be a potential gangster. The vulnerable parts of the enemy are the heart, spine, and privates. Kick him or knee him as hard as you can in the fork... Remember you are out to kill.'

The Basalt raid had repercussions of a very serious kind in the Islands too. The Germans responded vigorously to the attack on 'their' territory. First they dealt with their own. The Chief German Commandant in Sark was instantly court martialled and fired from his job for exercising an inadequate duty of care towards his men. Security was tightened up considerably. The German troops were thereafter garrisoned in one area alone and 4,000 mines were laid around the coastline, not only of Sark, but Guernsey as well, to prevent a repetition of such an assault.

These mines worked very well indeed as we shall see.

As for poor Mrs Pittard from La Jaspallerie, after a delay of four weeks the Germans came to question her. This they did quite forcefully, and eventually she told them what had happened on that night of 3rd October. It was an offence under German Occupation law to aid and abet enemy agents in acts of espionage. She could be shot if the strict letter of the law was observed, or at least be shipped across the sea to some terrible prison like the Cherche-Midi or worse, to a concentration camp. These thoughts must have been running through her head as she was placed in the Sark meat wagon, taken through the tunnel to the tiny Island harbour and shipped thence to Guernsey. She spent the first week of her eleven-week incarceration in solitary confinement, left alone with her tears and her fears. Thereafter she was moved into a much more congenial environment where she could be with other inmates. She suffered no real physical hardship in this prison. Indeed she was allowed lots of little comforts.

She was even allowed to dry her hair before the Governor's fire. After two months the cell door was opened and Francoise Pittard was told to go home. No explanation was ever given.

However the worst consequences of the Basalt Raid were yet to come. They came in the shape of a deportation order that, at first, was intended to apply to all of Sark. The whole population was originally to be evacuated, but this was later reduced to 52 of the Islanders. From Guernsey, 135 were to be taken. It was a hammer blow, particularly to Guernsey, with its population already massively depleted by the evacuation of June 1940 and by the subsequent forced deportation of 872 people in September 1942.

The Controlling Committee was asked to supply a list of a) all persons previously convicted; b) persons to be considered as unwilling to work; and c) young males without fixed occupation.

The Germans already had a list of the Island's ex-army officers who they were also intending to deport. More significantly, it soon became apparent that many high ranking government officials had been marked down for deportation as well, including the Bailiff himself, Victor Carey. John Leale, Dr Symons and Raymond Falla, together with a number of doctors and managers of essential services like electricity and water supply were also targeted, as was Ambrose Sherwill.

It was quite clear that removing such key personnel from the Island would inflict great damage on the running of the civilian administration. It was also abundantly clear that tearing people away from their homes and loved ones would create much grief and sorrow.

Representations were made by John Leale to the German Commander von Aufsess to grant exemptions to all those people on the list who they regarded as absolutely key to the administration of

Guernsey. They were largely successful but not entirely. Carey, Leale, Symons and Falla were allowed to stay but Ambrose Sherwill had to go; there was no reprieve for him.

Two parties of deportees left the Islands; the first, on 13th February 1943 was composed of 122 Guernsey folk plus 27 from Sark. Two Jews, Elda Brouard and Elisabet Duquemin (the friend of Therese Steiner), were in this first group, as was Robert Hathaway, the American husband of Sibyl Hathaway, the Dame of Sark. Her 'guests' had turned on her! There were ex-army officers and the families of some imprisoned Guernsey police officers and men deemed socially undesirable making up the remainder of this group.

The second group to leave was much smaller than the first in all ways, for it was 38 in number and included 21 children, 17 from Sark and four from Guernsey. It was nothing more or less than a brutal reprisal measure.

There was no publicity surrounding these deportations either in the press or anywhere else. They were carried out almost in secret, almost certainly to prevent civil unrest. Certainly not everyone in the Islands knew of them for instance, Julia Tremayne in her touching memoir *War on Sark* makes no mention of them at all.

The Basalt Raid had all kinds of nasty consequences for the Islanders in Guernsey and Sark. Nothing of much importance had been discovered but as a direct result of the action the safety, life and liberty of the Islanders were put even more at risk than before. The savage dog was growling.

It may confidently be asserted, however, that bad as these raids were for the Islanders, the results of some planned raids, had they been carried out, would have been worse. They would have been absolutely disastrous!

It was Vice Admiral Lord Louis Mountbatten who came up with the idea of Operation Constellation which was composed of three operations; Operation Condor being an attack on Jersey, Operation Coverlet, an offensive against Guernsey and Operation Concertina an assault on Alderney.

Constellation was certainly Mountbatten's proposal but its animating spirit was Churchill's, ever anxious to re-take the only British territory the enemy had occupied. What a propaganda coup that would be! But it would not be an easy job, far from it. The Germans had massively fortified each of the three Islands. As Mountbatten himself remarked:

'Each Island is a veritable fortress, the assault against which cannot be contemplated unless the defences are neutralised, or reduced to a very considerable extent by prior action.'

In other words, there would have to be a very heavy bombardment from the air and from the sea to 'soften up' the defensive capability of the Islands before attempting to put troops ashore. The possibility of civilian casualties would be very great should such a bombardment take place. The Islands are very small.

Any bombing or shelling, even that directed towards specific coastal defence installations could quite easily, within the margin of error that existed in such bombardments, kill large numbers of civilians. This was even more true if one considers the notorious inaccuracy of RAF bombing. It was said that the British bombers had to treat whole cities as a target because they could not hit anything smaller. The Butt Report of 1941 revealed that only one in five British bombers managed to drop their bombs within five miles of the target!

One estimate of the time reckoned that any bombing of the Island had the 'potential to pulverise two thirds of Guernsey's land surface and at least half of Jersey's.' Both Islands were densely populated. The danger to the Islanders was obvious. There were other objections to the projected attacks. A satisfactory reduction of the Islands' fortifications by bombardment from sea and air could not be guaranteed. Without this reduction very heavy losses indeed could be expected as the troops attempted to land.

And there was another, very serious, consideration.

It was pointed out by the RAF that any

flights by their aircraft over the Islands would be very vulnerable to attacks by the Luftwaffe, which had two airstrips just minutes away on the Cotentin peninsula. The nearest base to the Islands for the RAF was, in sharp contrast, over 70 miles away.

Taken altogether, the arguments against attempts to re-take the Islands outweighed the arguments for such attempts. In any case, it was said that the Islands were of no real strategic value and to risk so much merely to achieve a propaganda coup was frankly silly. Operation Constellation was abandoned. The Islanders were safe from friendly fire but ...

Towards the end of 1943 another series of attacks, referred to as 'pinprick' raids, were planned on the Cherbourg Peninsula and the Channel Islands. The code name was 'Hardtack.' Ten such raids were proposed, but only six were actually attempted – between Thursday 23rd and Friday 28th December 1943. It was a disaster. Not one of the raids was successful; indeed two commando units were completely destroyed, not a man surviving, and out of the other six units involved, not a single one escaped death and serious injury. Sadly, this was true of the raiding parties that went to Sark and to Jersey.

The first attempt on Sark was a failure. The ten men of Hardtack 7 and their leader, Lieutenant Ambrose McGonigal, landed on the rocks below Derrible Point (the promontory right next to the

Hog's Back where Appleyard and Lassen had embarked on Operation Ambassador), a little before midnight on Christmas Day 1943. But they couldn't find a way up the rocky cliff face and were forced to return to Dartmouth.

The party returned two nights later, this time landing at Hog's Back, and this time to they managed to scale the cliffs and find a path leading inland. The path was heavily mined. The Germans had done this immediately after Operation Ambassador. The men of Hardtack were using the same route as their predecessors in that operation. A mine exploded killing one man and injuring another. They tried to advance a little further but then two more mines exploded, severely wounding McGonigal in the leg and finally killing the previously-injured commando. Leaving their dead behind, the rest of the raiding party ran as best they could back to the base of Hogs Back. They were retreating through the minefield.

Four more mines exploded, injuring all but one of the remaining men but, wounded as they were, they managed to get down the cliff and into their escape boat, and thence to the waiting MTB. They arrived, bleeding and exhausted, into Dartmouth at five o'clock in the morning of 28th December. It had been a terrible night for the men of Hardtack 7. Two of their number had been killed, all but one of them had been wounded.

Nothing of any value had been gained.

It was an unmitigated disaster. The same could be said of the Hardtack raid on Jersey.

This, again was to take place on the night of Christmas – Boxing Day, to coincide with the Hardtack raid on Sark. Ten men and their Commander, Captain P. A. Ayton, landed unobserved at pretty little Giffard Bay on the north coast of the Island. They did encounter a minefield but this one, usefully and unlike the one encountered on Sark, had warning signs in German and English hung about its perimeter. They pressed on. Time was passing and they had seen not a single German soldier, so they knocked on the door of a farmhouse to see if they could get some information as to where enemy troops might be found. The Jersey lady who answered their midnight summons was anything but pleased to see these heavily armed men with blackened faces.

No Mrs Pittard she. She was not particularly frightened, just quite annoyed. No she would not tell them where German troops were. The people on the farm down the road might be able to help so why didn't they clear off and ask them. Captain Ayton's party did just that but the two brothers they found in the neighbouring farm, rather like Mr Crocker in Operation Ambassador, were so frightened that at first they could not speak. They did however finally calm down enough to tell the commandos that they did not know where any Germans were. Then, interestingly, they told Ayton that the

Islanders were not hostile to the Germans and furthermore there was no resistance movement in the Island.

The brothers then gave the soldiers a glass or two of milk (it was a small-holding with a couple of cows). The commando group then left and circled back via Les Platons towards Giffard Bay, their time running out, mission over. They had not come across a single enemy soldier to kill or take prisoner.

They had gathered a couple of bits of rather useless information and that was it. In no way could the enterprise be described as successful. This thought was probably running through Captain Ayton's mind when he stepped on a mine planted just above the bay. He was terribly injured and his men carried him the rest of the way to the boat.

The Captain made it back across the Channel but died in hospital a few hours later. Another brave man gone down in the Hardtack enterprise.

At this point, some three years into the war, with many men taken prisoner or killed, some realisation of the inadequacy of the 'pinprick raid' as a weapon of war must finally have permeated the British Military Command, for there were no further small-scale commando attacks on the Islands. In fact there were no further attacks of any kind for the rest of the War.

Ambrose Sherwill and many other Islanders were very pleased.

BEKANNTMACHUNG

PROCLAMATION

JERSEY,
den 24. 12. 40.

1. Die Ermittlungen der gerichtlichen Untersuchung haben eindeutig ergeben :

a) Leutnant Nicolle und Leutnant Symes, in der Nacht vom 3. 9. 40. zum 4. 9. 40. in Zivil mit einem Erkundungsauftrag auf Guernsey gelandet, sind der Spionage schuldig.

b) Emile Nicolle, Else Nicolle, Frank Nicolle, Hilda Nicolle, Louis Symes, Rachel Symes, Wilfred Bird, Walter Bird, Elise Bird, William Allan und Jessie Mariette haben die beiden Offiziere aufgenommen und ihnen Beihilfe geleistet. Sie haben sich damit des Landesverrates, beziehungsweise der Beihilfe zur Spionage schuldig gemacht.

c) Mr. Sherwill hat vor der Veröffentlichung der Bekanntmachung Erklärungen wider sein besseres Wissen abgegeben und seine gesetzliche Anzeigepflicht verletzt und sich dem Deutschen Inselkommandanten gegenüber illoyal verhalten.

d) Sämtliche Beteiligten haben nach ihrer Meldung auf Grund der Bekanntmachung vom 18. 10. 40. die deutschen Behörden vorsätzlich irrezuführen versucht.

2. Nach den mit der Haager Konvention in Einklang stehenden deutschen Kriegsgesetzen werden bestraft :

Spionage mit Todesstrafe,

Landesverrat mit Todesstrafe oder lebenslänglichen Zuchthaus.

Beihilfe zur Spionage mit Zuchthaus bis zu 15. Jahren,

Begünstigung mit Gefängnis bis zu einem Jahr.

3. Die deutsche Militärbehörde behandelt trotz der erschwerenden Vorgänge zu 1 c) und d), die oben genannten Fälle im Sinne der Zusicherungen vom 18. 10. 40.

Es wird keine kriegsgerichtliche Aburteilung stattfinden. Es bleiben daher sämtliche Beteiligten straffrei. Nach Abschluss des Ermittlungsverfahrens werden Leutnant Nicolle und Leutnant Symes in ein Kriegsgefangenenlager gebracht, die übrigen Beteiligten auf die Insel zurückgeführt. Der Vorfall ist hiermit erledigt.

4. Mr. Sherwill findet im Amte keine Verwendung mehr, da den deutschen Behörden eine weitere Zusammenarbeit mit ihm nicht möglich ist.

5. Die auf der Insel Guernsey eingezogenen Rundfunkgeräte werden auf Widerruf an die Eigentümer zur Benutzung zurückgegeben.

6. Sämtliche Massnahmen geschehen in der Erwartung und unter der Voraussetzung einwandfreien Verhaltens aller Inselbehörden und -bewohner für die Zukunft. Jedes illoyale und illegale Verhalten wird sofortige Gegenmassnahmen nach sich ziehen. Unter Verfehlungen Einzelner wird die Allgemeinheit leiden.

PROCLAMATION

JERSEY,
Dec. 24th, 1940.

(1) The findings of the Legal Investigations have proved conclusively :

(a) During the night from the 3rd to 4th September, 2nd Lieut. Nicolle and 2nd Lt. Symes having landed in Guernsey in civil clothing with a reconnaissance order are guilty of espionage.

(b) Emile Nicolle, Else Nicolle, Frank Nicolle, Hilda Nicolle, Louis Symes, Rachel Symes, Wilfred Bird, Walter Bird, Elise Bird, William Allan and Jessie Mariette have given refuge and assistance to the two officers. They have therefore been guilty of high treason and having lent assistance to espionage.

(c) Mr. Sherwill has, before the publication of the notice, made declarations contrary to the best of his knowledge and acted against his appointed duty of information. He has therefore been guilty of favouring the above and acting disloyally towards the German Inselkommandant.

(d) All the parties concerned have attempted to mislead the German Authorities even after having reported themselves in accordance with a notice of October 18th, 1940.

(2) In accordance with the German Military Law and in agreement with the Hague Convention, the penalties provided for are the following :

Espionage : death penalty.

High treason : death penalty or penal servitude for life.

Assistance to espionage : penal servitude up to fifteen years.

Favouring : imprisonment up to one year.

(3) In spite of aggravating circumstances, the German Military Authorities have treated the above mentioned cases 1 (c) and (d) with full consideration to the assurances given in the notice of October 18th, 1940.

No Martial Law condemnation will take place All the persons concerned will be exempted from punishment. After conclusion of the investigation proceedings, 2nd Lt. Nicolle and 2nd Lt. Symes will be sent to a camp as prisoners of war. The other persons concerned will be brought back to the Island. The matter is therefore settled.

(4) Mr. Sherwill will be released from his office as further co-operation with the German Authorities is no longer possible.

(5) The wireless receiving sets confiscated in the Island of Guernsey will be returned to their owners for use until further notice.

(6) All the above measures have been taken in the expectation and under the condition of a perfect loyalty on the part of the Island Authorities and population in the future Any disloyal or illegal behaviour will result in immediate counter measures. The whole community would bear the consequences of individual misconduct.

SCHUMACHER,
Oberst und Felkommandant.

Chapter 7
Precious Little Resistance

aptain Hans Kegelmann was transferred to Jersey after being wounded on the Eastern Front. He was asked about his experiences in the Island where he was based from 1944 to 1946:

'I felt almost at home I must say. The Island people were normal, they behaved normally, they were not afraid, they were in a relatively good situation, they were well dressed, they had beautiful houses, they had roads, in fact they had everything they needed there, there were water mains, waste disposal was provided; there were many, many things which we had at home too. And so there was a perfect impression. It was as if there was no war on. It was like being on holiday.

Of course I wasn't surprised that there were a few resistance groups. You find them wherever some enemy power keeps somewhere occupied, but I don't believe that there were strong resistance groups here in Jersey which aimed at real hard hits. Jersey is an island. The possibility of hiding and disappearing is not so great ... It was easy for us to search and comb through and find any would-be resister. That was no great problem.

The truth is that in the Islands the situation was not so serious or so threatening as to provoke the Islanders

to proceed with intensive force against the German occupation here.

There was perhaps a sense of national honour. They wanted to be doing something but really they had nothing to complain about on account of their treatment. After all, no great dangers had come from the Occupation, the German Occupation. Of course, they'd had enough and war is war and ... they just tried to make the best of it, and so I didn't come into contact with, see or hear anything like a resistance group. Naturally, sometimes, we monitored the Islanders, sometimes we carried out road checks, when there was a suspicion or it was obvious that something might be blown up or something set on fire. But it never happened. We were never confronted by any resistance groups'.

As we have heard when Captain P.A. Ayton was wandering about Les Platons up in the north-east of Jersey during the disastrous Hardtack raid he roused a couple of Islanders from their beds to enquire about the disposition of German troops and about conditions in Jersey generally. He was less than welcome at the little farm and no, they did not know where the German soldiers were and, in any case, they were not particularly hostile to them and what was more, there was no resistance movement in the Island. Not exactly music to the ears of the ill-fated captain but a largely true summation of the situation in Jersey if one thinks of resistance purely and exclusively in terms of killing the enemy, shooting him and blowing up the means he has to prosecute the war, as the Maquisards and the Front de L'Independence did on mainland Europe. Many German soldiers died in such attacks, but many more civilians died in reprisals such as in Oradour sur Glane and even more terribly, if that is possible, at Lidice. Such resistance has been called 'brave,' 'heroic' and 'noble' and nobody would say otherwise, but it came at a terrible price.

Both Winston Churchill and General de Gaulle counselled strongly against such forms of armed resistance for precisely this reason.

In the Islands there was no resistance of this kind at all – a cable or two was cut, but this was put down to cattle tramping across them and, true, a sleeper or two was stolen from the railway, but this was in order to burn and keep warm, certainly not to register a violent protest against the occupiers. A German officer was killed in Sark, but though an Islander was initially suspected, it turned out in the end that his batman had performed the bloody deed. Any violence visited upon the Germans was always imported, courtesy of the RAF or the Commando forces; it was never home grown. Resistance in the form of armed assault and sabotage simply did not happen in the Islands

during the Occupation; and it did not happen for very good reasons. It had nothing to do with a lack of courage and everything to do with the particular and complex nature of the German Occupation of the Islands, which differed markedly from that of Holland, Belgium or France.

The questions are many and have often been asked. Why was there no resistance movement in the Channel Islands as there was in every other occupied territory in Western Europe? Was there no Jean Moulin in the Islands? Was there not a small army of men and women ready and willing to lay down their lives in the cause of freedom from the Nazi yoke? Were the Islanders all so abjectly and cravenly subservient to their German masters that they could not offer up a squeak of protest, a murmur of dissent? Was it all collaboration and no confrontation?

For a resistance movement to flourish certain conditions must be met, and they are fairly obvious ones. For resistance to be possible, the resisters must first of all have somewhere they can take refuge from the enemy, somewhere they can hide both themselves and their weapons. Most importantly of all they would need to have ways to escape.

Now the Islands, unlike France, Belgium and Holland, are very small – Jersey, the largest of the group being only nine miles by five with the tide out. Not one of them provides anything like the amount of cover needed for a successful resistance movement to survive with any degree of security. The most that can be offered is a few clumps of woodland and small copses, utterly useless to any would-be resister. And there were no effective lines of retreat and escape, no vast hinterland in which to disappear.

There was no border to slip across, nor any great city to offer concealment. Every single avenue of escape was blocked by the exceedingly dangerous seas that surge about the Cotentin Peninsula. In short, there was nowhere to hide, nowhere to run. And there were many, many Germans to chase, capture and kill any resister who tried, for there were more German soldiers per head of population in the Islands than in any other occupied country in Western Europe. In fact for lengthy periods during the War the Islands were more densely populated with Germans than the Fatherland itself. This was particularly true in Guernsey where consequently it was virtually impossible to make a move without being seen.

It is also true to say in answer to the question, 'Where was the Island's fighting spirit?' that those young men who might have formed themselves into a resistance movement were nowhere to be seen in the Islands at this time for the very good reason that they were off 'resisting' the enemy as members of His Majesty's Armed Forces. Moreover, many of these young Islanders had not been conscripted: rather they had volunteered their services. The absence of these, the majority of the bravest and best of the Islands' youth, removed all possibility of a continental-style resistance movement.

'And, be it noted, not one native from the Channel Islands donned a German uniform to fight for Hitler, unlike every other country in Europe which all supplied tens of thousands of volunteers to form "Hitler's Foreign Legions" as they were known'.

(Michael Ginns)

The greatest deterrent to acts of resistance, however, came from the top. It came from the leaders of the Islands' civilian governments. It came from the Superior Council and the Controlling Committee, governing in the interests of the inhabitants as they had been instructed to do. They saw any act of resistance as liable to upset the delicate relationship that existed between the Germans and the Islanders in this 'model occupation'.

The principles of this 'model occupation' were, on the face of it, quite simple. In strict accordance with the Hague Convention the Island government and people would cooperate to a strictly limited extent with the occupiers and would offer no form of resistance. The Germans, for their part, would visit no violence upon the civilian community and guarantee the preservation of life, liberty and property.

THE 'V' SIGN NOTICE

In these circumstances did Victor Carey put up his notorious 'V' sign notice. In these circumstances did Ambrose Sherwill inveigh against the instigators of the commando raids as liable to destroy the understanding between the occupier and the occupied and thereby place civilian lives in danger. In these circumstances those who resisted were not war heroes but rather threats to the lives of the Islanders, lives which would undoubtedly be lost when the Germans carried out reprisals. (Victor Carey said that 80 civilians were threatened with the firing squad during the 'V' sign campaign and a further 20 'prominent citizens' were so threatened during the Nicolle–Symes fiasco). The view, particularly in Guernsey, was that those who committed acts against the Germans which were liable to bring the civil population into danger through reprisals were guilty of a crime. These acts included escaping from the Islands by sea, as happened in Guernsey when eight Islanders fled across the water to mainland Britain. Ambrose Sherwill published this comment:

'It must be known to a good many local inhabitants that eight persons recently left this Island in a boat with a view to reaching England. As a direct result, drastic control of boats has been instituted by the German authorities, resulting in the fisheries in the northern and western parts of our island being unable to follow their vocation and depriving the population of a very large proportion of the fish obtainable. Any

further such departures or attempts thereat can only result in further restrictions. In other words, any person who manages to get away does so at the expense of those left behind. In these circumstances, to get away or attempt to get away is a crime against the local population. In the event of a repetition of any such incident there is a grave possibility that, by way of reprisal, the male population of the Island will be evacuated to France.'

Sherwill was all too well aware that violent acts of defiance against the Germans would invite a more savage response than simple evacuation. People would be shot. To promote, even covertly, such acts would be to invite disaster and it would certainly not be governing 'in the interests of the inhabitants'. Quite the reverse. If you have to live with the tiger, don't tweak him by the tail. Besides, it cannot be too much emphasised that, at least in the opening months of the Occupation, the German invaders behaved unexpectedly well. There was no rapine, pillage, murder or mayhem.

'We do not pretend that we are happy at being in German Occupation but it is a fact that we are being treated with courtesy and consideration. The Civil government of the Island functions as before the Occupation and the churches and chapels are freely open for public worship. Every Island official is at his post, not a single civilian has been deprived of his or her liberty and the utmost correctness characterises relations

between the German forces and the civilian populations.'

Of course there was a reason for this 'soft' approach to the Islands. It was the strongly held belief that the English mainland was about to be invaded and that the Germans would be in Oxford by Christmas. The Channel Islands were the only British territory occupied by the Germans. Would it not be a good idea to demonstrate how civilised they were, how well behaved and respectful in their treatment of a British civilian population? Of course it would. Because thereby the will to resist might subtly be eroded, the short road to invasion smoothed and the international reputation of the Nazis enhanced.

It would be a propaganda coup of the greatest value to keep the bloody iron fist well wrapped in velvet!

For its part, the British Government did little or nothing to foster or help any domestic resistance in the Islands.

There was no Violette Szabo dispatched to the Islands, indeed there were no SOE interventions of any kind that are known, in the whole of the Occupation. There was no attempt to supply equipment, arms or explosives to any would-be resisters, no SOE agents sent in to organise and support resistance as happened in Holland and France. Perhaps the British Government believed that such help was impractical and also, agreeing with Sherwill, impolitic. They certainly believed that

the Islands had no strategic value.

However this may be, the Islanders could expect no help from across the Channel.

How, then, could the Islanders fight back at the invaders when all the obvious means to resist were denied them? Indeed should any attempt at all be made to defy the German occupiers if it would bring death and destruction to fellow Islanders?

In the event there was resistance in the Islands, and a lot of it too, but it was not of the 'sabotage and killing' style adopted by the Maquisards.

Resistance, Island fashion, had to take a different form if it was to take place at all. There was to be no blowing up of military installation, no killing of German troops and no destruction of the Islands' infrastructure. What there was to be was a great deal of resistance in the form of many other activities directed against the enemy. There was to be the creation of an underground press for the dissemination of news heard through illegally retained wireless sets or through home-made crystal sets. There were to be scores of minor acts of defiance directed against the enemy, including the 'V' sign campaign. There was, more importantly and dangerously, to be the provision of help, succour and refuge to many an escaped slave worker and also, even more dangerously, to at least two Jews, the most threatened people of all under Nazi rule.

The examples of this resistance are many, and many end horribly in torture and death. Taken together they form a resistance narrative which is shot through with ideals of common decency upheld against the most fearful odds.

It is a story to admire and to inspire and one of which the Islanders have every reason to be proud.

MAJOR MARIE

On a wet Sunday afternoon in November 1947, in the tiny Salvation Army hall in the parish of St Sampson, Guernsey, a very special ceremony took place. The Salvation Army General Albert Osborn was there to award the 'Order of the Founder' posthumously to Major Marie Ozanne. The mother of Marie, Sister Mrs D. Ozanne, accepted the award on her behalf.

The citation records that:

'After many years devoted service in France and Belgium, during the war years in her native Guernsey, under occupying forces, [she] maintained an outstandingly brave witness for God and for Salvation Army principles, was arrested and imprisoned. Until her death following shortly after her release, she revealed a self-sacrificing concern for men's freedom to serve God and for the saving of others.'

Marie Ozanne came back to her native Guernsey in May 1940 on the direct order of her Salvation Army Commander, Colonel Mary Booth. Marie had been over-working in Belgium and had become ill with the effort. It was thought best that she should rest and recuperate in her Island home with her parents. It was to be very far from a rest cure for, in the very next month, the Germans occupied the Islands and Marie saw that she had much more work to do in the service of her community.

After the massive evacuation of Guernsey in the June of 1940 the Island Salvation Army Corps was left without a leader. Marie Ozanne took on the role. When the 'V' campaign was at its height and the Germans were threatening hefty prison terms for the perpetrators, she wrote to the German authorities saying that she was quite prepared to serve the sentence for anyone who was found guilty of daubing the offensive sign around the Island. They did not take up her offer.

After the first six months of occupation the Germans, with their fear of anything in uniform, banned the Salvation Army altogether, closing down all the meeting places on 19th January 1941. Marie protested against this extraordinary order by standing outside the locked-up St Sampson's Citadel in her Salvation Army uniform in silent vigil.

More dangerously, because more publicly, Marie took to reading out passages of scripture in the St Peter Port marketplace with flagrant disregard for German authority. The Guernsey police, her friends and the townsfolk, all fully aware of the danger she was putting herself in, tried to stop her but to no avail. And more than this, Marie wrote to the *Feldkommandant*, not asking but demanding that the order banning the Salvation Army be rescinded.

Furthermore, whatever the Germans did or did not allow, she intended to open up the Salvation Army hall in Nocq Road and hold meetings there. The German authorities in the shape of Herr Zachau called her up to their headquarters at Grange Lodge. Marie arrived for the interrogation in full uniform. She refused to promise compliance with any of the German orders concerning her and the Salvation Army, and said that she would rather go to prison; indeed she asked to be put in prison. This was her way of protesting, her way of resisting.

Zachau plainly thought that she was mad and instead of punishing her for her intransigence he gave orders that she should be returned to the care of her parents and that she should get some medical help as a matter of urgency. He also ordered that all her uniforms should be confiscated and brought to him at Grange Lodge. Inspector William Sculpher, head of the Island police, oversaw the operation.

It must be said that not all the Island Salvationists approved of Marie's defiance of the Germans.

They saw it as an open invitation to the Germans to indulge in acts of reprisal, perhaps against all the members of the Salvation Army, which might result in fines, imprisonment and even deportation. Marie was only slightly deterred by this. She busied herself visiting Salvationists in their homes and conducting clandestine religious meetings, bible readings and scripture classes. For the next two years she wisely kept quite a low profile. That was until she heard the howling and the screams of the tortured workers in Paradise.

Paradise was the name of a house in the Vale district of Guernsey. Today it looks like what it is, a respectable, white-painted private dwelling by the side of an Island lane. But during the Occupation the Germans used it as a prison and punishment centre for the slave labourers who had in some way transgressed or defied their overseers. For these foreign workers shipped in from far Eastern Europe, Paradise became a hell. There was little subtlety about the way these *Untermenschen* were treated by their German captors, no sophisticated psychological torture, just plain straightforward whippings and beatings to the point of unconsciousness. The animal shouts and screams of these poor assaulted creatures filled the air around the Vale and came to the ears of Major Marie Ozanne. Again and again she wrote to the *Kommandant* protesting at the inhuman treatment meted out to the unfortunate inmates of Paradise. Her complaints reached such a pitch that the German authorities could no longer ignore her. Marie was arrested and imprisoned in St James' Street prison. In typical style she continued her ministry from within the prison writing many letters to her Salvationist flock, telling them to continue strongly in their faith despite the desperate times in which they were living, just as she was doing.

There was a story going round that she was roughly treated in the prison, even tortured, but according to her own account, in the diary she kept at the time, she was not maltreated in any obvious way at all by her German captors. What is certain is that, after a few weeks in the prison she was taken ill and suddenly collapsed.. She was immediately taken back to her parents' house where she stayed for three days, but she did not recover at all, in fact she got worse. Her health, which had deteriorated drastically during her incarceration, continued its downward slide. She was removed to the Castel Hospital. Here she lingered on for four months. The doctors did not have the drugs or the facilities to treat her condition and she died at the age of 37 in the springtime of 1943. The ultimate cause of her death was unknown, but traces of poison were found in her body at the post-mortem. The suspicion is that the Germans deliberately killed her by introducing a toxic substance into her meagre prison diet in the hope of removing this thorn in their side.

Again the evidence for this is far from certain but the Germans knew that her death might cause unrest in the civilian population. For this reason there was no account of her passing published in the Island press and only the briefest of brief ceremonies allowed at her burial in the Vale cemetery.

Marie Ozanne's protest achieved very little success in resisting the enemy, but it achieved a great deal in providing a glorious example of courage and sheer human decency in those morally difficult years of Occupation.

ANOTHER MOTHER'S SON

In the far north west of Jersey lies the parish of St Ouen, windswept, lying atop 300-foot cliffs. In this parish in the time of the Occupation there was a shop at La Fontaine called Millais Stores. This shop, a general store, was owned and run by Louisa Gould née Le Druillenec. She was a widow with two fine sons, and very fine sons at that. The oldest, Edward, was serving with the Royal Navy in the Mediterranean at the outbreak of war, one of the 10,000 Islanders serving with the British Armed Forces resisting Hitler's advance on all fronts.

The Bailiff himself, Alexander Coutanche, had a son in the Navy. John Coutanche was serving on HMS *Brissenden*.

The difference was that John Coutanche came home, Edward Gould did not. In the July of 1941 Louise received news that her brilliant and much-loved son had been killed in action serving King and Country.

A year passed. The character of the War changed. Life was getting harder. The Islands were to be heavily fortified, turned into great fortresses to protect the long German Western Front. And to build these massive military installations came the Todt workers, and with them hundreds of Russian slave workers captured on the terrifying Eastern Front.

Their appearance in Jersey went a long way to overturning the notion of the Germans as being rather benign invaders, for their treatment of these Russians who they regarded as *Untermenschen*, lower than the animals, beggared description. They were beaten, starved, tortured and shot as a matter of simple routine, and if they died, why it did not matter, for there were plenty more where they came from.

Among these Russian workers was 23-year-old Feodor Buryi Polykapovitch from Siberia, who was transported across Europe in a group of 200. They were all placed in a large labour camp at the bottom of the long Jubilee Hill in St Peter, and being a feisty fellow and judging that he was not in for a very pleasant time at all, Feodor made his first bid for freedom. It was a failure. He had no idea where he was, not even that he was on an island, and no idea where to go. Feodor was re-captured almost immediately.

By way of punishment and as a warning to others he was stripped naked, whipped and forced to pull a wheelbarrow filled to the limit with stones until his strength gave out and he fell to the ground unconscious. The guards revived him and then made him stand, unclothed as he was, all night outside the huts. Luckily for him it was August, it was summer and not freezing but the experience was bad enough. It did not, however, deter Feodor, but rather encouraged him to make another escape attempt. And this time he was to be successful, thanks to a number of Islanders who at considerable risk to themselves and their families gave help and refuge to the young Russian.

On Wednesday 23rd September 1942, Feodor slipped past the drunken guards (they had just been paid) and headed north up the bay into the parish of St Ouen and found refuge at the farm of Mr René Le Mottée who, at that time, was already hiding three other escapees. Feodor was given a mattress and shared a shed with one of these other Russian escapees and on Le Mottée's farm he stayed for three months. Conditions were not ideal but they were certainly better than in the camp at the bottom of Jubilee Hill.

The Parish of St Ouen is right up in the north-west corner of the Island and furthest away from St Helier. Bleak, windswept, relatively remote, it was probably the best place to hide if you were on the run. So it proved for Feodor up until the December of 1942 when the Germans made a great effort to round up Todt workers who had been escaping in increasing numbers during the autumn and committing robbery and murder in the process. For example, on the night of 1st December 1942, Mr Ernest Le Gresley and his sister were stabbed and beaten by two intruders seeking to rob their little shop in St Peter. Mr Le Gresley died of his wounds but, mercifully, his sister somehow survived. The perpetrators of this crime were declared by the *Feldgendarmerie* to be escaped foreign workers.

Leslie Sinel in his Occupation Diary for the autumn of 1942 records that:

'Robberies in the country parishes by foreign workers looking for food are on the increase, especially in the west, and it is not safe to leave anything about within reach of marauders. The Germans say that several Russians are missing and are at large in the Island, but if these poor creatures are guilty of robbing food, they are more to be pitied than blamed'.
(*Diary of Leslie Sinel, page 114*)

The 'country' folk were more than a little frightened. Robberies increased. Another Jerseyman was violently attacked by Russian escapees (it was assumed) in his home in the parish of St Mary on 18th December. The public were asked by the Germans to help in every way possible in the capture of escaped Russian prisoners. The Germans themselves launched house to house searches to discover the whereabouts of the absent workers in all the parishes including St Ouen.

Mr René Le Mottée was given advance notice of this search and thought it best that Feodor should leave the sanctuary of the La Villaise farm and take himself as fast as may be to another refuge.

Again the gods of good fortune smiled on Feodor Buryi for he found himself on the doorsteps of Louisa Gould. He told her he had nowhere to go. She took him in without hesitation, an act of kindness, as she said, 'for another mother's son'.

And she was to die for it.

Feodor Buryi Polykapovitch was taken into Louisa Gould's home and given refuge. He was also given the very English name of Bill, because, as Bob Le Sueur remarks, the good St Ouennais folk could not get their tongue around his Russian name of Polykapovitch.

'Bill' was dressed in Edward Gould's altered clothes and was treated as one of the family, looked after as if he were indeed Louisa's own son. Bill settled down, helped with the chores around the shop and was, generally speaking, wonderful company in that expansive Russian way. But he did suffer from depression and mood swings which could make him a little difficult at times.

English actors often complain when they are called upon to portray Russian characters, in Chekhov for example, that the emotional changes that are written happen too fast. They bemoan the fact that the almost instantaneous switch from euphoria to deep melancholy cannot be enacted 'realistically' or 'naturally'. What they mean is that an English sensibility, the English character, does not cater for such violent emotional shifts: 'we are not those kind of people'. However, the Russians are, and Bill was. In what we think of as typically Russian fashion he would have times of great happiness and good humour, he would work and, as he was a talented draftsman, do his drawings, then suddenly he would be plunged into deep depression. Bill also liked his drink and on one occasion, it is said, in the absence of vodka he drank methylated spirits as a substitute.

Whatever the difficulties of living with Bill may have been, they were more than outweighed by the happy times at La Fontaine. Bill was much-loved and stayed safely stored in St Ouens for two and a half years until May 1944, when, suddenly, unexpectedly, disaster struck.

Louisa Gould was betrayed. Luckily she had forewarning that the Germans were about to raid her home in search of an escaped Russian worker, and also her illegally-held wireless set. The letter of denunciation informing the Germans of Louisa's transgressions was intercepted. It had been sent to Victoria College. This was a mistake and an easy one to make (it was made many times in the course of the Occupation). The letter should have been sent to Victoria College House, another building entirely, the true headquarters of the *Feldkommandantur*. The deputy headmaster of Victoria College, Pat Tatum, who was no stranger to this kind of letter, steamed it open and instantly became aware of the danger to Mrs Gould. He got a message of warning through to Louisa, probably via the good offices of Norman Le Brocq's resistance

cell. He resealed the envelope and then waited 48 hours before forwarding it to the Germans at Victoria College House, judging that this delay would give Louisa time to move Bill out, remove any evidence of his stay in her house, and also hide the wireless. This was not the only warning she received. Bob Le Sueur says that Louisa received a warning from a most unlikely source, a 'Jerry bag' whose boyfriend was a German working just a short way down the road at L'Etacq:

'who told her there was a rumour of a Russian prisoner in that house and that the woman should be told or something would happen to her.'

Louisa and her sister Ivy Forster quickly began covering their tracks. Bill was instantly moved out of Louisa's house and into Ivy's. They set about frantically removing all trace of Bill's two and a half years' occupancy. But they did not succeed. When the Germans raided the house they found conclusive proof that Louisa had indeed harboured a Russian escapee.

They discovered little labels addressed to Bill from Louisa and Ivy which had been attached to Christmas presents. Expressions of affection become evidence of a 'crime'.

And there was more; a camera was discovered and, worse, the radio that had been concealed by the henhouse in the garden was also found. The German police, the *Geheimefeldpolizei* also found a shotgun and, most damning of all, a Russian-English dictionary.

On May 25th 1944 Louisa Gould, along with her maid Alice Gavey, was arrested. Seven days later Ivy Forster was likewise arrested. Bill had by this time been moved, along with another Russian who'd been hiding at the Forster's House, into Bob Le Sueur's office in St Helier. Seven days after that Berthe Pitolet and Dora Hacquoil, two of Louisa's greatest friends, were also arrested. Two days after their arrest Louisa's brother, Harold Le Druillenec, was arrested and imprisoned by the Germans, charged not with assisting escapees, but with listening to the radio.

On one of the very last shipping transports of the war, Louisa Gould, Harold Le Druillenec and Berthe Pitolet were conveyed to St Malo, arriving in the early hours of Sunday 2nd July. Mercifully Ivy Forster was not on that trip due to the fact that the Prison Governor of Gloucester Street had arranged to send her to the General Hospital where she was put in the care of a young doctor, Raymond Osmont. By substituting someone else's test results he pronounced with great verisimilitude that Ivy had tuberculosis and therefore could not be transported.

Louisa, Berthe and Harold were taken from St Malo to the prison in Rennes. Harold was moved on almost immediately, leaving the two women behind. The Allies bombed Rennes and

in that raid the prison was badly damaged and the walls of Louisa and Berthe's cell were blown down. Berthe escaped by simply running through the gap, but Louisa stayed put not wishing to endanger her friend by slowing her down.

When the smoke cleared Louisa Gould was herded onto a train heading north to the notorious Ravensbruck concentration camp. It was on this transport that she saw her brother Harold for the last time. It was a kind of miracle.

Thousands of people were being transported hither and yon to all points of the Nazi compass. Panic and chaos were everywhere, and yet it so happened that Louisa's train pulled to a stop at Belfort in the east of France. And who should she see in the train halted on the next track but her brother Harold! It was Harold Le Druillenec's birthday and Louisa contrived to get a tin of tobacco to him (he was a pipe smoker) by way of a present.

That meeting was the last piece of good fortune ever to fall Louisa's way.

Ravensbruck, 90 km north of Berlin, was a hellish place and had been since its creation by SS leader Heinrich Hurminster in 1938. Designed specifically for women, more than a 130,000 were interned in the death camp between 1939 and 1945. Of this number around 23,000 survived. Louisa arrived there in early August.

Her chances of survival were six to one against but survive she did but for just six months. On Tuesday 13th February 1945 Louisa Gould was taken into the gas chambers and killed. Her body was then burned.

No trace of her remained.

Bob Le Sueur believes that probably the greatest mistake of all happened to Louisa in Ravensbruck during her final days when she was wrongly categorised as being Jewish.

'There was a family theory that maybe the Germans thought that Gould was an Anglicisation of Goldberg and that she was a Jewess. I got to know Louisa quite well and she was the sort of woman who would not have been the soul of tact with the Germans whom she despised and loathed. And she was the sort of person, if you said to her "Are you Jewish?" if she said "No," which was true, she could have felt this was being disloyal to the Jewish women in that place. She was the kind of person who could have replied "That's none of your business!" or something of that sort.'

Louisa was probably thus classed as a Jew and was exterminated after she developed oedema and could no longer work, along with all the other Jewish women, one of the millions who perished in the Holocaust.

Louisa died, but Harold survived – just.

He found himself first in Wilhelmslaven,

which was terrible, and then in Bergen-Belsen, which was worse. In fact, he described it as *'the vilest spot that ever soiled the surface of this earth.'*

There was no food, little or no water. There was widespread disease, malnutrition and death. There was no way of disposing of the many, many corpses (35,000 dying of typhoid in the spring of 1945). Harold and other prisoners, scarcely alive themselves, would pile the naked bodies into obscene heaps around the camp.

Harold recalls:

'I noticed many of the corpses had a serious, deep wound in the thigh. There was no food, every blade of grass, every leaf of the tree had been eaten months before I ever got to the camp. At this stage one turned round to the corpses that were present and cut and ate, hence the wounds in the thighs, the favourite spot from which to remove a portion, although in fact, the favourite portion was the liver of a woman.'

Who had betrayed Louisa Gould? Who had written that letter of denunciation? And why?

Louisa's sister Ivy Forster and Harold Le Druillenec knew but would not say. Louisa's other son, Rex, did know and did say. Michael Ginns and Bob Le Sueur believe they know, and Eric Blakeney, who made what must be the definitive documentary of this sad episode, is certain he knows.

There were two people involved in the betrayal of Louisa Gould.

They were two of her nearest neighbours: Maud and Lily Vibert.

They were two elderly spinsters, sisters, who lived together in a single-storey house just over the road from Louisa's shop. Bob Le Sueur knew them and describes them as being:

'Two old biddies, the sort that in those days would wear long dresses, velvet collars and cameo brooches. Possibly they were jealous of Louisa with her two high-achieving sons and enjoying all kinds of little things the sisters did not have.'

It has been suggested that the sisters needed money like everyone else in the Island at this time, and so were attracted by the £100 reward offered to informers by the Germans. In other words they betrayed Louisa Gould for money. But if this had really been the case then they would surely have put their name on the infamous letter to College House so that the Germans would know to whom to send the reward. They did not do so. They were not motivated by greed then but rather, as Bob Le Sueur suggests, by jealousy and spite. A drama of parochial dislike finally played out in the Ravensbruck furnace.

There was an enquiry into the Louisa Gould affair at the end of the War, which was conducted by officers of the Civil Affairs Unit attached to Brigadier Snow's Liberation Force. Lily and Maud were questioned by Captain Bake. They denied everything, as they were bound to do, blaming another of Louisa's neighbours for the betrayal.

They signed a statement which includes the following:

'Maud and Lily Vibert hereby certify that Doris Le Gresley of Uplands, St Ouens, was the first person to tell that Mrs L. K. Gould was sheltering a Russian POW and listening to the radio. Mrs Gresley has told us that there was a reward of £100 and also that people had to sign to receive the money'.

Doris Le Gresley was the next neighbour of Louisa Gould and she lived with her sister Mary on the farm just across the road from La Fontaine. It was an ideal position from which to observe the comings and goings in the little shop. They would almost certainly have known that there was a Russian living in Louisa's house. But it was not the Le Gresleys who informed on Mrs Gould, despite Maud and Lily swearing that it was so. When the handwriting of the Vibert sisters was shown to the head of German security, Karl Lohse, he said it was exactly the same as that in the letter of denunciation sent in May 1944. Proof positive that Maud and Lily Vibert were the women who had betrayed Louisa Gould.

As in scores of other cases, no formal charges were ever brought against the two errant sisters. As in the matter of the 'Jerry bags' and the black-marketeers, the British liberating force under Brigadier Snow, working hard for a quick and quiet post-war settlement thought it best to leave such matters to the local community and whatever social sanctions they wished to employ. It was a local issue and should be dealt with locally. So Maude Mary and Lily Elsie Vibert were never dragged before a court. Instead they were left to the tender mercies of the little St Ouen's community they had so grievously betrayed.

They were ostracised for the rest of their lives.

Meanwhile, Bill and George were moved first into Bob Le Sueur's insurance office in St Helier and then into 'safe houses' about the town, at last ending up in the flat of two conscientious objectors, Mike Frowd and René Le Franoux. And here Bill stayed for the rest of the Occupation years. He perfected his English, helped with the household chores and even made a little money from selling his sketches of religious subjects at the shop of the Society for the Promotion of Christian Knowledge, work which must have meant a little suspension of his disbelief, Bill being an out and out communist and atheist.

Feodor finally returned to the Soviet Union at the end of the war but he was not accorded a hero's welcome. In common with all other Russian prisoners who had had contact with the West, he was regarded as 'tainted' and

'suspect' and true it is that the British Secret Service tried to recruit him as a spy but he refused the offer. Notwithstanding, he was kept under surveillance until the mid-1960s as a potential Western spy.

On 15th December 1965 the following message from Bill was published in the Jersey *Evening Post*:

'Greetings my dear friends on the far-away Island of Jersey which nevertheless remains close to my heart. A warm greeting to you and a Russian "thank you" from us all and from our relatives. My heart is wrung with pain that I shall never be able to greet nor affectionately shake the hand of that wonderful person who in a difficult period of my existence became a second mother to me – Mrs Louisa Gould. Yes, indeed she was a mother to me. She will remain forever in my heart.'

In that year too, Harold Le Druillenec and Norman Le Brocq, the communist leader of the small but highly effective resistance cell who had also helped Bill, went to Moscow to see Feodor, who by this time had ceased to be a suspicious character and had become quite a hero after a series of articles in *Pravda* on his experiences in Jersey.

RIGHTEOUS AMONG NATIONS
Bill was just one of a number of escaped Russian slave workers given refuge by the Islanders. Albert Bedane, for example, at one time had no less than three such Russians hidden in his home,

plus an escaped French prisoner of war. The Russian government some twenty years later in 1965 awarded Albert a rather large gold wrist watch by way of recognition of his great service to their countrymen.

But his courage went further than just helping the Russians, for Albert Bedane also hid a Dutch Jewish woman in his own home for well over two years, an infinitely more dangerous enterprise. By the German ordinances of Occupation the penalty for such concealment was summary execution by shooting. You might get away with a prison term for harbouring runaway *Untermenschen* Russian slave workers. There was no question but that you would be shot if you harboured a Jew. It was a brave man who would embark upon such a course. Albert Bedane was a brave man and was recognised as such by the State of Israel in January 2000 as 'Righteous Among the Nations' for saving of the life of a Jew.

Albert Gustave Bedane was, by all accounts, a quiet unassuming man. He had joined the Hampshire Regiment (the 'home' regiment for Channel Islanders) in 1917 at the age of 24 and then became a sergeant in the Royal Jersey Militia serving on the medical staff. After these years in the army he practiced as a qualified physiotherapist and at the commencement of the Occupation he was well established as a chartered masseur with a clinic adjoining his rather large house at 45 Roseville Street, St Helier. He lived there

on his own during these war years, his wife Clara and their teenage daughter having been evacuated to Devon immediately prior to the Occupation. The house itself was old and rambling with many rooms and attics and, best of all from Erica Olvenich's point of view, secret cellars – quite small, with low ceilings but nonetheless good enough to hide a person away from the eyes of the Jew killers. Erica Olvenich was a Dutch Jew, or so Albert Bedane thought, and everyone assumed. At the time of the Occupation she was known as Mrs Richardson for she had married a Captain Edmund Richardson who hailed from the mainland. She must have had a well-founded suspicion that no good would come of registering under that first anti-Jewish Order of October 1940 and so she did not do so. However everyone had to register in February of the following year under the Identification of Persons Order. Every single Islander had to sign up to this in order to obtain the identity cards without which life just became impossible.

Erica knew she would be in a lot of trouble if in the process of registration it was discovered that she was Jewish. She resorted to subterfuge. Freddie Cohen, in his definitive account of the Channel Islands' Jews, believes that she invented a couple of names for herself to throw the Germans off-track. First she registered her name as being Mary Richardson, Mary being a good English-sounding name. There is no record of her ever using that name before the registration of 1941. Secondly, and more tellingly, she entered her maiden name as Algernon rather than her actual maiden name of Olvenich, again with the same intention of hiding her Jewish background.

And it worked – for a time. It worked for over two years in fact, but then things went disastrously wrong for Erica. In the May of 1942 every single person was required to have his or her photograph taken so it could then be attached to their Identity Card. It appears that Erica did not comply with the instructions, for in the June of 1943 we find Mrs Richardson, Erica, being 'escorted' by Jersey's Aliens Office officials along to Scotts the photographers to have her photograph taken for precisely that purpose.

On that same day Erica was also taken to the *Feldkommandantur* at Victoria College House to be 'interviewed' by the Germans. It is reasonable to assume that her true Jewish identity was discovered in the course of this interrogation for as Albert Bedane himself recounts in an interview he gave to Jeanne Milne in the Jersey *Evening Post*:

'She [Erica] was allowed to go home and collect her jewels and valuables because, she was told, she was to be sent to a 'very nice, special camp,' where she would be well looked after and she would need her best things with her.'

It would appear from Norman Longmate's 1970 interview with Albert Bedane (recorded in the book *If Britain Had Fallen*) that Erica was accompanied back to her home in Dicq Road, St Saviour by German soldiers. Despite being so guarded, Erica, guessing at the nature of the 'very nice, special camp' she was promised, took to her heels and fled the 200 yards round the corner to Bedane's clinic in Roseville Street. This on 25th June 1943:

'The bell rang on the door of my clinic one day and I thought it was a patient. I went to the door and it was Mrs R and she was agitated and shaking. I said, "What's wrong with you?"
"Well, can I come in?"
I said, "Yes, come in", and she said, "The Germans are after me."
I said, "Where are they?" and she said, "I don't know. I left them in my flat. They made me pack up all my jewellery and good stuff and told me as I was married to an English officer … I was going to a special camp which was much better than any camp in Germany, so I was to bring all my best things … trunks, never mind how much, and I'd be well treated. Well," she said, 'during this time my husband, who was an invalid downstairs, he called out to ask if we'd like some tea and I said, 'Yes.' A German soldier came to me. I was at the passage by then. I said 'You go down and tell my husband to make the tea and we'll come down and fetch it'. He did, but I went into the next room which gave on to the fire escape, and escaped down it and ran here.'
(Longmate *If Britain Had Fallen*, page 200).

And Albert Bedane took Erica into his home and hid her from the Germans who had immediately mounted a search. They did not find Erica for she was down in the secret three-roomed cellar beneath Albert's house where she stayed for eight long months, never daring to venture out. And then in the spring of 1944 Albert moved her out of the cramped cellars and up into a more spacious upstairs room, the windows hung with net curtains to prevent people seeing in. Moreover Erica, to make assurance doubly sure, changed her hairstyle and took to wearing dark glasses, particularly on the very few occasions when she was allowed to get out of her prison and sit in the garden.

It wasn't much of a life but it was a life, and not the certain death in the 'very nice camp' in Germany.It was a life she owed to Albert Bedane. It must have been a long, fearful time for him, and indeed at the War's end Albert found himself in hospital on the mainland being treated for post-traumatic stress disorder, a direct result of his experience during the Occupation.

In the final few months of the War, with the Islands completely cut off from mainland Europe, the situation was adjudged to have changed so much that it was safe for Erica to return to her little house in Dicq Road and to her ailing husband, and here she stayed until the end of the Occupation, safe from the Nazi threat.

Albert Bedane returned to his practice in Jersey after recovering from his Occupation experiences and also from the tragic loss of his wife, Clara, who died in 1944. There was no recognition of his bravery by the Island, or the British government during his lifetime. He had the watch from the Russians and that was all. Albert Bedane died in his 87th year on 8th January 1980, and his body was cremated at Westmount crematorium. Nobody came to witness his passing. In the Jeanne Milne interview in the Jersey *Evening Post* he said of his Occupation, which could fairly be described as a near-death experience:

'I had a few nightmares occasionally, but I thought if I was going to be killed I would rather be killed for a sheep than a lamb anyway.'

Prime Minister Gordon Brown posthumously awarded the 'Hero of the Holocaust' medal to Albert Bedane.

THE UNDERGROUND NEWS

Jean Terfve of the Belgian *Front de l'Independence*, working at the end of the War, wanted and needed, for reasons of national pride, to produce a definition of resistance in order to identify all of his countrymen who were deserving of honour and recognition. The Belgians wanted to regain their pride, so badly hurt during their terrible war. He produced a very good description of the different types of resistance. And these apply very much to the anti-German activities in the Channel Islands during the Occupation.

Terfve listed three major forms of resistance. Firstly there was the most obvious form of resistance, sabotage. Then, secondly, there was the production of an underground press. And thirdly, helping people who needed to hide from the enemy. The common and defining feature was that those who pursued these activities should be in danger; their lives should be at risk.

As we have seen, resistance in the form of sabotage, blowing up military installations and killing German soldiers was just not an option in the Islands. But the other two types of resistance were.

Certainly many refugees from German persecution were given sanctuary by Islanders who risked their lives to do so and there was an underground press in the Islands, especially so in Guernsey in the shape of GUNS – the Guernsey Underground News Service. This was produced by professional newsmen at huge risk to themselves.

It is impossible to overestimate the need the beleaguered Islanders felt for news and information from a source other than Germany. During these Occupation years, disinformation, rumour and downright lies were everywhere. The official press, the *Evening Post* in Jersey, the *Gazette* and the *Star* in Guernsey, were all heavily censored. Items were deleted or re-written to accord with the aims of enemy propaganda on the command of the specially-appointed German censor.

And it was not just articles about the progress of the War that were interfered with. The German censor micro-managed the press to the point of altering the Reverend Hartley Jackson's little sermon published in the Guernsey *Star*. Violet Carey records this in her diary entry for 27th December 1941:

'Mr Hartley Jackson is livid with rage. The Star *asked him to write a Christmas message and he did, a very nice one. In the middle of this message came this paragraph: "What of the present? The recognition that Christ was born into the world to save the world and bring peace on earth is the need of Britain and her Jewish and Bolshevik allies"! He went to see the editor and was told the German censor had inserted that paragraph. He went to see him and he agreed to withdraw the paragraph, so he went back to tell the editor and the editor had allowed the article to be printed. It is rotten.'*

(Diary of Violet Carey, page 68)

News that could be trusted by the Islanders came courtesy of BBC radio broadcasts, but many wireless sets had been confiscated and it was forbidden to listen to such broadcasts.

Nevertheless a few people did listen to the news from London, concealing their sets in many an unlikely place – Louisa Gould hid her set under a step leading down to the henhouse in her garden. And, more than this, some of them copied down such news for publication via the underground press. The whole process: listening to the bulletins, writing out the content, printing it up and then disseminating it Island-wide was fraught with danger. One informer, one break in the chain, and the whole enterprise could collapse, with disastrous consequences for the organisers, as happened with the GUNS outfit.

This underground news sheet was set up in Guernsey during the May of 1942. It was the brainchild of Charles Machon, a typesetter with the *Star*, and it was intended to bypass the censored newspaper and provide the Islanders who did not possess a wireless set with news broadcast by the BBC in printed form. Machon was aided in his task by a core group of three men, fellow newspapermen Frank W. Falla, and friends Cecil Duquemin, Joe Gillingham and Ernest Legg. This group of Guernsey men managed to produce news sheets at the rate of around two dozen copies a day, every day bar Sunday, for almost two years. It was an incredible achievement.

But suddenly disaster!

On 11th February 1944 the operation was discovered and shut down by the Germans. And they had found out who was organising it through an informer called Peter Doyle, nicknamed Paddy, an Irishman who was to become one of the most reviled figures in the whole history of the Occupation of the

Channel Islands. Despite this, he got away scot-free with his crime at the War's end.

Peter Doyle was a communist and, being Irish, was thought of as neutral. He was also thought of as a friend by Charles Machon who would give him a copy of the GUNS news sheet as a matter of course on a daily basis.

Then at 11 p.m. on the night of 11th February 1944, two Guernsey police officers, PC J.W. Salmon and Police Sergeant Edward Dill, saw Peter Doyle with a group of Germans. He was leading them to Victoria Road where Charles Machon, and, a few houses down, Cecil Duquemin, lived. Peter Doyle had betrayed them.

The two men were arrested and taken to the German headquarters. They were 'interviewed'. Each day they would be taken from their cell and questioned harshly for hours on end.

This went on for 14 days.

Charles Machon was given a particularly hard time and suffered all the more because he had a stomach ulcer which caused him a deal of exquisite pain and discomfort, intensified by the Germans denying him the special food he needed because of that condition. Finally, at the end of days of interrogation, the German inquisitors played their trump card – they threatened to imprison Machon's mother if he did not confess all he knew.

She was 74 years old and in poor health.

He made his confession and was sentenced to two years imprisonment along with Cecil Duquemin. The other three 'offenders', Joseph Gillingham, Frank Falla and Ernest Legg were given lesser terms.

Charles Machon, deprived of proper medical care and without a proper diet, could not endure the conditions of his German prison and died a painful death in the September of 1944. He was interred in the Wehl Cemetery.

The other four GUNS men, Duquemin, Gillingham, Falla and Legg, were sent to Nuremberg prison near Frankfurt on Main where they suffered much from over-work and malnutrition, beatings and solitary confinement, to say nothing of lice infestations which were a particular source of aggravation. Frank Falla in his account of his experience in *The Silent War* says that:

'The trouble was the manner in which you acquired lice. Prisoners who were approaching death and couldn't care less about anything got infested, and their vests and shirts went to the prison laundry, carrying lice and eggs in their seams. Back came the garment which was then given out as clean to any other prisoner. Good though the cleaning should have been, it did not dispose of the lice eggs, and once they got in contact with the warmth of a prisoner's body, they came to life, and you, like it or not, were lousy.'

Conditions in the German prisons were truly appalling. One of the few relieving factors was an exercise in *schadenfreude* at the sound of the thousand bomber raids roaring overhead on their mission to level every German town and city to the ground. Even then the prisoners were not allowed to smile for fear of a beating.

At the time of his release by the Americans, Frank Falla was an angry man: angry at the Germans who had inflicted so much pain and suffering on him and his fellow Islanders and angry most of all at Peter Doyle, the Irishman who had betrayed the GUNS operation to the Germans. Immediately on his return to Guernsey he rushed to the British army officer who was there to hear any and every accusation of collaboration, ill-treatment, profiteering and treason that might be made by the Islanders. Frank Falla told the officer of Doyle's betrayal, and by way of corroborating evidence for the crime he advised the officer that he would find Wolfle and Einert, the Germans who had conducted the investigation, still in the Island at the POW camp. Peter Doyle would be found and punished severely – or so Frank Falla thought. But much to Falla's surprise, not to say disgust, the major refused to proceed with the matter saying, as Falla reports:

'Well personally, Mr Falla, I am very sorry about this. But I am afraid we are powerless to do anything in this matter, for we just could not take the words of Germans against those of an Irish

national. You'll have to forget it.'

And there the matter ended as far as Mr Doyle was concerned. He had by this time, it is thought on the advice of the British army Intelligence, fled to mainland UK. Had he not done so it is a certainty he would have been killed.

GUNS was a splendid acronym for the Island's underground press, and the other clandestine news sheet also had a memorable title. It was GASP, the letters standing for the Guernsey Active Secret Press, which indeed stayed secret until the very end of the War, signing off with the publication of Churchill's speech on 12th May, Liberation Day. They were lucky. There was no Peter Doyle on their doorstep. Their chief enemy was a carelessness born of over-confidence, leaving copies lying around in public places where German eyes might see them. The creator of GASP was Mr Ludovic Bertrand and he was assisted by Reginald Warley, who would type up Bertrand's long-hand copy of the BBC news. The news sheets would then be distributed by the man and wife team of Madeleine and Irwin Sims. These news sheets, printed on the ubiquitous tomato packing paper, found their way not only into the hands of locals and foreign workers, but also onto the desk of the Bailiff himself, Victor Gosselin Carey. And Martin Finch down at the emergency hospital would read out the news sheets, believing (correctly) as did Clifford John Cohu in Jersey, that the uncensored news from London would have a significant therapeutic

value for the patients.

And there were others who were anxious to spread the news of German defeats, like:

THE SURREAL SISTERS
St Brelade's bay is one of the most beautiful bays in the whole of the Channel Islands, with the great La Cotte cave at its eastern side and the lovely little church and fishermen's chapel by the perquage on the western wall. In the south-west corner of the graveyard the gravestones of two Jewish women stand side by side. On the one is inscribed the name of Lucille Schwab and on the other Suzanne Malherbe. Immediately behind these grave stones, just two steps away in fact, is that of Clifford Orange, Chief Aliens Officer for Jersey during the Occupation. But Orange never encountered the two women in his official capacity for, being wise French ladies with an understanding of what the Germans were up to, they did not register under the First Order against the Jews of October 1940.

Suzanne Malherbe and Lucille Schwab were French and they were half-sisters. During the pre-War years they had spent many a happy holiday in the Island, so much so that in 1937 the two came to live permanently in Jersey. They took up residence in a delightful Jersey granite home by the western slip looking out over the smooth sand towards the sea.

Beyond question Lucille and Suzanne

were the most exotic creatures in the Islands. Lucille Schwab, or Claude Cahun, which was her pseudonym, was a writer and photographer of note. Suzanne Malherbe, or Muriel Moore as she liked to be known, was a graphic artist. They had put together a wonderful art collection consisting not only of their own works but also some by the great painters of the time, including Picasso.

Lucille and Suzanne, who had been part of a left-wing anti-Nazi group *Centre-Attaque* in Paris during the 1930s, conducted a daring operation to undermine the German troops' morale, to destroy their confidence and their will to continue the fight. The sisters would, like Machon in Guernsey, note down items of news broadcast by the BBC on their *verboten* wireless sets. These items, containing as they did, news of endless German defeats and the apocalyptic bombing of German cities, were translated into German, typed onto small pieces of paper, together with anti-Hitler propaganda, and then signed 'the soldier with no name'. The little slips of paper were rolled up, placed in cigarette packets and left where the German soldiers were bound to find them as they walked along the top of St Brelade's beach or disported themselves on the sands.

It was a dangerous activity. As in so many cases of resistance in the Islands, the sisters fell victim to an informer, and this time we do not know who this was.

Lucille and Suzanne were arrested by the German police. They knew only too well what their fate was going to be.

Von Aufsess in his diary entry for 28th October 1944 wrote:

'There are very few Jews in the Islands. The two Jewish women who have just been arrested belong to an unpleasant category. These women had long been circulating leaflets urging German soldiers to shoot their officers. At last they were tracked down. A search of the house, full of ugly cubist paintings, brought to light a quantity of pornographic material of an especially revolting nature. One woman had had her head shaved and been thus photographed in the nude from every angle. Thereafter she had worn men's clothes. Further nude photographs showed both women practising sexual perversion, exhibitionism and flagellation. At the moment pronouncement of sentence is being postponed. Normally, on the charge of inciting the troops to rebellion they could be condemned to death, but women cannot be executed here.'

Lucille and Suzanne took poison in a bid to commit suicide. It failed and they were indeed both sentenced to death.

At this point the Jersey Bailiff, Alexander Coutanche, made a successful intervention on behalf of the sisters. It was not customary to execute women in Jersey he said. It was certainly not the Island way, and if the sentence were carried out, there was every possibility of civil unrest.

The German authorities listened carefully to Coutanche and then decided to commute the sentence to life imprisonment. This of course really meant imprisonment for the duration of the German Occupation, which lasted for another five months. Come the liberation the two women were freed and, though much damaged in health, they returned to their beautiful seaside home in St Brelade – only it was not so beautiful anymore. It had been looted and vandalised. The paintings by Picasso and Miró so disliked by Von Aufsess had disappeared, along with all the other works of art, photographs and pictures.

The furniture had also been removed – there was not a chair or a table in the place. The two sisters had suffered a fate common to many Islanders who for one reason or another were absent from their houses for any length of time. They would return to find the whole place plundered by their neighbours. The two sisters spent weeks hunting down their possessions with limited success. The paintings were never found and it is believed that they were burnt by the Germans, probably at the behest of the resident art connoisseur, von Aufsess himself.

Lucille and Suzanne, despite their horrendous ordeal and their narrow escape from death, could count themselves lucky, certainly as compared to the Reverend Clifford John Cohu.

THE GREAT CANON

Clifford Cohu was a Guernseyman, born in Câtel on 30th December 1883. He was educated at Keble College, Oxford, ordained in 1908 and saw many years of ministerial service in London where he was hugely popular and successful. Indeed he became for some little while the Canon of Allahabad Cathedral. In 1937, Cohu returned to the Channel Islands but this time to Jersey. He was so much looking forward to a long and happy retirement with his devoted wife Harriet. But it was not to be, for in 1940 he was called to serve as a Minister in Charge and Rector of St Saviour on the death of the Reverend Balleine (another wonderful eccentric, much given to showing off by proudly driving his sparkling Model T Ford round about his parish).

Clifford Cohu quickly established himself firmly in the affections of his Jersey flock, not least because of his extravagant and colourful behaviour. A friend of his described him as being a complete and utter extrovert who cared nothing for the Germans. He also cared nothing, it seems, for his own safety, defying in a most public fashion many of the German orders – he must have understood that riding his bicycle down the Parade in St Helier shouting out anti-German news to everyone within earshot would not endear him to the Secret Police. He must have known, too, that recounting stories gleaned from from the BBC of wonderful British victories to cheer his patients up when he did his hospital rounds at the general hospital would put him at risk. Terrible risk as it turned out, for the Reverend Cohu had made himself into something of a local hero, a fine example to the local populace of defiance in the face of the enemy.

There is no doubt that the Germans wanted this turbulent priest removed from the Island society as quickly as possible – and in the spring of 1943 they got their man.

Leslie Sinel in his diary entry for March 13th writes:

'The Germans are hot on the trail of persons who are alleged to be spreading wireless news; several well known residents of St Saviour's parish, from the church district, are in prison for this 'offence'; these include the acting Rector (Canon Cohu, who is also Hospital Chaplain), the Deputy (who is also a churchwarden), the Parish Clerk, a Vingtenier and his son, and the gravedigger. If every person who spreads news were arrested there would be more in jail than out, for there are large numbers of wireless sets still in use, hidden in all sorts of queer places.'

The wireless set which was the source of all Cohu's news was in the possession of a vingtenier farmer, Mr Nicolle, in the parish of St Saviour, and his son John. These two passed on the news they received through the radio to the gravedigger in St Saviour, a Joseph Tierney, a supremely cheerful individual

despite his depressing calling. He in his turn passed it on to Clifford Cohu.

Joseph was the first to be arrested by the Field Police on Wednesday 3rd March 1943. Many more arrests took place in the next three weeks, including that of Clifford Cohu.

The Reverend Cohu was delivering his sermon in his church when he was taken by the Germans. The congregation was large, and at the very back sat two German soldiers in uniform who were regular worshippers at the church. They would sing the hymns in German as they spoke but little, if any, English. They certainly would not have understood that Cohu was inserting little pieces of news about the Allies' progress in his sermon as he was wont to do.

On this day he was half way through his news bulletin disguised as a sermon when the doors of the church burst open and six Geman soldiers with rifles and fixed bayonets charged down the aisle. They dragged the Reverend gentleman from his pulpit in a most irreverent manner and marched him away, a prisoner of the Reich.

On 9th April the trial was held of 17 people accused in the St Saviour's wireless case. The sentences varied between two years and two weeks. Tierney received a two-year sentence and Cohu 18 months, which would appear at first glance to be unduly severe, but as Paul Sanders points out, 'a hidden agenda was at work seeking to isolate "troublemakers" and emblematic figures like Cohu.'

Quite simply, the Germans wanted to get rid of any focus for defiance and resistance in order to render the civilian population quiescent and more manageable. By this time too, it must be noted, the morale of the German soldier was in danger from the dissemination of BBC news. It was a bad thing for the rank and file to hear of all the Allied victories north, south, east and west, and the great number of cities across Germany being continually bombed, day and night. Their countrymen, their loved ones, their nearest and dearest being horribly done to death in their thousands.

The aim was to stop the flow of any news detrimental to the Nazi cause and only allow Goebbels to tell the story of the War – the spin-doctor of all spin-doctors pointing the way through the ruins, the defeats and the heaps of German dead onwards and upwards, towards the Final Victory!

Clifford Cohu, lightly built (he weighed only 10st 7lbs), ageing but strong in spirit was taken eventually to a prison in Frankfurt, right under the flight path of the Allied bombers. There was little food, it was very cold and the work was impossibly hard. Frank Falla of GUNS fame, in his account of his time in that Frankfurt prison, recalls that many executions took place there – up to 30 a week courtesy of Madame Guillotine. And the men who were executed were mostly the victims of Roland Freisler's 'Peoples Court' – tried for actions hostile to the Nazi regime.

Falla recalls that he was very much impressed by Cohu's courage and endurance and also that of his fellow prisoner, Jo Tierney.

And they had a lot to endure.

Freezing cells, long periods of solitary confinement, a starvation diet, often hard and gruelling physical labour, abuse and assault. Falla, Cohu, and several of the Channel Islanders were transferred from the Frankfurt prison to Nuremberg in the July of 1944. Conditions here were truly terrible, even more so than at Frankfurt. Rations were far below subsistence level. Disease was rife and there was no medication made available to the wretched prisoners. When Frank Falla asked Dr Hohner, the prison doctor, for some aspirin by way of treatment for his pneumonia, the good doctor, having discovered Frank was English, screamed at him:

'Nein, alles für die Wehrmacht! Nicht Englander'.

A statement that had nothing to do with the Hippocratic oath and everything to do with the massive bombing of German cities.

After liberating the prison in April 1945 the Americans found a great stock of medical supplies in the prison stores: bandages, dressings, disinfectant, lice powder and soap, the distribution of which would have gone a long way to alleviate the suffering of the Nuremburg inmates. Dr Hohner simply withheld these life-saving supplies. He was accused of maltreatment and was imprisoned by the Americans in one of the cells, where he died from unknown causes some three weeks later.

Frank Falla was free but Clifford John Cohu was definitely not. He had been delivered into the hands of the SS and taken to an *Arbeitserziehungslager* (a work education camp) in Zöschen. There were over 200 of these camps.

The prisoners who were incarcerated in these hellish places were mostly labourers, both German and foreign, who had proved recalcitrant in some way, refusing to toe the party line or disobeying orders at work. It was thought that a period in the extra-primitive conditions of these camps would bring the inmates round to a more positive way of thinking and behaving.

For Cohu it would bring more increased suffering and eventually death.

Clifford Cohu was already skeletal and enfeebled when he arrived in Zöschen. He had lost one third of his body weight. Moreover he was the only Englishman in the camp and a priest to boot. This made him mortally vulnerable to the attention of the German guards. They could take out all their hatred of the English on him as he

stood weak and defenceless before them. They starved him, mocked him, inflicted terrible beatings on him and abused him in most ways known to man. 'You English swine, you want to bomb us we'll bloody well show you,' said they.

He did not last long. Clifford came to Zöschen on Wednesday 13th September 1944. On Wednesday 20th September 1944 he died. It had taken seven days to finally kill the man. His death was witnessed by fellow prisoner Przemysl Polacek, a Czech who managed to survive the camp. He recalls that when he was stripping Cohu prior to incineration he discovered a miniature bible hidden on his chest. How he had contrived to keep the precious book away from the Germans is little less than miraculous, but Canon Clifford John Cohu died as he had ever lived, with the words of Christ beside him.

MUTINY AND REVOLUTION

From the other end of the theological spectrum, over in Jersey, came Norman Le Brocq, an avowed communist, to be numbered amongst the successful, if not the most successful of the Island resisters.

To be a communist in a Nazi-occupied country was to invite imprisonment and death. To pursue a course of active resistance against Germans was doubly dangerous. Had he been caught, there is not the slightest doubt he would have been swiftly transported to a concentration camp as a mortal enemy of the Third Reich and there he would probably have died.

Norman Le Brocq was not caught, because he was a clever and resourceful man, despite being only 18 years old when the Germans came marching into Jersey. A stonemason by trade, he was a member of the Transport and General Workers Union as well as of the Communist Party. There was no great communist cell in Jersey in the immediate pre-War years, indeed the Island group was tiny having only six members. This was reduced to three when three members left in the evacuation. But though small in number, the remaining trio carried on a highly successful resistance operation for the whole of the five years of Occupation. First, they increased their manpower by creating an alliance with a small cadre of centrist socialists and titling the union the JDM or Jersey Democratic Movement.

Having no access to weapons or explosives the resistance of the JDM took the form, in the first instance, of producing leaflets printed off on a duplicating machine which Le Brocq had carefully concealed in his great aunt's attic. These leaflets, produced at the rate of 300 or 400 at a time, were distributed at regular intervals for the rest of the War and the authors were never discovered. There was none of the GUNS disaster in Jersey, no Paddy Doyle to play the informer. Given the number of informers in the Island and given the amounts of money offered by the Germans for information on such resistance activity, this is remarkable, and a tribute to Le Brocq's organisational skills.

The leaflets themselves were full of anti-fascist material and information designed to bolster opposition morale – and not only among the Islanders. Some of the leaflets were published in Russian and found their way into the labour camps where the Soviet slave workers might read some hopeful news to ease their suffering. These leaflets also found their way to those Russians in the Island who had volunteered for service in the German army to fight against the Bolsheviks. Leaflets were also published in German, particularly towards the end of the Occupation when the Axis powers went into full retreat on every front and disaffection was thought to be spreading in the rank and file of the Island garrison.

Norman and his men were very anxious to fan the flames of insurrection in the *Wehrmacht*, and it seems they were on the verge of a great success when the War ended.

In the meantime the chief aim of the JDM was to provide refuge and safety for escaped slave workers. Slave workers such as 'Bill' Feodor Polykapovitch. Le Brocq and the party secretary Les Huelin would find the escaped prisoners and send them to 'safe houses'. They would regularly move then from one such place to another either to avoid one of the German searches or simply to escape detection by local informants as in the case of Bill. Wisely, a degree of anonymity was introduced into the running of this network of safe houses. The two conscientious objectors Mike Frowd and René Le Franoux who gave Feodor refuge when he was moved from Louisa Gould's house in St Ouen would not know who had looked after the Russian prior to his arrival on their doorstep. In that way the integrity of the network could be preserved. If one refuge was discovered it would not follow that all such refuges would be compromised. Moving circumspectly, the JDM resistance group managed to maintain their anti-German campaign for the whole of the Occupation, saving the lives of many a Russian and providing a regular flow of information and anti-Nazi propaganda to all sides involved in the Occupation of Jersey.

The big opportunity for the JDM group to achieve a more spectacular anti-German strike came in the spring of 1945, the last year of the War. They made contact with Paul Mülbach, a mutinous anti-Nazi German solder who had fought in Spain in the International Brigade. While fighting unsuccessfully against Franco's forces he was captured and returned to Germany and, like many men at that time, he was told to either join the army or go to the notorious Dachau concentration camp.

It was in this terrible place that Mülbach's father had died after being imprisoned there for opposing the Nazi regime. Mülbach saw it was no choice at all and so, not wishing to follow his father to an early grave, he joined the German army and found himself on the Eastern Front. He survived the experience but suffered a serious injury which meant he had to wear a surgical boot and had a pronounced limp.

More importantly he had a great ambition to incite mutiny amongst the German troops and there was never a better time to achieve this than in that spring of 1945.

No one with eyes to see and ears to hear could doubt that the Third Reich was doomed. Berlin was in ruins. Every day, every night, bombs rained down on the virtually defenceless cities and industrial centres of the Fatherland; every day, every night the Allied armies from east and west advanced further towards Germany. Hitler might try a blitzkrieg assault in the Battle of the Bulge. The new 'wonder weapons,' the V1 and V2 might take to the skies, the Volksturm might be mobilised, the very children of the Reich be conscripted, but nothing could change the course of the War. The last scene of the last act was being played out. Hitler was in his bunker and German defeat inevitable.

And what of the German soldiers left behind in the Islands? Their kinsfolk, wives and children were being blasted into oblivion all across Germany. They themselves were ill, starving and fainting with hunger. They were dressed in rags.

They were thoroughly demoralised to the point where, for many of them, peaceful surrender would be a wonderful release. But then Admiral Friedrich Hüffmeier took over as German commander-in-chief from General von Schmettow. As we have seen, Hüffmeier was not much of a seaman (though he liked to pretend otherwise) but he was very much a Nazi with an unswerving party loyalty to Hitler. There would be no surrender, no capitulation, only armed resistance to the very end. 'We will eat grass rather than surrender' he informed an understandably alarmed Bailiff Coutanche. As late as 29th March 1945 he was declaring to a mass meeting of officers and men in the Forum Cinema:

'I shall hold out here with you until final victory – we cannot be shamed before the Fatherland.'

The Admiral was plainly prepared to die in a last battle and, even more plainly, expected his men to die alongside him. Many of the Island garrison recognised only too well that this was a nothing short of a suicide mission. Dying for a lost cause was not an appealing prospect. Mutiny was in the air.

The Jersey Democratic Movement and Paul Mülbach were very anxious to encourage it. Calling themselves the Free Germany Movement, *Es Leben des Freies Deutschland*, they produced little leaflets in German aimed at rousing the troops to mutiny and encouraging them to kill those officers intent on holding out to the last. More than this, it seems, they dabbled in more violent forms of resistance. Together with Mülbach they destroyed a part of a German bakery in St Helier using explosives stolen from the German military.

It was not a particularly successful foray into the land of armed resistance, but it was a gesture.

It is claimed too that Paul Mülbach set fire to the Palace Hotel in St Helier on 7th March 1945. This was followed by a massive explosion that brought down the entire building. It would seem however that this explosion might have been an accident rather than design.

Hauptmann Kegelmann, the Adjutant, tried to create a firebreak to stop the spread of the fire by laying demolition charges in the central three floors of the hotel. He hoped in this way to contain the blaze and allow time for the army personnel to be evacuated and all the explosives and ammunition stored in preparation for the Granville raid to be removed. In the event, everything went up in a mighty explosion and one officer and nine NCOs lost their lives. From Mülbach and the JDM's point of view a great, if unintended, result. Sinel records in his diary entry for 7th March:

'A fire broke out at the Palace Hotel this morning; when this spread to an ammunition dump, there was a violent explosion which shook the town and did widespread damage, windows being

shattered in districts far removed from the scene of the fire. In the immediate vicinity many houses suffered damage to windows, doors, ceilings, etc, and flying debris was found in neighbouring fields. In addition, 15 gas meters exploded and ammunition was heard going off until late in the evening, the fire brigade having an unenviable task. The main part of the building was gutted. The Germans have been at the Palace since the start of the Occupation. At night a shed at the Todt depot at Georgetown also caught fire and was burnt out. It is understood the Germans suspect sabotage.'

If indeed it was sabotage then it is certain that Paul Mülbach, aided by the JDM, was a prime mover, and he was upping his game; moving towards his ultimate goal of a mass mutiny among the troops of the German garrison in order to bring about immediate surrender. The time was ripe for such an insurrection in the German ranks but there was something else going on at the heart of the Jersey Democratic Movement which was truly shocking. Bob Le Sueur, a founder member of the JDM, tireless in his resistance, says:

'I learned by chance that the inner group of the JDM was actually proposing in the chaos of the mutiny and with the help of rogue elements in the German army, to liquidate several members of the Jersey administration, including the three Crown Officers, and set up a kind of 'People's Democracy' on the pattern of those which were established in Eastern Europe.'

Having this knowledge impaled Bob Le Sueur firmly on the horns of a dilemma. He was very desirous of the mutiny taking place in order to stop the Admiral's plan to hold out to the very last, but on the other hand:

'The thought that senior members of the Jersey administration would be dealt with summarily by mutinous soldiers at the behest of a few unrepresentative individuals intoxicated with the heady prospect of power was totally unacceptable.'

Bob Le Sueur considered his options:

'I thought of seeking an interview with the Bailiff but decided against it. It would have placed him in an impossible situation of possibly feeling that he had to report it to the Platzkommandantur in the interest of the safety of the Island population as a whole and for which he had responsibility. People I knew, and in most cases respected as individuals, would have been shot. The Bailiff would have survived but would have been branded a traitor. If I did nothing there was an image of soldiers with guns storming past the States buildings, shooting anybody who moved, any terrified typist.'

It was an impossible dilemma, weighing the worth of one life against another. Whatever decision he took would result in unwanted deaths for which he would be responsible.

'It would be satisfying if I could report

here that I worked on some brilliant alternative strategy. Sadly I can claim no such glory. On the premise that sometimes in life it is better to delay, to hope for the best, I did absolutely nothing.'

Events then overtook the plotters. On 3rd May 1945 this appeared in the *Evening Post*:

'Adolf Hitler falls at his post fighting to the last breath. He has met a hero's death in the capital of the German Reich'.

Admiral Doenitz was declared Hitler's successor. Admiral Doenitz dallied with the notion of a re-alignment of the warring parties by which Germany would join with Britain and America to fight the common enemy, the Jewish Bolshevist armies of Russia. It is quite remarkable how many of the German commanders thought that such a re-alignment of the warring parties was even a remote possibility. Himmler certainly thought it was a viable solution to Germany's problems and Göring openly boasted of the part he would have to play in the new alliance. Even Albert Speer subscribed to the view.

Down in Jersey, Bailiff Coutanche recalls a conversation he had on 6th May with Admiral Hüffmeier, who said:

'Of course, everything has changed. I don't know how much you know, but the fact is that your country and the Americans are going to join forces with us and we are all going to fight the Russians.'

The grand admiral was living in a dreamland.

Of course no such alliance of the three powers was possible. This was made crystal clear at Lüneburg Heath when Field Marshal Montgomery told the German generals that there would be no peace on negotiated terms.

Absolute and unconditional surrender was what the Allied Powers wanted and what they were going to get.

On 7th May Doenitz ordered the surrender of all German forces everywhere.

That the admiral surrendered without, as he had threatened, blowing up all the arms and ammunition, was due to the orders he received directly from Supreme Commander Doenitz. On 8th May Von Aufsess spoke in the States of Guernsey. He spoke in English and he spoke plainly.

'The War is over, we herewith hand back the Islands to you.'

The formal surrender of the Islands took place the next day aboard the HMS *Beagle* off Jersey. It was all over as far as the Germans were concerned – no need for mutiny now, no need for any more resistance, nothing left, only a desire in the Islands to express their overwhelming joy for their deliverance that had been five long years in the coming. Time too for the band of Islanders who had, in ways both great and small, resisted the Nazi invaders, to celebrate their liberation. Sadly there were those who could not be there on that glorious May day in 1945, Louisa Gould, Charles Machon , Clifford Cohu, John Nicolle, Joe Tierney and all those who lives had been destroyed in this the most terrible of wars the world had ever seen.

HAROLD LE DRUILLENEC'S TESTIMONY IN THE POST-WAR TRIALS

Harold was first examined by Colonel BACKHOUSE:

- I am a British subject, a schoolmaster by profession, and my address is 7 Trinity Road, St. Helier, Jersey. On 5th June, 1944, I and most of the members of my family were arrested by the Germans because we had helped a Russian prisoner to escape some 18 months before, and we were also in possession of wireless sets which were forbidden. I was taken to a prison near Rheims in Brittany, to Belfort, and finally to Neuengamme, where I arrived, as far as I can remember, on 1st September, 1944. From there I was sent on a Kommando to Wilhelmshaven, where I was made an oxy-acetylene welder in the region of the arsenal. Eventually I went to Belsen, arriving there about 5th April, around 10 o'clock in the evening. I received no food on arrival, but some fortunate individuals who had a few cigarettes or a bit of bread from the journey had soup – swede, turnip or mangel – offered to them in exchange. I was taken to Block 13. I should think, on that night, there must have been somewhere around 400 to 500 people in that block.

I would like you to describe to the Court in your own words, just what conditions were like in that block that night?
- To begin with, a French Colonel, an old friend of mine from the previous camp, and myself turned into one of the few beds, three-tiered bunks they were, in the hut. About five minutes later some severe blows on the head made us realize that we were not supposed to be there. We gathered from this language of blows that these beds were reserved for the officers and orderlies amongst the prisoners themselves. The Colonel and I made a point of finding some other French people – there was safety in being in groups – and sat with legs wide apart and other people sitting in between in a group on the floor. Sleep was impossible; the whole hut I should describe as a babel gone mad. Actually that proved to be my luckiest night in Belsen, because the next day or two the next Kommandos were sent in and had to sleep in this already overcrowded hut. The floor was wet and abominably foul and we had to lie in that, but we were allowed two very tattered blankets. The next morning, about half-past three, we were roused and sent out of the hut, again the language of blows being the only way of giving orders.

Did anybody die in that hut that night?
- After we had been out on the Appell, or roll call, for some time the next morning the hut was cleared of the superficial debris, litter, etc, and then some seven or eight dead were taken out and put in a latrine trench, which ran the whole length of most of these huts.

Were there any rafters in the hut?

- Yes, boards were usually put across two rafters by some enterprising prisoners, and rather than sleep on the murderous floor below they slept across these narrow boards. Most of the people in the hut were suffering from dysentery, and, as many of those people on the boards were suffering from this, I think I can leave the rest to your imagination. It was possible for people below to move out of the way, but if they had they would probably never have found a place to get down again, so after a little experience they learned it was better not to.

Were you allowed out of the hut at all during the night?

- No. It was humanly impossible to get out since the whole floor was just one mass of humanity, it would have meant walking across people in order to get out; in any case the door was shut. People were lying against it, and I think that it was locked as well.

What was the atmosphere inside that hut like?

- Well, it is rather difficult to put into words. I do not think it is humanly possible to describe that – it was vile. I think I have told you sufficient to make you realize that the smell was abominable; in fact it was the worst feature of Belsen Camp. A night in those huts was something maybe a man like Dante might describe, but I simply cannot put into words.

The next morning you say you left the

hut. Please go on from there?

- For the first three or four days I was in Belsen we had nothing in particular to do. The Appell, which used to last from about half-past three – I am judging times, as I had no watch, of course – till about eight or nine o'clock in the morning, was in itself a terrible strain. The Appell is the normal concentration camp roll call, during which time you are supposed to stand in ranks of five, at attention, I presume to make the ranks easy to count, and you are counted and then counted again ad infinitum for some hours – apparently no two men could make the total the same. If you moved you received the usual blow on the head, the weapon used being a stick some four or five feet long and one and a half inches thick; it was usually a very hard blow.

Were you given any food before the Appell?

- No, nor drink.

What food did you have during the day?

- The first day I had precisely nothing.

How were you employed during the day?

- We did nothing that day. Most of us went out into the yard adjoining the block and slept, as was the custom at Belsen, in heaps. At the end of the morning a French friend of mine asked me if I had inspected the long grey brick-built hut on the other side of our yard, and invited me to go and look through the windows, or rather, holes in the walls. The first window showed only a wash-house room, a very crude place with one or two dead bodies floating about, or rather reclining on the flooded floor. The second window gave me a terrible shock. This room was absolutely filled up, and I really mean filled up, with dead bodies. These dead were arranged with the crown of one's head touching the chin of the one just below him, and in that way I should think there were many hundreds per room. We strolled down the yard looking into each window in turn, and in every room of that very long hut the sight was precisely the same. I had some experience with dead people before, both at Bremen and at Lüneburg, but this particular sight made me wonder all the more, after the first night at Belsen, what sort of hell I had entered. The rest of the day was just spent lying about on the ground outside hoping against hope some food would turn up.

What was the next night like?

- Rather worse. Some more Kommandos had arrived by then and the hut was more crowded than on the previous night. By the second day we realized that although some rather primitive type of sanitation existed, it was not used by the vast majority.

Did you receive any food or water on the second day?

- I had that day about an inch and a half of soup in an ordinary army enamel mug which I had to go and pick up off a certain heap of discarded effects of the dead, and there being no water to wash it in, I just had to eat out of that like many hundreds of others. We used to have the food given us in the hut; actually everyone had to get into the hut first. Then we went out with our little portion, and we had to keep giving furtive looks behind and chasing from one corner to the other, so as not to drop even a spot of rather precious food.

What was the attitude of the SS guards to the prisoners?

- I did not see very much of the SS during my short stay in Belsen, but on one occasion later I did see an SS officer whipping the women in the women's compound near the burial pits because they had lit some fires to do some rather primitive cooking.

What was the attitude of the Blockältesten?

- Particularly vile. They used to have some soup apparently sent to the block at midday, and distributed to the other officers, and to anyone who had a few cigarettes to exchange. The usual rate of exchange being three cigarettes to one plate of soup, though the vast majority of ordinary prisoners in the hut never even saw that soup – if we did have a little it was at night. The SS made no attempt to control the block leaders. On the fifth day I began work, and worked roughly for the last five days.

Prior to beginning to work were the other days much the same as the day you have described?

- More or less.

There were one or two rather startling events, of course. I remember seeing my first friend, not quite dead, brought out of the hut in the morning and lined up with the people actually dead, then later on, still alive, dragged off to the hut east of Block 13, which was being used as a mortuary. In the first four days at Belsen I had, all told, about a pint of soup, about an inch and a half depth, in an army mug each day for about four days. On the fourth day the water was turned on for maybe half an hour in the hut used as a mortuary and after negotiating three or four corpses you could get to the taps, and there, despite the warning of one of my friends that I would catch typhoid if I drank, I did have one mugful of water.

Will you now tell the Court about the first day you began work?

- In the beginning the work was rather interesting because we were herded as a block, some six or seven hundred maybe into the mortuary yard by means of blows, the language we understood pretty well by then; we were made to understand that we had to drag these dead bodies a certain route to what we were to find to be large burial pits. The procedure was to take some strands of humid blanket from a heap where the effects and clothing of the dead had been put, tie these strips of blanket or clothing to the ankles and wrists of the corpses and then proceed to walk to the pits. We started work at sunrise and were up quite a long time before that. We got no food before we started and worked till about 8 o'clock in the evening. In those five days or so I spent on this burial work neither a spot of food nor a drop of water passed my lips.

Will you describe one of these days?

- After the usual terrible night we started the Appell first. After about two hours of that we would be herded in the usual manner to this yard. We tied the strips of blankets to the wrists and ankles of the dead bodies, which we picked out most carefully. Firstly, we found the shortest corpse possible; they were all emaciated and more thin than anything I had imagined before, so by getting the shortest we were bound to get the lightest. Secondly, we chose one that was not too black. Our first task in the morning was to bury the fresh dead that had been brought from the various huts in my portion of the camp to the mortuary yard, not those which were in the hut. Despite the fact that there must have been over 2,000 all told occupied in this work, it used to take us nearly the whole morning to empty that yard prior to going into the rooms to start burying the old dead. We then left the northernmost gate of the yard with the body dragging behind, usually allowing maybe two metres between the foremost people dragging and the body in front. If you allowed more than that a hit on the head made you hurry up to reduce the distance. We made our way along the central road towards the burial pits. Along this road, stationed at intervals, were orderlies to see that the flow of dead to the pits carried on smoothly; they were particularly numerous near the kitchen and the reservoir water. One of the most cruel things in this particular work was the fact that we passed this water regularly on every trip, and although we were dying of thirst we were not allowed to touch it or get anywhere near, nor were we allowed to get to the heap of swede peelings near the kitchen. A few of those would have made us a very fine meal indeed in the state we were in. Nearing the pits I found out that the pits themselves were being dug by so-called free foreign workers. I cannot very well explain my feelings when I first saw one of those pits which already contained many dead, and had to throw my particular corpse on top of those others already there. During the dragging process I noticed on many occasions a very strange wound at the back of the thigh of many of these dead. First of all I dismissed it as a gunshot wound at close quarters, but after seeing a few more I asked a friend and he told me that many prisoners were cutting chunks out of these bodies to eat. On my very next visit to the mortuary I actually saw a prisoner whip out a knife, cut a portion out of the leg of a dead body and put it quickly into his mouth, naturally frightened of being seen in the act of doing so. I leave it to your imagination to realize to what state the prisoners were reduced for men to chance eating these bits of flesh taken out of black corpses.

What was the attitude of the SS and of the orderlies you have mentioned while all this was going on?

- To get on with the job as quickly as possible. My own idea is that it was to make a good impression on the advancing British army. We knew it was coming. We could hear the guns; and I think the whole idea was to clear the camp of as many dead as possible before they arrived. I would like you to picture what this endless chain of dead going to the pits must have looked like for about five days from sunrise to sunset. How many were buried I have no idea. It must have been vast numbers – certainly five figures.

What happened to a prisoner who fell out on this parade?

- You didn't dare to fall out, but many collapsed on the way – just lay dead by the roadside, or died. They in turn were lifted by a team of four and taken to the pits. People died like flies on the way to these pits. They did not have the necessary energy to drag even those very light bodies. A man who faltered was usually hit on the head, but many people were cunning, and if no orderlies were round about they used to leave their corpses stranded by the roadside and go back to the mortuary for another, because they would pass the kitchen or reservoir, and they still had hopes that they would reach some food or water.

Were you struck at all yourself during this period?

- Oh, many times. You were bound to get hit in the normal course of the day. You were bound to get hit on the head in the morning getting out of the hut, whether you were out first or last. You were bound to be hit in getting to the mortuary, and all along the way to the pits. They were just odd blows here and there, given, I suppose, for the fun of the thing. One ceases to question in a concentration camp why things happen. One is taught from the very beginning just to accept things as they are.

Were any of the guards armed with firearms?

- Yes. All the SS and Hungarian guards in the look-outs and who walked about in the camp. The first few days I did hear some shots, but saw no results, and in the last few days the shooting was almost furious, barely a minute of the day or evening passed without hearing a shot somewhere. Usually it was a whole volley of shots. I saw plenty of shooting, usually for no reason at all. Sometimes there was a hidden reason which we learned of only after many dozens had been killed; for example, at the north entrance of the mortuary yard many people had been killed before we realized that the particular guard in charge of that gateway wanted to see people go through at the double dragging the dead body behind. He was a member of the Hungarian guard, but the shooting was not confined to Hungarians; it was simply terrible, hundreds were shot per day.

Did you see the results of any beatings?

- The beatings were usually confined to blows on the head. I did see one receive 25 strokes. They were not particularly terrible – nothing like as bad as my previous camp – but the slapdash blows on the head during the day were very frequent, and very, very nasty.

I think almost immediately the camp was liberated, you were released?

- Yes. As far as I know I was the first man out, and I have been in hospital up to last Saturday week.

Can you recognise any particular guard who either shot or ill-treated people when you were there?

- No, they all looked. similar to me at the time; I don't think I could pick one out.

Did you ever see any guard help or assist any of the prisoners?

- Never. May I add that guards in the concentration camp – I am talking in general when I say this – are brutish, and the prisoners in time become brutish and such a thing as human kindness is quite unknown in such a place. I would like to try to make everyone realize what starvation, absolute starvation, no water at all for some six days, lack of sleep – for sleep near the burial pits was quite impossible – to be covered in lice and delousing oneself three or four times a day proving absolutely useless, is like.

Then there is the fatalistic attitude between the prisoners towards what the end would certainly be – the crematorium or the pits. Add to this the foul stench and vileness of the place, the scenes which apparently horrified the whole of the world, which we saw by the whole of daylight day by day, the blows on the head, the hideous work, and in the last three days the Hungarian guards shooting at us just as if we were rabbits, from all directions. If you can picture all this, the sum total as it were, then maybe you will get a remote inkling of what life was like in Belsen in those last three days.

Cross-examined by Major WINWOOD:

What was the condition of the other prisoners who arrived at Belsen with you?
- I don't know exactly how many died, but I know that many did. About 150 of us all told reached Belsen, only a remnant, and I know that many thousands died in these ten days.

What was their condition when they first got to Belsen?
- Most of the Kommandos arrived by marching there, and were pretty fit. We came by transport because we had been bombed in Lüneburg by the RAF. I have no idea whether our transport was expected at Belsen or not.

Were you always in Block 13?
- The day the British tanks first appeared we were transferred to Block 26. Block 13 was swept and garnished early that morning, and we found ourselves transferred to this new block – again, I think, in order to make a good impression on the British Army. There had been some grass growing round this hut, and when the tanks passed through I was actually having

my first meal for five days; I was eating grass.

Is it true that every day you were in Belsen the cookhouses were actually working?
- I think they were working.

Was the food brought to Block 13 every day?
- Some was brought in the first few days, but on the last five days when we came back from our work in the burial pits at dusk there was no soup.

In Block 13 how many of the inmates had blankets?
- I cannot answer that. There was a pile of blankets on the left of the door as you went in. The first ones in took one or two blankets, and I presume the rest did not have any. When I arrived at 10 o'clock at night I had brought one myself and I picked up one of these humid ones on the left-hand side of the door. The hut was not so crowded then as it was a night or two later. I think you said that the Appell started at half-past three in the morning? - We were told it was half-past three. We had no watches. It was pitch dark.

Is it true to say that during the time you were at Belsen some real attempt was being made to bury the corpses?
- An attempt was made. In fact, it was more than an attempt, I think it was successful. We did bury many thousands in the last four or five days. I have no idea from whom the order to bury the bodies came.

Cross-examined by Major CRANFIELD:

Were all the SS personnel and Blockältesten you came into contact with men?
- Yes. I saw some SS women the first night, but only at the entrance to the camp watching the Kommandos coming into the camp from various directions.

Cross-examined by Captain ROBERTS:

At the time of the arrival of the British was your health as good as any of the internees?
- I thought it was, but it proved not to be the case.

Cross-examined by Captain FIELDEN:

Were all the SS men in Belsen responsible for ill-treatment and shooting?
- No, the shootings I saw on the last three days were by Hungarian guards. Most of the guards who were in charge of the huts were not SS at all, but, on the orders of the SS, were *Blockältesten*, *Kapos*, *Vorarbeiter* and the like. I did not see the SS men in the vicinity of my compound during my stay there. I did see one ill-treating a woman, as I have mentioned, and a few others just strolling around. In the three concentration camps I have seen, the SS in every case have lived in a very well protected compound outside the actual concentration camp area, and the discipline and administration of the concentration camp itself is deputed to prisoners. That is the viciousness of this concentration camp system, to have prisoners in charge of prisoners.

Cross-examined by Captain CORBALLY:

When the time came for the prisoners to have a meal was food brought to your hut and had you all to go inside before it was distributed to you?
- Yes. Quite a few methods were tried and failed absolutely. It meant that perhaps 20 or 30 prisoners got food, and the rest went without. In the first days the method was to go into the hut - the soup bin was near the door - and pass outside into the yard with your mug or plate of soup. The best way was the last time I had any food. We were behind some barriers and the people were called out one by one and got their soup near the doorway and walked out into the yard. The person who ladled out the soup in our case was the *Blockältesten* or an assistant.

Did you ever seen internees employed trying to rejoin the queue after they had their ration?
- Yes.

Was there any system employed to prevent that happening?
- Yes. People were stationed at all the windows and at the doors or breakages through the side of the hut to prevent people doing that.

Have you ever seen an internee come up to where the soup was being ladled out just too late, to find that it had all disappeared?
- Yes, that occurred on quite a few

occasions. It was very rare at any one distribution to find there was enough to go around, even with the small amount that was put in.

Did you ever see anyone caught coming up for a second bowl of soup?
- I cannot swear that I did.

Would you agree that one of the reasons why the soup did not go round all the internees in the hut was that some people succeeded in getting a second helping?
- No, I would not agree with that.

Cross-examined by Captain MUNRO:

You said that the *Blockältesten* and *Kapos* were under the control of the SS Would it be true to say that these internees were as frightened of the SS as you were?
- I don't know. I did not come into contact sufficiently with the SS to make a genuine answer to that.

Would you think that they would be punished by the SS if they did not do their job as the SS thought they should?
- I have no idea. I have never been a *Kapo* or *Blockältester*.

By the JUDGE ADVOCATE:

Did you or did you not get the impression that the *Blockältesten* and the *Kapos*, in addition to being under the control of the SS, were under

their protection in the sense that if any attack had been made upon them they could have relied upon the SS men to support their authority?
- Yes, I think so.

Do you know how the internee officials came to get their posts?
- I don't know.
In the first four days you said that you got about an inch and a half depth of soup on each day in a mug.

Was that the sort of quantity that everybody was getting, or was it just accidental you got that amount?
- That was the regular quantity that was being given to the whole lot.

There was some kind of attempt to organize that each prisoner should get a certain amount?
- In those first days, yes.

Do you think that conditions were deteriorating towards the end in the sense that many more internees were flooding into the camp and that such arrangements as there had been for distribution of soup – little in amount as it was – and water were getting worse?
- I did not quite get that impression. Things were deteriorating, but not necessarily because of the numbers flowing into the camp. Conditions got worse and worse, and finally ended with the shooting in the last three days, for which I could find no excuse at all.

By a Member of the Court:

Would you tell the Court how conditions in Belsen compared, in general terms, with the other camps you had been in?

- In the two previous camps in which I had been there was an attempt made at cleanliness, though the atrocities probably or sadism in the other camps at Wilhelmshaven and Neuengamme were worse than Belsen. I think I can fairly describe Belsen as probably the foulest and vilest spot that ever soiled the surface of this earth.

By another Member of the Court:

Did you actually see anyone except the Hungarians shoot an internee?

- No.

By the PRESIDENT:

Were these Appelle all run by the prison leaders as distinct from the SS personnel in the camp?

- Yes.

Do you know, in those last four days when you said no food was issued, whether it was actually issued to other prisoners in your hut or to the prison leaders and you merely missed it because you were away, or was there no issue at all so far as you know?

- I don't know, but I know I didn't see any soup at all in the last five days.

Chapter 8

The Jews in the Channel Islands

If even one state, for whatever reason, allows even one Jewish family to live in it, then this family will become the bacillus source for a new decomposition. If there were no more Jews in Europe then the unity of the European States would no longer be destroyed. Where one will send the Jews, to Siberia, or Madagascar, is all the same to me.
(Adolf Hitler. July 1941)

Every day for a year and a half, until I was deported to a German concentration camp, I lived in fear and terror. I lived in trauma all the time. Every day I was frightened, and did not know if they would take me away, or my baby daughter, or my husband.
(Elisabet Duquemin a Guernsey Jew, finally deported with her baby daughter and her husband in February 1943)

On 19th June 1940 Jurat Edgar Dorey flew back to the Islands after his meeting at the Home Office with Sir Alexander Maxwell, the permanent UnderSecretary of State. He bore with him a letter addressed to the Lieutenant Governors of Guernsey and Jersey. It read:

> *Home Office*
> *19th June, 1940*
>
> Sir,
> *I am directed by the Secretary of State to say that, in the event of a recall, it is desired by this Majesty's Government that the Bailiff should discharge the duties of Lieutenant Governor, which would be confined to civil duties, and that he should stay at his post and administer the government of the Island to the best of his abilities in the interest of the inhabitants, whether or not he is in a position to receive instructions from His Majesty's Government. The Crown Officers should also remain at their posts.*
>
> *I am, Sir*
> *Your Obedient Servant*
> *Maxwell*

This is the story of how the Islands' governments served the interests of one tiny section of the Islands' community – the Jews.

In the years leading up to the Occupation the whole world became aware of the Nazi policy towards Jews and the philosophy which informed it. A vicious and virulent anti-Semitism informed all their actions: internment in concentration camps, cultural, economic, political disenfranchisement, insult and hideous assault. All means to establish the new Nazi world which belonged as of right:

'... to the fair-skinned and the superior Aryan race, and all others belonged to subhuman culture.'

The images from those pre-War years still live with us: *Kristellnacht*, destruction of the synagogues and shops, the shaving of Jewish men, the yellow star of David everywhere, the kickings and the beatings, Jews cleaning the streets with toothbrushes, and, of course, the lines of Jewish refugees crowding onto ships, planes and trains to take them as far away from savage Germany as it was possible to go.

Many did not run. Some stayed to die. It is said the only gunfire to be heard when the Germans marched into Austria was the sound of the Jews shooting themselves.

It must be true that in 1939 no one knew how far the Nazis could and would go in their destruction of European Jewry, for Wannsee, Posen and the Final Solution, the *Geheimie Reichssache* – Secret Reich Matter – were all two years in the future. But anyone who was not deaf or blind must have known that the fate of any Jew, man, woman or child, who fell under German control would be very far from pleasant. Certainly the small numbers of Jewish residents in the Channel Islands were aware of the danger they were in and many of them left the Islands before that June of 1940. And it must be assumed that many other people in the Islands would have known of the Nazi treatment of the Jews, not least because the Jersey newspaper, the *Evening Post* during January and February of 1939 published upwards of 15 articles detailing the vicious anti-Semitic measures being imposed at that very moment in mainland Europe.

In Jersey too, the Aliens Office had received many letters from Jewish people seeking asylum and escape from German persecution. These were seen, not just by Clifford Orange but also by the Bailiff himself, Alexander Coutanche.

These letters contained many a detailed story of the harassment and persecution the Jews were suffering in the Fatherland.

In Guernsey on 23rd June Ambrose Sherwill was told that a certain doctor in the Island, Dr William Montague, was a Jew and that, given the certainty of Occupation, his friends were fearful for his safety and that:

'The worst might happen to him at the hands of the Germans.'

Sherwill knew perfectly well of Jews in Germany itself and in the rest of occupied Europe being:

'... jeered at in the streets, pelted with filth and generally harassed.'

Having a proper and careful regard for the best interests of his fellow citizen, Sherwill arranged for the doctor to be sent on a mission to the Home Office (to ask for total evacuation) but with this added instruction. That for 'racial reasons', he was on no account to return. It may be assumed that there was a widespread awareness of the dangers facing any remaining Jews in the Islands. Insular, cut off and isolated the Islanders may have been, but they could by no means have been oblivious to the cries of anguish from across the water, or to their cause.

STRAW MAN

The Jews were in especial danger. Everyone knew it. Above all, the Jews themselves knew it.

In particular the Island's few Jewish business owners in Jersey knew it, and made good their escape from Jersey before the Germans, with their Aryan policy of racial reduction, arrived in 1940. Alfred and Wilfred Krichevski, father and son, who owned the large gentlemen's outfitters in Halkett Street; Simon and Rebecca Peretz, costumiers and milliners of King Street, and Louis Feldman, 'trading in ladies' gowns, millinery etc' at 5 New Street all left their Jersey homes and businesses for the blessed safety of mainland UK.

They were all too right in assuming that, when the Germans arrived, they would all be deprived of their businesses which would be handed over to administrators who would sell them to the 'racially superior' and therefore 'more deserving' Aryans.

This is exactly what happened.

Notices such as those that had appeared all over the conquered territories in Western Europe declaring the establishments to be 'Jewish Undertakings,' *Judisches Geschaft*, duly appeared in the shop windows.

Advertisements were placed in the *Evening Post* and also in the Guernsey *Star*, announcing that these undertakings were for sale by tender.

They were to be sold and Aryanised in strict accordance with the Nazi racial agenda.

The whole process was in the hands of the Jersey Advocates Le Cornu, Le Masurier, Giffard and Poch. It was, however, a process that was closely overseen and monitored by the German officers of the *Feldkommandantur* who, driven by the Hitlerian imperative, were very anxious indeed that the sale should be genuine, real and above board. And it was not only the Germans who were casting a beady eye over the proceedings. The local Island officials were doing the same thing, but for the different reason that they saw obedience to the letter and spirit of the German directives as being essential to the maintenance of good relations with their unwelcome guests. The rule had to be, 'Do not upset the Germans in any way that might invite reprisals or cause the Island government to be replaced by direct SS rule.'

The 'savage dog' was not to be annoyed!

Given the amount of scrutiny that the transactions attracted it is quite remarkable that the Jersey Advocates managed to pull a fast one on both the German and the Island observers. And they did so by the creation of 'straw man' agreements.

At first sight it appears that the Aryanisation was successfully achieved.

The shops were sold to proper racially qualified Islanders at a proper, independently-assessed price. The fact that the purchasers of the businesses were all managers or employees of the previous owners might have aroused some suspicion. But it did not. Nor did the fact that the new buyers could not, by any stretch of the imagination, be considered rich enough to have the means to buy these rather large concerns give rise to any investigation as to the integrity of the sales. They all went through without a single objection being raised.

Mr Beaton, senior manager for the Krichevski business, was the buyer of that business.

Miss Hawkins, manager for Louis Feldman, bought his business 'Louis and Cie.'

And a Miss White, an employee of Simon and Rebecca Peretz, bought their costumier store.

It was all done and dusted.

But not really. The sale of the shops was fraudulent. It was not a genuine transaction at all. The buyers were not really buyers at all but 'straw men', dissembling and pretending in order to protect and preserve the interests of their Jewish employers. And it had all been organised by the Jersey Advocates Le Cornu, Le Masurier, Giffard and Poch.

At the end of the War the businesses were simply handed back, intact, to the owners. It was a notable victory against the German racists and more than that, a clever, not to say courageous, act of resistance against the occupying power.

Even David Fraser, in his work in which he generally and viciously attacks the Islands' legal profession for their anti-Semitism concedes:

'There is convincing evidence that ... some Jersey lawyers saw that in order to protect their clients' interest, and to do what they perceived to be the right thing, they would have to appear to be complying with the legal requirements of declaration of sale, while they were in fact engaged in an act of subversion of, and resistance to, the existing judicial norm.'
(David Fraser)

But what of the Jews who remained in the Islands?

The Germans wasted no time. It did not take long for the first directive against the Jews to be registered in the Royal Courts of Jersey and Guernsey as one of the laws applicable to the Islands. There were to be nine in all.

'Registration having the effect of promulgating an enactment has to be authorised by the Royal Court sitting as a Full Court i.e. composed of the Bailiff or a Lieutenant Bailiff and at least seven of the twelve Jurats.'
(Ambrose Sherwill)

If there was to be an objection to any of

these directives it would have to be made at this stage in the Judicial process.

With reference to this First Order against the Jews, in his evidence given before the Home Secretary after the War Alexander Coutanche stated:

'The Court had no options but to register this German Order. There was no conversation. The number of persons affected was extremely small and moderation was shown in the execution of the order. It could be shown that other oppressive measures against the Jews were entirely avoided by proper intervention by the Insular Authorities.'
(PRO 3 July 1945 HO 45/22399)

The purpose of that First Order of October 1940 was to discover and identify all the Jews remaining in the Islands.

In Jersey they were required to report and register at the Aliens Office run by Chief Aliens Officer, Clifford Orange; in Guernsey they had to go to the office of the Inspector of Police, William Robert Sculpher, and in Sark to the Seneschal. It was the beginning of a long and painful process of imposing and implementing the Nazi anti-Semitic programme, and it was the thin end of a very thick and very nasty wedge.

No objection was raised by any of the Islands' authorities when this October directive was registered in the Courts,

and no objections were raised on the introduction of the further eight orders, except on one, or maybe two, occasions. The Jersey Bailiff, Alexander Coutanche, remembered, in a somewhat removed fashion:

'The Jews were, I think, called upon to declare themselves. Some did, some didn't ... Those who didn't weren't discovered. I've never heard they suffered in any way.'

In Guernsey, Attorney General Ambrose Sherwill records that when he knew of the intended registration of this Order:

'I made such enquiries as I could and learned, accurately as it turned out, that the few Jews who had settled in Guernsey had all evacuated.

I am virtually certain that I conveyed to the Bailiff and Jurats in private that the [registration of the Order] would harm no one in the Island.'

In Jersey that October of 1940, twelve Islanders, asked as they thought by a benevolent authority dedicated to protecting their best interests, presented themselves before the Chief Aliens Officer, Clifford Orange, and were duly registered as Jews. They included Marianne Blampied who was a Dutch Jew married to the extraordinarily gifted Jersey artist, Edmund Blampied.

For whatever reason, she was left unharmed and not harassed, in any way that is recorded during the Occupation.

Others were not so fortunate. Subsequent Orders passed, without demur, into Island law deprived the Jews of their ability to make a living. Their businesses were taken from them. They were barred by the Third Order from being employed in:

'wholesale and retail, hotel and catering, insurance, navigation, dispatch and storage, guides, banking and money exchange, and businesses concerned with dealings in apartments, land and mortgages.'

More than this, no Jew was to be employed as a:

'higher official or as an employee who comes into contact with customers.'

Jewish employees were to be sacked and their jobs taken by 'non Jewish employees.' In short there was nothing they could do – nothing they were allowed to do.

They also became prisoners in their own homes. The Sixth Order imposed a curfew from 8.00 p.m. until 6.00 a.m., and the Ninth (and last) Order, registered in Jersey on 15th August 1942, forbade them to shop except between the hours of 3.00 p.m. and 4.00 p.m. They were also banned from places of public entertainment, so for them no visits to the Forum Cinema to see *Sieg im Westen* or to the Opera House to see, maybe a performance of *The Merchant of Venice*, or anything else for that matter.

They had nothing.

They were deprived of everything.

And in those early years of the War the future looked terrible. The suffering and fear of many in this small beleaguered group, unprotected by their own government, threatened by a powerful and vicious occupying power, cannot be overestimated.

It drove two of them into madness and death.

British-born Samuel Selig Simon had registered as a Jew according to the requirements of the First Order of October 1940. He and his wife were old, frail and frightened. His great-granddaughter recalls visiting the 78-year-old Simon and his wife Beatrice at their house in Grand Vaux, St Helier, and says they lived:

'... in a terrible state of fear and kept their curtains drawn at all times.'

They were even more frightened, if that were possible, when they received a deportation notice. The night before his deportation order was due to take effect in November 1943, he was found dead at home, ostensibly from a heart attack. Old people do not live long under such conditions.

Samuel Selig Simon died on 7th November 1943 of heart failure.

Victor Emanuel, a naturalised Briton

who also registered in the October of 1940, hanged himself on 9th April 1944. According to the coroner his death was 'suicide whilst of an unsound mind.'

Nathan Davidson, an Egyptian born in Romania, who had been in Jersey for eight years by the time of the Occupation, likewise registered in October 1940. As a consequence he was deprived of his very small grocery store at 38 Stopford Road, St Helier. He had no income. No means to live. No way of looking after his family. His situation got worse by the month. He was reduced to selling his confiscated wireless set to a German officer to buy a little food. He and his wife were forced to move house. But the final blow came when they received their deportation order in the December of 1942. Nathan Davidson had a good idea of the fate that awaited them and the prospect was too much for him. His mind gave way. He was taken to St Saviour's Mental Institution on 25th February 1943. He lasted four days. On 29th February he died.

Official cause of death was given as 'maniacal exhaustion, insanity.'

Hyman Goldman, although he was not deported from Jersey, was traumatised by his experience during the Occupation years, eventually committing suicide by drowning himself in a water tank at his home in St Peter's Valley.

Across the water in the sister Isle of Guernsey, the work of compiling the list of Jews required by the First Order registered on 23rd October 1940 in the Royal Courts, was in the hands of Inspector William Sculpher. He was an ex-London policeman who had been the Chief Officer since 1930. Prior to the arrival of the Germans, for want of better things to do, he seems to have spent most of his time complaining about the low pay and the lack of a police car. Sculpher only managed a very small increase in pay and he didn't have much luck with the car either. A shiny, new and altogether splendid Wolseley did appear for him in Guernsey on the very eve of the outbreak of war. William rejoiced in it.

But his happiness was short-lived. One of the first acts of the invading Germans was to commandeer the motor for their own use. The Inspector was not pleased.

It may safely be assumed that he had never experienced a situation like the one of 1940, and had never had so much detecting, analysing and compiling of lists to do. But do it he did, serving both his German and his Guernsey masters with an assiduity and attention to detail which rivalled that of Clifford Orange – his opposite number in Jersey.

THERESE, AUGUSTE AND MARIANNE
The Viennese Jews

Mercifully, however, it appeared there were fewer Jews in Guernsey than in Jersey. Only five Jews appeared in response to the notice published on

24th October in the Guernsey *Evening Press*.

There was Italian-born Elda Brouard, née Bauer, who had been married to an Englishman. He had died before her arrival in the Island. She was a widow but would still be counted a British citizen.

Then there was divorcee Annie Wranowsky from Czechoslovakia, living in Sark, who had come to the Islands in 1934. Her German passport was marked with a 'J' though she vigourously maintained that this was a mistake. Dr Casper, whose name appears on every anti-Semitic order, evidently believed her for her name does not appear on the list of Island Jews that he sent to the SS Headquarters in Paris in the June of 1942.

The last three were all from Vienna and two of them were at special risk.

Therese Steiner and Auguste Spitz were single women and thought of as German nationals and not Guernsey residents for whom the Island government would have a responsibility. There would be no interventions on their behalf by any Island official. The fate of Steiner and Spitz was none of their business. They were foreigners.

Last on the list is Elisabet Fink, who had come to Guernsey in 1937. She married Henry Duquemin just prior to the outbreak of war and thereby became a British citizen and so afforded a degree of protection from German anti-Semitism.

The three Viennese women formed a tight, friendly little group. Auguste Spitz was bridesmaid at Elisabet's wedding. They had good times together.

There was at least one other Jew on the Island but she did not declare herself. She was the handsome, sandy-haired, 30-year-old Marianne Grünfeld, who worked on Duvaux farm. The farm was owned by Mr Edward Ogier, a benign and caring employer who, when the Germans came for Marianne, would have saved her had it been even remotely within his power.

John Leale tried desperately to save Therese Steiner from transportation, arguing that she was an essential worker at Castel Hospital and could not be spared. He was as unsuccessful in trying to save Therese as Edward Ogier was to be in trying to save Marianne Grünfeld.

Therese Steiner was born in Vienna in 1916. She was just 26 in the spring of 1942 when she received her deportation order. Her family had been fairly prosperous and middle-class. She had two brothers, Karl and Paul. Karl was a well respected classical musician and he it was who taught Therese to play the piano. They gave concerts together in Vienna and by all accounts Therese was a happy, out-going and talented girl.

She was also one of the most unlucky.

Therese left Austria just as the Germans were preparing to walk into the country in 1938. By this time she was a qualified dental assistant and in that capacity she travelled to England to take up a post in the practice of Mr Edgar Potts in Kent. According to Karl, who was the only member of the Steiner family to survive, Therese was a little miffed to find herself demoted, as she thought it, from the position of dental assistant to that of nanny to the Potts' two children.

In November 1939, as war was declared in Europe, the Potts family – mother, father, two daughters and Therese, travelled to Sark, probably believing that, as all the holiday adverts proclaimed, the Channel Islands were a safe haven from the dangers of war. There is a pretty photograph, taken by Edgar Potts, of them all enjoying the sunshine on a little Sark beach. However, their happiness was short-lived. In the next year, 1940, Edgar went back to the mainland to work. His wife Marjorie and children with Therese, moved across the little stretch of water to live in Guernsey.

Towards the end of May 1940 it became more and more apparent that there was a very real danger of the Islands being invaded and occupied by the Germans.

Suddenly the little Islands did not seem so safe after all.

Marjorie Potts and her two children made haste to leave Guernsey and return to Edgar on the mainland.

They would have taken Therese, their nanny, with them of course, but they found they were unable to do so because Therese, with her Austrian passport, was classified as an 'enemy alien' and refused permission to travel out of the Island. Indeed she was interned as an 'enemy alien' on 4th June 1940. But the internment didn't last long.

On 25th June, three days before the bombing of St Peter Port, Therese was freed and given a job in Castel Hospital as an auxiliary nurse.

The Germans occupied Guernsey and as in all territories that they occupied, they immediately set about discovering what Jews lived in the Island.

Therese Steiner and Auguste Spitz were registered as Jews, and thus immediately caught up in the Nazis' net.

Therese registered as a Jew according to the requirements of The First Order Relating to Measures against the Jews of 23rd October 1940. Her name appears on the list of five compiled by Inspector Sculpher. This list was passed to the Germans on 25th November 1940.

Meanwhile, up at the Castel Hospital, Therese quickly settled into her new role; her good humour, her efficiency and most especially, her brilliant piano playing, made her a great favourite with staff and patients alike.

'But after about 18 months, Therese still had no news of her family, her father, her mother and her two brothers Karl and Paul, and they were a close family, always looked out for each other. She thought she might go to the Germans to ask if they could find out about them. She went to Matron Hall and Doctors Rose and Sutcliffe to ask their advice. They said, "Whatever you do, don't approach the Germans or talk to them because you will put your life in danger!" But, you see, she was German, she was Austrian, she did not believe all the rumours that were running about; she thought it was just enemy propaganda. So one day when it was her time off, she went to the German High Command in Grange Lodge and when she came out she was very pleased, she told matron that they had been very kind to her and that they were going to find out all about the family for her. Well, at this time there was a great surge of Nazism against the Jews and of course, then, you see it was when the camps started. They issued an anti-Jewish Law in Guernsey. A few weeks later Therese heard she had to leave Guernsey and go, as she believed, back home to Austria.'

(Lily Mauger from the account of her mother, the Assistant Matron of Castel Hospital)

Assistant Matron of Castel recalls that she left the Island in quite a happy frame of mind, really believing she was to be reunited with her family.

The Reverend Ord however, in his Occupation diary says that Therese was very far from being in a 'happy state of mind':

'When I last spoke to her, she had orders to go to France. She was in great distress and seemed to feel that her feet were now set upon the via dolorosa. I did what I could to comfort her, but what can you say or do?'

Therese and Auguste went to see their fellow Jewish refugee from Vienna, Elisabet Duquemin, nee Fink. She was not in as much danger as the other two women for she had married a Guernseyman, Mr Duquemin, which meant she was protected from deportation at least for the time being. (The whole Duquemin family were deported later on in 1943, but not to their deaths.) She was powerless to help Auguste and Therese. She recalls the visit from the two women on the day before they were transported:

'They had to report the next morning to be taken away to France and were in a terrible state of anxiety.'

Further, a Guernsey policeman of the time, Sergeant Ernest Plevin, stated

'I do remember – well – Therese coming into the office where I conveyed to her the instructions given to the Guernsey police by the German military authorities. Therese became extremely distressed, bursting into tears and exclaiming that I would never see her again. At that time I was unaware of the cause of her

outburst, but shortly after I learned of the atrocities being committed by the Germans.'

(Guernsey Evening Press. Major E. Parks. File on Jews during the Occupation)

Whatever her state of mind may have been, Therese, along with Auguste Spitz and Marianne Grünfeld, was taken down to White Rock and shipped thence to France.

Not nearly as much is known of Auguste Spitz except that she, like Therese, was from Vienna and, again like Therese, had come to Guernsey as a nanny in 1937. She too had been interned as an 'enemy alien.' She too had been registered as a Jew on 25th November 1940. On her release, along with Therese, the States had found her employment at Catel Hospital.

41-year-old Auguste, or 'Gustie' as she was known, became a hugely popular member of the staff: humorous and full of fun. She named the hospital pet cat 'Churchill' because he was rotund, forever growling, being confrontational and fighting on all fronts.

She received her deportation order on 20th April 1942 and, as far as is known, she did not have a John Leale or an Edward Ogier to plead on her behalf against that deportation. Auguste joined Therese Steiner and Marianne Grünfeld in the White Rock section of St Peter Port harbour ready for her journey into mainland Europe.

Therese was right. It was the start of their via dolorosa.

Marianne Grünfeld, unlike Therese and Auguste, had not registered as a Jew, as she was required to do under the terms of the First Order of October 1940, although she did register to obtain an identity card in that month. On the face of it she appeared to have a very good chance of going undiscovered – she was petite and sandy-haired with a Slavic look, so physically she corresponded to none of the Jewish stereotypes. Moreover she had become a much loved honorary member of Edward Ogier's family at the Duvaux Farm.

Marianne had come to Guernsey by a somewhat circuitous route. Born in Kartourcie in Poland in December 1912 to a fairly well off German Jewish family, Marianne was a bright, endlessly cheerful girl. She came to England in 1937 and enrolled at Reading University to study horticulture. She was deeply interested in animals and their welfare and worked for some little time in a veterinary practice. Then in 1939, her university life behind her, she saw an advert for a farm assistant in Guernsey whose prime responsibility would be to look after a herd of Guernsey cows (very like the Jersey cows only better, as the Guernseyman would say). Marianne replied to the advert, was given the job and thus it was she arrived in Guernsey in the April of 1940 to live and work on Ted Ogier's farm.

Somehow and some way, in the spring of 1942, the Germans found out about her. She was summoned to the *Nebenstelle* (the Guernsey branch of the *Feldkommandantur*) at The Grange and grilled as to her 'Jewishness'. The Germans were satisfied that Marianne fell within the definition of a Jew as described in the Third Order of Regulations against the Jews of May 1941, and she received notice of deportation on 20th April 1942.

Edward Ogier tried to prevent her being taken from them.

The Reverend Douglas Ord, the wise, kindly and, on this occasion despairing, Guernsey Methodist Minister has this entry in his diary on the 18th April:

'A friend [Ogier] stopped me outside the Grand Lodge, the Civil Kommandantur, to vent his rage and sorrow. He had gone to appeal for a girl employee who is only just within the forbidden degrees of Jewish birth and is to be carried off. The officials listened to his arguments but were powerless to resist the inhuman decree of the Nazi Frankenstein.'

Edward's vehement appeals were unsuccessful and Marianne joined Therese and Auguste down on the harbourside on 21st April 1942.

But how had Marianne been found out?

Had she been betrayed by someone? If so, for what reason?

There is a story from those times which does assert that she was indeed betrayed, and not by a Nazi sympathiser or an anti-Semite either. No, Marianne had been betrayed by a spurned lover. This is what happened according to the story.

There were two other women working at Duvaux farm at this time: Mary Edwards from London who looked after the poultry was one, and the other was Dorothy Susan Harvey, young, upper-class English lady. Her father was the noted editor of the *Oxford Companion to English Literature*. Francis herself was rather famous too, at least in London, where she was known as a brilliant photographer for glossy magazines like the *Picture Post* for whom she worked under the more exotic name of Merlyn Severn.

As war approached nearer and nearer in 1939 Merlyn Severn was planning a photographic expedition to Java but one night, as she stood by her bedroom window, she heard the many sirens howling into the blackness:

'I stood for a long minute entranced by this eerie howling of the dogs of war. And in that minute life changed its course for me. When it ended, I knew that if my ship sailed for the East Indies it would sail without me. The Javanese drama must wait: there was another drama, nearer home, in which I was cast for a very minor part.'

She signed on in the Women's Auxiliary

Air Force (WAAF) as Airwoman Class 2.

But what was the role she was about to play in these dangerous years of war?

'I was taken on a long bus ride and unloaded at a Gothic-looking country house surrounded by gloomy trees. After signing a blood-curdling oath of secrecy, we were admitted to the mystery of "Special Duties". At that time I did not dare confide, even to my diary, what they were, but at this date there can be no harm in revealing that "Special Duties" meant "Radar."'

Now radar, its use and development, was a cutting-edge technology at the very forefront in the battle against Germany. It was of vital importance to know how far the enemy had got in its development, where their radar installations were, of what type and how powerful.

So Merlyn Severn was learning of something that was to have a huge effect on the outcome of the war.

Then suddenly she was discharged from the WAAF for unknown reasons. Perhaps she was ill and needed to rest but nothing is known for certain. There might have been another reason.

The next we know of Merlyn Severn is that she was in Guernsey. She herself does not say why she was there. She is silent on the subject.

So here we have in the Island a WAAF

officer who is an expert in photography and also has a special knowledge of radar, working as a farmhand at Ogiers farm alongside Marianne Grünfeld.

And the Germans are about to move in.

It is an odd state of affairs to say the least.

Given that, unlike Marianne, Merlyn had no skills that would be remotely useful on a farm, it has been assumed that she had been sent over to Guernsey as a spy to discover information about troop numbers, disposition of fortification and, most especially, radar installations, together with anything else that might be of use to the British.

The story continues, intriguingly enough, that Merlyn was a lesbian and that she made advances towards Marianne. These Sapphic advances were strongly rebuffed. This being so and hell having no fury like a woman scorned, Marianne's would-be lover rushed to tell the Germans of an undeclared Jew residing at Duvaux Farm. This was her revenge.

The story is as unlikely as it is lurid. Merlyn may have been a lesbian and she may have been a British spy but there is not a scrap of evidence to suggest that she betrayed Marianne to the Germans out of spite as a spurned lover. If, in fact, she was a British agent it is inconceivable that she would have advertised her presence to the Germans by marching up to The Grange to inform on an unregistered Jew, however crossed in love she might have been. A much more likely explanation of how Marianne came to the notice of the Germans is that advanced by Freddie Cohen.

The name Grünfeld is a recognisably Jewish name. That name was on the list of all the Islanders compiled in August 1940. Any German trawling through that list would have spotted it.

However, it's even more likely that she was identified from the list of 'Key Aliens' given by the Controlling Committee to the Germans in the October of 1941. This list most certainly would have been carefully examined by the *Feldkommandantur,* and the name Grünfeld would have stood out as being obviously Jewish.

No lover, just a list. More prosaic but still deadly.

From Guernsey the women were taken to Laval and there registered as Jews in the Department of Mayenne. Here their names were put on yet another list, this time in accordance with the requirement of the Eighth Order against the Jews which made compulsory the wearing of the yellow star.

Then they were left alone for two months during which time they found lodgings. Therese took up employment again as a nurse. Marianne became an interpreter. No record exists of what

Auguste did for a living during this time.

On 15th July 1942 Therese and Auguste were arrested. On the following day, Marianne too was detained by the Germans. On 20th July 1942 Therese, Auguste, Marianne and 82 other Jews were loaded onto the cattle trucks which formed Convoy No. 8.

After three days they arrived at Auschwitz Birkenau. The three women were young and healthy and therefore fit for work so it is quite possible that they survived the initial 'left-right' selection process.

But none of them lived through to the end of the War. Only 14 people from Convoy No. 8 survived that long, and they were all men. Therese, Auguste and Marianne had all been swallowed up by the Auschwitz Birkenau fires.They were among the first of thousands of Jews from Western Europe transported to the death camps and the Final Solution.

No more Jews were transported from the Islands for the sole reason that they were Jews, until the February of 1943. Their deportation came about as a direct result of Hitler's huge anger at the conduct of British commandos in Sark. As we have seen in a previous chapter the Basalt raid had resulted in two Germans with their hands tied being done to death. As Ambrose Sherwill had predicted, such a raid caused nothing but trouble and disaster for the civilian population of the Islands. And this was the trouble.

The enraged Fuehrer ordered a wholesale deportation of Islanders from all sections of the community. Included on the list were Freemasons, communists, political agitators, religious leaders and, inevitably, Jews. Of the final 202 who were transported on the 12th and 13th February 1943, nine were Jews or part of a family with a Jewish member. So, for example, Henry Duquemin was deported because his wife was a Jew and, even more cruelly, 18-month-old Janet Duquemin was sent away because she was the child of Elisabet Duquemin who, as we have seen, was a registered Austrian-born Jew. However, the family of Esther Pauline Lloyd – her ill husband and her two children – were not included in the final list for deportation, though she herself was.

Unlike Therese, August and Marianne, these Jews, together with the rest of the deportees were not taken to concentration death camps initially but to the internment camps Lager Laufen and Lager Compiègne. Later in the year all the Channel Islands deportees found themselves in Germany, in Lager Biberach.

Esther Pauline Lloyd had a very nasty time. John Max Finkelstein, the elderly retired Egyptian government official had a worse time. He was a Romanian Jew and had registered as such in Jersey in October 1940. He did not make it to Biberach, and as we have already heard ended up in the dreaded Buchenwald concentration camp with the legend

Jedem das Seine hung over the entrance. Here prisoners were worked to death, starved, beaten, crucified, shot and subjected to the most hideous 'medieval' experiments. It was a place as far removed from the Channel Islands as hell is from heaven.

Between 1939 and 1945 it is believed that 56,545 died there. Miraculously the 63-year-old John Finkelstein survived not only the two years in the Buchenwald camp but also the forced march to Theresienstadt when the Germans evacuated the camp in the April of 1945. But he was in a terribly emaciated state, so much so that he was unable to return to Jersey immediately upon liberation. It took nearly five months for him to recover sufficiently to return to the Island. He finally made it home at the very beginning of 1946.

But his troubles were not over. The motto *Jedem das Seine* fixed over the gates of Buchenwald camp means 'everyone gets what he deserves.' John Finkelstein would have known it very well. But after his cruel incarceration in that hellish place John did not get what he deserved, at least not for some little time.

He had no money, no means of supporting himself. For the entire period of the Occupation he had not received the pension due to him from the Egyptian government as an ex-civil servant. He asked the British government via Edward Le Quesne, the

President of the States Committee of Public Works, to help him get the money due from the Egyptian Government. He eventually got his money but not before the Foreign Office had notified the British Ambassador in Egypt that John Max Finkelstein was:

'a technical enemy on two counts, as a Romanian and as having been in enemy territory.'

The enemy territory he had been in was Germany when he was imprisoned in Buchenwald!

Despite all his trials and tribulations John at last settled back in Jersey to enjoy a long retirement. He died in 1972 aged 90.

Meanwhile, Esther Pauline Lloyd appealed against her incarceration in Biberach. She wrote in her diary during 1943:

'Never shall I be honest again – if I had not declared myself this wouldn't have happened.'

Esther was successful in her appeal and she was returned to Jersey in the April of 1944. She fired off a letter of complaint to Alexander Coutanche from her home in St Brelade. In it she says

'I went alone (to Biberach) and left my two small children here and my husband who was ill most of the winter and is still

far from well today. My home and everything has all been neglected, also I have lost all my personal stuff . I have had to pay out for necessary winter underwear which is very hard considering my husband's business has been closed since last January by order of the German authorities.

I went to register at the Aliens Office at the time an order was brought out concerning Jews, as I am of Jewish origin on my grandmother's side only. I thought at the time it concerned me, but if all the facts concerning myself had been fully explained to the German authorities, there would have been no question of my being sent away. I wish to know why these facts have been suppressed.'

Clifford Orange wrote to the Bailiff on 23rd September 1944 defending his dealing with Esther saying, basically, that it was her own fault for:

'In each case of registration, the person concerned was told by me that the responsibility for registering or not registering under the Order rested entirely with the individual concerned and Mrs Lloyd was informed accordingly. I wish to state in conclusion that I had no knowledge whatever of the intended transportation of Mrs Lloyd and other registered Jewish persons in 1943 until after it had actually taken place.'

Esther Lloyd herself, however, did not recall having been offered such a choice when she was sitting opposite Clifford Orange down at the Aliens Office. Nor did any other possibly Jewish person remember such an offer in the same situation.

Freddie Cohen, in his definitive work *The Jews in the Channel Islands 1940–1945*, points to this incident as an example of 'over-inclusiveness' on the part of the Chief Aliens Officer in his identification of Jewishness. The bias was towards inclusion rather than exclusion, and indeed he managed to include people in the October 1940 lists who could quite easily, on a more sympathetic interpretation of the facts, have fallen outside the definition of a Jew, particularly as described in the First Order of October 1940 – John Max Finkelstein being a case in point.

To best protect the Jews he should have tried to keep them off the lists and not been so bureaucratically precise and anxious to put them on. But nowhere in his work on the Jews is there the smallest recognition, awareness or indication that the Jews he dealt with, small in number though they might have been, were in especial danger from the Germans, as evidenced by the treatment meted out to them in Germany itself and in every single one of the occupied territories, or that to place these Jews on a specifically Jewish register would not be to protect their interests at all, precisely the reverse.

Chief Aliens Officer Orange was very assiduous too in hunting down and identifying Jewish interests in the Jersey business world, identifying as Jews at least two men who had not registered as such in October 1940. Orange's persistence in identifying the Jews in Jersey led David Fraser in his study of the problem in *The Jews of the Channel Islands and the Rule of Law*, to characterise him as even more than a 'faithful and loyal enforcer of anti-Semitic Laws' doing his job as a 'good bureaucrat', but as an anti-Semite himself. It is more likely, however, that Clifford Orange was, and saw himself as being, an excellent and painstaking officer of the law, a man bound in duty to implement to the full and to the letter those measures registered in the Royal Court of Jersey and so legitimised by the ultimate States authority.

There was, it seems, a late recognition of what he was doing for he does seem to have abandoned his work of providing lists of all kinds when he discovered why the Germans wanted such lists. Clifford Orange was questioned after the war by MI6 officers and stated:

'As from September 1942 when it became obvious the purpose to which lists of persons supplied long before were being put, I refused to supply any further lists to the German authorities'.

The sound of another stable door being locked – and it was not enough to prevent severe criticism of the Islands in their handling of the Jewish issue. An Intelligence report of August 1945 states:

'When the Germans proposed to put

their anti-Jewish measures into force, no protest whatever was raised by any of the Guernsey officials, and they hastened to give the Germans every assistance. In Jersey the attitude of the States and of the Bailiff Alexander Moncrieff Courtanche does not seem to have been quite so gratuitously friendly as it was in Guernsey, but was still far from being satisfactory'.

And indeed it is true beyond question that no substantive protest was raised against the Orders Relating to Measures against the Jews when they were registered in the Royal Courts of Guernsey and Jersey, nor, it seems, was any attempt made in either bailiwick to prevent their implementation or at least lessen their impact, except on two, possibly three, occasions.

Sir Abraham Lainé, a member of the Guernsey Controlling Committee, objected to the registration of the First Order of October 1940. There is only one source for this and that is Ambrose Sherwill in his autobiography *A Fair and Honest Book*:

'I read the 'VOBIF' (the official German journal in occupied territories), which applied primarily to occupied France and noted its provisions, which included the required wearing by all Jews of the yellow Star of David. It disgusted me and I visualised Jews being jeered at – not in Guernsey – in the streets pelted with filth and generally harassed but I had no premonition of the appalling atrocities which were to be perpetrated upon them

by the Nazi regime.

I made such enquiries as I could and learned, accurately as it turned out, that the few Jews who had settled in Guernsey had all evacuated.

I am virtually certain that I conveyed to the Bailiff and Jurats in private that the VOBIF, to the best of my belief, would harm no one in the Island in these circumstances, I felt that no purpose would be served in opposing the registration of the VOBIF or in advising the Court to refuse to register it.

Nevertheless, I still feel ashamed that I did not do something by way of protest to the Germans; a vital principle was at stake even if no human being in Guernsey was actually affected. The honour of refusing to concur fell to Sir Abraham Lainé KCIE, who, when called on as Jurat to vote on the matter, openly and categorically refused his consent and stated his grave objections to such a measure. He has now gone to his rest but this courageous act of his should never be forgotten. As I sat listening to him, I realised how right he was.'

(Ambrose Sherwill)

Sherwill has a somewhat confused memory of this unique principled objection by Abraham Lainé, in that the first anti-Jewish measures of October 1940 in Guernsey contained no mention of Jews having to wear the six-pointed star of David. That instruction appeared in the infamous Eighth Order registered in the Royal Court of Guernsey in the June of 1942, two years later.

But there was a later and better-documented objection to anti-Jewish legislation, and that was raised by the Bailiff of Jersey, Alexander Coutanche, and also concerned the wearing of the yellow star by Jews as commanded by the Eighth Order. This Order was registered in Guernsey but not in Jersey due to the direct intervention in the process by the Bailiff and his Attorney General, Duret Aubin who:

'... visited Dr Casper ... and advised that this Order should not be registered or put into execution.'

There is no record of precisely why Coutanche decided, at this very late stage in the imposition of anti-Jewish measures, to object to this particular one. He had not objected to any before, but one may reasonably assume that he was animated by feelings of revulsion, akin to those felt by Abraham Lainé in the sister Island, at the thought of Jews having to wear the yellow Star of David.

The Bailiff's intervention in this matter is the only recorded time that an objection was raised against anti-Jewish measures in the Bailiwick of Jersey, and it was successful.

The Eighth Order was never registered in Jersey. No yellow stars appeared in the Island. None appeared, either, in Guernsey, where the Order was indeed registered, although this was due to a shortage in the supply of yellow stars from France and in any case, as Dr Casper, the Chief non-

military administrator in the Islands remarked, in a letter to Paris headquarters:

Die Angelegenheit ist in Nebrigen überholt, da der Abtransport der juden in Aussicht steht.

('In any case the matter is superseded as the deportation of the Jews is in sight.') And, yes indeed, the cattle trucks were rolling all across Europe.

Alexander Coutanche also intervened with the Germans on behalf of Lucille Schwab and Suzanne Malherbe, who were tried in the November of 1944 for the crime of undermining the morale of German troops by distributing news from the BBC. The details of their case are described elsewhere. Sufficient here to happily record that the two women were sentenced to death but had their sentences commuted to life imprisonment due to Alexander Coutanche's direct appeal to the German authorities.

POST-WAR ANGST

In recent years no aspect of the Occupation has aroused more passion and angry debate than that of the treatment of the Jews by the Island authorities. There have been heated exchanges between, on the one hand, those like Madeleine Bunting and David Fraser who accuse the Guernsey and Jersey governments of a gross dereliction of duty towards an unlawfully oppressed minority, and (in Fraser's case) of outright anti-Semitism: and on the other, outraged Islanders like

Bob Le Sueur, who reject absolutely these charges, arguing that the Island authorities did all they could possibly do for the Jews in the circumstances – and those circumstances were very difficult, the room for manoeuvre being tiny, the prospect of success very limited. They could not do as they wished. They could only do what they were told.

Here is Madeleine Bunting talking of Steiner, Spitz and Grünfeld:

'... Islanders defensively claimed that no one had any idea of what was happening to the Jews in Europe. They may not have known of the horror of the Holocaust, but they did know the Jews were in grave danger ... The truth is that no official in either Guernsey or Jersey considered the welfare of a handful of Jews sufficiently important to jeopardise good relations with the Germans.'

And even more damningly:

'A mixture of ignorance, indifference and anti-Semitism all contributed to these British officials playing their tiny part in the tragedy of the Holocaust.'

These officials made no significant protest against the implementation of the Nazi anti-Jewish directives.

If we include the Schwab and Malherbe case, there were only three recorded objections raised by the Island Governments against the treatment of the Jews by the occupying Germans.

It is argued that people in the positions of authority in the Islands, people like Alexander Coutanche, Ambrose Sherwill, Duret Aubin, Victor Carey, John Leale, even Clifford Orange and William Sculpher, must have known that the Jews were a specially endangered people and yet no effort at all was made to help them, either by objecting on principle to the imposition of anti-Jewish measures or by trying to administer the legislation in such a way as to shield them from its full effect. For example, at the very beginning when the 12 Jersey folk presented themselves to Clifford Orange for classification as 'Jew' or 'non-Jew':

'Undoubtedly a sympathetic interpretation of the definitions [of Jewishness] of the First Order would have allowed the exclusion of a number of those subsequently listed as registered Jews.'

(Cohen)

If that had happened, most, if not all of the pain and hardship, madness, perjury and death associated with the Jewish experience in the occupied Islands would not have occurred.

In the letter from Sir Alexander Maxwell to the Bailiffs of Jersey and Guernsey, His Majesty's Government had desired the Bailiffs to:

'stay at his post and administer the government of the Island to the best of his abilities in the interests of the inhabitants.'

With the implication that all the officers of the two administrations – in the bureaucracy, the judiciary and the police force, would assist and support the two men.

At the end of the War it was said with some degree of certainty that the governors of the two Islands carried out the instruction with a great deal of success, not to say creative ingenuity.

They did indeed administer the government of the Islands to the best of their abilities in the interests of most of the inhabitants, but, so the complaint runs, it can scarcely be said they governed with any regard whatsoever to the interests of the remaining Jews. They didn't even try.

Indeed the opposite appears to be the case, for by registering anti-Jewish measures in the Royal Courts without demur, and by helping to implement those measures, the Jews were actually deprived of any interests or rights of citizenship at all. The Island governments actively helped and connived in a process designed to reduce them to non-persons with no legitimate interests of any kind. And in the case of the foreign nationals, Steiner, Spitz and Grünfeld, they were not regarded as native inhabitants and therefore their interests were no concern of the Guernsey authorities.

But the wishes of their German masters were. Carey, Leale, Sculpher, Coutanche and Orange actively helped the Germans by providing them with information as to their identity and whereabouts, information which led to their arrest, deportation and eventual death in Auschwitz. In other words, the Island's civilian authorities, on however small a scale, were uncomplaining assistants and helpers in the Nazi destruction of Jews.

That is the charge levied against the Islands' civilian authorities during those Occupation years, and it is a charge which even now, 70 years after the War, generates a lot of heat and passion.

On 24th January 2004, an article by Madeleine Bunting appeared in the *Guardian*:

OUR PART IN THE HOLOCAUST

In this article she says of the work of the Islands officials:

'The level of petty detail pursued by Island officials calls to mind Hannah Arendt's phrase, "the banality of evil". It was these kinds of small actions on the part of thousands of police and town officials all over Europe that had such terrible consequences. What has always made the Channel Islands' record so important is that it punctures the complacent British assumption of a national immunity to this combination of amoral bureaucracy and anti-Semitism.'

Bunting's accusations roused the ire of the Islanders and in particular Robert Le Sueur, who found the journalist's judgement offensive in the extreme. On 4th February he fired off a letter to the *Guardian*. Remarkably that newspaper, self-proclaimed promoter of honest debate and defender of free speech, declined to publish it. But it should have done so, for it is an important, succinct and precise explanation of the Islanders' point of view.

This is an extract from Bob Le Sueur's letter:

'*The article by Madeleine Bunting on January 24th really is insufferably tendentious, not least in its inflammatory headline 'Our Part in the Holocaust,' implying that the governments of the Channel Islands had a part in that unspeakable mass genocide of six million people.*

What really happened?

One Jersey Jewish resident, a Mr Finkelstein, ended up in a concentration camp, Buchenwald, but managed to survive. He was a Romanian and his country entered the war on the German side. There was nothing the Jersey authorities could do effectively on his behalf although I understand they tried.

In Guernsey, three Jewesses, all citizens of the Third Reich, were moved to France in 1942 by their government, the German government. It was learned after the war that, tragically, all three perished in the gas

chambers at Auschwitz. Can Miss Bunting tell us how the Guernsey authorities could have intervened to prevent the Germans from moving their own citizens?

Of the remaining Jews in both Islands, a small number and all British citizens, for all their understandable fears, in fact nothing happened to them that did not happen to the rest of us. None ever wore the hated yellow star. The official curfew was published on German orders but not imposed. The authorities connived at the paper 'sales' of their businesses to their Gentile employees who 'sold them back' after the War.

Of those Jews who were wise enough not to register, not one was ever denounced, not even those with rather obvious Jewish surnames like Leopold.

Those few Jews who were sent to internment camps in Bavaria were with the interned British Gentiles from the Channel Islands and were sent for the same reasons. These were not concentration camps in the usual sense of the word. They were frustrated and possibly apprehensive but they were not physically ill-treated, received Red Cross parcels, were able to write censored letters to friends in the Channel Islands and the UK.

Is that really such a 'scandalous wartime past' as claimed by Miss Bunting, one about which we as a community must now 'make a clean breast?'

Chapter 9

Festung Alderney

The Island of Alderney lies to the north-east of the main group of Channel Islands, closer to the coast of France than to Guernsey. The apprehensive Islanders could hear the firing of the guns and the exploding bombs. They could see the fires raging on the Cherbourg Peninsula, the great columns of smoke rising up in the hot summer skies of June 1940. The Germans were on their way! The Alderney folk needed hardly any encouragement at all to drop everything and run as fast as the boats would take them, away, over the sea, to England. Only a handful of people remained behind to greet the conquering Germans when they first landed in the Island on 2nd July 1940, one day after the other Islands had been occupied. Not that the Germans attached any great importance to the occupation of Alderney. For most of the Germans the belief was that Britain would be overrun and conquered within a matter of weeks. Herman Goering's Luftwaffe would blow the RAF out of the skies, the great cities of the United Kingdom could then be bombed with impunity and into submission to an invading German force. It was all so simple and seemingly inevitable.

There was no great strategic role for little Alderney to play in this coming operation, entitled 'Sea Lion', and this lack of importance was reflected in the tiny number of troops who actually arrived in the Island that hot summer's day in July 1940. There were just 80 of them. Their commanding officer was a Sergeant Schmidt who became the first *Inselkommandant* of Alderney – there was to be no aristocratic general for this little place, and no great plans either for much more than a token occupation. In fact, initially the German interest in Alderney was more agricultural than military. Within weeks of the occupation of the larger Islands Jersey and Guernsey, serious food shortages were making themselves felt. It was thought a good idea to grow food in the depopulated island for the supply of Guernsey. But it was just short-term thinking as far as the Germans were concerned. Soon the War would be over. The Islands would remain under German rule in perpetuity, most probably as holiday resorts for the deserving German people. There would then be no shortage of anything. The Islands wafted by Channel breezes would flow with milk and honey. 'Strength through Joy' in the former English land.

But the times they were a-changing.

The nature of the War changed.

The British could thank God for the

lone and damaged German bomber that dropped its bombs onto the West End of London rather than on the 'legitimate' military target of the docks and the East End. This action so enraged Churchill that he ordered the bombing of the German capital, Berlin. This action in turn enraged the febrile lord of the Third Reich. Hitler had promised that no German cities would ever be bombed in his war, and so had Goering. Outraged at the temerity of the RAF in launching this attack, Hitler ordered that the Luftwaffe should switch its attacks away from the RAF Fighter Command and its aerodromes and direct them instead to the cities of Britain, particularly London. The timing of this order was, from a German perspective, catastrophic, for the Luftwaffe were on the brink of defeating the RAF. When they turned their firepower towards London and away from the RAF, they gave Fighter Command a much-needed respite from constant deployment and a heaven-sent time to repair, regroup and re-energise the fight against their mighty foe.

The Battle of Britain won, it became clear that Churchill was not going to negotiate a peace, far from it. Britain would hold out to the last, praying the while that America would join with her sooner rather than later to fight the Germans.

Hitler was nonplussed by this setback to his plans. He wanted to begin the 'real war' in the East and here were the British holding up the Fuehrer's divine mission to exterminate the Jewish Communist state of Russia for the good of mankind and certainly Germankind. No, he would not wait for the war in the West to be won. Yes, he would open up the Eastern Front and march against Stalin. He was advised against trying to fight a war on two fronts. Indeed every relevant military precedent in German history, particularly from the First World War, spoke loudly against it. Nonetheless Hitler, enamoured to the point of madness by the strategy of blitzkrieg, and hopelessly ill-served by German intelligence about the strength of the Russian forces, believed he could turn away from the West, fight and win a lightning war against the Russians, and then come back to the British problem later. Of course while thus turned away from the Channel he would take the elementary precaution of securing the Western Front in a purely defensive way to prevent incursion and invasion by the enemy.

And in this new strategy Alderney had an important part to play.

In Alderney this process of building up defensive positions, which found its full expression in the creation of the Atlantic Wall, began quite early. As we have seen, the 'pin prick' commando raids on the Islands convinced Hitler that the first place the British would attack would be the Channel Islands, as much for propaganda reasons as for strategic advantage. They must not be allowed to succeed. Preparatory work to provide accommodation for the proposed increase in the number of German troops coming to Alderney was begun as early as April 1941. Little Braye Harbour was made ready for the import of men and material needed for the construction of the fortifications.

In the autumn of that same year, 1941, Hitler issued his famous Directive on the Fortification and Defence of the Channel Islands.

20.10.41

1. English operations on a large scale against the territories occupied by us in the West are not, as before, unlikely. But under pressure of the situation in the East and for reasons of politics and propaganda small-scale operations must at any moment be reckoned with, particularly an attempt to regain possession of the Channel Islands which are important to us for the protection of our sea communications.

3. With regard to the permanent fortifying of the Islands to convert them into an impregnable fortress, (this) must be carried forward with the utmost speed.

Immediately there was an intensification of activity. Troops poured into the Island by the hundred. Come the Christmas of 1941 there were 3,000 Germans from army, navy and air force in the Island. And there was a new *Inselkommandant*, no sergeant he, but a Lieutenant Colonel Gleden. But finally the task of making Hitler's wish a reality fell to Major Hoffman. It was time to start serious construction work on Festung Alderney.

To put fortifications in place on such a massive scale required a huge labour force and as ever on such occasions, this was provided by the Organisation Todt (OT) as was the practice all along the Atlantic Wall. There were hundreds if not thousands of them, and, of course, they came principally from Eastern Europe. There were Russians, Ukranians and Poles afforced by 'volunteers' from France and Spain. There was also a large contingent of German workers.

As Major 'Bunny' Pantcheff, who conducted a thoroughgoing investigation into the Alderney Occupation, remarks:

'Foreign workers in the forced labour contingents, with certain exceptions like the Jews and civilian prisoners who arrived in October 1943, were, in theory, volunteers. Some of the Russians, for example, had been invited to volunteer for agricultural work in France. The Spaniards had been given the option of work on military construction sites or being returned to Franco's Spain, from which they were Republican refugees in France. The degree of compulsion in recruitment varied, but the conditions under which they were held and employed may justify their own description of themselves as forced labour.'

These 'volunteers' were placed in four camps named after German Islands in the North Sea; Helgoland, Borkum, Norderney and Sylt. Of these four camps Borkum had the best conditions for the workers. These men were not from Eastern Europe at all, but from the West: Belgium, Holland and France. They were paid for their labour and enjoyed more freedom and more food than the inmates of the other three camps. The overall administration of the camps was in the hands of the OT *Frontführer* and the individual camp commanders were answerable to him.

Sylt was much smaller than the other three but it was to become the most notorious of the four camps because in March 1943 it was taken over by a murderous SS *Totenkopf* unit from Neuengamme concentration camp. Sylt, camp number four, itself became a concentration camp – the only one on British soil. The population of this desperate place was quite special and distinct from that of the other three camps. These were the special enemies of the Third Reich. Germans, some highly decorated in the First World War; Jews, of course; homosexuals; conscientious objectors, and 'politicos', which is to say principled objectors to Nazism and Hitler, usually Communists. There was also an admixture of so called 'habitual criminals' – a catch-all category which included anyone and everyone who had offended against the regime. Whatever they had done, or were alleged to have done, was indicated by differently-coloured patches sewn onto the arms of their stripped clothing. Red for a 'politico',

pink for a homosexual, green for a habitual criminal, purple for a conscientious objector and the usual yellow for a Jew.

The camp commander of Sylt was SS *Haupsturmführer* Maximilian List who had been an admired administrator at the Neuengamme camp. His staff included equally dedicated hard-line Nazis Lieutenants Klebeck and Braun. Lieutenant Braun, an uncured syphilitic, was promoted to Camp Commandant when Maximilian List was sent to Norway in March 1944.

The treatment of prisoners in Sylt camp was, as might be expected from a Death's Head unit, much worse than that afforded the prisoners in the other three camps. They had less to eat and the punishments were more severe. So severe in fact that on one occasion the OT Commander of Alderney complained to the Alderney Military Commander that prisoners from Sylt working on the work sites had their 'capacity for work adversely affected' – meaning they were beaten to death's door and certainly to a point where they could not work at all.

The punishment expertise practised by List and his men was recognised and put to good use in that Sylt became not only a concentration camp but also a place where convicted offenders against OT ordinances could serve a term of imprisonment. The SS liked this arrangement very much, because once they had hold of the wretched OT

German Navy personal adrift in St. Anne, Alderney.

Marching past in a deserted Alderney.

Hans Herzog the Sonderfuehrer for Alderney, third from the left, seen here with members from the Feldkommandantur 515 Guernsey and Jersey.

A huge observation tower in Alderney.

Last resting place for slave workers who died horribly in Alderney.

The Survivors

Churchill addresses the troops.

The Submarine used to take Hubert Nicolle to Guernsey.

Commandos in training for attacks on France and the Channel Islands.

Collapsible landing-craft used in the commando raids.

Second Lieutenant Hubert Nicolle.

Nicolle as a P.O.W.

Bill

Slave workers

Louisa Gould and her two sons in happier times circa 1937.

Marie Ozanne of the Salvation Army

Louisa Gould.

Canon Clifford Cohu.

Harold Le Druillenec.

The Germans go shopping for luxury goods at the start of the Occupation.

offenders they could indent for more rations which they themselves could appropriate. The rule was 'keep hold of the OT men as long as possible'. So sentences were extended up to three times their original length. Good times for the *Schutzstaffel*!

THE DEVIL'S ISLAND?

There is a great problem in discovering what really went on in this little island during the Occupation years, and it is the problem of finding the evidence for the many seemingly fantastic and lurid allegations that have been made about the brutalities, the torture and the wholesale killings that are said to have taken place during these war years.

This, of course, is because the civilian population had, with the notable exception of the Pope family, fled to the mainland UK before the Germans and their slave workers ever arrived in the Island. There were no Islanders left to actually see and bear witness to what the Germans were doing, which made Alderney unique amongst the Islands. In Jersey and Guernsey and even in tiny Sark, there were thousands of eyes watching every move the Germans made. In Alderney there were only a few, and these belonged to workers shipped over from Guernsey and Jersey. Some, like Gordon Prigent, were sent there for punishment; some went voluntarily, enticed by the relatively high pay; others were selected to go there to repair houses:

'I knew one such in the last named

category and he related that they lived in houses, ate in German army cookhouses, were well-paid but had nothing on which to spend the money! Occasionally they had the luxury of a shower in the SS bath house at Sylt where the showers were operated by a "trusty" prisoner.'

(Michael Ginns)

There are stories of scores of dead slave workers being taken in the rubbish carts down to the coast and flung into the sea as a special 'treat for the crabs'; workers thrown alive into wet cement and entombed; the crucifixion of Russian slave workers; casual shootings; strangulations, and, always, malnutrition and starvation. Some reckon the number of dead in the thousands.

Major Pantcheff found actual records of only 389 dead:

'But the German records in Alderney were so confusing that one cannot but doubt whether these so traditionally renowned for meticulous and efficient administration were in this instance really aiming at clarity.'

(Pantcheff)

Perhaps the records were deliberately incomplete in order to disguise a much larger number of fatalities. Certainly the treatment meted out to the inmates of the three slave worker camps, Helgoland, Norderney and Sylt would point to a much greater figure than 400. Madeleine Bunting, in her excellently researched account of the Alderney camps, records a conversation she had with Georgi Kondakov, a survivor of Helgoland (and that was the best of the slave labour camps) in which he says:

'About 400 people died in Helgoland while I was there; many died at the beginning of January 1945, when it was cold. One of the most common signs of the approach of death was that people started to swell. When we were woken in the morning (around 5 a.m.) there were corpses in the beds beside us.

Those who had been allowed off work because they were sick had the job of collecting the bodies which were then thrown from the breakwater into the harbour. When I was building a round in the harbour, I saw special lorries come to the breakwater and tip bodies into the sea two or three times. Each lorry contained at least eight corpses.'

Another survivor, Kirill Nevrov, again in conversation with Madeleine Bunting, says that:

'We worked sometimes for as long as 16 hours a day, building concrete walls around the Island. Often we worked for 24 hours at a stretch, and we were then given half a day rest before resuming work. My only wish was to rest.'

And later:

'Many people died at the construction sites. After two or three months people started to die at the rate of about twelve men a day. There was a yard in the centre of the camp where people were shot for

stealing cigarettes. In the morning, people were found dead in their beds, and the naked corpses were loaded into trucks. A truck would tip the corpses at low tide into pits dug in the beach fifty to a hundred metres off the shore. There would be about twelve people in each pit. You could never find the grave after the tide had been in and out because sand had been washed over it. I saw the bodies being buried with my own eyes because I was working about 50 metres away on a concrete wall.'

The mortality rate was certainly very high and it is beyond question that the two major causes of this were malnutrition and overwork. These men in the three slave labour camps of Helgoland, Norderney and Sylt worked up to a 16- hour day, and often round the clock when 'concrete pours' had to be completed. The food they were given to sustain them in their very heavy physical labour was ludicrously little. The menu available to the workers during the last six months of 1942:

Breakfast
½ litre of coffee substitute, without milk or sugar. This was consumed in camp before going out to work.

Lunch
½ litre of thin cabbage or other vegetable soup. This was served at the working site and known as *Bunkersuppe* (bunker soup).

Supper
½ litre of similar soup and a 1 kilo loaf of bread to be shared among five to six

men. This was eaten in camp. In theory the bread was for use at breakfast next day also.

In addition, 25 grams of butter per head were issued twice, sometimes three times a week, and on isolated occasions a portion of sausage, jam, cheese or fresh vegetable. There was not any meat or sugar until 1944 when most of the OT workers had left Alderney.

In other words a starvation diet. Little wonder that many died and many were driven mad through hunger. And the plight of the forced workers was made worse by misappropriation of those rations which should have been available to them. The food ration was delivered to the OT administrators by army officers. The two quartermaster officers employed in this distribution, *Oberzahlmeister* Frank and *Oberzahlmeister* Kruger, would habitually retain part of the supply and then sell it for personal gain. It was common knowledge that they were doing this but no one cared enough about it to bring charges against the two men until 1944 when most of the OT workers had left (most of them to work on the V1 and V2 launching sites in northern France, Belgium and Holland). All the SS guards at Sylt were involved to a greater or lesser extent in keeping food from the prisoners and either keeping it for themselves or, more often selling it on the black market. And this stealing went right to the top. The camp *Kommandant* of Sylt, Maximilian List, and his second, Lieutenant Klebeck,

were actually court martialled in an SS court for stealing foodstuffs and black marketeering. The sentence was light.

SPEHR'S STORY

Hans Spehr was a German policeman and he was a brave man. He was audaciously anti-Nazi. He detested Hitler and all his works. In 1934, the year after Hitler had assumed supreme leadership of the Third Reich, Spehr was busy distributing anti-Hitler leaflets and carrying out all kinds of subversive activities against the new Nazi state.

But, like so many opponents of the regime, he was found out, hunted down, and then imprisoned,first in Berlin Tegel, then in Neuengamme concentration camp and finally in Sachsenhausen, where he stayed for six years. In the autumn of 1940 an SS building brigade was set up, of which Spehr was a member. This workforce was later sent to Dusseldorf to clear the debris caused by the British bombing and to search for unexploded bombs. As Spehr himself said, it was a suicide squad. He survived but a 100 of his fellow-prisoners were killed.

In the Spring of 1943 workers were desperately required in Alderney to build the fortifications to turn the little island into a mighty fortress or *Festung*. The Saschenhausen Brigade was made up to 1,000 men by the addition of prisoners from the notorious Buchenwald concentration camp, and sent, post-haste, to Alderney. They found themselves in the half-built Sylt camp which was run by the SS and which meant they were in for a very hard time:

'The conditions were catastrophic. Officially we were provided with the same rations as the armed forces got because we were classed as manual labourers. But unfortunately we didn't get it because the SS asked for double helpings of breakfast for themselves and sold too much on the black market. Our camp leader, the camp commandant, SS Haupsturmführer Liszt, went on leave and was checked by the military police, naturally under protest. He had whole chests full of sugar, lard, dripping, bacon and all the foods which were rather scarce. He had whole chests full.'

The days were long, starting at 5.00, when the men had to get up, clean the barracks and have a tiny breakfast if there was any breakfast at all. Then it was off to work by 6.00. A watery soup with bits of cabbage or turnip in it was served up for lunch. Work finished at 6.00 and supper was served out back in the camp. Everyone got a piece of bread. That is to say, one loaf, which was 1,000 grammes, was divided up amongst six people. And then there were 10 grammes of margarine and sometimes a slice of sausage or a slice of cheese. Lastly there was something to drink that was called coffee.The work was hard and the food utterly inadequate. But worst of all was the mistreatment.

'For example, one man moved a few steps from his place of work. This was then reported to the camp leader, and from him he got 25 lashes with the horse whip in the evening. And so it was for every little thing, at least 25 lashes.
And inmates were not only beaten, they were also hanged. They were all supposed to have committed suicide. They weren't hanged officially, but in reality the prisoners themselves were made to do it, and most of the orders to do this were given by Obersturmführer Klebeck. He gave the order and the inmates would hang their fellow prisoners. And they were rewarded for it. Particularly outstanding was what's his name ... Fahrenbacher, then there was von Trauer, and a few others too. They hanged the prisoners.'*

That the workers were maltreated to an astonishing degree, particularly in Norderney and Sylt, is beyond question. What is also true is that none of these camps was a 'death' or extermination camp. They were primarily labour camps in which the unwilling workers for the Third Reich could be housed. Admittedly the conditions under which the labourers, the *Untermenschen*, worked were horrible, bestial even, but the purpose was not to kill them but to get as much work out of them as possible. If the men died, then that was collateral damage and not the main ambition of their overlords. There was no Treblinka or Sobibor in Alderney, or anywhere else in the Channel Islands, but life was cheap when it came to the Russian *Untermenschen*, and it was taken casually and often viciously by the Germans.

Pantcheff records this account of a Polish forced labourer held in Sylt, the dreaded Camp No. 4:

'The Truppführer *gave an order to cut ten sticks on which they then fitted rubber tubes. Then we were beaten with them. Very often we were beaten without reason; sometimes we were accused of laziness; but mostly we were beaten out of hatred. They called us 'Communist swine' and 'bloody Poles' etc. Often the men were beaten so long that they fell down from sheer weakness ... we were beaten every day. My friend Antoni Anchrowski died that way. He was from my native village and of course I knew him very well. He had stayed behind in Sylt camp for a few days because of illness. He had swollen feet. Afterwards he got a bit better, but he was still very weak and could not walk properly. One day after work, when our squad was marching back to camp, he could not keep up and fell behind. I saw the* Truppführer *remain with him and get to work out his truncheon. Later we lost sight of him. All the evening we kept waiting in the camp for him but he never returned. The next morning when I went to the latrine after reveille, Antoni lay there on the other side of the barbed wire at the side of the camp. His face was covered with red weals and when we later brought his body into the camp and undressed it, we could distinctly see the weals and blotches on his body.'*

It appears from accounts given to Soloman Steckoll, Bunny Pantcheff and Madeleine Bunting that this was by no means an isolated occurrence, in fact it was a regular occurrence, particularly in the three camps of Helgoland, Norderney and Sylt. For instance the Camp Commander, or *Lagerleiter*, of Helgoland, Ludwig Becker, took his daily exercise by beating any prisoner who failed to show enough respect at roll call or did not snap to attention quickly enough. He would attack the offender about the head, arms and body with a truncheon. He would be helped in his joyful work by his second in command, who would also hit the unfortunate worker with a similar stick:

'... on all parts of the body until their faces were covered with blood and they could not rise from the ground, when he would call the prisoner's mates to carry the prostrate body away.'

Violence and serious injury were endemic in the camps, and so was disease. Workers suffering acute malnutrition and working long hours in a harsh climate they were unused to, often with no protective clothing beyond adapted cement bags and rags, suffered serious degeneration of the immune system and were consequently prey to every disease imaginable.

Beaten up, diseased and weak, workers were often in need of medical attention, but there wasn't any available, at least none worth the name. There was, it is true, an OT doctor assigned to the Alderney camps, but he seems not to have given any medical care at all to the inmates. There was a medical unit of sorts at the Norderney Camp, which was run by a Russian with the assistance of one nurse and two untrained orderlies.

There is no evidence that any constitutionally sick foreign forced labourer working for the OT ever received proper medical attention. There was a much better chance of being beaten or shot than of getting medical treatment.

So said Albert Pottingine, as reported by Madeleine Bunting in her book *The Model Occupation*:

'They used dynamite at the quarry to blow the rock out. On one occasion we were told to take shelter from the explosion, but the force of it came from exactly the opposite direction and I received the full blast. My ankle was hit by a rock and to this I am lame. I couldn't walk back to the camp and an old Russian sailor hid me in sacking at the quarry for three days. He brought me water, but the only food he could give me was wild blackberries. I had to start work again to get my food rations. People helped me by loading the trolley and pushing it to the beach. First my foot started to swell and then the other leg started to swell and then my face. I would have recovered if the wound had been cleaned but there was no medical care. The Lagerführer's method of curing people was to beat them. People were either dead or working, you couldn't be ill.'

Albert Pottingine was a Ukranian, only

16 years old when war began, but young as he was, he could not escape being taken by the Germans for use by the OT men in Alderney.

He remembered nothing so much of the Island of Alderney as the leaving of it for, hurt and weak as he was, he was put aboard the ill-fated ship, the *Xaver Dorsch* along with 600 other damaged OT men. She was meant to sail, along with another ship, the *Franka*, also packed with OT workers, out across the small expanse of water to Cherbourg, only they didn't make it, at least not at the first time of asking.

The seas about the Channel Islands are dangerous and those about Alderney doubly so. The waters that run along the north-west coast of the Island are aptly named 'The Swinge' and those on the other side of the Island, 'The Screech'. A winter storm can turn them into a raging torrent and have a ship helpless before it. So it was with the *Xaver Dorsch* and her sister ship the *Franka*. They and their wretched human cargo were forced back and wedged firmly on the Alderney rocks – and there they stayed for 14 days – 14 hellish days imprisoned in the hold. For food the Germans made a kind of soup from soya flour stirred into barrels of water. The prisoners were allowed six barrels a day of this barely-edible gunk. The Germans themselves would not go into the hold in order to avoid the verminous and potentially dangerous crush of *Untermenschen*. Instead they appointed certain of the

Russians to do the work of distribution and, as was the custom in Alderney, those who controlled the distribution of the food always kept some back for themselves. In this case the suffering men on the *Xaver Dorsch* only got five barrels of 'food' instead of six, and this meant there was not enough to go round. Consequently some of the prisoners got none at all. Porttingine says that:

'The prisoners crowded around the barrels, knowing there might not be enough for the last queue. In the rush, about six people were crushed to death every day.

The Russian police then found a big long stick and stood on the ladder which led up to the deck and beat those who were near the front of the queue on their heads. These prisoners lost consciousness and fell, and the people behind them would rush forward and trample them to death. After the stick was introduced, the number who died went up to ten or more a day.'

But the worst of the prisoners' experience was caused by the lack of any remotely adequate sanitary arrangements. There was one solitary barrel which served as a toilet for over 600 men. It got full very quickly, full to overflowing. The heavy seas meant that the ship was inconstant, often violent, motion which shook the barrel so that excrement would slop and pour over the rim and along the floor of the hold. The prisoners were lagged with it:

'Everyone was wet with excrement and the lice multiplied so quickly you could collect handfuls under your armpits, but there was nowhere to drop them other than on your neighbours. There was no room to lie or stretch your legs. We were covered with wounds and our skin was eaten up with lice and sores.'

It was a scene from Dante's Inferno with the sole difference that the torment of the men on the Xaver Dorsch and the Franka did not last an eternity, though it felt like it to those on board. After 14 days the storms and the heavy seas abated. The Germans managed to ease the ships off the rocks and take them for repair. This took three days, after which time the prisoners, wearing little more than blankets with holes cut in them for the head, were shipped off again to Cherbourg aboard the *Xaver Dorsch* and the *Franka*.

The *Xaver Dorsch* was named after *Reichsminister*, Franz Xaver Dorsch. Ferret-faced and sporting a Hitler moustache, Dorsch had seen long service as deputy to Fritz Todt, and on Todt's mysterious death he became Albert Speer's second in command of the Organisation Todt. Miraculously he was not charged with any crime against humanity at the War's end, far from it. The US Army were anxious to use his knowledge of labour deployment on massive engineering projects for their own purposes and he was commissioned to write a comprehensive study of the workings of the Organisation Todt, published in 1947. Five years after the War's end he set up a hugely successful engineering consultancy company, Dorsch Consult. It is certain that the advice he and his company gave out to the industrialists of post-War Germany did not include recommendations to beat, starve and kill their workforce.

German soldiers often referred to their experience of the Channel Islands as 'coming to a place flowing with milk and honey.' But for the OT slave workers it was a place stinking of ordure, full of hurt, disease and death, and a place from which there was no getting away. The sea blocked every escape route. The Island was covered with barbed wire and everywhere the sign 'Achtung! Minen' gave notice of the ever-present danger. Alderney was indeed the 'accursed rock,' as it was named by the French Jews who found themselves there. It was called 'Devil's Island' too, again with good reason, the Devil in question being Adolf Hitler, whose Christian name was used as the code-word for Alderney.

Alderney was known as 'Adolf '.

Curiously, it seems that when the Islanders took to the boats and fled, the bird population went too. Time and again this strange phenomenon is remarked – no birds, no birdsong, the skies empty, not a bird to be seen for the entire duration of the War. It is said they did not reappear about the Island until five years later.

QUITE A LOAD OF HARDWARE FOR A LITTLE ISLAND
(Pantcheff on Alderney)
Not much thought was expended on

Alderney's strategic role in the imminent conquest of Britain, which was expected to take place certainly before the Christmas of 1940. There was some vague notion that the little Island might be used as a small springboard for Operation Sealion, perhaps a few invasion barges could be launched against the southern coast of England from Braye harbour. But nothing was certain or decided about the German plans for the Island.

This was to change as the nature of Hitler's war changed in the West. It changed from an offensive to a defensive war for two reasons. Firstly Goering, despite all his boastful promises, failed to win the Battle of Britain with his Luftwaffe. Britain was not bombed into negotiation or submission. The conditions for a land invasion were not established.

Dr Peter Schentz gives us the other reason:

'By October 1940, it was clear to everybody that the menace of the German invasion was receding. It is still commonly believed that this was due to the failure of the German air offensive over Britain, but the true reasons lay in the weakness and unwillingness of the German Navy to provide cover for the invasion force against the British Home Fleet. The RAF alone would not have stopped the invasion fleet of some 4,000 units just as the Luftwaffe could not prevent the evacuation of Dunkirk.'

The second reason why the nature of the War changed was, of course, because Hitler turned away from the West to attend more urgent business in the East. Operation Sealion was put on hold. It could be activated 'if necessary' after the brief war against the Russian Jewish Bolshevik forces had been won.

The Channel Islands, including Alderney, now found themselves with a more important military role to play in the defensive war. They were to be heavily fortified to defend themselves against the British attack which the Fuehrer was sure would come to the Islands, for propaganda as well as military purposes. Eventually the fortified Islands could be considered part of the Atlantic Wall, keeping the Allies out and the Germans safe within. Alderney's particular role in this massive defensive structure was, obviously, to control the Channel approaches toward Cap de la Hague and the seas running along the western coast of the Cherbourg Peninsula. Little Alderney was to become *Festung* Alderney. There was much work to be done – starting at Braye harbour.

Huge quantities of building material and munitions had to be imported into the Island. The Alderney harbour hiding behind the Admiralty Breakwater was not up to the job of offloading such huge amounts of material and so it was decided to extend the north-eastern arm of the harbour by adding two four-legged Krupp units to its length. These units were ingeniously designed bridge units originally intended for use in Operation Sealion. Now two of them were to help the new defensive war by facilitating the flow of men, machinery, guns, munitions and cement needed to turn Alderney into a fortress with a firepower extending all across the bay of St Malo. And what a great number of guns there were! To say nothing of the mines.

There were five medium and light batteries about the Island on strategic sites. There was the Giffone Battery up in the north-west corner of the Island known as the Batterie Annes; the Alsace Battery housed at the old Victorian Fort Albert; the Batterie Blücher by Balmoral House on the Longis Road. These batteries were almost self-contained units – they had their own electricity and own water supply, their own workshop, supply store and even their own recreation hut which would surely be of use in the long and largely uneventful years of occupation that were to follow.

And there were more, slightly smaller batteries; the Rose Battery (later known as the General Marcks Battery) and the Falcon Battery together with no less than 16 casemated 10.5 defence guns carefully positioned around the Island. All their firepower would be concentrated on any would-be invading force coming in from the sea, but of course there was also the more present threat of attack from the skies. The Germans in Alderney took great pains to counter that threat by deploying four Anti-Aircraft (AA) units, one to the cliffs overlooking Fort Clonque, another to the side of Alderney's tiny airfield, a third to the north of the Russian cemetery on Mannez Hill, and the fourth south-west of Longis Bay by Essex Castle. Smaller AA guns were situated over Telegraph Bay, and by Simons Place. There was more AA artillery positioned at Chateau à L'Etoc on the northernmost tip of the Island and at Simon's Place just south of Whitegates. There were also guns placed on the Admiralty breakwater and some by the stone jetty of Little Crably harbour.

To prevent any enemy landing with armoured vehicles the Germans built a defensive wall on Platte Saline Beach which they considered a very likely spot for an invading force attack. At Longis beach, another potential landing site, they did not go so far, but blocked all the possible exits from the beach with huge lumps of concrete. On all the beaches there were anti-tank devices, tetrads, steel railings, and, of course, mines. From figures obtained by Pantcheff just after the War, it appears that no less then 30,000 mines were laid in the Island from 1941 onwards. There was a ring of minefields all around the coast and especially by the beaches. They were surrounded by barbed wire and their contents advertised on signs surrounded by skull and crossbones with the simple message 'Achtung! Minen.'

But the most powerful discouragement offered to the potential invader was the anti-tank gun. There were 17 of them in all guarding Alderney from Braye to Longis Bay. The OT workers built massive casements to house the 4.7 cm anti-tank Guns. If you came at Alderney with an ambition to invade, you would find yourself looking straight down the barrel of at least one, if not more, of these powerful weapons. And if you did manage to get off the beach you would run into the guns positioned alongside all major roads. There was indeed 'quite a lot of hardware for a little Island.'

By 1943 Alderney had become a massively fortified Island, a kind of stationary battleship in the bay of St Malo. It was covered in barbed wire, laid end-to-end with mines and a hundred guns small, large and massive pointed up to the skies or out over the seas. Thousands of tons of concrete had been poured. Scores of slave workers had suffered horrible deaths but nobody cared about that, least of all the Germans. Their ambition had been achieved. Alderney was now powerful enough to play a major role in the war in the West, which it might well have done had the Constellation Operations for the invasion of all three Channel Islands, Jersey, Guernsey and Alderney, been carried forward. As we have seen elsewhere, Constellation was shelved on the grounds that re-taking the Islands would mean an unacceptable number of civilian casualties and would in any case involve the Allies in a great expenditure of effort for very little return. It was a long way to Berlin. The effort to get there must be intense and concerted. The Allied commanders could not afford to have a significant number of their forces embroiled in a struggle to dislodge the foe from three tiny Islands, which even if they were successful in so doing would afford tiny Islands, would afford them not one iota of strategic advantage. It was a military nonsense to attack Alderney. Therefore, come D-Day, the Allies just bypassed Alderney along with all the other Channel Islands. All that effort, all that cost of men and material and all that display of power, in the end, meant absolutely nothing. Alderney, exactly like many a place designated *Festung* by the Fuehrer, particularly on the Eastern Front, was simply ignored. These fortresses did not figure in any military planning. They were not attacked, they were just ignored and were left increasingly far behind the advancing Allied lines. For them and for Alderney, the War was over.

THE SURRENDER

Even so, Alderney was the very last of the Channel Islands to surrender to the Allies. A detachment from Force 135 repossessed the Island on 16th May. The delay in this operation was caused by a lingering suspicion that the German garrison in the Island would attempt a last-ditch defence and go down fighting to the last man. In the event there was no such struggle and the Germans quietly laid down their arms and surrendered. The job of cleaning the place up was begun and this was an almost Herculean endeavour. A workforce made up of German POWs from Alderney garrison began the

arduous task of dismantling the military machinery that had taken so much effort to put in place, and they started with the most dangerous first. The mines were lifted by the hundred and exploded under German supervision. The miles of barbed wire were taken away. Now it was possible to move safely around the Island. Now it was possible to transport guns and munitions to the harbour and then dump them far out to sea. Work was begun to destroy the concrete gun emplacement with sharply contrasting results. The smaller and simpler gun emplacements could very quickly be destroyed or removed, but the great watchtower and the massive coastal concrete casements proved altogether more intractable. As in the two sister Islands of Jersey and Guernsey, the decision was taken just to leave them as they were and as they became, enduring reminders of the German Occupation.

CRIME AND PUNISHMENT

But what of the suffering endured by the thousands of OT workers who had built all these seemingly immoveable fortifications. What about these men from the East who had been brutalised, beaten, tortured and shot by the Germans? Shouldn't someone be held to account for these war crimes, these offences against humanity? The answer should have been a resounding 'Yes!'. But in fact hardly anything at all was done to call the guilty parties to justice because of the crimes committed in the Island. For example, *Lagerluter* Karl

Tietz, who had been in charge of Norderney camp from 1942 to 1943. As we have already noted, he and his assistant visited brutality upon the prisoners on a daily basis. They would batter them with specially designed truncheons about their arms, legs, trunk and head, until bloody and unconscious they finally collapsed on to the ground.

Tietz was tried by a German court in 1943 but not for mistreating the prisoners. He was tried for running a black market in cigarettes! A much more serious crime than assaulting defenceless prisoners, at least in German eyes.

It must be added though, that the two OT officers who ran the brutal Norderney Camp after Karl Tietz had left were dragged before a court, not in Britain or Russia, but in France, where they were charged with war crimes and subsequently sentenced to many years imprisonment.

It appears from Steckoll's investigation that Alderney's *Inselkommandant* Major Karl Hoffman never saw the inside of a court, though he had been offered by the British to the Russians for trial. At one time it was thought that he had been taken by the Russians and hanged in Kiev's central square before 40,000 Russian onlookers but this, apparently, was not the Karl Hoffman who had figured in the grim Alderney occupation but someone else entirely. That Karl

Hoffman never went to Russia. Instead, along with thousands of other POWs, he was taken to a camp in England from which he was not released until April 1948. He returned to his homeland and, according to reliable reports, lived quietly in West Germany until his death in 1979.

Proceedings were never instituted against *Hauptsturmführer* Liszt. He was interrogated by the Director of Public Prosecutions in Hamburg but he simply stated that he did not know Alderney at all and had nothing whatever to do with the crimes that had been committed there. It was, he maintained, obviously a case of mistaken identity. He was released without any of the former inmates of Sylt being allowed to confront and identify him, and without any charge being brought against him.

Hans Spehr, the former Sylt inmate, went looking for his tormentors after the war and:

'I was told, for instance at the National Records Office in Freiburg, that was a branch of the National Office, I enquired after a few people and I was told by the officials, we can't give you any information because of State security, but just let the people die in peace.'

The British themselves put no one on trial for crimes committed in Alderney because it was their decision to let the countries against whose nationals the war crimes had been committed mount their own prosecutions of the perpetrators on their own soil. In the case of Alderney the race most sinned against had been the Russian, therefore the Russian state should try the accused in Russia. Britain effectively washed its hands of the whole process of bringing German war criminals in Alderney to justice. All the investigative work contained in Major Pantcheff's report was passed over to the Russians in the belief that they would conduct their own trials into the crimes that had been committed in Alderney. Scores of their people had died in the most awful circumstances during the course of the Occupation of the Island. Surely they would be only too anxious to exact a heavy price from those responsible. But they weren't.

Nobody was prosecuted in a Russian court, or summarily executed even by the Russians for war crimes committed in Alderney. As has been remarked in the case of 'Bill' Buryi Polykapovitch in Jersey, the Russians were not really interested in what had been done to their nationals who had been used as forced labour in the West. Indeed, they treated the survivors of the labour camps who made it home as being tainted by their contact with the West. They mistrusted these ex-OT men as being spies for the Capitalist states. The concern was for the present threat they posed rather than for their previous suffering and those who had caused it. They had betrayed their country by working for the Germans and now they were to repeat the offence by working for the Western Allies as spies. There were, it is actually true, a few half-hearted attempts by the British to turn the returning Russian slave workers into spies for the West. 'Bill' Buryi Polykapovitch was approached at the War's end by British officers who wanted to turn him into a 'sleeper' agent. Unfortunately for these cunning officers, anxious to strike a blow in the expected Cold War, Bill did not understand what the term 'sleeper' meant in this context. He thought it meant simply 'one who sleeps'. He knew nothing of its usage to describe a deeply embedded latent spy who could be activated maybe many years down the line. That particular definition had not appeared in the Russian-English dictionary he'd been thoughtfully provided with by that feisty Jersey lady, Louisa Gould. Bill did not become a spy but even so, he, along with many others, was suspected of being one, and for 25 years he was denied freedom of movement, denied the right to work where he wanted and kept under constant surveillance. Not a good life, as Bunny Pantcheff says at the end of his authoritative history of the Alderney Occupation:

'Finally let us not forget those unfortunates in the worst case of all who, having survived one inhumanity, may have returned home to another; not welcomed, their wounds not healed nor their life restored, but blamed by their rulers for working for the German enemy

and consequently condemned as traitors.'

The intense fortification of this little Island was as fine an example of Hitler's *Inselwahn* as can be found. It was predicated upon a mistaken assessment of strategic advantage and the expectation of an attack that never materialised. It was a gross waste of material and men's lives. It was all for nothing.

Well, not quite nothing, for a Lancaster bomber was shot down over the Race in June 1944 by the *Flakbatterie* near Essex Castle. The crew bailed out and hit the water. D-Day had just happened.

Kommandant of the Harbour, Captain Massman, was not in a forgiving mood. He expressly refused to allow rescue ships to leave the harbour to save the fallen crew.

And prior to that in March 1943, AA artillery at Les Auteuils by the airport managed to hit and bring down another Fortress, but this time a Flying Fortress of the US Air force. There were no survivors to pick up.

Two 'kills' in five years. Alderney was not exactly in the thick of the fighting. And it cannot possibly be said that the embattled isle played a significant role in any part of the War. Just like her two sister islands, Jersey and Guernsey, Alderney was completely ignored by the Allied Forces as they invaded mainland France on D-Day, 6th June 1944.

Chapter 10

It Was Over

---

*Hostilities will end officially at one minute after midnight tonight...
and our dear Channel Islands will also be free today.*
Winston Churchill 3pm on May 8th 1945

The Islands were in a truly terrible state after five years of German Occupation. Scores of gun emplacements, huge and ugly observation towers and great anti-tank installations littered the countryside, the beaches and the coastline. The roads too were in a parlous state of disrepair, cracked and pot-holed beneath the weight of military traffic.

And perhaps worse than all this, many houses, particularly in Guernsey, had suffered severe damage. Some had been destroyed altogether. Those that had been occupied by the imported Todt workers had been left in a disgusting state. Overburdened sanitation systems had broken down. Furniture left by evicted owners had been smashed up, and in many cases all the wooden fitments, door frames, skirting boards and even floorboards had been ripped out for firewood.

Vandalism and looting seem to have been the order of the day – and it was not confined to the Germans and their agents. A minority of the remaining Islanders were not averse to helping themselves to their absent neighbours' goods and chattels. In one notorious instance in Jersey during the deportations a family had gone to the harbour as they had been ordered to do, to embark for an internment camp on mainland Europe. However, due to lack of room, the ship taking them could not sail and they were sent home. They had spent only a few hours away, but when they arrived back at their house they discovered that most of their furniture had disappeared, along with some carpets. They went next door to their neighbours' house to see if they knew what had happened. They certainly did. One of the carpets was on the floor of their kitchen and a lot of the furniture was stacked in their front room. Of course, as they explained, they were not looting or stealing their neighbours' goods. Far from it! They were simply acting in a good neighbourly fashion and taking the said property in to their own house for 'safe-keeping'.

There was, as could be expected, great euphoria at this release from German captivity. It was a joy shared by the whole world. But still it was not an easy time in the post-Occupation Channel Islands and, most of all, it was not an easy time for all those many children who had been evacuated in the June of 1940 and were now returning. These boys and girls had been away from their mums and dads, away from their small insular community, for five long years. Most of their formative years had been spent away on the mainland in huge cities like London, Liverpool and Glasgow.

Inevitably in this time they had grown away from their roots. Their style became mainland British and urban, their speech grew towards cockney, Scouse and Glaswegian. They had in many ways ceased to be Islanders, but it was back to the Islands that they came. Re-adjustment and re-integration often proved difficult and in some cases impossible. The pleasure of being reunited with their families was not unalloyed.

There was a lot of celebration, flag-waving and happy triumphalism in the weeks following liberation, but there was also burgeoning discontent bubbling in toxic fashion just beneath the surface. People were critical of the conduct of the Island leaders.

Accusations of collaboration, toadying to the enemy, corruption and cowardice were all levelled at the heads of Victor Carey, John Leale, Alexander Coutanche, Duret Aubin and indeed all members of the Superior Council and the Controlling Committee.

Brigadier Snow was very much aware of what was happening in the Islands. His brief was to address the myriad problems attendant on the transition from war to peace. He laid out the tasks for the Liberating Force 135 in what he was pleased to call an 'Appreciation of the Situation' on 30th May 1945:

1. To land and occupy the CHANNEL ISLANDS.

2. To disarm and take prisoner the GERMAN garrison, returning all but 3,200 immediately to the United Kingdom.

3. To maintain law and order.

4. To administer the Government of the CHANNEL ISLANDS until their normal civil Governments are reinstated and functioning fully.

5. To begin the rehabilitation of the Islands.

The Brigadier realised quite quickly that there were difficulties ahead:

'There is considerable evidence that amongst the population that remained throughout the Occupation there is growing discontent with the previous somewhat archaic and undemocratic form of government in the Islands. Having experienced a more modern form of government in the United Kingdom (even if under somewhat authoritarian forms it has taken on account of War conditions of control), it appears that the

Tommies being welcomed in Guernsey.

A gaunt Huffmeier and a very youthful aide on his last day in the Islands.

A Happy day! Members of the Controlling Committee in the background.

The price that was paid.

Brigadier Snow tells Zimmerman to bring someone of a higher rank to sign the surrender.

At last a decent cigarette!

Victor Carey and Brigadier Snow on Liberation Day. John Leale can be seen over Snow's left shoulder.

Sibyl, Bob and their friendly German, Dr Maass.

Alexander Coutanche and a haggard Victor Carey pictured towards the end of the Occupation.

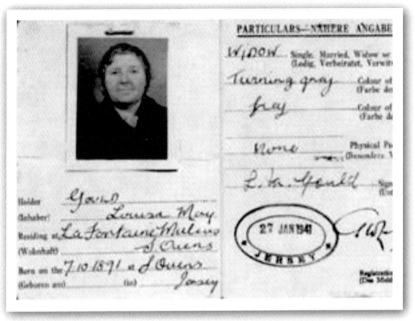

Louisa's Identity Card.

The Wehrmacht terrorises Polish women and children, 1939.

The Nuremberg Laws are applied in Jersey.

Inspector William Sculpher's motor car falls into German hands.

ROYAL COURT

Before A. M. Coutanche, Esq., Bailiff, and Jurats Dorey and Labey.

MONDAY, October 21st, 1940.

MORE ORDERS REGISTERED

There was a special sitting of the Court this morning for the registration of Orders issued by the German authorities.

JEWS TO REGISTER

The Bailiff said he had received two Orders from the German authorities, the first relating to measures to be taken for the registration of Jews.

This was read by the Attorney-General, and on his conclusions was lodged au Greffe and its promulgation ordered.

The Bailiff announced that he had entrusted the Chief Aliens Officer with the registration of Jews under the Order.

NOTICE
concerning the Registration of Jews in Jersey.

IN pursuance of an Order of the Chief of the German Military Administration in France (registered by Act of the Royal Court, dated October 21st, 1940, and in virtue of the power delegated to me by the Bailiff, all Jews must present themselves for registration at the Aliens Office, No. 6, Hill Street, St. Helier, on Wednesday and Thursday, October 23rd and 24th, 1940, between the hours of 10 a.m. and 4 p.m.

For the purposes of this Order, persons are deemed to be Jews who belong or have belonged to the Jewish religion or who have more than two Jewish grandparents.

Grandparents who belong or have belonged to the Jewish religion are deemed to be Jews.

The particulars to be provided upon registration are :—

1. Surname.
2. Christian name.
3. Date of birth
4. Place of birth.
5. Sex.
6. Family status.
7. Profession
8. Religious faith.
9. Length of uninterrupted residence in the Island.

The declaration of the head of the family will suffice for the whole family

CLIFFORD ORANGE,
Chief Aliens Officer.

October 21st, 1940.

NOTICE
concerning the marking of Jewish business undertakings.

NOTICE is hereby given that, for the purpose of §4 of the Order of September 27th, 1940, relating to measures against Jews (registered by Act of the Royal Court, dated October 21st, 1940), the marking of Jewish businesses, particularly shops, hotels, etc., must be carried out by means of a printed notice to be affixed to the inner side of all shop windows or, where there are no such windows, to be displayed in some other conspicuous place.

Printed notices are to be 20 cm x 40 cm in size, and yellow in colour.

Upon them in black letters, are to be printed the following words :

JUEDISCHES GESCHAEFT

Jewish Undertaking

Businesses are deemed to be Jewish if an interest therein exceeding 50% is owned by Jews.

"Jew" means a person who belongs or has belonged to the Jewish religion or who has more than two Jewish grandparents. Grandparents who belong or have belonged to the Jewish religion are deemed to be Jews.

American Jews are exempt from the provisions of the Order.

The marking of premises must be completed before October 30th, 1940.

C. W. DURET AUBIN,
H.M. Attorney-General.

October 22nd, 1940.

The first steps on the road to the camps

(from left to right) Therese Steiner, Auguste Spitz, Marianne Grunfeld.

Liberation joy.

Swastika daubed on the wall of the home of a suspected collaborator.

returning evacuees may well add to the numbers of those who are not content with the Islands' form of government.'

Brigadier Snow was a worried man. The 'dear Channel Islands' were not simply pretty little holiday resorts, they were hotbeds of political unrest and disaffection. The people were mutinous, the Islands' governments unpopular, even despised. There was a real possibility of violence.

'Should this unpopularity produce a situation in which civil government is paralyzed, even temporarily, as for instance by a general strike, the Force Commander will need all his present powers and resources to continue the effective administration of the Islands and maintain law and order.

It is seriously put forward that if this discontent does, in fact, exist, the discontented elements of the population have not had, during the events of the last three weeks, sufficient breathing space to organise a blunt and open expression of their opinion.

It is suggested that even should there be an expression of such discontent to occur in the near future, there is an equal possibility that after the return of these Channel Islanders, more evacuees in the United Kingdom, wider discussions of, and comparisons with the methods of government in the United Kingdom, may produce a renewed and even exacerbated expression of discontent.

Until it is apparent that such a situation will not develop, it is unwise to reduce

either the Internal Security strength of the Force in Infantry and Provost, or its administrative strength in staffs and services. It is considered that Internal Security and administration of the Force should be maintained to cover the repatriation period.'

John Leale mounted a massive defence of his governance during the Occupation years in an epic speech to the Guernsey States.

His conduct and that of the Controlling Committee was so comprehensively explained and justified that even Stopford's 1(b) gang (the small intelligence group attached to Snow's Force 135) were forced to the conclusion that no charges of criminal collaboration could be brought against him. Victor Carey, too, was vigorous and very precise in his own defence, to the satisfaction of everyone except, predictably, Stopford, Dening and d'Egville. But whatever they thought, there would be no neck-stretching exercise in Guernsey or anywhere else in the Channel Islands.

Coutanche was, typically, more understated in his own defence, and in particular of his conduct at the time of the deportations. Most of Coutanche's thoughts on the conduct of his government during the war years were probably shared with the ebullient little cockney, Home Secretary Herbert Morrison, who stayed at the Bailiff's house during his visit. They had stayed up most of the night discussing the occupation and Coutanche's role in it, and it was on the morning after this nocturnal discourse that Morrison said, in a jocular and somewhat undiplomatic way, after praising the Bailiff's 'sterling' work, that:

'I am not sure everything was always within the law, but if anything has been done which needs whitewashing at the other end, I will take care of it!'

But not everyone was so conciliatory. Not everyone wanted a simple return to the status quo and government in the old oligarchic and decidedly undemocratic way. This was particularly true in Jersey, and in the vanguard of the dissenting parties was the noted communist Norman Le Brocq with the Jersey Democratic Movement. He and they had not come through five years of occupation just to see the old gang of oligarchs back in the driving seat. They wanted constitutional reform. Norman Le Brocq was very careful not to mention his previous intention to assassinate Coutanche and his two chief law officers, judging, no doubt, that what the discontented Islanders wanted was political reform, not bloody revolution.

Norman Le Brocq's post-war career is described by Michael Ginns thus:

'In the post war period, Norman le Brocq continued his communist activity and this during the Cold War. When he tried to hold outdoor meetings he would be pelted with over-ripe tomatoes.

He stood for election to the States and was eventually elected as a Deputy in the 1960s. Once he had got several items (which would have been seen as Red Revolution in 1945) passed into law, he turned his attention to environmental issues and his ultimate accolade came in the 1990s when he was elected as President of the National Trust for Jersey, of which, they say that to be a member you have to be female, fifty and vote Tory!!

It was quite a journey for Norman – from bloody revolutionary to pillar of the establishment.

But in 1945 he was in the van of the movement for change. The pressure was most definitely on.

There was a petition to the King, (he, acting in Privy Council, being the ultimate authority in the Islands' constitution), begging for a referendum to determine the extent of the desire for closer incorporation into the UK and for doing away with the old form of government, which was seen as collaborationist, corrupt, inefficient and undemocratic.

Feelings were running high and the situation was hardly helped by the British government heaping honours upon the Islands' political leaders while largely ignoring those who had bravely and honourably risked, and sometimes lost, their lives resisting the enemy.

As Alan and Mary Seaton Wood

pointed out in their authoritative and sympathetic account of the Occupation, *Islands in Danger*:

'It is understandable that the Island authorities, fearing everything might bring reprisal on their people, should have felt that they could not countenance anything like sabotage or resistance. But it seemed strange for this attitude to be carried over by the Home Office to the bestowal of awards after the war... even more strange that no attempt had been made to compile a Roll of Honour of those who, like Canon Cohu, died for their courage.'

Sir John Leale wrote to the Seaton Woods about this odd state of affairs, explaining it by reference to the statement he had made just before the Germans arrived. In it he had stated that anyone who resisted the occupying power in any way, thereby inviting reprisals against the civilian population, was a criminal enemy of that population, deserving not of honour, but of prosecution.

Sir John described the situation more coolly in his letter to the Woods:

'It might be difficult for a government which is a signatory to the Hague Convention to recommend Honours for those who broke the Convention.'

Whatever the reasoning behind the award of honours it only served to exacerbate the angry feelings of many of those outside the governing circle who saw themselves as betrayed, and politically disenfranchised. Norman Le Brocq put it succinctly in the postscript to the optimistically-entitled pamphlet *Jersey Looks Forward*:

'Just as after the First World War, the island witnessed a great upsurge of class struggle, precipitated by the ever-worsening conditions of the local workers, so now Jersey, liberated from the Nazi Occupation, prepares itself for the further liberation from its paternalist and semi-feudal system of government.'

And his wish was partly granted by way of a typically British compromise. A lot of the old was retained in the government, but new democratising elements were introduced to leaven the feudal mix. The reforms were largely self-generated as it was the States in each Island that submitted proposals and recommendations for the restructuring.

And so it was that in Jersey the twelve Jurats who had been elected for life by popular franchise no longer sat in the States but were replaced by twelve Senators elected for a term of nine years (which was reduced to six years in 1966). The Jurats remained members of the Royal Court, being chosen by an electoral college. The twelve rectors nominated by the Crown no longer sat in the Assembly, although the Dean was left with the right of addressing the States without a vote. The number of deputies elected by popular franchise by parish (members of parliament) was increased from 17 to 28. It was not a revolution such as Norman Le Brocq and Les Huelin would have liked, but rather a small but important devolution of power to the people.

Over in Guernsey the Attorney General and Solicitor General appointed by the Crown, who had the right to speak and vote in the States, lost the right to vote. The twelve Jurats who were appointed by an electoral assembly and sat for life were no longer to be members of the States. A new office of Conseiller was created, twelve being elected by electoral assembly for a turn of six years. As in Jersey, the Rectors lost their seats and the 15 Douzeniers were reduced to ten. The 18 deputies, elected by parish by popular franchise for three years were increased to 33. As in Jersey the people were given a louder voice in government.

Just as in Britain, the war years in Jersey had brought about great changes in the way people thought of their society and of the rulers they had. The War had seen the greatest and most sustained attack on civilised values ever in the history of mankind. Forty million people died in those five years. No one in the world was left untouched by the cataclysmic experience, certainly no one in the little Channel Islands. Time for the voice of the people to be heard, raised in support of those principles of common decency that had been so outrageously traduced, betrayed and

trampled underfoot by the mad dictator and his savage armies.

A new order was called for. The old order must be swept away from the Islands and a properly democratic, newly accountable States Assembly, governing for, by and through the people, instituted to guide the little Island communities wisely through the difficult and traumatised post-War world.

Let John Leale have the last word on the days of Occupation. These words form the peroration of his great speech delivered in the States of Guernsey at the close of the war:

'From the Occupation of this Island by German forces, grim though the experience has been, we have all doubtless learned salutary lessons. But there is one, I think, we have been taught above all others, and it is this: never in the past have we valued liberty as we shall value it in the future. If that thought dominates our political, social and industrial lives then good may yet come out of evil. If, because of our trials, we realise, as we have never realised before, the meaning of freedom to the human spirit, then those cruel years from 1940 to 1945 will not after all have been wasted, but on the contrary, out of the wreckage of the weary and useless years, we shall have rescued and indeed refined that conception of life which alone entitles us to bear the name of men.'

Chapter 11
Crime and Punishment

9th May 1945. Hitler was dead. The Allies were shaking hands in the ruins of Berlin while a glum and defeated Grand Admiral Hüffmeier was shipped off to Plymouth. Most importantly the Channel Islands were free. Brigadier Snow, looking unnervingly like a larger version of Captain Mainwaring from *Dad's Army*, at the head of Force 135 of cheerful Tommies took control of the Islands in the name of the king. There was joy unbounded, delight unlimited that this long and dreadful Occupation had finally come to an end.

Bailiff Coutanche sent a message to the king:

'With my humble duty I send to Your Majesty this assurance of the devotion of the States and People of Jersey to your Majesty's throne and person.
We have kept ourselves informed of the Armed Forces of your Majesty and of your Majesty's Allies and of the ceaseless efforts behind them, and on this day of our liberation we rejoice that we can once more take our place and play our part within Your Majesty's Empire.'

It was a truly happy time for the Islands:

'Nobody had to work so as to enjoy a real holiday with something to thrill one every minute. Crowds watched the arrival of sailors and soldiers from assault boats or 'ducks', these coming from part of a convoy of over 50 ships which had been sent to the Channel Islands. Tank-landing craft came up right under the seawall of St Aubin's Bay, and these discharged all sorts of vehicles; so great was the enthusiasm of the onlookers that even German prisoners who were working in the vicinity applauded excitedly. More and more men arrived all day and these received a great welcome – everyone cheered, children clamoured for autographs, and the soldiers and sailors were very generous in showering chocolate, sweets and cigarettes on new-made friends.'

(Leslie Sinel)

The new and very British military commander of the Islands addressed the assembled crowds:

People of the Channel Islands: It having pleased His Majesty by Order in Council to vest in the officer of the armed forces in the Channel Islands all powers necessary for the success of our operation, the safety of our forces, and the safety and well-being of his subjects in the islands, I, Alfred Ernest Snow, as the officer commanding the forces, give you greeting on your liberation from the enemy.
I rely upon you all to work cheerfully and loyally to restore the normal life of your

islands. Your ready compliance with such regulations and orders as may from time to time be issued. It will be my firm duty to exercise my authority that your own government may rapidly be restored to your Islands and that you may enjoy in peace and prosperity, your customary rights, laws and institutions.

A.E. SNOW, Brigadier.

It all sounded lovely. There would be a short period of military rule under the wise brigadier so that the dirt and mess left after five years of German Occupation could be swept up and cleared away in proper soldierly fashion. Then, when that task was completed, Churchill's 'dear Channel Islands' could be returned restored to their own governance. A gentle and peaceful way back to normality was envisaged. But alas for such expectations, it was not going to be as easy as that, not by a long chalk. Things had happened in those years of Occupation. It appeared as though the civil administrations of the Islands had collaborated with the enemy. People had been taken from their homes and deported across the sea to Biberach, Wurzach and Laufen. Other Islanders had been brutally battered and beaten, starved and mistreated. And most dreadful of all, a few, but too many, had been done to death in extermination camps. There had been a deal of suffering for many but there was a belief, well founded, that a favoured few seemed to have profited from their misfortune. like the black marketeers who had so much of what others had so little.. Like the hundreds of informers who had betrayed their fellow-Islanders for money or out of spite. Like the 'Jerry bags' who had fraternised with the *Wehrmacht* men. Island women laying back and not thinking of England at all.

And what of the work of the Island leaders in the Controlling Committee in Guernsey and the Superior Council in Jersey? Had they not, as many voices proclaimed, abandoned their duty of protecting their people? Had they not become quislings to a man, more anxious to please their German masters than to care for the welfare of their flock? Had they not registered the Anti-Jewish Orders without a murmur? Had they not supplied lists of those Islanders that the Germans wanted to harm? Had they not administered the coercive and oppressive German ordinances of Occupation, serving the enemy at each and every turn to the detriment of the interests of the native Islanders?

Many were the voices raised in accusation that the Islanders had been grossly betrayed by their collaborationist governments, sold down the river by the likes of Coutanche and Carey, Leale and Aubin, Orange and Sculpher, left without defence against the depredations of the enemy. Should not those responsible for such a state of affairs be made to answer for their sins?

And more than that, should not the old and failed form of government in the

Islands be swept away and a more modern constitution be put in its place? Retribution for the past and a new constitution for the future, that was what was wanted by a significant number of the Island folk. But that was not quite what the British Government wanted, and they were very quick off the mark to make known what their attitude toward the Occupation was going to be.

On 15th May Herbert S. Morrison, British Home Secretary, accompanied by Lord Munster, Parliamentary Undersecretary, came hurrying to the Islands. The Right Honourable Herbert Morrison was famously monocular and was, it seemed, determined not to see very much with his good eye either. He only stayed in the Islands for two days and most of that time was taken up with telling the assembled Island folk what great work their leaders had done during the Occupation, and how well and courageously the civilian population had behaved.

Norman Le Brocq, member of the Jersey Communist Party and of the Jersey Democratic Movement, he who had plotted to assassinate the Bailiff, reports that he was shocked when he heard Morrison say that he thought that while there had been some minor collaboration and blemishes by people during the German Occupation, the majority of Islanders had shown great loyalty, and that any misdemeanours that had happened would not be followed up.

Off the street, and in the States Assembly no less, Morrison was even more explicit:

'If anything has been done that needs whitewashing at the other end, I will take care of it.'

In other words there were not, absolutely not, going to be any recriminations, quisling trials, or any accusations of betrayal levelled against any of the Islands' leaders. A discreet veil would be drawn over any darker and more morally ambiguous activities that had been pursued during those long years of Occupation. The Islanders could look forward to seeing their wartime leaders showered with honours for their courageous behaviour in such adverse conditions, and for not subverting the Churchillian notion of British exceptionalism, so essential in the telling of the nation's brave and glorious struggle against a monstrous enemy. It was just so unfortunate for the preferred British narrative of the War that the Channel Islands had been occupied.

Here was one group of British people who had surrendered without fighting on the beaches, on the streets or anywhere else come to that, and what was more, no Island resistance resulting in a single German death had been offered to the invader. Islanders were accused of being 'servile,' 'obsequious,' 'quisling,' 'pusillanimous' and 'cowardly' before their German lords and masters; not heroic, defiant, death-defying and brave as the Churchillian model required them to be. Something had to be done to bring the Islanders back into the fold along with the rest of the nation, and it had to be done quickly!

Clearly the fact of the Occupation could not be disputed. The Channel Islands had been well and truly occupied for five long years, the only British soil under enemy rule. But what if the story of this peculiar occupation could be told in terms of honourable, courageous, plucky and determined endurance, if not actual resistance, in the face of overwhelming force? Would not that be a good way of making the Channel Island experience into another wonderful chapter in the book of Britain's glorious war? Thought of in this way, the defeat which the Occupation represented could be turned into yet another triumph for the indomitable British spirit even in the most terrible adversity, a great victory born of an unfortunate reverse. Of course, if this were to be the dominant narrative, there could be no contrary talk of collaboration or helping the enemy in any significant way. Certain minor lapses could, of course, be allowed, even the noble British race contained unsatisfactory elements. But these would not, could not, must not, spoil the overall picture of a typically British and brave defiance of the German aggressor. Thus identified as true possessors of all the expected national virtues, the Islanders could, after five years in the wilderness, be readmitted to the British 'family', honour

untarnished, behaviour applauded. Despite everything, they had come through with Union Jacks flying and heads held high. There was nothing to be ashamed of and everything to praise. The Islanders had done their best and now time could be called on this extraordinary period in their history, a longed-for end.

There was, however, behind all the cheery talk of a rapid and honourable closure to the whole Occupation experience, another large and complicating factor driving the Whitehall agenda in the Channel Islands, and it was this ...

It is not quite true to say that the Islands surrendered to the enemy. Rather, they were surrendered to the enemy by the British government in London which had taken from the Islands all means of defence. All the soldiers had been evacuated, there was no air cover and no naval forces to defend the Islands. The British had fled. They had given up entirely. The Islands were declared a de-militarised zone but the Germans were not told of this and, as we have seen, they bombed the Islands in the belief that they remained a legitimate military target. 44 people were killed unnecessarily because of what Lord Portsea called the 'sheer, stark buffoonery' which characterised the behaviour of the British government towards the Islands. The widespread belief in the Islands was that they had been ditched, abandoned and betrayed by the British in a most shameful manner, and Portsea pushed the idea that this was a true belief time and time again. And he had right on his side. The British had indeed abandoned the little Islands to their fate and, worse than that, had put them in mortal danger, a danger that had been realised. This betrayal of the Islands was seen as some kind of offence against the Island folk, a sin even, for which atonement was due. In pursuit of this there appears to have been a kind of tacit deal intended, that if the Islanders would forget the great British betrayal at the start of the War, the British themselves would not only forgive any bad behaviour by the Islanders during the Occupation, but also forget it. It was as pretty a quid pro quo arrangement as could be imagined in the circumstances, and many government officials involved in the post-War settlement tried very hard with this quietist approach which would allow all the parties to emerge from the Occupation years with some degree of honour and respectability.

- Forgive and forget.
- Whitewash (if necessary).
- Walk away from the Occupation without looking back.

This was certainly the view adopted by Morrison.

But the clamour for some sort of investigation into the grave charges of collaboration at every level during the Occupation was rising more and more. Many Islanders were not prepared to forgive and forget, not so much the alleged 'betrayal' by the British in 1940, they were not bothered by that too much. What really incensed the protesters was the behaviour of their leaders in 'collaborating' with the Germans, the activities of the profiteers in the black market, to say nothing of the 'Jerry bags', 'troop-carriers' (Island women who had German-fathered babies), and informants. The Island people were not happy and the man with the immediate responsibility of dealing with all the anger and complaint was the military commander, Brigadier A. E. Snow.

Snow was a very able man, not to be rushed into judgement, always willing to listen and, most importantly, to understand and sympathise with the Islanders in their peculiar and difficult situation that summer of 1945. And it was a difficult situation. There was anger and real hatred in the air, particularly in Jersey, to such an extent that Snow requested that the military presence should be maintained for more than the three months originally intended.

Brigadier Snow, aided by a twenty-strong Civil Affairs Unit attached to the Liberation Force, began his investigation into the allegations of wrong-doing and accusations of craven collaborative behaviour and criminal activity during the Occupation. Brigadier Snow was not the only one interested in such investigations, particularly those that involved the Islands' political leaders in the civil administrations. Questions had to be asked about these men. The Home Office turned to a man who might have been expected to have a special insight into Island affairs, Lord Justice du Parcq. He was a Jerseyman who, along with Lord Portsea, had done sterling work during the war helping the Channel Islanders who had fled to the mainland prior to the Occupation. He was president of the Channel Island Refugee Committee, which raised money to provide funds, clothing and advice to the evacuees who had come in their thousands to the mainland in June 1940. He was a persuasive man, for in that same year of 1945 he went on the BBC to broadcast an appeal on behalf of the Island refugees and raised more money than had ever been raised before!

Du Parcq took himself off to the Islands to pursue his enquiries. He did not stay much longer than Morrison had done before him but he took the results of his exceedingly brief investigation along to the Home Office.

He identified two areas of possible concern. The first had to do with the attitude of the two Islands' governments towards the 1942 deportations:

'I think that a strong case can be made... that the authorities ought to have refused to give any assistance in the performance of this violation of international law. I have had some communication with the War Crimes Commission on the subject, and I know that the Commission has recommended the prosecution of the Germans responsible... I should feel happier if I thought a strong line had been taken.'

In this instance, so the Lord Justice believed, the Island authorities had been weak and ineffective and had possibly colluded in the commission of a war crime.

His second concern, predictably enough, was about the behaviour of the Guernsey Bailiff, Victor Carey. In particular he was concerned about Carey's reference to British forces as 'the enemy' in a notice signed by him at the time of the commando raids, and also the publication of the infamous 'V' notice offering a reward of £25 to those who informed on their fellow-Islanders who had painted that victory sign about the place. A touch of the quisling there thought the noble Law Officer.

This charge of collaborative conduct has been repeatedly levelled against Victor Carey, despite the fact that he himself provided a quite robust and very plausible rebuttal as early as 25th June 1945. Many of the notices over his signature were, he averred, not written by him at all but by the Germans. The wording was theirs, not his, though this was not true in the case of the 'V' notice:

'I, and I alone am responsible for it, as at that time I was very much alarmed at the reaction of the Germans when they discovered that, in spite of the first

warning, more 'V' signs were being painted up all over the Island, and even on gate-posts of houses in which German officers and soldiers were billeted. I had a very stormy interview with the Feldkommandant at which all kinds of things were threatened, and I was afraid they would take hostages (of which I understand they had a list of 80) and thought therefore that a notice of this kind would be the only way to stop the matter, which it did for a few days.'

Next into the Islands enquiring after the truth about Occupation sins came the Director of Public Prosecutions himself, Theobold Matthew. He talked exclusively to the Islands' leaders and not at all to the agitators in the street. He looked at those grave issues that du Parcq had concerned himself with, particularly the Victor Carey problem. He also looked at the Islanders' role in the implementation of the 1942 deportation order by the Islands civil administrations. He listened very closely indeed to Bailiff Coutanche's defence of his actions which was, put simply, that he had to comply with the German deportation order to prevent the government of the Island falling entirely into German hands, which would have happened if he and his Superior Council had resigned in protest.

It was, he said, a matter of 'comply or have direct German rule', probably of the SS variety, thrust upon them. The DPP understood his position perfectly. On this and other matters, Matthew thought, Alexander Coutanche had acted with great skill and wisdom and deserved not censure or prosecution but rather praise and commendation.

Things were going very well for the Home Office policy of forgive and forget. Indeed, they were going much better than that, for no sins had been discovered which actually needed forgiveness and a politic amnesia. Sure there had been 'weakness of judgement' in certain cases, and certainly the Island authorities had worked with the Germans, but this was not collaboration in the quisling or Vichy style, this was more a kind of enforced cooperation between an all-powerful occupier and an occupied land left defenceless by the British government. The Islanders had complied with German orders because they had to. They had not collaborated in any substantive way. The Home Office, in the shape of James Chuter Ede, Morrison's successor in the newly-elected Atlee government, was very happy indeed. But not everyone on the Channel Island case was so pleased.

Into the Islands rode a small group of MI5 intelligence officers on a mission: a mission to identify every act of 'collaboration', and to hunt down every 'collaborator' that could be found. Not for them the accommodating attitude of the Home Office towards the behaviour of the Islands' leaders during the Occupation – or anyone else's come to that. They would be zealous in their searching and unforgiving in their judgement.

This little hit squad was headed up by young Major J.R. Stopford, seconded by gimlet-eyed Major Alan d'Egville. The latter might have been expected to have an intimate knowledge of the Islands as he had been the Port Security Officer for the Channel Islands in the immediate pre-War period. It was not an expectation that was much fulfilled.

These two men were aided and abetted in their crusade against collaborators by Captain Bake and Captain Palmer of the Civil Affairs Unit, who worked in Guernsey, and more importantly by a member of Brigadier Snow's staff, Captain J. R. Dening.

They set about their work with a will. They found nothing at all to please them!

'When our forces arrived in Guernsey it is a remarkable fact that they found that not the slightest attempt had been made by any official whatsoever to accumulate any information which might have been of value to the Force, nor to prepare the ground in the way that might have been expected if they had been wholeheartedly zealous British officials.'
(*Report to the Home Office 1945*)

So from the very beginning of the investigation, the Islands' governments' attitude was to be condemned and castigated as falling far short of those standards expected of the British patriot. It almost constituted a betrayal, but then what more could be expected from an Island people described thus by Captain Dening in a memorandum of 3rd July 1945. (Interesting to note that his description of the Island population accords quite closely with that in the Pfeiffer report):

'It was generally agreed that the majority of inhabitants of this Island – Norman peasants with all their limitations of character and outlook – view German and English men with almost equal indifference as long as their material prosperity is unaffected. Throughout the Occupation they enjoyed an administration which faithfully protected their parochial interests and which to achieve its ends was quite willing to discard a loyalty to Britain which appears merely nominal.'

They were not slow in finding fault in the sub-species and, of course, the first target had to be the Bailiff of Guernsey, Victor Gosselin Carey, a collaborator if ever there was one. And how heinous were his crimes!

'In Guernsey the attitude of the Bailiff towards the Germans was friendly and cooperative. We have articles in the Guernsey newspapers written by the Bailiff, one of which condemned in no uncertain terms the maliciousness of a Guernseyman for the cutting of German telephone wires, and extolled the virtues of the Germans for their kindliness and gentlemanly behaviour, while the other article recommended the Islanders to attend a German musical concert, saying how pleasant it would be and making quite unnecessary complimentary remarks about the Germans.'

Then this report to the Home Office, delivered in August 1945, talks in highly critical fashion of the infamous two notices signed by Carey in the summer of 1941: the 'V' notice and this one concerning any help given to British soldiers:

IMPORTANT NOTICE

Attention is called to the fact that under the Order Relative to Protection against Acts of Sabotage dated October 10th 1940, any person who hides or shelters escaped prisoners of war shall be punished with death. The same applies for the sheltering or hiding of members of enemy forces (for instance, crews of landing aircraft, parachutists, etc). Anyone lending assistance to such persons in their escape is also liable to the death sentence.

It was the use of the phrase 'enemy forces' in referring to British servicemen that was found to be so offensive, indicative, as it was thought to be, of a quisling mentality.

But there was worse to come!

A letter was found 'in his own handwriting' (no dispute about authorship then) which clearly made Carey the Laval of the Channel Islands. Here it is, in full:

Le Vallon
Guernsey

The Lieutenant Governor and Bailiff requests the pleasure of the company of the *Inselkommandant, his adjutant, Prince Oettingen and Dr Reffler with the interpreter to take wine with him at Le Vallon on Sunday July 6th at 5.30 p.m. (17.30)*

For the MI5 investigation team this was proof positive of a criminally collaborative attitude. Fortunately for the aged Bailiff, it was not accepted as such by the Director of Public Prosecutions, Theobold Matthew. He took a much more kindly, not to say lenient point of view as regards all of Carey's actions during the Occupation, including the 'V' notice. A venal not a mortal sin thought the sagacious DPP.

Dening glumly reported the news to Stopford:

'The offence, as such, was not considered worthy of more than four days in the market square stocks of an English country town. We found ourselves wishing for a pillory in ST PETER PORT, with a population rightly incensed at the unsavouriness of its leaders, and plentifully furnished with their own, preferably unmarketable, vegetable produce.'

Next up for censure was Sibyl Hathaway, the Dame of Sark. Victor Carey had behaved in such an un-British fashion as to actually invite the Germans to take wine with him. The Dame went several steps further down the unpatriotic road, for she invited the Hun to dinner and not just once, but several times!

'The Dame was a particular friend of Dr MASS (sic), Prince von OETTINGEN and General von Schmettow, who were frequent visitors at weekends. At Easter 1945 ZACHAU, SCHNEEBERGER and others were invited to a lobster lunch. The Dame of Sark has preserved her property and privileges intact throughout the Occupation; her gardens have not even been modified by wartime agriculture.'

German Generals, German aristocrats and German intellectuals eating at the same table as a British ruler! Wasn't this 'ingratiating and friendly behaviour towards the Germans' a form of collaboration deserving of punishment?

Stopford, d'Egville and Dening certainly thought so.

The boys from British Intelligence were not quite so quick to find fault and condemn John Leale, the President of the Controlling Committee in Guernsey. In fact John Leale had got his defence in prior to any investigation when he addressed the Guernsey States in an extremely long speech during which he eloquently and persuasively justified his conduct during the Occupation. Dening reported that:

'The Director (of Public Prosecutions) was also interested in the record and character of Jurat LEALE, whose ability and astuteness are fully recognised. It is unlikely, in view of the tenuous evidence available, that his defence of acting always in the public interest could be overthrown.'

This was undoubtedly true, for John Leale's defence was as near perfect as could be hoped for in the difficult and complex moral circumstances of the Occupation. As he himself had announced at the very beginning:

'Should the Germans decide to occupy this Island, we must accept the position. There must be no thought of any kind of resistance; we can only expect that the more dire punishment will be meted out. I say this; the man who even contemplates resistance should the Germans come is the most dangerous man in the Island and its most bitter enemy. The military have gone. We are civilians.'

The Islands' leaders had been commanded to carry on governing to the best of their ability even if no instructions or directives were received from London, and they had to govern so as to serve the best interests of the people. That was the order and Leale, along with his fellow Committee members, obeyed it dutifully. He judged that the best way to protect and promote the interests of the Island folk was to pursue a policy of non-resistance and cooperation with the occupying power. He might have thought, along with the Reverend Ord, that it was better to try and make friends with a potentially savage dog than to bite it on the bum! With that in mind he pursued a course of prudent cooperation with the Germans. This wasn't collaboration to further German war aims, rather it was the considered construction of a détente with the enemy to protect the life, liberty and property of the Islanders.

In other words, Leale and his men were trying to conduct a civil government in the best interests of their people, as he had been commanded to do. It seemed, despite all the misgivings of British Intelligence, that John Leale was an honourable man doing an honourable job to the best of his ability – no quisling he!

MI5 moved on across the water to Jersey to consider the behaviour of Bailiff Alexander Moncrieff Coutanche, and here again found little substance in the charges of wholesale collaboration.

Grudgingly they observed:

'The attitude of the States and of the Bailiff does not seem quite so gratuitously friendly as it was in Guernsey.'

(Alexander had certainly not asked the Germans to take wine with him, nor invited them round for a lobster dinner!)

But it was still far from being satisfactory. Over one question, that of the deportations, there is almost universal bitterness. The States provided the Germans with the names and addresses of all persons likely to be wanted by the Germans for this purpose. Their doing this is bitterly resented, the general comment being that the Germans should have been left to do their own dirty work. There are

too, numerous allegations about the way in which members of the States and heads of departments abused their position by obtaining for themselves commodities which were not available to the general public. The States argument is that there was not enough for everyone to have a share. There seems however to have been slightly less collaboration by the States of Jersey, and correspondingly, the behaviour of the Jerseymen has been less reprehensible than that of the inhabitants of Guernsey.

In both Islands there was much charge and counter-charge, rumour and allegation, insult and accusation of all kinds to assail the ears of Stopford and his team. The difficulty was in discovering what truth, if any, there was in all of this. It was hard, if not impossible, work, as d'Egville remarked despairingly in a long letter to Stopford on the 8th July 1945 about the progress of his investigations in Guernsey. At the heart of this missive is an observation about the Channel Island folk:

'The people of these Islands as a whole may be said to have accepted the Germans as not a bad substitute for the other 'foreigners' (ourselves) and to have lived with them on the best of terms. When you go to a dance or a party, where such a fuss is made of us, you can be sure that the same people but three months ago were gushing over the Germans as they are with us. And that applies to all ranks of society.'

And d'Egville had indeed talked to many Islanders of every class, from the highest to the lowest, but he did not make much progress for:

'One found that everyone had something to say about everyone else, that everyone accused the next man of collaboration, only to have the same accusation made against himself.'

The somewhat frustrated Major goes on to bemoan the fact that the Island folk are so intermarried, interrelated and interdependent that:

'There are few people, if there are any, who can be relied on to supply information, because anyone on whom they may be called to report is bound in some way to be connected to them by marriage, in business or in society.

Thus many of those whom I had in mind as possible contacts are now found to be wholly unsuitable. You find them covering up and covering each other up very quickly. This does not mean that they do not criticise certain actions of the Bailiff, for instance. But then he is rather remote from them. And on balance they will support the Bailiff and all the other state officials.

The population is so small and so concentrated that a man's business may easily suffer unless he keeps in with everyone, so that he is forced to wink at a good deal, if only to be winked at in return.'

The going was tough for the MI5 officers in their search for collaborators, and it was about to get tougher.

The DPP, Matthew Theobold, declared that, even if charges of collaboration were brought against certain individuals, there was no law under which they could be tried. The appropriate legal machinery would have been the Defence Regulations Act of 1939 Article 2a:

'If with intent to assist the enemy, any person does any act which is likely to assist the enemy or prejudice the public safety, the defence of the realm or the efficient prosecution of the war, he shall be liable to penal servitude for life.'

This was clear enough. Anyone collaborating with the enemy to help in the prosecution of his War aims could be charged with a criminal offence. However the question was whether or not this Defence Regulations Act could be applied to the Channel Islands during the period of Occupation 1941-45. The Act, insofar as it applied to the Channel Islands, had been revoked in London in the August of 1941 by an Order in Council, but because the Islands were then occupied, this Order revoking the Defence Regulations Act in the Channel Islands was not registered in the Royal Courts of Jersey and Guernsey. All Orders in Council, in order to become laws in the Islands, had to be so registered as a matter of constitutional obligation. This Order had not been so registered but did that mean that it ceased to have any legal significance at all and if so, what of the legal status in the Islands of the 1939 Act that had been so registered? In other words was the registered Defence Regulations Act of 1939 still in force in the Islands during the Occupation or had it been effectively revoked by the unregistered Order of August 1941? If it had been revoked, there could be no trials for crimes of collaboration.

The man who mattered in this situation was, of course, Matthew Theobold. He informed Major Stopford that the Act could not be held to apply to the Islanders during the period of the Occupation. There was some thought that perhaps in lieu of the Defence Regulations Act, trials could be held under the English 'Common Law' concerning 'misdemeanours' liable to cause 'a public mischief'.

But Stopford, d'Egville and Dening were not too pleased with that suggestion. Downgrading what they saw as acts of collaboration to the level of 'misdemeanours' was nowhere on their agenda. Too small a charge for so great a crime, thought the men from MI5.

There was another suggestion, and that was to apply the Treason and Treachery Act in cases of alleged collaboration, but this was seen as going too far in the opposite direction. Those convicted under this law would actually be hanged and that was too much even for the zealous Major Stopford to countenance. But he and his team were increasingly frustrated by their inability to bring the collaborators to justice,

and irritated by the lack of any real encouragement or support from the Home Office, from the DPP or, most importantly, from the interim Military Governor of the Islands, Brigadier Snow, who was extremely and almost insultingly dismissive of their efforts. The MI5 team had assembled a grand list of collaborators, eleven in all, whom they wanted sent for trial, along with a number of lesser offenders, mostly black-marketeers and 'Jerry bags'.

Brigadier Snow would have none of it!

He condemned the evidence they had produced in support of their accusations as 'useless' in any court of law, based as it was on hearsay, second-hand accounts and sheer 'tittle-tattle'.

According to Snow they had not begun to prove the cases of collaboration they claimed to have found. They had 'talked up' instances of association with the Germans (lobster dinners for example) until they became full-blown acts of collaboration. They had made 'mountains out of molehills' and, in hyperbolic fashion, thought of Carey as if he were Laval.

Dening recalls the concussive encounter with the somewhat annoyed Brigadier:

'It seems clear that he did not expect that my findings and conclusion – with which he was fully conversant – would one day cause consternation at the Home Office, whose officials have preferred to accept opinions not related to the existing

evidence but based rather upon the apparently accepted policy of appeasement and the social impression of high ranking officers.

The Force Commander asserted that the report gave only one side of the picture, and that while he agreed with it, the individuals against whom criticism could be levelled were insignificant and unimportant.'

The disappointment is palpable.

Despite his best efforts, Dening could see the quarry escaping from him, collaborators walking free even though their guilt was obvious. He continues:

'In my view the evidence is irrefutable and I cannot see how the present embarrassment of the Home Office can be alleviated in a major degree by any extenuating circumstances which the Force Commander may see fit to put forward in due course. Even when all allowances are made, the character of the Administration of the Islands during the Occupation remains pusillanimous – particularly so in Guernsey.'

Alas for Stopford, d'Egville and Dening, all their efforts to 'decontaminate' the Channel Islands, to bring the scores of criminal collaborators to justice were being wasted, reduced to nothing. Nobody believed that what they had uncovered amounted to very much at all, certainly not enough to drag people into a criminal court. Furthermore, nobody wanted to

believe that there had been significant collaboration in the Islands. Charles Markbreiter, secretary with special responsibility for the Channel Islands, still in office at the end of the Occupation as he had been at the beginning, was 'uninterested' in pursuing charges of collaboration. Matthew Theobold, Chuter Ede and Brigadier Snow were likewise reluctant to lay any charges of unlawful association with the enemy on the Islanders' doorstep. Dening was right.

Appeasement and reconciliation was the name of the Home Office game, and anything that ran counter to that would be kicked into the long grass and largely ignored.

And this is precisely what happened to the work of Major Stopford and his little group of troublemakers and boat-rockers. They failed to put a single Islander in court to be charged with collaboration. Perhaps the sinners should be left to be dealt with by the Islanders themselves. The high-minded Major wrote this in a letter to Dening on 31st May 1945:

'I am sending you herewith papers and photographs which were taken from German prisoners of war. These show the extent of collaboration of certain unpleasant individuals, mostly in Guernsey. In the case of most of the women, they look thoroughly unsatisfactory types, but I see that there are certain men involved, and in their cases, their behaviour is likely to be more sinister.

The policy as I see it at the moment is that we are unlikely to be able to bring prosecutions against most of these people or in fact any of them, unless there is direct evidence of their having been of active assistance to the enemy against the United Kingdom. Therefore it seems the best way to deal with the women and possibly the men, is to have them up before you, grill them thoroughly, take down what they say, and make pretty public the fact that they have been seen and why, so that their fellow citizens can make their lives as unpleasant and uncomfortable as possible. The way these girls have behaved is a perfect disgrace, and the more people who know about it the better.'

Name, shame and leave the sinners to the tender mercies of their fellow Islanders. It looked very much like an invitation to the Islanders to indulge in vigilante justice. Not, one might think, the wisest or the most responsible course to take to bring about a peaceful post-Occupation settlement in the Islands. But it was not so far removed as all that from the official British Government approach adopted as a means of solving the problem of how to deal with alleged criminal actions during the Occupation.

Having given the Islands' leaders a clean bill of health, the question remained of how to deal with those charges of consorting with the enemy, collaboration and black-marketeering, to say nothing of horizontal collaboration, aimed at those a little

further down the social scale. There was a unanimous reply from the Brigadier and the Home Office. Given the difficulty of finding the evidence to bring charges in a court of law anywhere in the United Kingdom, the whole issue should be left to the Island authorities. It was for them to impose some kind of retribution on offenders. Black marketeers, as Timmer in Guernsey was alleged to have been, should be made subject to a punitive tax on their war-time profits. The 'Jerry bags' should be left alone by the courts in the expectation that they would suffer ostracism, exclusion and denigration in their own society. Punishment enough it was thought, and the only one that was considered politic and practicable in the circumstances.

The end was in sight as far as the Home Office was concerned. An enquiry, in fact several enquiries, had been conducted into the conduct of the Islanders during the Occupation and, as the British Government hoped, hardly anything of a criminal nature had been discovered, despite Stopford's claim to the contrary. The Islands' leaders Coutanche and Leale were in the clear, no quislings they. Victor Carey was found to have been perhaps a little weak in his dealings with the Germans but that was very forgiveable in the circumstances. Certainly he was not guilty of collaboration. He could join the other ennobled Island leaders in the pantheon of Occupation heroes who had upheld that tradition of British exceptionalism in the most trying circumstances. The British family welcomed the Islanders home from their long exile.

On 20th August 1945 Home Secretary James Chuter Ede delivered this commendation of the Islands to the expectant House of Commons:

'The Islands have every reason to be proud of themselves and we have every reason to be proud of them. That after a period of great suffering there should have been a tendency in certain quarters, not fully informed of all the facts, to indulge in recriminations, is not surprising, but I hope, in the interests of the future of the Islands, nothing will be said in this House to encourage any such tendency.'

The Islands' leaders were pleased, very pleased indeed. They were not to be hanged for collaboration but knighted for patriotic service. Alexander Coutanche, John Leale, and even Victor Carey all received their knighthoods in the Christmas Honours List of 1945. Oddly enough, given the nature of his contribution to public service in the Occupation, Ambrose Sherwill was only given a CBE. He had to wait another four years, until 1949, before he joined his fellow-Islanders in the knightly ranks.

Epilogue

What was the effect of these five long years of Occupation by the 'most hated people in the world', as von Aufsess himself called his fellow-countrymen? What was the damage? What was the loss? After all, the Occupation of France had had terrible implications for the moral well-being of that society. Did the Occupation of the Channel Islands have similar traumatic effects on the native Islanders and, if so, what were they?

Occupation of the kind endured by the Channel Islanders was never going to be an easy affair. It was not going to be, either, a 'model occupation' of the kind envisaged by Ambrose Sherwill and John Leale in which occupiers and occupied could interact in a properly-prescribed, ethical manner within the framework of the Hague Convention. It would have been wonderful, not to say miraculous, had there been such an occupation – one in which the Germans kept their word to safeguard the life and liberty of the Islanders in return for a certain quiescence from them, legitimised by international law. No room in such a scenario for moral ambiguity, no need for dishonourable conduct and no justification for acts of resistance against the invader. All would be quiet on this tiny section of the Western Front. Everyone observing the letter and the spirit of international law.

But that was not the way it worked out in practice. That was not the kind of occupation it was. What it was, what it became, as we have seen, was an increasingly nasty and often traumatic experience for the Islanders. All those promises to protect the essential rights of the people and preserve their life and liberty proved hollow as Islanders were variously thrown out of their homes, deported, beaten up and starved by the increasingly desperate Germans. Their actions had very little to do with the niceties of the Hague Convention and everything to do with military expedience and Hitler diktat.

Things turned ugly. Dissensions and fractures appeared in Island society. Many Islanders did not trust their own leaders and thought, in the absence of any evidence to the contrary, that they were craven collaborators, quislings to a man.

The moral fabric of Island society seemed to decay as quickly as the physical fabric. There was the scourge of informers running to the Germans to tell tales against their nearest neighbours, often with terrible consequences. There were the black marketeers making money by the barrowload out of the misery and suffering of their own countrymen. There were the 'Jerry bags' and 'troop-carriers', women and girls not concerned with any kind of resistance at all, lying down with the enemy, much to the horror of those upright officers from the virtuous mainland charged with investigating this heinous behaviour in 1945.

And then there was the sight and knowledge of the slave workers shipped across from Russia and Ukraine to help transform these pleasant islands into great impregnable fortresses ready to play their part in the biggest, and certainly the most horrendous, war the world had seen since time began.

An Islander would not have to look much beyond his front door to see the ugly images of venality, violence, death and destruction. From Sylt to Paradise, from Foulon to Gloucester Street prison, man's inhumanity to man was never so unkind. Yet this was the world of the Occupation in which the Islanders were forced to live, day after day, month after month, year after year. A world, moreover, where for most of the time there was not enough food, clothes, fuel or medicine to supply basic needs. And of course this awful circumstance had an effect on them. And of course this effect varied enormously from person to person. But each Islander, in his or her own way, was trying to answer the same question. And that question tended to be more existential than ethical: 'What do I have to do to survive?' rather than, 'How ought I to behave to maintain my moral integrity?' Times without number during the Occupation that second question had to be ignored in

order to answer the first with any prospect of success. Or, as Berthold Brecht, with welcome if unusual Germanic brevity remarked, *Erst komm das fressen, dan kommt die Moral!* ('Food comes first, then morals!').

Scarce an Islander there was, from the highest to the lowest, who did not recognise the truth of this; who was not, to a greater or lesser extent, forced to 'dodge and palter in the shifts of lowness,' to ensure their survival and that of their children – and no one was about to blame them in any way for doing so.

Many of these same Islanders showed outstanding courage born of moral steadfastness in the service of their fellow-Islanders, and, as is ever the case, quite a few did not. Hardship sorted all. Bob Le Sueur, who knew, and knows, his fellow-countrymen well, says this of those times:

'People you've known well, or thought you knew well, when really faced with difficult circumstances, the naturally kind, good-hearted people can become saintly and those with a mean streak in them become – must be careful of the word I'm using here, well, just what they are.'

Now if the ordinary Channel Islander (should such a creature have existed) found it difficult to breathe in the poisoned atmosphere of the Occupation, then their leaders too were in difficulty. In fact, on occasion, they were almost asphyxiated.

There was a problem. And it was this. Cooperation to any degree and of whatever kind with the Germans was seen by many, including Winston Churchill himself, as being morally repugnant and downright wrong. Any such accommodation with the enemy was seen as but a small step away from treason. It was certainly a dishonourable subversion of that sustaining belief in British exceptionalism which held that the true Brits in the Channel Islands, unlike their pathetic and pusillanimous French neighbours just across the water, should and could never cease to oppose the Germans absolutely and at all times.

The Islands' leaders, living in the real and rather nasty world, were light years away from mounting any such opposition, as far away as they could possibly be. For apart from registering German decrees in the Royal Courts, they made any and all resistance to Hitler's men a criminal offence!

Deep and stormy waters for the Islands' leaders, and many were the critics to say that the first thing lost overboard, almost before the Occupation began, was the precious moral compass that would have helped them avoid the reefs and shoals of collaboration and subservience.

And subservient, craven collaboration appeared to be the name of the game. But appearances can be deceptive, particularly in these extraordinary days of wartime Occupation. Both John Leale in Guernsey and Alexander Coutanche in Jersey (we may safely leave Dame Sibyl of Sark out of this as she seemed aristocratically unaware that there was any problem at all) were slick and quick to remove any doubts about their wartime governance by pointing to the reality which gave the lie to the appearance.

They had not been 'collaborating' with the enemy at all. Certainly not! They had been pursuing a far more subtle approach in a war of damage limitation, which was the only kind of war it was in their power to fight. It might well appear that they were being unnecessarily obsequious and pusillanimous in kow-towing to the Germans. But what they were in fact doing was trading a limited cooperation in return for the retention of such sovereignty as they still possessed, and which they so much needed in order to carry out the instruction they had been given at the start of the Occupation. Which was to carry on and govern in the best interests of the inhabitants.

In other words, they used the influence they still had to help and protect their community for the five years of the Occupation. The appearance was that of helping the Germans. The reality was that they were serving their people.

This justification of their behaviour was accepted at least by the British, but it was never tested in a court. There were no prosecutions. No one was executed for treasonable behaviour. Carey, Leale and Coutanche were knighted. Peace and quiet should have returned to the

Islands, and indeed it did in no small measure. But something was missing in this post-War settlement and it was this.

The gloriously outspoken Joe Mière, who we've had the pleasure of meeting before in these pages, identifies it perfectly. There were no trials at the end of the Occupation. There were no public enquiries into the alleged criminal conduct of some Islanders. No one laid any charges of dishonourable or traitorous conduct against anyone in a properly constituted court of law, either in the Islands or in mainland UK. There was no officially-acknowledged public airing of all the trials, tribulations, crimes and misdemeanours that had occurred, or were supposed to have occurred, during the Occupation.

Accusation and malicious rumour, charge and counter-charge lingered on and on. And they are still with us, for what was missing from the Islands in that autumn of 1945 was any kind of truth and reconciliation process which would have helped the Island communities know exactly what had happened to them during those Occupation years. Who had done what to whom? Who had betrayed his neighbour? Who had robbed his absent countryman? Who had made themselves rich from the suffering of others? Who were the guilty people?

Without knowing all these things, which would have been revealed by such a process, there could be no healing of the wounds inflicted on the community, no punishment for the guilty and no naming of the betrayers. There could be no closure and there was no closure. And the inevitable consequence is that there is unfinished business from the Occupation, years on, hanging unhappily over the Islands to this day. And, even as living memory turns to recorded history, it still provokes sorrow, anger, outrage and, sometimes, even disgust.

This is the worst part of the Occupation legacy, and it happened quite simply because, in the euphoria of that summer in 1945, almost all the people with any kind of influence at all, like Morrison and Brigadier Snow, opted for a quietist approach to all the problems in the Islands. They just refused to address them at all. Certainly, a series of public trials or open judicial enquiries was to be avoided. Anything 'untoward' that had happened, particularly in the actions of the Islands' leaders would be comprehensively whitewashed in Whitehall. And as for the 'Jerry bags', local collaborators and black marketeers, they should be left to endure whatever form of social ostracism their neighbours felt like inflicting upon them.

There was nothing of truth or reconciliation in this, just an anxiety to forgive, deny and forget, brush all the difficulties under the carpet, shut the door on the whole unfortunate experience and march, without a backward glance, into the bright new post-War world.

But too much had happened in the Occupation – too many people had been hurt, too many people had died – for those years to be so easily forgotten. And nor have they been, as the work of Paul Sanders, Louise Willmot, Gill Carr, David Fraser, Madeleine Bunting, Freddie Cohen and Hazel R. Knowles Smith so eloquently testifies.

The fierce debates and the heated arguments go on and on. And this is as it should be, for the story of the German Occupation of the Channel Islands, in all its richness and complexity, can tell us so much about the way people react to oppression, about the way we would react *in extremis*, that it must be told over and over again. How these tiny, peace-loving communities tried to cope with Hitler's men for the five years of the Occupation.

One thing is for certain. Very few of the Islanders who survived the concussive encounter with the Third Reich came away from it loving the Germans. How could they? The Occupation was an outrage. It was a violation. A horrible affair, in which the Islanders were, as we have seen, starved, thrown out of their homes, deported in their hundreds, assaulted and sometimes killed. Five years of misery inflicted by the Germans.

It is said that the Occupation of the Channel Islands was a mild affair compared with what happened in Holland, Belgium and France during these same years. And this is true, but still it was bad enough to provoke a deep and abiding loathing of the Germans and all their works – a loathing shared by countless millions across the entire world. Even today, many of the survivors in the Islands speak of the hatred and contempt they still hold for that enemy.

Many others have come to think beyond the rage and the anger and have come to believe that the way forward out of the Occupation world is one of forgiveness and reconciliation. And they have pursued this path with tremendous belief and energy. The Islander stretched out his hand to the former oppressor in a spirit of friendship and it was accepted gratefully for what it was: a brave, if not heroic, gesture to bring a gentle and proper end to the traumatic experience of the Occupation.

Understanding would take the place of condemnation. There might not be forgetting but there would be forgiving. And the hatred would end, for as Michael Ginns sagely remarks:

If you go on hating forever, you don't promote peace.

As a result of this reconciliation process, Germans now come to visit the Channel Islands, and Islanders, in their turn, visit the German towns like Bad Wurzach where they were once interned. There are German members of the Channel Island Occupation Society. The former enemy is now a friend.

The embrace has now replaced the gun. This is perhaps the better part of the legacy of Occupation.

Bibliography

Bell, William M., *Guernsey Occupied but Never Conquered*, Guernsey Press, 1992

Bell, William M., *I Beg to Report*, Guernsey Press, 1992

Bell, William M., *The Commando who Came Home to Spy*, Guernsey Press, 1998

Bonnard, Brian, *Alderney at War*, The History Press, 1993

Briggs, Asa, *The Channel Islands: Occupation and Liberation 1940–45*, Batsford and The Imperial War Museum, 1995

Bunting, Madeleine, *The Model Occupation: The Channel Islands Under German Rule 1940–45*, Pimlico, 2004

Cohen, Frederick, *The Jews in the Channel Islands during the German Occupation*, London, 1998

Cruikshank, Charles, *The German Occupation of the Channel Islands*, Oxford University Press, London, 1975

Evans, Alice (ed.), *The War Diaries of Violet Carey*, Phillimore, 2011

Falla, Frank, *The Silent War*, New English Library, 1967

Forty, George, *Channel Islands at War*, London, 1999

Fraser, David, *The Jews of the Channel Islands and the Rules of War, 1940–45*, Sussex Academic Press, 2000

Ginns, Michael, *Jersey Occupied*, Channel Island Publishing, 2009

Harris, Roger, *Islanders Deported*, CISS Publishing, 1983

Hathaway, Sibyl, *Dame of Sark, an Autobiography*, Heinemann, 1961

Herzog, Rudolf, *Dead Funny*, Melville House, 2011

Hilberg, Raul, *The Destruction of the European Jews*, Yale University Press, 2003

Lamerton, Mark, *Liberated by Force 135: The Liberation of the Channel Islands, 1945*, ELSP, 2000

Lewis, John, *A Doctor's Occupation*, NEL, 1983

McLoughlin, Roy, *Living with the Enemy*, Starlight Publishing, 1995

Mière, Joe, *Never to be Forgotten*, Channel Island Publishing, 2004

Nowlan, K. J. (ed.), *The Von Aufsess Occupation Diary*, Phillimore, 1985

Pantcheff, T. X. H., *Alderney, Fortress Island*, Phillimore, 1981

Pocock, H., *The Memoirs of Lord Coutanche*, Phillimore, 1975

Le Ruez, Nan, *Jersey Occupation Diary*, Seaflower Books, 2003

Sanders, Paul, *The British Channel Islands Under German Occupation*, Société Jersiaise, 2005

Sinel, Leslie, *The German Occupation of Jersey*, JEP, 1946

Steckoll, Solomon H., *The Alderney Death Camp*, Granada, 1982

Stephenson, Charles, *Fortifications of the Channel Islands 1941–45*, Osprey Publishing, 2006

Tabb, Peter, *A Peculiar Occupation*, Ian Allan, 2005

Le Tissier, Richard, *Mined Where You Walk: The German Occupation of Sark, 1940–45*, Seaflower Books, 2008

Le Tissier, Richard, *Island Destiny: A True Story of Love and War in the Channel Island of Sark*, Seaflower Books, 2006

Trevor-Roper, Hugh (ed.), *Hitler's Table Talk 1941–44*, London, 2000 (reprint)

Turner, Barry, *Outpost of Occupation*, Aurum, 2011

Wood, Alan and Mary Seaton, *Islands in Danger*, London, 1955

Index